# ATROCIOUS JUDGES.

# LIVES OF JUDGES

## INFAMOUS

AS

## TOOLS OF TYRANTS AND INSTRUMENTS OF OPPRESSION.

COMPILED FROM THE JUDICIAL BIOGRAPHIES OF

JOHN LORD CAMPBELL,

LORD CHIEF JUSTICE OF ENGLAND.

WITH AN APPENDIX,

CONTAINING THE

CASE OF PASSMORE WILLIAMSON.

Edited, with an Introduction and Notes,

BY

RICHARD HILDRETH.

NEW YORK AND AUBURN:

MILLER, ORTON & MULLIGAN.

NEW YORK: 25 PARK ROW.—AUBURN: 107 GENESEE STREET.

1856.

STEREOTYPED AT THE
BOSTON STEREOTYPE FOUNDRY.

# ADVERTISEMENT.

---

THE text of the following BOOK OF JUDGES has been derived from Lord Campbell's *Lives of the Chief Justices, and Lives of the Chancellors*, with only a few verbal alterations for the sake of connection, some transpositions, the omission of some details of less interest to the American reader, and the insertion of a few paragraphs, enclosed in brackets, thus [ ].

Most biographers have been arrant flatterers. Lord Campbell is a distinguished member of that modern school, which holds that history is of no dignity nor use, except so far as it is true; and that the truth is to be told at all hazards and without reserve. Hitherto social and political position, obtained no matter by what means, has in general secured not only present but future reputation. It can hardly fail to be a serious check upon those who struggle for distinction to understand, that, however they may cheat or dazzle their contemporaries, they must expect to encounter from posterity a Rhadamantine judgment.

The object of the present work, prepared as it is in the interest of justice and freedom, and designed to hold up a mirror to magistrates now sitting on the American bench, in which "to show virtue her own feature, scorn her own image, and the very life and body of the time his form and pressure," will, I hope, induce Lord Campbell to pardon the liberty I have ventured to take with his writings.

R. H.

BOSTON, *November* 20, 1855.

# CONTENTS.

## INTRODUCTION.



## CHAPTER I.

### ROGER LE BRABANCON.



## CHAPTER II.

### ROBERT TRESILIAN.



## CHAPTER III.

### THOMAS BILLING.



## CHAPTER IV.

### JOHN FITZJAMES.

## CHAPTER X.

### ROBERT HYDE.



## CHAPTER XI.

### JOHN KELYNGE.



## CHAPTER XII.

### WILLIAM SCROGGS.



## CHAPTER XIII.

### FRANCIS NORTH.

## CHAPTER XIV.

## EDMUND SAUNDERS.



## CHAPTER XV.

## GEORGE JEFFREYS.



## CHAPTER XVI.

## ROBERT WRIGHT.

# INTRODUCTION.

Hume observes, in his History of England, that "among a people who lived in so simple a manner as the Anglo-Saxons, the judicial power is always of greater importance than the legislative." The same comparison will hold good even in communities far more advanced in civilization than the Anglo-Saxons. It has indeed been well said that the great end of the complicated machinery of the existing British government is to get twelve men into a jury box. It might even be laid down as a general principle that the freedom or servitude of a people will mainly depend upon the sort of administration of justice which they have — especially of criminal justice.

The whole course of British history will serve to justify this observation, since it has not been so much by the aid of mercenary soldiers, as by the assistance of lawyers and judges, that tyranny has sought to introduce itself into that country. It is in the history of the English courts, still more than in the history of the English Parliament, that we are to trace the origin and growth of those popular rights and of that idea of public liberty, propagated from England to America, and upon which our Anglo-American free institutions are mainly founded.

The origin of British liberty, by an ancient, constant, and affectionate tradition, has uniformly been traced back to the times of the Anglo-Saxons. It was, however, by judicial, far more than by legislative institutions, that among those progenitors of ours private rights and public liberty were guarantied.

The smallest political subdivision among the Anglo-Saxons was the tything, (*teothing*,) consisting of ten families, the members of which were responsible for the good conduct of each other. The head man of this community, denominated tything-elder, (*teothing ealdor*,) seems to have acted as a kind of arbitrator in settling disputes about matters of a trifling nature; but whether he had actually a court for administering justice does not appear. Next in order came the hundred, (*hundrede*,) or, as it was called in the north of England, the *wapentake*, in its original constitution consisting of ten tythings, or a hundred families, associated together by a similar bond of mutual responsibility. Its head man was called the hundred's elder, (*hundredes ealdor*,) or simply reeve, (*gerefa*,) that being the generic term for the officer of any district, or indeed for any officer.* This gerefa, along with the bishop of the diocese, acted as the presiding officer of the hundred court, which met once at least every month, and had both

* The German *graf*, for which the Latin *comes* (in English, *count* or *earl*) was employed as an equivalent, is a form of the same word. The law Latin for sheriff is *vice-comes*, a name given, it would appear, after the title of earl or count had become hereditary, to the officer who still continued to be elected by the people for the official functions originally discharged by the earl.

civil and criminal jurisdiction, and cognizance also of ecclesiastical causes, which were entitled to precedence over every other business.

There was besides a shire or county court (*shir-gemot*) held twice every year, or oftener if occasion required, convened by the sheriff, (*shir-reeve,*) or, as he was sometimes also called, the alderman, (*ealdor-man,*) who presided over it, assisted by the bishop. Here causes were decided and business was transacted which affected the inhabitants of several of the hundreds.

The highest court of all was that of the king, the Wittenagemot, (*witan-gemot,*) in which he himself was present, attended by his councillors, or *witan*. This body, which united the functions of a legislative, judicial, and executive council, had no fixed times or place of meeting, but was held as occasion required, wherever the king happened to be. As to its judicial functions, it was in general only a court of extraordinary resort; it being a rule of the Anglo-Saxon law that none should apply for justice to the king unless he had first sought it in vain in the local courts.*

Hence the hundred and county courts occupied by far the most conspicuous position in the Anglo-Saxon judicial polity. The Anglo-Saxon shires, it may be observed, having been originally principalities, nearly, if not altogether, independent, but gradually united into one kingdom, were rather tantamount to our Anglo-American states than to our counties, of which the Saxon hundreds may be taken as the equivalent; the tythings corresponding to our Anglo-American townships; while (to carry out the parallel) the central authority of the

* See Forsyth's *History of Trial by Jury*, ch. iv. sec. 4.

king and the wittenagemot may be considered as represented by our federal system generally.

But though the reeve and the bishop presided in the local Anglo-Saxon courts, it was rather in the character of moderators than of judges; that latter function being performed by the freeholders of the county, all of whom, not less than the bishop and the reeve, had the right and were bound to give their attendance at these courts.

"Suits," says Hume,* "were determined in a summary manner, without much pleading, formality, or delay, by a majority of voices; † and the bishop and alderman had no further authority than to keep order among the freeholders, and interpose with their opinion."

These county courts, though traces of them are to be found in all the old Teutonic states of Europe, became ultimately peculiar to England. None of the feudal governments of continental Europe had any thing like them; and Hume, with his usual sagacity, has remarked that perhaps this institution had greater effects on the political system of England than has yet been distinctly pointed out. By means of this institution, all the freeholders were obliged to take a share in the conduct of affairs. Drawn from that individual and independent state, so distinctive of the feudal system, and so hostile to social order and the authority of law, they were made members of a political combination, and were taught in the

* History of England, Appendix, I.

† The decision of this majority would seem to have been principally determined, if the party complained against denied the charge, by the method of compurgation, in which the oath of the defendant was sustained by that of a certain number of his neighbors, who thereby certified their confidence in him; or, if he could not produce compurgators, and dared to venture upon it, by a superstitious appeal to the ordeal.

most effectual manner the duty and advantages of civic obedience by being themselves admitted to a share of civic authority. Perhaps, indeed, in this Anglo-Saxon institution of hundred and county courts we are to seek the origin of that system of local administration and self-government still more fully carried out in America than in England, by which English and Anglo-American institutions are so strongly distinguished from those of Europe, and in the judicious combination of which with a central administration, for matters of general concern, British and American liberty, as a practical matter, mainly consists.

One of the first procedures of the Norman Conqueror, by way of fixing his yoke upon the shoulders of the English people, was gradually to break down and belittle this local administration of justice. He did not venture, indeed, to abolish institutions so venerable and so popular, but he artfully effected his purpose by other means. He began by separating the civil and ecclesiastical jurisdictions. The bishops, according to a fashion recently introduced on the continent, were authorized to hold special courts of their own. These courts were at first limited to cases in which ecclesiastical questions were involved, or to which clergymen were parties; but by the progress of an artful system of usurpations, familiar to the courts of all ages and nations, they gradually extended their authority to many purely lay matters, under pretence that there was something about them of an ecclesiastical character. It was under this pretence that the English ecclesiastical courts assumed jurisdiction of the important matters of marriage and divorce, of wills, and of the distribution of the personal property of intestates — a jurisdiction which they still retain in England, and which, though we never had any ecclesiastical courts in the United States of America, has left deep traces upon our law and its administration as to these subjects.

In establishing these separate ecclesiastical courts, the Conqueror made a serious departure from his leading idea of centralization; and he thereby greatly contributed to build up a distinct theocratic power, which afterwards, while intrenching on the rights of the laity, intrenched also very seriously on the authority of his successors on the throne. But this was a danger which either he did not foresee — since he possessed, though his next successor relinquished it, the sole power of appointing bishops — or which he overlooked in his anxiety to diminish the importance of the old Saxon tribunals.

Both the civil and criminal authority of the local courts was greatly curtailed. Their jurisdiction in criminal cases was restricted to small matters, and even as to questions of property was limited to cases in which the amount in dispute did not exceed forty shillings; though, considering the superior weight of the shilling at that time, the greater comparative value in those ages of the precious metals, and the poverty of the country, this was still a considerable sum.

The general plan for the administration of justice of the Anglo-Norman government was a court baron in each of the baronies into which the kingdom was now parcelled out, to decide such controversies as arose between the several vassals or subjects of the same barony. Hundred courts and county courts still continued from the Saxon times, though with restricted authority, to judge between the subjects of different baronies; and a court composed of the king's great officers to give sentence among the barons themselves. Of this court, which ultimately became known as *Curia Regis*, (King's Court,) and sometimes as *Aula Regis*, (King's Hall,) because it was held in the hall of the king's palace, and of its instrumentality in extending the royal authority, Hume * gives the following account: "The king himself often sat in his court, which always attended his person: he there heard causes and pronounced judgment; and though he was assisted by the advice of the other members, it is not to be imagined that a decision could easily be obtained contrary to his inclination or opinion. † In the king's absence, the chief justiciary presided, who was the first magistrate of the state, and a kind of viceroy, on whom depended all the civil affairs of the kingdom. ‡ The other chief officers of the crown, the constable, marshal, seneschal, or steward, chamberlain, treasurer, and chancellor, were members, together with such feudal barons as thought proper to attend, and the barons of the exchequer, who at first were also feudal barons appointed by the king. This court, which was sometimes called the King's Court, sometimes the Court of Exchequer, judged in all

* History of England, Appendix, II.

† We may observe that even at present, whether in England or America, though the depositaries of the legislative and executive authority (which in those times the king was) sit no longer openly and personally on the bench, it still remains no easy matter, in cases in which they take an interest, to obtain in either country a judicial decision contrary to the inclination of these two authorities.

‡ In the king's absence — and the Anglo-Norman kings were often absent on visits to their continental dominions — this chief justiciary acted in all respects as the king's substitute, no less in military than in civil affairs, those who held it being selected quite as much for warlike prowess as for judicial skill. Such was the case with Ranulphus de Granville, chief justiciary of Henry II., A. D. 1180–1191, whose treatise in Latin, *On the Laws and Customs of the Kingdom of England*, is the oldest book of the common law. He went with Richard I. on the third crusade, and was killed at the siege of Acre.

causes, civil and criminal, and comprehended the whole business which is now shared out among four courts — the Chancery, the King's Bench, the Common Pleas, and the Exchequer.

"Such an accumulation of powers was itself a great source of authority, and rendered the jurisdiction of the court formidable to all the subjects; but the turn which judicial trials took soon after the conquest served still more to increase its authority, and to augment the royal prerogatives. William, among the other violent changes which he attempted and effected, had introduced the Norman law into England, had ordered all the pleadings to be in that tongue, and had interwoven with the English jurisprudence all the maxims and principles which the Normans, more advanced in cultivation, and naturally litigious, were accustomed to observe in the administration of justice.

"Law now became a science,* which at first fell entirely into the hands of the Normans, and even after it was communicated to the English, required so much study and application that the laity of those ignorant ages were incapable of attaining it, and it was a mystery almost solely confined to the clergy, and chiefly to the monks.

"The great officers of the crown, and the feudal barons who were military men, found themselves unfit to penetrate into these obscurities; and though they were entitled to a seat in the supreme judicature, the business of the court was wholly managed by the chief justiciary and the law barons, who were men appointed by the king, and entirely at his disposal.

* It might rather be said, a scholastic art, in which forms and words became matters of much greater consideration than substantial justice, and in which technical rules were substituted for the exercise of the reasoning faculties.

This natural course of things was forwarded by the multiplicity of business which flowed into that court, and which daily augmented by the appeals from all the subordinate judicatures of the kingdom. For the great power of the Conqueror established at first in England an authority which the monarchs in France were not able to attain till the reign of St. Louis, who lived near two centuries after: he empowered his court to receive appeals both from the courts of barony and the county courts, and by that means brought the administration of justice ultimately into the hands of the sovereign.*

"And lest the expense or trouble of the journey to court should discourage suitors and make them acquiesce in the decision of the inferior judicatures, itinerant judges were afterwards established, who made their circuits through the kingdom and tried all cases that were brought before them. By this expedient the courts of barony were kept in awe, and if they still preserved some influence it was only from the apprehensions which the vassals might entertain of disobliging their superior by appealing from his jurisdiction. But the county courts were much discredited; and as the freeholders were found ignorant of the intricate principles and forms of the new law, the lawyers gradually brought all business before the king's judges, and abandoned that convenient, simple, and popular judicature."

The innovations of the Conqueror and his successors having reduced the old local Anglo-Saxon tribunals to comparative insignificance, the whole judicial authority, except that which had been seized upon by the ecclesiastical courts,

* Not merely were these appeals introduced, but process was invented by which suits commenced in these local courts might, before they were finished, be removed into the king's courts, by the writ of *pone* and others.

remained for a hundred and fifty years after the conquest concentrated in the Aula Regis. But as Norman and Saxon became thoroughly intermixed, with the first faint dawn of modern English liberty the judicial power thus thoroughly centralized became again subdivided and distributed, though in a manner very different from that of the Saxon times.

The Anglo-Norman kings of England were perpetually on the move: the only way of disposing of the products of the landed estates which scattered over England afforded the main part of the royal revenue, was to go thither with the royal household and consume it on the spot. Wherever the king went, the Aula Regis followed, occasioning thereby great inconvenience and delay to suitors. This was complained of as a grievance, and the barons who extorted Magna Charta from their reluctant sovereign insisted, among other things, that *Common Pleas*, that is, civil suits between man and man, should be held in some certain place. It was in this provision of Magna Charta that originated the English Court of Common Pleas, which became fixed at Westminster Hall, the place of session of the Aula Regis when the king was in the vicinity of London. This Court of Common Pleas, or Common Bench as it was sometimes called, seems to have been at first but a mere committee of the Aula Regis; and the disintegration of that tribunal, thus begun, was, on the accession of Edward I. in 1272, completed by its resolution into three or rather five distinct tribunals.

Of these new courts, that which more immediately represented the Aula Regis was the Court of King's Bench, which still continued to follow the king and to be held in his presence. In the language of its process, such is still supposed to be the case; but like the other English courts, it has long since been fixed at Westminster Hall, and admits nobody to participate in its proceedings save its own members — a chief justice, who, though of inferior position in point of precedence, may be considered as in some respects the successor of the chief justiciary, which office was now abolished — and three or four puisne judges, the number having varied at different times.

The Court of Common Pleas was now also organized like the King's Bench, with a chief justice and three or four puisne judges. As this court had exclusive jurisdiction of civil suits, (except those relating to marriage, divorce, wills, tithes, and the distribution of the personal property of intestates, which had been usurped by the ecclesiastical courts,) *Pleas of the Crown*, that is, the criminal jurisprudence of the realm, (except prosecutions for heresy, of which the ecclesiastical courts claimed jurisdiction,) and also the hardly less important duty of superintending the other tribunals, even the Common Pleas itself, and keeping them within their due limits, was assigned to the King's Bench.

To a third court, that of Exchequer, of which, besides a chief baron and three or four puisne barons, the treasurer and the chancellor of the exchequer originally formed a part, were assigned all cases touching the king's revenue, and especially the collection of debts due to him, in which light were regarded not only all fines, forfeitures, and feudal dues, but the imposts and aids occasionally granted by Parliament.

There was also a Court of Chivalry or "Honor Court," presided over by the constable and marshal, and having jurisdiction of all questions touching rank and precedency; and another, over which the steward of the household presided, to regulate the king's domestic servants; but these courts, which have long since vanished, could never be considered as having stood on a par with the three others, the judges of which esteemed themselves the grand depositaries of the knowledge of the common or unwritten law of England; that is, of such customs and forms as had obtained the force of law previous to the existence of the regular series of statutes beginning with Magna Charta. Indeed, these judges of England, as they were called, were in the habit of meeting together in the Exchequer Chamber, for the purpose of hearing arguments on law points of importance or difficulty, adjourned thither for their consideration, and which they decided by a majority of their whole number present, thus presenting down to the recent abolition, or rather modification, of the Court of Exchequer Chamber, a shadow, as it were, of the ancient Aula Regis.

Already, previous to this fracture of the Aula Regis into the various courts above named, the legal profession, so far as practice in the lay courts was concerned, had begun to separate itself from the clerical; and places for the education and residence of a class of laymen who began to devote themselves to the study of the common law were established in the vicinity of Westminster Hall. Of these, Lincoln's Inn, founded at the commencement of the reign of Edward II., (about A. D. 1307,) under the patronage of William Earl of Lincoln, who gave up his own hostel or town residence for that purpose, was the earliest, and has always remained the principal. On this model were established before long the Inner and Middle Temple, (so called because a residence of the Knights Templars, forfeited by the dissolution of that order, had been devoted to this purpose,) Gray's Inn, Serjeant's Inn, and the Inns of Chancery.

Such was the origin of the profession of law as it still exists in England and America; of that body of lawyers whence all our judges are taken, arrogating to itself, after the example of the churchmen, of which it originally consisted, a certain mystical enlightenment and superiority, scouting the idea that the laity, as the lawyers too affect to distinguish all persons not of their cloth, — in plain English, *the people*, — should presume to express or to entertain any independent opinion upon matters of law, or that any body not a professional lawyer can possibly be qualified for the comprehension, and much less for the administration, of justice.

In the Anglo-Saxon courts the parties had appeared personally, and pleadings had been oral. The Anglo-Norman practice gave rise to appearance by attorney in all civil cases, and to that system of special written pleadings, prepared by counsel learned in the law, of which the operation was to give the victory to ingenuity and learning rather than to right, and which, after undergoing many modifications, has at length been abolished in many of our Anglo-American states, as an impediment to justice and an intolerable nuisance. Even in conservative England itself, though the system of special pleadings, greatly modified by modern changes, still exists, the recent return, by the examination of the parties, to the old popular system of oral pleading has been attended by the happiest results.

The preparation of these written pleadings, by which we are here to understand not arguments, but allegations of facts relied upon by the respective parties, was engrossed by the serjeants at law, whose distinguishing badge was a coif or velvet cap — wigs being a comparatively modern invention. To obtain admittance into this order, by which the entire practice of the Court of Common Pleas was engrossed, (that is, originally, the entire practice in civil suits,) and from which the judges were exclusively selected, sixteen years' study was required. The degree of barrister, or, as it was called, of apprentice, might be obtained by seven years' study; and it was to these two classes of serjeants and apprentices that the practice in the courts of Westminster Hall was originally confined.* But subsequently there sprang up a third inferior and still more numerous class, called attorneys, a sort of middle-men between the client and his counsel, not permitted to speak in court, for which purpose they must retain a serjeant or barrister, but upon whom was shifted off all the drudgery and responsibility of preparing the case, in which, however, no step of consequence could be taken without the advice of counsel learned in the law, *i. e.*, a serjeant or barrister.†

As the law and its practice thus became more and more a mystery, only to be learned by frequenting the courts of Westminster Hall, and by the study of the obscure and ill-prepared reports of their proceedings, which began now to be compiled by official reporters, and published under the name of Year Books, the old local Anglo-Saxon courts fell still more into contempt. Already in the reign of Henry III. the freeholders had been released from their obligation of attendance

* Originally, and down to a comparatively recent period, the Inns of Court were real schools, "readers" or lecturers being appointed for the instruction of the students, who were only admitted to practice after a sharp examination. Now, the examination is a mere form, and the student seeks instruction where he pleases. Even the nominal term of study has been reduced to five, and in some cases to three years.

† This distinction between attorneys and barristers, though still in full vogue in England and in several of the British colonies, is not recognized in the United States, where, indeed, it never had but a feeble and transient existence.

upon them, and another blow was given to these ancient tribunals when, in the reign of Edward II., the appointment of sheriffs, hitherto chosen by the freeholders, was assumed by the crown; and still another when, in the following reign, the election of conservators of the peace was also taken from the people and assumed by the king. To the magistrates thus appointed by the king the new name of Justices of the Peace was soon afterwards given, and the criminal jurisdiction conferred upon them, whether acting singly as examining and committing magistrates, or met together at the courts of Quarter Sessions, gradually superseded the small remains of criminal authority hitherto left to the old popular tribunals.

Two circumstances, however, combined to transfuse a certain portion of the spirit of these old tribunals into the newly established courts, thus standing in the way of the entire monopoly of the administration of justice at which the lawyers aimed, and securing to the body of the people a certain participation in the most important function of the government, to wit, the administration of justice; which participation, derived from the old Anglo-Saxon customs, and transmitted to our times, constitutes to-day the main pillar of both British and American liberty.

Contemporaneously with the new organization above described of the courts of common law, the British Parliament had taken upon itself that organization which it still retains — an upper house, (House of Lords,) composed of great nobles and bishops,* successor of the Anglo-Saxon Wittenagemote and of the Anglo-Norman Great Council, and a lower house,

* Down to the period of the reformation the abbots of the greater monasteries sat also in this house.

(House of Commons,) in which met together the elected representatives of the smaller landed proprietors, holding by knight's service immediately of the crown, (knights of the shire,) together with the newly-admitted representatives of the cities and chief towns, (burgesses.) The Parliament thus constituted claimed and exercised, probably as successor of the Wittenagemote, appellate jurisdiction from the decisions of all the courts of law. In the time of Edward III. it was even a common practice for the judges, when any question of difficulty arose in their several courts, to take the advice of Parliament on it before giving judgment. Thus in a case mentioned in the Year Book, 40 Ed. III., Thorpe, chief justice of the King's Bench, went with another judge to the House of Lords, to inquire the meaning and effect of a law they had just passed for amending the system of pleadings;* and many other instances occur of the same sort.

This appellate power vesting in Parliament from the decisions of all the courts was the first of the circumstances above alluded to as serving to prevent the monopoly of the administration of justice by the lawyers. But this check with the process of time has almost entirely disappeared. In England this appellate power in Parliament has long since fallen into the hands exclusively of the House of Lords, who themselves in giving judgment are ordinarily only the mouthpiece of the judges called in to give their advice. In what are now the United States of America the same appellate jurisdiction was

* If the Lords, says Campbell, were still liable to be so interrogated, they would not unfrequently be puzzled; and the revival of the practice might be a check on hasty legislation. It certainly would be a check upon the practice of courts, now so frequent, of putting an interpretation on statutes totally different from the intentions of those who frame them.

originally exercised by the colonial assemblies. With us, however, it has entirely vanished under the influence of the idea of a total separation of the legislative, executive, and judicial functions.

The other, and by far the most important check upon the monopoly of the lawyers, was the introduction and gradual perfecting of the trial by jury, by which the more ancient methods — the compurgation and ordeal of the Anglo-Saxons, and the trial by battle, the favorite method of the Anglo-Normans — were entirely superseded. The history of the trial by jury is exceedingly obscure. The petit jury may, however, be traced back to the old Anglo-Saxon method of trial by compurgation, the jury in its origin being only a body of witnesses drawn from the vicinage, who founded their verdict not upon the evidence of witnesses given before them, but upon their own personal knowledge of the matters in dispute.*

The grand jury seems to have originated in the old Anglo-Saxon custom imbodied in one of the laws of Ethelred, by

* Hence the necessity of venue, that is, the allegation in all declarations and indictments of some place in some county where the matter complained of happened, in order to a trial by a jury of the vicinage. In personal actions this necessity of trying a case in the county where the transaction occurred was got rid of by first setting out the true place of the transaction, and then alleging under a *videlicet* a venue in the county where the action was brought, which latter allegation the courts would not allow to be disputed. But in criminal proceedings and real actions the necessity of a trial in the county where the offence was committed or the land lies still continues.

The origin of the jury in a body of neighbors who decided from their own knowledge will seem less remarkable when we recollect that by the customs of the Anglo-Saxons all sales of land, contracts, &c., between individuals took place in public at the hundred and county courts, the memory of the freeholders present thus serving in place of written records. See Palgrave's *English Commonwealth*, vol. i. p. 213.

which was imposed upon the twelve senior thanes of every hundred the duty of discovering and presenting the perpetrators of all crimes within their district — a custom revived by the constitution of Clarendon, enacted A. D. 1164, by which twelve lawful men of the neighborhood were to be sworn by the sheriff, on the requisition of the bishop, to investigate all cases of suspected criminality as to which no individual dared to make an accusation. At first this accusing jury seems also to have served the purpose of a jury of trial. In what way the grand jury came to be separated from the petit jury, and how the former came to be increased to a number not exceeding twenty-three, of whom at least twelve must concur in order to find an indictment, is a point which still remains for the investigation of legal antiquaries.*

The trial by jury, though of the progress of its development little is known, appears to have taken on substantially its existing form, both in civil and criminal cases, nearly contemporaneously with the new organization of the English courts, with the rise of the legal profession as distinct from that of the clergy, and with the commencement of the series of English statutes and law reports — all of which, as well as the existing constitution of the British House of Commons, may be considered as dating from the accession of Edward I., A. D. 1272, or somewhat less than six hundred years ago. In certain cases of great importance this trial took place and still takes place in bank, as it is called; that is, in Westminster Hall, before all the judges of the court in which the suit is pending;† but in general, the trial is had

* See Forsyth's *Trial by Jury*, ch. x. sec. 1.

† Down to the time of Elizabeth *all* cases occurring in Middlesex county, in which Westminster lies, were thus tried in bank.

in the county in which (if a criminal case) the offence had been committed, or (if a civil case) in which the venue is laid, before certain commissioners sent into the counties for that purpose, and who, under the new system, were the successors of the justices in eyre, or itinerant justices, who had formed a part of the ancient Aula Regis. Originally, separate commissions appear to have issued for criminal and civil cases — for the former a commission of oyer and terminer, (to hear and determine,) and of general jail delivery; and for the latter a commission of assize, so called from the name of a peculiar kind of jury trial introduced as a substitute for trial by battle, in real actions, that is, pleas relating to land, villainage, and advowsons. In the times in which land, villains, and the right of presentation to parishes, constituted the chief wealth, these real actions constituted also the chief business of the Common Pleas, which then had exclusive jurisdiction of civil controversies; but to this commission of assize was annexed another, called a commission of *nisi prius*, authorizing the commissioners to try all questions of fact arising in any of the courts of Westminster. This latter commission was so called because the writ issued to the sheriff of the county in which the cause of action was alleged to have originated, to summon a jury to try the case, directed such jury to be summoned to appear at Westminster on a day named, unless before (in Latin, *nisi prius*) that day commissioners should come into the county to try the case there. Hence the term *nisi prius* employed by lawyers to designate a trial by jury before one or more judges, commissioned to hold such trials within certain circuits, but whose directions to the jury, and other points of law decided by them in the course of the trial, are liable afterwards to be reviewed by the whole bench.

Ultimately these commissions for both criminal and civil trials were given to the same persons, who also received a commission of the peace; and the whole territory of England being divided into six circuits, two of the judges, to whom other assessors were added, held assizes twice a year in each county,* for the trial of issues found in Westminster Hall — a system closely imitated in all our American states.

But the distribution of authority above described as having been originally made to the different courts of Westminster Hall, into which the Aula Regis was divided, did not long remain undisturbed. Courts have at all times, and every where, exhibited a great disposition to extend their jurisdiction, of which we have already had an example in the authority over marriages, wills, and the personal property of intestates, assumed by the English ecclesiastical courts; and considering the double jurisdiction under which we citizens of the United States live, — that of the federal and that of the state courts, — and the disposition so strongly and perseveringly exhibited by the federal courts to enhance their authority, while the state courts continue to grow weaker and tamer, this is, to us, a subject of no little interest.

Besides the general love of extending their jurisdiction characteristic of all courts, and indeed only one of the manifestations of the universal passion for power, the English Courts of King's Bench and Exchequer had a special motive for seeking to encroach on the exclusive civil jurisdiction of the Common Pleas. The salaries of the judges were very small — originally only sixty marks, equal to £40 sterling, or

* In London and Middlesex four sessions were held a year; in the four northern counties only one.

about $200 a year; nor was their amount materially increased down to quite recent times; but to this small salary were added fees paid by the parties to the cases tried before them; and the judges of the two other courts were very anxious to share with their brethren of the Common Pleas a part of the rich harvest which their monopoly of civil cases enabled them to reap from that source. Not only did the Court of King's Bench start the idea that all suits in which damages were claimed for injuries to person or property, attended by violence or fraud, came properly within its jurisdiction as "savoring of criminality;" it found another reason for extending its jurisdiction, by suggesting that when a person was in the custody of its officers, he could not, with a due regard to "legal comity," be sued on any personal claim in any other court, since that might result in his being taken out of the hands of their officer who already had him in custody, and was entitled to keep him. If any body had any claim against such a person, (such was the position plausibly set up,) it ought to be tried before the court in whose custody he already was. Having thus prepared the way, the Court of King's Bench did not stop here; but by a fiction, introduced into the process with which the suit was commenced, that the defendant was already in the custody of their marshal for a fictitious trespass which he was not allowed to deny, jurisdiction was gradually assumed in all private suits except real actions.

The Court of Exchequer in like manner claimed exclusive jurisdiction of suits for debt brought by the king's debtors, since by neglecting to pay them they might be prevented from paying their debts to the king; and under the pretence, which nobody was allowed to dispute, that all plaintiffs were the king's debtors, that court, too, gave an extent to their jurisdiction similar to that of the King's Bench. The exclusive jurisdiction of real actions, which alone remained to the Common Pleas, by the disappearance of villainage and the great increase of personal property, every day declined in importance; but even this was at last taken from the Common Pleas by the invention of Chief Justice Rolle, during the time of the Commonwealth, of the action of ejectment, which proceeds from beginning to end upon assumptions entirely fictitious, but which by its greater convenience entirely superseded real actions in England and in most of the Anglo-American States.

But while these three common law courts were thus exercising their ingenuity to intrench upon each other's jurisdiction, their pertinacious adherence to powers and technicalities, and their unwillingness, except in matters where the alleged prerogative of the crown was concerned, to do any thing not sanctioned by precedent, led them to refuse justice or relief to private suitors in many crying cases. Such cases still continued to be brought by petition before the king, and by him were referred to his chancellor, who in the earlier times was commonly his confessor, and who since the abolition of the office of chief justiciary had become the first official of the realm. Undertaking in these cases to prevent a failure of justice by rising above the narrow technicalities of the common law, and guided by the general principles of equity and good conscience, the chancellor gradually assumed a most important jurisdiction, which in civil matters ultimately raised his court to a rank and importance above that of all the others. With the advance indeed of wealth and civilization, appeals to chancery became more and more frequent; and if the common law courts had not altered their policy, and adopted upon many points equitable ideas, it seems probable that so far as civil suits were concerned, those courts would long since have been superseded altogether.* What indeed greatly contributed to save them was, the falling of the chancellorship of and the practice in the Equity Court entirely into the hands of lawyers bred in Westminster Hall, by whom equity itself was made subservient to precedent, and the whole procedure involved in forms and technicalities even more dilatory and expensive than those of the common law courts.

The same disinclination on the part of these common law courts to go beyond the strict limit of technical routine, led, with the progress of commerce and navigation, to the erection, in the time of Edward III., of the Admiralty Court, mainly for the trial of injuries and offences committed on the high seas, of which, on technical grounds, the courts of common law declined to take jurisdiction. After the foundation of English colonies,† branches of this court, to which also was given an exchequer jurisdiction, were established in the colonies, and on that model have been formed our federal District Courts.

* This history holds out to our state tribunals significant warnings as to the danger to which they are exposed on the part of the federal judges, especially those of the District Courts, who sitting singly on the bench, and with powers enormously and most dangerously extended by recent legislation, have from the unity and concentration of the one-man power, a great advantage over courts liable to be retarded in their action, if not reduced to imbecility by divisions among their members.

† The appeal from the English colonial courts to the king in council — the appeal cases being heard and decided by a committee of the privy councillors learned in the law — is another remnant of the old system, in which the constitution of the ancient Aula Regis has been very accurately preserved.

While the common law courts, through their preference of technicalities to justice, thus enabled the chancellors to assume a civil jurisdiction by which they themselves were completely overshadowed, driving the Parliament also to the necessity of creating, for both civil and criminal matters, a new Court of Admiralty,* they gave at the same time the support of their acquiescence and silence to other innovations, prompted not by public convenience, but by the very spirit of tyranny.

In every reign, at least from the time of Henry VI. down to that of Charles I., torture to extort confessions from those charged with state crimes was practised under warrants from the Privy Council. In the year 1615, by the advice of Lord Bacon, then attorney general, the lustre of whose philosophical reputation is so sadly dimmed by the infamy of his professional career, torture of the most ruthless character was employed upon the person of Peacham, a clergyman between sixty and seventy years of age, to extort confessions which might be used against him in a trial for treason, as to his intentions in composing a manuscript sermon not preached nor shown to any body, but found on searching his study, some passages of which were regarded as treasonable, because they encouraged resistance to illegal taxes. Thirteen years afterwards, when it was proposed to torture Fenton, the assassin of Villiers, Duke of Buckingham, to extort from him a confession of his accomplices, the prisoner suggested that if tortured he might perhaps accuse Archbishop Laud him-

* Both these courts proceeded according to the forms of the civil law, and without a jury. But occasionally the court of equity directed questions of fact arising before it to be settled by jury trial, and by a statute of Henry VIII. the trial of all maritime felonies before the Admiralty Court was directed to be by jury.

self. Upon this, some question arose as to the legality of torture; and the judges being called upon for their advice, thus at length driven to speak, delivered a unanimous opinion that the prisoner ought not to be tortured, because no such punishment was known or allowed by the English law; which English law, it now appeared, had for two hundred years been systematically disregarded under the eye and by the advice of judges and sworn lawyers, members of the Privy Council, and without any protest or interference on the part of the courts!

Another instance of similar acquiescence occurred in regard to the Court of Chivalry, which in the reign of Charles I. undertook to assume jurisdiction in the case of words spoken. Thus a citizen was ruinously fined by that court because, in an altercation with an insolent waterman, who wished to impose upon him, he deridingly called the swan on his badge a "goose." The case was brought within the jurisdiction of the court, by showing that the waterman was an earl's servant, and that the swan was the earl's crest, the heavy fine being grounded on the alleged "dishonoring" by the citizen of this nobleman's crest. A tailor, who had often very submissively asked payment of his bill from a customer of "gentle blood" whose pedigree was duly registered at the herald's college, on a threat of personal violence for his importunity, was provoked into saying that "he was as good a man as his debtor." For this offence, which was alleged to be a levelling attack upon the aristocracy, he was summoned before the earl marshal's court, and mercifully dismissed with a reprimand — *on releasing the debt!*

No aid could be obtained from the common law courts against this scandalous usurpation, by which, without any trial by jury, enormous damages were given.* Legal "comity" perhaps prevented any interference. Presently, however, the long Parliament met, and a single resolution of that body stopped forever this usurpation.

But while a scrupulous adherence to technicalities and to legal etiquette prevented the common law courts, on the one hand, from doing justice in private cases, and on the other from guarding the subject against official injuries and usurpations, they showed themselves, as the following biographies will prove, the ready and willing tools on all occasions of every executive usurpation. If the people of Great Britain and America are not at this moment slaves, most certainly, as the following biographies will prove, it is not courts nor lawyers that they have to thank for it.

How essential to liberty is the popular element in the administration of criminal law — how absolutely necessary is the restraint of a jury in criminal cases — was most abundantly proved by the proceedings of the English courts of Star Chamber and High Commission. The Court of Star Chamber, though of very ancient origin, derived its chief importance from statutes of Henry VII. and Henry VIII., by which it was invested with a discretionary authority to fine and imprison in all cases not provided for by existing laws, being thus erected, according to the boasts of Coke and Bacon, into a "court of criminal equity." The Court of High Commission, whose jurisdiction was mainly limited to clergymen, was created by a statute of Elizabeth as the depository of the ecclesiastical authority as head of the church assumed

* Hyde, (afterwards Lord Clarendon,) himself a lawyer, by whom the usurpations of this court were brought to the notice of Parliament, stated that more damages had been given by the earl marshal in his days, for words of supposed defamation, of which the law took no notice, than by all the courts of Westminster Hall during a whole term.

after the reformation by the English sovereigns. Both these courts consisted of high officers of the crown, including judges and crown lawyers; and though not authorized to touch life or member, they became such instruments of tyranny as to make their abolition one of the first things done after the meeting of the Long Parliament. The only American parallel to these courts is to be found in the authority conferred by the fugitive act of 1850, upon certain commissioners of the Circuit Court of the United States, to seize and deliver over to slavery peaceable residents in their respective states, without a jury, and without appeal.

History is philosophy teaching by example. From what judges have attempted and have done in times past, and in England, we may draw some pretty shrewd conclusions as to what, if unchecked, they may attempt, and may do, in times present, and in America. Nor let any man say that the following pages present a collection of judicial portraits distorted and caricatured to serve an occasion. They have been borrowed, word for word, from the *Lives* of the Chief Justices and of the Chancellors of England, by Lord Campbell, himself a lawyer and a judge, and though a liberal-minded and free-spoken man, by no means without quite a sufficient share of the *esprit du corps* of the profession. Derived from such a source, not only may the facts stated in the following biographies be relied upon, but the expressions of opinion upon points of law are entitled to all the weight of high professional authority.

Nor let it be said that these biographies relate to ancient times, and can have no parallelism, or but little, to the present state of affairs among us here in America. The times which they include are the times of the struggle in Great Britain between the ideas of free government and attempts at the establishment of despotism; and that struggle is precisely the one now going on among us here in America, with this sole difference, that over the water, among our British forefathers, it was the despotism of a monarch that was sought to be established; here in America, the despotism of some two hundred thousand petty tyrants, more or less, in the shape of so many slaveholders, who, not content with lording it over their several plantations, are now attempting, by combination among themselves, and by the aid of a body of northern tools and mercenaries, such as despots always find, to lord it over the Union, and to establish the policy of slaveholding as that of the nation. In Great Britain, the struggle between despotism and free institutions closed with the revolution of 1688, with which these biographies terminate. Since that time the politics of that country have consisted of hardly more than of jostlings between the Ins and the Outs, with no very material variance between them in their social ideas. Among us the great struggle between slaveholding despotism and republican equality has but lately come to a head, and yet remains undetermined. It exhibits, especially in the conduct of the courts and the lawyers, many parallels to the similar struggle formerly carried on in Great Britain. That struggle terminated at last with the deposition and banishment of the Stuart family, and the reëstablishment in full vigor of the ancient liberties of England, as embodied in the Bill of Rights. And so may ours terminate, in the reduction of those who, not content with being brethren seek to be masters, to the republican level of equal and common citizenship, and in the reëstablishment of emancipation, freedom, and the Rights of Man proclaimed in our Declaration of Independence, as the national and eternal policy of these United States!

# ATROCIOUS JUDGES.

## CHAPTER I.

### ROGER LE BRABACON.

ROGER LE BRABACON,* from the part he took in settling the disputed claim to the crown of Scotland, is an historical character. His ancestor, celebrated as "the great warrior," had accompanied the Conqueror in the invasion of England, and was chief of one of those bands of mercenary soldiers then well known in Europe under the names (for what reason historians are not agreed) of Routiers, Cottereaux, or *Brabançons.*† Being rewarded with large possessions in the counties of Surrey and Leicester, he founded a family which flourished several centuries in England, and is now represented in the male line by an Irish peer, the tenth Earl of Meath.

* The name is sometimes spelt Brabaçon, Brabançon, Brabason, and Brabanson.

† Hume, who designates them "desperate ruffians," says "troops of them were sometimes enlisted in the service of one prince or baron, sometimes in that of another; they often acted in an independent manner, and under leaders of their own. The greatest monarchs were not ashamed, on occasion, to have recourse to their assistance; and as their habits of war and depredation had given them experience, hardiness, and courage, they generally composed the most formidable part of those armies which decided the political quarrels of princes." — Vol. i. 438. In America we have no mercenary soldiers, but plenty of mercenary politicians, almost as much to be dreaded. — *Ed.*

The subject of the present sketch, fifth in descent from "the great warrior," changed the military ardor of his race for a desire to gain distinction as a lawyer. He was regularly trained in all the learning of "Essions" and "Assizes," and he had extensive practice as an advocate under Lord Chief Justice de Hengham. On the sweeping removal of almost all of the judges in the year 1290,* he was knighted, and appointed a puisne justice of the King's Bench, with a salary — which one would have thought must have been a very small addition to the profits of his hereditary estates — of 33*l.* 6*s.* 8*d.* a year. He proved a most admirable judge; † and, in addition to his professional knowledge, being well versed in historical lore, he was frequently referred to by the government when negotiations were going on with foreign states.

* They were removed because, during the king's absence on the continent, they had been guilty of taking bribes, and other misdemeanors. Of De Wayland, one of their number, and the first chief justice of the Common Pleas, Lord Campbell gives the following account: When arrested, on the king's return from Aquitaine, conscious of his guilt, he contrived to escape from custody, and, disguising himself in the habit of a monk, he was admitted among friars-minors in a convent at Bury St. Edmund's. However, being considered a heinous offender, sharp pursuit was made after him, and he was discovered wearing a cowl and a serge jerkin. According to the law of sanctuary, then prevailing, he was allowed to remain forty days unmolested. At the end of that time the convent was surrounded by a military force, and the entry of provisions into it was prohibited. Still it would have been deemed sacrilegious to take him from his asylum by violence; but the lord chief justice preferred surrendering himself to perishing from want. He was immediately conducted to the Tower of London. Rather than stand a trial, he petitioned for leave to abjure the realm; this favor was granted to him on condition that he should be attainted, and forfeit all his lands and chattels to the crown. Having walked barefoot and bareheaded, with a crucifix in his hand, to the sea side at Dover, he was put on board a ship and departed to foreign parts. He is said to have died in exile, and he left a name often quoted as a reproach to the bench till he was superseded by Jeffreys and Scroggs.

† That is, in the ordinary discharge of his duties. His attempt to take away the liberties of the Scotch we shall presently see. — *Ed.*

Edward I., arbitrator by mutual consent between the aspirants to the crown of Scotland, resolved to set up a claim for himself as liege lord of that kingdom, and Brabacon was employed, by searching ancient records, to find out any plausible grounds on which the claim could be supported. He accordingly travelled diligently both through the Saxon and Norman period, and — by making the most of military advantages obtained by kings of England over kings of Scotland, by misrepresenting the nature of homage which the latter had paid to the former for possessions held by them in England, and by blazoning the acknowledgment of feudal subjection extorted by Henry II. from William the Lion when that prince was in captivity, without mentioning the express renunciation of it by Richard I. — he made out a case which gave high delight to the English court. Edward immediately summoned a Parliament to meet at Norham, on the south bank of the Tweed, marched thither at the head of a considerable military force, and carried Mr. Justice Brabacon along with him as the exponent and defender of his new *suzeraineté*.

It is a little curious that one of these competitors for the Scottish throne had lately been an English judge, and a competitor for the very place to which Brabacon, for his services on this occasion, was presently promoted.

From the time of William the Conqueror and Malcolm Canmore, until the desolating wars occasioned by the dispute respecting the right of succession to the Scottish crown, England and Scotland were almost perpetually at peace; and there was a most familiar and friendly intercourse between the two kingdoms, insomuch that nobles often held possession in both, and not unfrequently passed from the service of the one government into that of the other. The Norman knights, having conquered England by the sword, in the course of a few generations got possession of a great part of Scotland by marriage. They were far more refined and accomplished than the Caledonian thanes; and, flocking to the court of the Scottish kings, where they made themselves agreeable by their skill in the tournament, and in singing romances, they softened the hearts and won the hands of all the heiresses. Hence the Scottish nobility are almost all of Norman extraction; and most of the great families in that kingdom are to be traced to the union of a Celtic heiress with a Norman knight. Robert de Brus, or Bruis, (in modern times spelt *Bruce*,) was one of the companions of the Conqueror; and having particularly distinguished himself in the battle of Hastings, his prowess was rewarded with no fewer than ninety-four lordships, of which Skelton, in Yorkshire, was the principal. Robert, the son of the first Robert de Brus, married early, and had a son, Adam, who continued the line of De Brus of Skelton. But becoming a widower while still a young man, to assuage his grief, he paid a visit to Alexander I., then King of Scots, who was keeping his court at Stirling. There the beautiful heiress of the immense lordship of Annandale, one of the most considerable fiefs held of the crown, fell in love with him; and in due time he led her to the altar. A Scottish branch of the family of De Brus was thus founded under the designation of Lords of Annandale. The fourth in succession was "Robert the Noble," and he raised the family to much greater consequence by a royal alliance, for he married Isabel, the second daughter of Prince David, Earl of Huntingdon, grandson of David I., sometimes called St. David.

Robert, son of "Robert the Noble" and the Scottish

princess, was born at the Castle of Lochmaben, about the year 1224. The Skelton branch of the family still flourished, although it became extinct in the next generation. At this time a close intercourse was kept up between "Robert the Noble" and his Yorkshire cousins; and he sent his heir to be educated in the south under their auspices. It is supposed that the youth studied at Oxford; but this does not rest on any certain authority. In 1245, his father died, and he succeeded to the lordship of Annandale. One would have expected that he would now have settled on his feudal principality, exercising the rights of *furca et fossa*, or "pit and gallows," which he possessed without any limit over his vassals; but by his English education he had become quite an Englishman, and, paying only very rare visits to Annandale, he sought preferment at the court of Henry III. What surprises us still more is, that he took to the gown, not the sword; and instead of being a great warrior, like his forefathers and his descendants, his ambition seems to have been to acquire the reputation of a great lawyer. There can be little doubt that he practised as an advocate in Westminster Hall from 1245 till 1250. In the latter year we certainly know that he took his seat on the bench as a puisne judge, or justiciar; and, from thence till 1263, extant records prove that payments were made for assizes to be taken before him — that he acted with other justiciars in the levying of fines — and that he went circuits as senior judge of assize. In the 46th year of Henry III. he had a grant of 40*l.* a year salary, which one would have supposed could not have been a great object to the Lord of Annandale. In the barons' wars, he was always true to the king; and although he had no taste for the military art, he accompanied his royal master into the

4*

field, and was taken prisoner with him at the battle of Lewes.

The royal authority being reëstablished by the victory at Evesham, he resumed his functions as a puisne judge; and for two years more there are entries proving that he continued to act in that capacity. At last, on the 8th of March, 1268, 52 Henry III., he was appointed "capitalis justiciarius ad placita coram rege tenenda," (chief justiciary for holding pleas before the king); but unless his fees or presents were very high, he must have found the reward of his labors in his judicial dignity, for his salary was very small. Hugh Bigod and Hugh le Despencer had received 1000 marks a year, "ad se sustentandum in officio capitalis justitiarii Angliæ," (for sustaining themselves in the office of chief justice of England,) but Chief Justice de Brus was reduced to 100 marks a year; that is, 66*l.* 13*s.* 4*d.* Yet such delight did he take in playing the judge, that he quietly submitted both to loss of power and loss of profit.

He remained chief justice till the conclusion of this reign, a period of four years and a half, during which he alternately went circuits and presided in Westminster Hall. None of his decisions have come down to us, and we are very imperfectly informed respecting the nature of the cases which came before him. The boundaries of jurisdiction between the Parliament, the Aula Regis, and the rising tribunal afterwards called the Court of King's Bench, seem to have been then very much undefined.

On the demise of the crown, Robert de Brus was desirous of being reappointed. He was so much mortified by being passed over, that he resolved to renounce England forever; and he would not even wait to pay his duty to Edward I., now returning from the holy wars.

The ex-chief justice posted off for his native country, and established himself in his castle of Lochmaben, where he amused himself by sitting in person in his court baron, and where all that he laid down was, no doubt, heard with reverence, however lightly his law might have been dealt with in Westminster Hall. Occasionally he paid visits to the court of his kinsman, Alexander III., but he does not appear to have taken any part in Scottish politics till the untimely death of that monarch, which, from a state of peace and prosperity, plunged the country into confusion and misery.

There was now only the life of an infant female, residing in a distant land, between him and his plausible claim to the Scottish crown. He was nominated one of the negotiators for settling the marriage between her and the son of Edward I., which, if it had taken place, would have entirely changed the history of the island of Great Britain. From his intimate knowledge both of Scotland and England, it is probable that the "Articles" were chiefly of his framing, and it must be allowed that they are just and equitable. For his own interest, as well as for the independence of his native country, he took care to stipulate that, "failing Margaret and her issue, the kingdom of Scotland should return to the nearest heirs, to whom of right it ought to return, wholly, freely, absolutely, and without any subjection."

The Maid of Norway having died on her voyage home, the ex-chief justice immediately appeared at Perth with a formidable retinue, and was in hopes of being immediately crowned king at Scone; — and he had nearly accomplished his object, for John Baliol, his most formidable competitor in point of right, always feeble and remiss in action, was absent in England. But, from the vain wish to prevent future disputes by a solemn decision of the controversy after all parties should have been heard, the Scotch nobility in an evil hour agreed to refer it, according to the fashion of the age, to the arbitration of a neighboring sovereign, and fixed upon Edward I. of England, their wily neighbor. The Scottish nobles being induced to cross the River Tweed, and to assemble in the presence of Edward, under pretence that he was to act only as arbitrator, Sir Roger de Brabacon by his order addressed them in French, (the language then spoken by the upper classes both in Scotland and England,) disclosing the alarming pretensions about to be set up.

A public notary and witnesses were in attendance, and in their presence the assumed vassals were formally called upon to do homage to Edward as their *suzerain*, of which a record was to be made for a lasting memorial. The Scots saw too late the imprudence of which they had been guilty in choosing such a crafty and powerful arbitrator. For the present they refused the required recognition, saying that "they must have time for deliberation, and to consult the absent members of their different orders." Brabacon, after advising with the king, consented that they should have time until the following day, and no longer. They insisted on further delay, and showed such a determined spirit of resistance, that their request was granted; and the first day of June following was fixed for the ceremony of the recognition. Brabacon allowed them to depart; and a copy of his paper, containing the proofs of the alleged *superiority* and *direct dominion* of the English kings over Scotland, was put into their hands. He then returned to the south, where his presence was required to assist in the administration of justice, leaving the Chancellor Burnel to complete the transaction. Although the body of the Scottish nobles, as well as the body of the Scottish people, would resolutely have withstood the demand, the competitors for the throne, in the hopes of gaining Edward's favor, successively acknowledged him as their liege lord, and their example was followed by almost the whole of those who then constituted the Scottish Parliament.*

Bruce afterwards pleaded his own cause with great dexterity, and many supposed that he would succeed. Upon the doctrine of *representation*, which is familiar to us, Baliol seems clearly to have the better claim, as he was descended from the eldest daughter of the Earl of Huntingdon: but Bruce was one degree nearer the common stock; and this doctrine, which was not then firmly established, had never been applied to the descent of the crown.

When Edward I. determined in favor of Baliol, influenced probably less by the arguments in his favor than by the consideration that from the weakness of his character he was likely to be a more submissive vassal, Robert de Brus complained bitterly that he was wronged, and resolutely refused to acknowledge the title of his rival. He retired in disgust to his castle of Lochmaben, where he died in November, 1295. While resident in England, he had married Isabel, daughter of Gilbert de Clare, Earl of Gloucester, by whom he had several sons. Robert, the son of Robert the eldest, became Robert I. of Scotland, and one of the greatest of heroes.

When judgment had been given in favor of Baliol, Brabacon was still employed to assist in the plan which had been

* Just like our northern candidates for the presidency, and the dough-face politicians who contrive to get chosen to Congress by northern constituencies, whose rights they then barter away and betray. — *Ed.*

formed to bring Scotland into entire subjection. There being a meeting at Newcastle of the nobles of the two nations, when the feudatory king did homage to his liege lord, complaint was made by Roger Bartholomew, a burgess of Berwick, that certain English judges had been deputed to exercise jurisdiction on the north bank of the Tweed. Edward referred the matter to Brabacon and other commissioners, commanding them to do justice according to the laws and customs of his kingdom. A petition was then presented to them on behalf of the King of Scotland, setting forth Edward's promise to observe the laws and customs of that kingdom, and that pleas of things done there should not be drawn to examination elsewhere. Brabacon is reported thus to have answered: —

"This petition is unnecessary, and not to the purpose; for it is manifest, and ought to be admitted by all the prelates and barons, and commonalty of Scotland, that the king, our master, has performed all his promises to them. As to the conduct of his judges, lately deputed by him as SUPERIOR and DIRECT LORD of that kingdom, they only represent his person; he will take care that they do not transgress his authority, and on appeal to him he will see that right is done. If the king had made any temporary promises when the Scottish throne was vacant, in derogation of his just *suzeraineté*, by such promises he would not have been restrained or bound." *

Encouraged by this language, Macduff, the Earl of Fife,

* This is the very ground upon which it is attempted, now, to justify the repeal of the Missouri prohibition of slavery, while Brabacon's defence of English judges in Scotland is a counterpart to the justification by our federal judges of the authority given to slave-catching commissioners. — *Ed.*

entered an appeal in the English House of Lords against the King of Scotland; and, on the advice of Brabacon and the other judges, it was resolved that the respondent must stand at the bar as a vassal, and that, for his contumacy, three of his principal castles should be seized into the king's hands.

Although historians who mention these events designate Brabacon as "grand justiciary," it is quite certain that, as yet, he was merely a puisne judge; but there was a strong desire to *reward* him for his services, and, at last, an opportune vacancy arising, he was created chief justice of the King's Bench.

Of his performances in this capacity we know nothing, except by the general commendation of chroniclers; for the Year Books, giving a regular account of judicial decisions, do not begin till the following reign.

On the accession of Edward II., Brabacon was reappointed chief justice of the King's Bench, and he continued very creditably to fill the office for eight years longer. He was fated to deplore the fruitless result of all his efforts to reduce Scotland to the English yoke — Robert Bruce being now the independent sovereign of that kingdom, after humbling the pride of English chivalry in the battle of Bannockburn.*

At last, the infirmities of age unfitting Brabacon for the discharge of judicial duties, he resigned his gown; but, to do him honor, he was sworn a member of the Privy Council, and he continued to be treated with the highest respect till his death, which happened about two years afterwards.

* May the pending attempts of the Southern States, countenanced and supported by the federal judges, to establish a "superiority" and "direct dominion" over the north, be met and repelled with similar spirit and success! — *Ed.*

## CHAPTER II.

### ROBERT TRESILIAN.

We next come to a chief justice who actually suffered the last penalty of the law — and deservedly — in the regular administration of retributive justice — Sir Robert Tresilian — hanged at Tyburn.

I can find nothing respecting his origin or education, except a doubtful statement that he was of a Cornish family, and that he was elected a fellow of Exeter College, Oxford, in 1354. The earliest authentic notice of him is at the commencement of the reign of Richard II., when he was made a serjeant at law, and appointed a puisne judge of the Court of King's Bench. The probability is, that he had raised himself from obscurity by a mixture of good and evil arts. He showed learning and diligence in the discharge of his judicial duties; but, instead of confining himself to them, he mixed deeply in politics, and showed a determination, by intrigue, to reach power and distinction. He devoted himself to De Vere, the favorite of the young king, who, to the great annoyance of the princes of the blood, and the body of the nobility, was created Duke of Ireland, was vested for life with the sovereignty of that island, and had the distribution of all patronage at home. By the influence of this minion, Tresilian, soon after the melancholy end of Sir John Cavendish,* was appointed chief justice of the King's Bench; and

* He had been murdered by a body of insurgent peasants headed by Jack Straw, one of the leaders in Wat Tyler's insurrection. — *Ed.*

he was sent into Essex to try the rebels. The king accompanied him. It is said that, as they were journeying, "the Essex men, in a body of about 500, addressed themselves barefoot to the king for mercy, and had it granted upon condition that they should deliver up to justice the chief instruments of stirring up the rebellion; which being accordingly done, they were immediately tried and hanged, ten or twelve on a beam, at Chelmsford, because they were too many to be executed after the usual manner, which was by beheading."

Tresilian now gained the good graces of Michael de la Pole, the lord chancellor, and was one of the principal advisers of the measures of the government, being ever ready for any dirty work that might be assigned to him. In the year 1385, it was hoped that he might have got rid, by an illegal sentence, of John of Gaunt, who had become very obnoxious to the king's favorites. But the plot got wind, and the Duke, flying to Pontefract Castle, fortified himself there till his retainers came to his rescue.

In the following year, when there was a change of ministry, Tresilian was in great danger of being included in the impeachment which proved the ruin of the chancellor; but he escaped by an intrigue with the victorious party, and he was suspected of having secretly suggested the commission signed by Richard, and confirmed by Parliament, under which the whole power of the state was transferred to a commission of fourteen barons. He remained very quiet for a twelvemonth, till he thought that he perceived the new ministers falling into unpopularity, and he then advised that a bold effort should be made to crush them. Meeting with encouragement, he secretly left London, and, being joined by the Duke of

Ireland, went to the king, who was at Nottingham, in a progress through the midland counties. He then undertook, through the instrumentality of his brother judges, to break the commission, and to restore the king and the favorite to the authority of which it had deprived them. His plan was immediately adopted, and the judges, who had just returned from the summer assizes, were all summoned in the king's name to Nottingham.

On their arrival, they found not only a string of questions, but answers, prepared by Tresilian. These he himself had signed, and he required them to sign. Belknappe, the chief justice of the Common Pleas, and the others, demurred, seeing the peril to which they might be exposed; but, by promises and threats, they were induced to acquiesce. The following record was accordingly drawn up, that copies of it might be distributed all over England: —

"Be it remembered, that on the 25th of Aug., in the 11th year of the reign of K. Rich. II., at the castle of Nottingham, before our said lord the king, Rob. Tresilian, chief justice of England, and Robt. Belknappe, chief justice of the common bench of our said lord the king, John Holt, Roger Fulthorp, and Wm. de Burg, knights, justices, &c., and John de Lokton, the king's serjeant-at-law, in the presence of the lords and other witnesses under-written, were personally required by said lord the king, on the faith and allegiance wherein to him the said king they are bound, to answer faithfully unto certain questions hereunder specified, and to them then and there truly recited, and upon the same to declare the law according to their discretion, viz.: —

"1. It was demanded of them, 'Whether that new statute, ordinance, and commission, made and published in the last parl. held at Westm., be not derogatory to the loyalty and prerogative of our said lord the king?' To which they unanimously answered that the same are derogatory thereunto, especially because they were against his will.

"2. 'How those are to be punished who procured that statute and commission?' — *A.* That they were to be punished with death, except the king would pardon them.

"3. 'How those are to be punished who moved the king to consent to the making of the said statute?' — *A.* That they ought to lose their lives unless his Maj. would pardon them.

"4. 'What punishment they deserved who compelled, straightened, or necessitated the king to consent to the making of the said statute and commission?' — *A.* That they ought to suffer as traitors.

"5. 'How those are to be punished who hindered the king from exercising those things which appertain to his royalty and prerogative?' — *A.* That they are to be punished as traitors.

"6. 'Whether after in parl. assembled, the affairs of the kingdom, and the cause of calling that parl. are by the king's command declared, and certain articles limited by the king upon which the lords and commons in that parl. ought to proceed; if yet the said lords and commons will proceed altogether upon other articles and affairs, and not at all upon those limited and proposed to them by the king, until the king shall have first answered them upon the articles and matters so by them started and expressed, although the king's command be to the contrary; whether in such case the king ought not to have the governance of the parl. and effectually overrule them, so as that they ought to proceed first on the matters proposed by the king: or whether, on the contrary, the lords and commons ought first to have the king's answer upon their proposals before they proceeded further?' — *A.* That the king in that behalf has the governance, and may appoint what shall be first handled, and so gradually what next in all matters to be treated of in parl., even to the end of the parl.; and if any act contrary to the king's pleasure made known therein, they are to be punished as traitors.

"7. 'Whether the king, whenever he pleases, can dissolve the parl., and command the lords and commons to depart from thence, or not?' — *A.* That he can; and if any one shall then proceed in parl. against the king's will, he is to be punished as a traitor.

"8. 'Since the king can, whenever he pleases, remove any of his judges and officers, and justify or punish them for their offences; whether the lords and commons can, without the will of the king, impeach in parl. any of the said judges or officers for any of their offences?' — *A.* That they cannot; and if any one should do so he is to be punished as a traitor.*

"9. 'How he is to be punished who moved in parl. that the statute should be sent for whereby Edw. II. (the king's great grandfather) was proceeded against and deposed in parl.; by means of sending for and imposing which statute, the said late statute, ordinance, and commission, were devised and brought forth in parl.?' — *A.* That as well he that so moved, as he who by pretence of that motion carried the said statute to the parl., are traitors and criminals, to be punished with death.

"10. 'Whether the judgment given in the last parl. held at Westm. against Mich. de la Pole, Earl of Suffolk, was

* Some of our federal judges would no doubt like very much to see this rule established among us. — *Ed.*

erroneous and revocable, or not?' — *A.* That if that judgment were now to be given, they would not give it; because it seems to them that the said judgment is revocable, as being erroneous in every part of it.

"In testimony of all which, the judges and serjeants aforesaid, to these presents have put their seals in the presence of the rev. lords, Alex. abp. of York, Rob. abp. of Dublin, John bp. of Durham, Tho. bp. of Chichester, and John bp. of Bangor, Rob. duke of Ireland, Mich. earl of Suffolk, John Rypon, clerk, and John Blake, esq.; given the place, day, month, and year aforesaid."

Tresilian exultingly thought that he had not only got rid of the obnoxious commission, but that he had annihilated the power of Parliament by the destruction of parliamentary privilege, and by making the proceedings of the two houses entirely dependent on the caprice of the sovereign.

He then attended Richard to London, where the opinion of the judges against the legality of the commission was proclaimed to the citizens at the Guildhall; and all who should act under it were declared traitors. A resolution was formed to arrest the most obnoxious of the opposite faction, and to send them to take their trials before the judges who had already committed themselves on the question of law; and, under the guidance of Tresilian, a bill of indictment was actually prepared against them for a conspiracy to destroy the royal prerogative. Thomas Ush, the under sheriff, promised to pack a jury to convict them; Sir Nicholas Brambre, who had been thrice lord mayor, undertook to secure the fidelity of the citizens; and all the city companies swore that they would live and die with the king, and fight against his enemies to their last breath. Arundel, Bishop of Ely, was still chancellor; but Tresilian considered that the great seal was now within his own grasp, and, after the recent examples of chief justices becoming chancellors, he anticipated no obstacle to his elevation.

At such a slow pace did news travel in those days, that, on the night of the 10th of November, Richard and his chief justice went to bed thinking that their enemies were annihilated, and next morning they were awoke by the intelligence that a large force, under the Duke of Gloucester and the Earls of Arundel and Nottingham, was encamped at Highgate. The confederate lords, hearing of the proceedings at Nottingham, had immediately rushed to arms, and followed Richard towards London, with an army of 40,000 men. The walls of London were sufficient to repel a sudden assault; and a royal proclamation forbade the sale of provisions to the rebels, in the hope that famine might disperse them. But, marching round by Hackney, they approached Aldgate, and they appeared so formidable, that a treaty was entered into, according to which they were to be supplied with all necessaries, on payment of a just price, and deputies from them were to have safe conduct through the city on their way to the king at Westminster. Richard himself agreed that on the following Sunday he would receive the deputies, sitting on his throne in Westminster Hall.

At the appointed hour he was ready to receive them, but they did not arrive, and he asked "how it fortuned that they kept not their promise." Being answered, "Because there is an ambush of a thousand armed men or more in a place called the Mews, contrary to covenant; and therefore they neither come, nor hold you faithful to your word,"—he said, with an oath, that "he knew of no such thing," and he ordered the sheriffs of London to go thither and kill all they could lay hands on. The truth was, that Sir Nicholas Brambre, in concert with Tresilian, had planted an ambush near Charing Cross, to assassinate the lords as they passed; but, in obedience to the king's order, the men were sent back to the city of London. The lords at last reached Westminster, with a gallant troop of gentlemen; and as soon as they had entered the great hall, and saw the king in his royal robes sitting on the throne, with the crown on his head and the sceptre in his hand, they made obeisance three times as they advanced, and when they reached the steps of the throne they knelt down before him with all seeming humility. He, feigning to be pleased to see them, rose and took each of them by the hand, and said "he would hear their plaint, as he was desirous to render justice to all his subjects." Thereupon they said, "Most dread sovereign, we appeal of high treason Robert Tresilian, that false justice; Nicholas Brambre, that disloyal knight; the Archbishop of York; the Duke of Ireland; and the Earl of Suffolk;" — and, to prove their accusation to be true, they threw down their gauntlets, protesting by their oaths that they were ready to prosecute it to battle. "Nay," said the king, "not so; but in the next Parliament (which we do appoint beforehand to begin the morrow after the Purification of our Lady,) both they and you, appearing, shall receive according to law what law doth require, and right shall be done."

It being apparent that the confederate lords had a complete ascendency, the accused parties fled. The Duke of Ireland and Sir Nicholas Brambre made an ineffectual attempt to rally a military force; but Chief Justice Tresilian disguised himself, and remained in concealment till he was discovered, after being attainted, in the manner to be hereafter described.

The election for the new Parliament ran strongly in favor of the confederate lords; and, on the day appointed for its meeting, an order was issued under their sanction for taking into custody all the judges who had signed the opinion at Nottingham. They were all arrested while they were sitting on the bench, except Chief Justice Tresilian; but he was nowhere to be found.

When the members of both houses had assembled at Westminster Hall, and the king had taken his place on the throne, the five lords, who were called APPELLANTS, "entered in costly robes, leading one another hand in hand, an innumerable company following them, and, approaching the king, they all with submissive gestures reverenced him. Then rising, they declared their appellation by the mouth of their speaker, who said, 'Behold the Duke of Gloucester comes to purge himself of treasons which are laid to his charge by the conspirators.' To whom the lord chancellor, by the king's command, answered, 'My lord duke, the king conceiveth so honorably of you, that he cannot be induced to believe that you, who are of kindred to him, should attempt any treason against him.' The duke, with his four companions on their knees, humbly gave thanks to the king for his gracious opinion of their fidelity. And now, as a prelude to what was going to be acted, each of the prelates, lords and commons then assembled, had the following oath administered to them upon the rood or cross of Canterbury, in full Parliament: 'You shall swear that you will keep, and cause to be kept, the good peace, quiet, and tranquillity of the kingdom; and if any will do to the contrary thereof, you shall oppose and disturb him to the utmost of your power; and if any will do any thing against the bodies of the five lords, you shall stand with them to the end of this present Parliament, and maintain and support them with all your power, to live and die with them against all men, no person or thing excepted, saving always your legiance to the king and the prerogatives of his crown, according to the laws and good customs of the realm.'"

Written articles to the number of thirty-nine were then exhibited by the appellants against the appellees. The other four are alleged to have committed the various acts of treason charged upon them "by the assent and counsel of Robert Tresilian, that false justice; and in most of the articles he bears the brunt of the accusation. Sir Nicholas Brambre alone was in custody; and the others not appearing when solemnly called, their default was recorded, and the lords took time to consider whether the impeachment was duly instituted, and whether the facts stated in the articles amounted to high treason. Ten days thereafter, judgment was given "that the impeachment was duly instituted, and that the facts stated in several of the articles amounted to high treason." Thereupon, the prelates having withdrawn, that they might not mix in an affair of blood, sentence was pronounced, "that Sir Robert Tresilian, the Duke of Ireland, the Archbishop of York, and Earl of Suffolk, should be drawn and hanged as traitors and enemies to the king and kingdom, and that their heirs should be disinherited forever, and that their lands and tenements, goods and chattels, should be forfeited to the king."

Tresilian might have avoided the execution of his sentence, had it not been for the strangest infatuation related of any human being possessing the use of reason. Instead of flying to a distance, like the duke, the archbishop, and the earl, none of whom suffered, although his features were necessarily well known, he had come to the neighborhood of Westminster Hall on the first day of the session of Parliament; and, even after his own attainder had been published, trusting to his disguise, his curiosity induced him to remain to watch the fate of his associate, Sir Nicholas Brambre.

This chivalrous citizen, who had been knighted for the bravery he had displayed in assisting Sir William Walwort to kill Wat Tyler and to put down the rebellion, having been apprehended and lodged in the Tower of London, was now produced by the constable of the Tower, to take his trial. He asked for further time to advise with his counsel, but was ordered forthwith to answer to every point in the articles of treason contained. Thereupon he exclaimed, "Whoever hath branded me with this ignominious mark, with him I am ready to fight in the lists to maintain my innocency whenever the king shall appoint!" "This," says a chronicler, "he spake with such a fury, that his eyes sparkled with rage, and he breathed as if an Etna lay hid in his breast; choosing rather to die gloriously in the field, than disgracefully on a gibbet."

The appellants said "they would readily accept of the combat," and flinging down their gages before the king, added, "We will prove these articles to be true to thy head, most damnable traitor!" But the lords resolved "that battle did not lie in this case; and that they would examine the articles with the proofs to support them, and consider what judgment to give, to the advantage and profit of the king and kingdom, and as they would answer before God."

They adjourned for two days, and met again, when a number of London citizens appeared to give evidence against Brambre. For the benefit of the reader, the chronicler I have before quoted shall continue the story: —

"Before they could proceed with his trial, they were interrupted by unfortunate Tresilian, who, being got upon the top of an apothecary's house adjoining to the palace, and descended into the gutter to look about him and observe who went into the palace, was discovered by certain of the peers, who presently sent some of the guard to apprehend him; who entering into the house where he was, and having spent long time in vain in looking for him, at length one of the guard stepped to the master of the house, and taking him by the shoulder, with his dagger drawn, said thus: 'Show us where thou hast hid Tresilian, or else resolve thy days as accomplished.' The master, trembling, and ready to yield up the ghost for fear, answered, 'Yonder is the place where he lies;' and showed him a round table covered with branches of bays, under which Tresilian lay close covered. When they had found him they drew him out by the heels, wondering to see him wear his hair and beard overgrown, with old clouted shoes and patched hose, more like a miserable poor beggar than a judge. When this came to the ears of the peers, the five appellants suddenly rose up, and, going to the gate of the hall, they met the guard leading Tresilian, bound, crying, as they came, 'We have him, we have him.' Tresilian, being com- into the hall, was asked 'what he could say for himself why execution should not be done according to the judgment passed upon him for his treasons so often committed;' but he became as one struck dumb; he had nothing to say, and his heart was hardened to the very last, so that he would not confess himself guilty of any thing. Whereupon he was without delay led to the Tower, that he might suffer the sentence passed against him. His wife and his children did with many tears accompany him to the Tower; but his wife was so overcome with grief, that she fell down in a swoon as if she had been dead. Immediately Tresilian is put upon an hurdle, and drawn through the streets of the city, with a wonderful concourse of people following him. At every furlong's end he was suffered to stop, that he might rest himself, and to see if he would confess or acknowledge any thing; but what he said to the friar, his confessor, is not known. When he came to the place of execution he would not climb the ladder, until such time as being soundly beaten with bats and staves he was forced to go up; and when he was up, he said, 'So long as I do wear any thing upon me, I shall not die;' wherefore the executioner stript him, and found certain images painted like to the signs of the heavens, and the head of a devil painted, and the names of many of the devils wrote in parchment; these being taken away he was hanged up naked, and after he had hanged some time, that the spectators should be sure he was dead, they cut his throat, and because the night approached they let him hang till the next morning, and then his wife, having obtained a licence of the king, took down his body, and carried it to the Gray-Friars, where it was buried."

Considering the violence of the times, Tresilian's conviction and execution cannot be regarded as raising a strong presumption against him; but there seems little doubt that he flattered the vices of the unhappy Richard; and historians agree that, in prosecuting his personal aggrandizement, he was utterly regardless of law and liberty. He died unpitied, and, notwithstanding the "historical doubts" by which we are beset, no one has yet appeared to vindicate his memory.

## CHAPTER III.

### THOMAS BILLING.

THE crown of England, transferred on the deposition of Richard II.* in 1399 to the Lancaster family in the person of Henry IV., was worn successively by him and by his son and grandson, Henry V. and Henry VI. After the lapse, however, of sixty-two years, the imbecility of Henry VI. enabled the Legitimist or Yorkist party to triumph by placing Edward IV. on the throne.

At this time Sir John Fortescue, an able man and distinguished by his treatise *De Laudibus Legum Angliæ*, (Praises of the Laws of England,) was chief justice of the King's Bench; but being an ardent Lancastrian, and having written pamphlets to prove that Richard II. was rightly de-

* The persistence of Richard II. in the same arbitrary principles of which the advocacy cost Tresilian his life, caused his deposition a few years afterwards, as to which, Lord Campbell observes, —

"While we honor Lord Somers and the patriots who took the most active part in the revolution of 1688, by which a king was cashiered, hereditary right was disregarded, and a new dynasty was placed on the throne, we are apt to consider the kings of the house of Lancaster as usurpers, and those who sided with them as rebels. Yet there is great difficulty in justifying the deposition of James II., and condemning the deposition of Richard II. The latter sovereign, during a reign of above twenty years, had proved himself utterly unfit to govern the nation, and, after repeated attempts to control him, and promises on his part to submit to constitutional advice, he was still under the influence of worthless favorites, and was guilty of continued acts of tyranny and oppression; so that the nation, which, with singular patience, had often forgiven his misconduct from respect to the memory of his father and his grandfather, was now almost unanimously resolved to submit no longer to his rule."

posed, that Henry IV. had been called to the throne by the estates of the kingdom and the almost unanimous voice of the people, and that now, in the third generation, the title of the House of Lancaster could not be questioned, he was by no means the man to suit the new dynasty. He was removed to make way for Sir John Markham, who had been for nineteen years a puisne judge of the same court, and who, though he had not ventured to publish any thing on the subject, yet in private conversation and in "moots" at the Temple, such as that in which the white and red roses were chosen as the emblems of the opposite opinions, did not hesitate to argue for indefeasible hereditary right, which no length of possession could supersede, and to contend that the true heir of the crown of England was Richard, Duke of York, descended from the second son of Edward III. His sentiments were well known to the Yorkist leaders, and they availed themselves of the legal reasoning and the historical illustrations with which he furnished them; but he never sallied forth into the field, even when, after the death of Richard, the gallant youth his eldest son displayed the high qualities which so wonderfully excited the energy of his partisans. However, when Henry VI. was confined as a prisoner in the Tower, and Fortescue and all the Lancastrian leaders had fled, Markham was very naturally and laudably selected for the important office of chief justice of the King's Bench. Although he was such a strong Legitimist, he was known not only to be an excellent lawyer, but a man of honorable and independent principles. The appointment, therefore, gave high satisfaction, and was considered a good omen of the new *régime*.

He held the office above seven years, with unabated credit. Not only was his hand free from bribes, but so was his mind from every improper bias. It was allowed that when sitting on the bench, no one could have discovered whether he was Yorkist or Lancastrian; the adherents of the reigning dynasty complaining (I dare say very unjustly) that, to obtain a character for impartiality, he showed a leaning on the Lancastrian side.*

At last, though he cherished his notions of hereditary right with unabating constancy, he forfeited his office because he would not prostitute it to the purpose of the king and the ministers in wreaking their vengeance on the head of a political opponent. Sir Thomas Cooke, who inclined to the Lancastrians, though he had conducted himself with great caution, was accused of treason and committed to the Tower. To try him a special commission was issued, over which Lord Chief Justice Markham presided, and the government was eager for a conviction. But all that could be proved against the prisoner was, that he entered into a treaty to lend, on good security, a sum of 1000 marks for the use of Margaret, the queen of the dethroned Henry VI. The security was not satisfactory, and the money was not advanced. The chief justice ruled that this did not amount to treason, but was at most misprision of treason. Of this last offence the prisoner being found guilty, he was subjected to fine and imprisonment; but he saved his life and his lands. King Edward IV. was in a fury, and swearing that Markham, notwithstanding his high pretensions to loyalty, was himself little better than a traitor, ordered that

* Fuller, in praising Fortescue and Markham, says, "These I may call two chief justices of the chief justices, for their signal integrity; for though the one of them favored the house of Lancaster, and the other of York, in the titles to the crown, both of them favored the house of Justice in matters betwixt party and party."

he should never sit on the bench any more; and appointed in his place a successor, who, being a *puisne*, had wished to trip up the heels of his chief, and had circulated a statement, to reach the king's ear, that Sir Thomas Cooke's offence was a clear, overt act of high treason. Markham bore his fall with much dignity and propriety — in no respect changing his principles or favoring the movement which for a season restored Henry VI. to the throne after he had been ten years a prisoner in the Tower.

Upon the dismissal of Sir John Markham, Edward IV., who no longer showed the generous spirit which had illustrated his signal bravery while he was fighting for the crown, and now abandoned himself by turns to voluptuousness and cruelty, tried to discover the fittest instrument that could be found for gratifying his resentments by a perversion of the forms of law, and with felicity fixed upon Sir Thomas Billing, who, by all sorts of meannesses, frauds, and atrocities, aided by natural shrewdness, or rather low cunning, had contrived to raise himself from deep obscurity to a puisne judge of the King's Bench; and in that situation had shown himself ready to obey every mandate, and to pander to every caprice of those who who could give him still higher elevation. This is one of the earliest of the long list of politico-legal adventurers who have attained to eminence by a moderate share of learning and talent, and an utter want of principle and regard for consistency.*

His family and the place of his education are unknown. He was supposed to have been the clerk of an attorney; thus

* A list by no means limited to England, but very much lengthened out in America. — *Ed.*

making himself well acquainted with the rules of practice and the less reputable parts of the law. However, he contrived (which must have been a difficult matter in those days, when almost all who were admitted at the inns of court were young men of good birth and breeding) to keep his terms and to be called to the bar. He had considerable business, although not of the most creditable description, and in due time he took the degree of the coif, that is, became a serjeant.

His ambition grew with his success, and nothing would satisfy him but official preferment. Now began the grand controversy respecting the succession to the crown; and the claim to it through the house of Mortimer, which had long been a mere matter of speculation, was brought into formidable activity in the person of Richard, Duke of York. Billing, thinking that a possession of above half a century must render the Lancastrian cause triumphant, notwithstanding the imbecility of the reigning sovereign, was outrageously loyal. He derided all objections to a title which the nation had so often solemnly recognized; enlarging on the prudence of Henry IV., the gallantry of Henry V., and the piety of the holy Henry VI., under whose mild sway the country now flourished, happily rid of all its continental dependencies. He even imitated the example of Sir John Fortescue, and published a treatise upon the subject, which he concluded with an exhortation "that all who dared, by act, writing, or speech, to call in question the power of Parliament to accept the resignation of Richard II., or to depose him for the crimes he had committed, and to call to the throne the member of the royal family most worthy to fill it, according to the fashion of our Saxon ancestors, should be proceeded against as traitors." This so pleased Waynflete, the chancellor, and the other

Lancastrian leaders, that Billing was thereupon made king's serjeant, and knighted.

When the right to the crown was argued, like a peerage case, at the bar of the House of Lords, Billing appeared as counsel for Henry VI., leading the attorney and solicitor general; but it was remarked that his fire had slackened much, and he was very complimentary to the Duke of York, who, since the battle of Northampton, had been virtually master of the kingdom.

We know nothing more of the proceedings of this unprincipled adventurer until after the fall of Duke Richard, when the second battle of St. Alban's had placed his eldest son on the throne. Instantly Sir Thomas Billing sent in his adhesion; and such zeal did he express in favor of the new dynasty that his patent of king's serjeant was renewed, and he became principal law adviser to Edward IV. When Parliament assembled, receiving a writ of summons to the House of Lords, he assisted in framing the acts by which Sir J. Fortescue and the principal Lancastrians, his patrons, were attainted, and the last three reigns were pronounced tyrannical usurpations. He likewise took an active part in the measures by which the persevering efforts of Queen Margaret to regain her ascendency were disconcerted, and Henry VI. was lodged a close prisoner in the Tower of London.

Sir John Markham, the honorable and consistent Yorkist, now at the head of the administration of the criminal law, was by no means so vigorous in convicting Lancastrians, or persons suspected of Lancastrianism, as Edward and his military adherents wished; and when state prosecutions failed, there were strong murmurs against him. In these Mr. Serjeant Billing joined, suggesting how much better it would be for the public tranquillity if the law were properly enforced. It would have appeared very ungracious, as well as arbitrary, to displace the chief justice, who had been such a friend to the house of York, and was so generally respected. That there might be one judge to be relied upon, who might be put into commissions of oyer and terminer, Billing was made a puisne justice of the Court of King's Bench. He was not satisfied with this elevation, which little improved his position in the profession; but he hoped speedily to be on the woolsack, and he was resolved that mere scruples of conscience should not hold him back.

Being thus intrusted with the sword of justice, he soon fleshed it in the unfortunate Walter Walker, indicted before him on the statute 25 Edward III., for compassing and imagining the death of the king. The prisoner kept an inn called the Crown, in Cheapside, in the city of London, and was obnoxious to the government because a club of young men met there who were suspected to be Lancastrians, and to be plotting the restoration of the imprisoned king. But there was no witness to speak to any such treasonable consult; and the only evidence to support the charge was, that the prisoner had once, in a merry mood, said to his son, then a boy, "Tom, if thou behavest thyself well, I will make thee heir to the Crown."

Counsel were not allowed to plead in such cases then, or for more than three centuries after; but the poor publican himself urged that he never had formed any evil intention upon the king's life, — that he had ever peaceably submitted to the ruling powers, — and that though he could not deny the words imputed to him, they were only spoken to amuse his little boy, meaning that he should succeed him as master of the Crown Tavern, in Cheapside, and, like him, employ himself in selling sack.

Mr. Justice Billing, however, ruled —

"That upon the just construction of the statute of treasons, which was only declaratory of the common law, there was no necessity, in supporting such a charge, to prove a design to take away the natural life of the king; that any thing showing a disposition to touch his royal state and dignity was sufficient; and that the words proved were inconsistent with that reverence for the hereditary descent of the crown which was due from every subject under the oath of allegiance; therefore, if the jury believed the witness, about which there could be no doubt, as the prisoner did not venture to deny the treasonable language which he had used, they were bound to find him guilty."

A verdict of guilty was accordingly returned, and the poor publican was hanged, drawn, and quartered.*

Mr. Justice Billing is said to have made the criminal law thus bend to the wishes of the king and the ministers in other cases, the particulars of which have not been transmitted to us; and he became a special favorite at court, all his former extravagances about cashiering kings and electing others in their stead being forgotten, in consideration of the zeal he displayed since his conversion to the doctrine of "divine right."

Therefore, when the chief justice had allowed Sir Thomas Cooke to escape the penalties of treason, after his forfeitures had been looked to with eagerness on account of the great

* Some of our American advocates of constructive treasons have laid down the law much in the same spirit. — *Ed.*

wealth he had accumulated, there was a general cry in the palace at Westminster that he ought not to be permitted longer to mislead juries, and that Mr. Justice Billing, of such approved loyalty and firmness, should be appointed to succeed him, rather than the attorney or solicitor general, who, getting on the bench, might, like him, follow popular courses.

Accordingly, a *supersedeas* to Sir John Markham was made out immediately after the trial of *Rex* v. *Cooke*, and the same day a writ passed the great seal, whereby "the king's trusty and well-beloved Sir Thomas Billing, Knight, was assigned as chief justice to hold pleas before the king himself."

The very next term came on the trial of Sir Thomas Burdett. This descendant of one of the companions of William the Conqueror, and ancestor of the late Sir Francis Burdett, lived at Arrow, in Warwickshire, where he had large possessions. He had been a Yorkist, but somehow was out of favor at court; and the king, making a progress in those parts, had rather wantonly entered his park, and hunted and killed a white buck, of which he was peculiarly fond. When the fiery knight, who had been from home, heard of this affair, which he construed into a premeditated insult, he exclaimed, "I wish that the buck, horns and all, were in the belly of the man who advised the king to kill it;" or, as some reported, "were in the king's own belly." The opportunity was thought favorable for being revenged on an obnoxious person. Accordingly he was arrested, brought to London, and tried at the King's Bench bar on a charge of treason, for having compassed and imagined the death and destruction of "our lord the king."

The prisoner proved, by most respectable witnesses, that

the wish he had rashly expressed was applied only to the man who advised the king to kill the deer, and contended that words did not amount to treason, and that — although, on provocation, he had uttered an irreverent expression, which he deeply regretted — instead of having any design upon the king's life, he was ready to fight for his right to the crown, as he had done before; and that he would willingly die in his defence.

"Lord Chief Justice Billing left it to the jury to consider what the words were; for if the prisoner had only expressed a wish that the buck and his horns were in the belly of the man who advised the king to kill the buck, it would not be a case of treason, and the jury would be bound to acquit; but the story as told by the witnesses for the crown was much more probable, for sovereigns were not usually advised on such affairs, and it had been shown that on this occasion the king had acted entirely of his own head, without any advisers, as the prisoner, when he uttered the treasonable words, must have well known: then, if the words really were as alleged by the witnesses for the crown, they clearly did show a treasonable purpose. Words merely expressing an opinion, however erroneous the opinion, might not amount to treason; but when the words refer to a purpose, and incite to an act, they might come within the statute. Here the king's death had certainly been in the contemplation of the prisoner; in wishing a violence to be done which must inevitably have caused his death, he imagined and compassed it. This was, in truth, advising, counselling, and commanding others to take away the sacred life of his majesty. If the wicked deed had been done, would not the prisoner, in case the object of his vengeance had been a subject, have been an accessory before the fact?* But in treason accessories before the fact were principals, and the prisoner was not at liberty to plead that what he had planned had not been accomplished. Therefore, if the jury believed that he had uttered the treasonable wish directed against his majesty's own sacred person, they were bound to convict him."

The jury immediately returned a verdict of guilty; and the frightful sentence in high treason, being pronounced, was carried into execution with all its horrors. This barbarity made a deep impression on the public mind, and, to aggravate the misconduct of the judge, a rumor was propagated that the late virtuous chief justice had been displaced because he had refused to concur in it.

Lord Chief Justice Billing, having justified his promotion by the renegade zeal he displayed for his new friends, and enmity to his old associates, was suddenly thrown into the greatest perplexity, and he must have regretted that he had ever left the Lancastrians. One of the most extraordinary revolutions in history, — when a long continuance of public tranquillity was looked for, — without a battle, drove Edward IV. into exile, and replaced Henry VI. on the throne, after he had languished ten years as a captive in the Tower of London.

There is no authentic account of Billing's deportment in

* It was, we may suppose, from this charge that Mr. Justice Curtis, of the Supreme Court of the United States, got the law retailed in his charge to the grand jury of the Massachusetts District, in consequence of which indictments were found against Wendell Phillips and Theodore Parker for obstructing the execution of the fugitive slave act — on the ground that certain speeches of theirs in Faneuil Hall against that statute "referred to a purpose" and "incited to an act" of resistance to it, thereby making their expression of opinion criminal. — *Ed.*

this crisis, and we can only conjecture the cunning means he would resort to, and the pretences he would set up, to keep his place and to escape punishment. Certain it is, that within a few days from the time when Henry went in procession from his prison in the Tower to his palace at Westminster, with the crown on his head, while almost all other functionaries of the late government had fled, or were shut up in jail, a writ passed the great seal, bearing date the 49th year of his reign, by which he assigned "his trusty and well-beloved Sir John Billing, Knight, as his chief justice to hold pleas in his court before him." There can be as little doubt that he was present at the Parliament which was summoned immediately after in Henry's name, when the crown was entailed on Henry and his issue, Edward was declared a usurper, his most active adherents were attainted, and all the statutes which had passed during his reign were repealed. It is not improbable that there had been a secret understanding between Billing and the Earl of Warwick, (the king maker,) who himself so often changed sides, and who was now in possession of the whole authority of the government.

While Edward was a fugitive in foreign parts, the doctrine of divine right was, no doubt, at a discount in England, and Billing may have again bolted his arguments about the power of the people to choose their rulers; although, according to the superstition of the age, he more probably countenanced the belief that Henry was a saint, and that he was restored by the direct interposition of Heaven.

But one would think he must have been at his wits' end when, in the spring of the following year, Edward IV. landed at Ravenspurg, gained the battle of Barnet, and, after the murder of Henry VI. and the Prince of Wales, was again on the throne, without a rival. Billing does seem to have found great difficulty in making his peace. Though he was dismissed from his office, it was allowed to remain vacant about a twelvemonth, during which time he is supposed to have been in hiding. But he had vowed that, whatever changes might take place on the throne, he himself should die chief justice of the King's Bench; and he contrived to be as good as his word.

By his own representations, or the intercession of friends, or the hope of the good services he might yet render in getting rid of troublesome opponents, the king was induced to declare his belief that he who had sat on the trials of Walker and Burdet had unwillingly submitted to force during the late usurpation; and on the 17th of June, 1472, a writ passed the great seal, by which his majesty assigned "his right trusty and well-beloved Sir John Billing, Knight, as Chief Justice to hold pleas before his Majesty himself."

For nearly nine years after, he continued in the possession of his office, without being driven again to change his principles or his party. One good deed he did, which should be recorded of him — in advising Edward IV. to grant a pardon to an old Lancastrian, Sir John Fortescue. But for the purpose of reducing this illustrious judge to the reproach of inconsistency, which he knew made his own name a by-word, he imposed a condition that the author of *De Laudibus* should publish a new treatise, to refute that which he had before composed, proving the right of the house of Lancaster to the throne; and forced him to present the petition in which he assures the king "that he hath so clearly disproved all the arguments that have been made against his right and title, that now there remaineth no color or matter of argument to the hurt or infamy of the same right or title by reason of any such writing, but the same right and title stand now the more clear and open by that any such writings have been made against them."

There are many decisions of Chief Justice Billing on dry points of law to be found in the Year Books, but there is only one other trial of historical importance mentioned in which he took any part; and it is much to be feared that on this occasion he inflamed, instead of soothing, the violent passions of his master, with whom he had become a special favorite.

Edward IV., after repeated quarrels and reconciliations with his brother, the Duke of Clarence, at last brought him to trial, at the bar of the House of Lords, on a charge of high treason. The judges were summoned to attend, and Lord Chief Justice Billing was their mouthpiece. We have only a very defective account of this trial, and it would appear that nothing was proved against the first prince of the blood, except that he had complained of the unlawful conviction of Burdet, who had been in his service; that he had accused the king of dealing in magic, and had cast some doubts on his legitimacy; that he had induced his servants to swear that they would be true to him, without any reservation of their allegiance to their sovereign; and that he had surreptitiously obtained and preserved an attested copy of an act of Parliament, passed during the late usurpation, declaring him next heir to the crown after the male issue of Henry VI. The Duke of Buckingham presided as high steward, and in that capacity ought to have laid down the law to the peers; but, to lessen his responsibility, he put the question to the judges, "whether the matters proved against the Duke of Clarence amounted, in point of law, to high treason." Chief

Justice Billing answered in the affirmative. Therefore a unanimous verdict of guilty was given, and sentence of death was pronounced in the usual form. I dare say Billing would not have hesitated in declaring his opinion that the beheading might be commuted to drowning in a butt of malmsey wine; but this story of Clarence's exit, once so current, is now generally discredited, and the belief is, that he was privately executed in the Tower, according to his sentence.

Lord Chief Justice Billing enjoyed the felicitous fate accorded to very few persons of any distinction in those times — that he never was imprisoned, that he never was in exile, and that he died a natural death. In the spring of the year 1482, he was struck with apoplexy, and he expired in a few days — fulfilling his vow — for he remained to the last chief justice of the King's Bench, after a tenure of office for seventeen years, in the midst of civil wars and revolutions.

He amassed immense wealth, but dying childless, it went to distant relations, for whom he could have felt no tenderness. Notwithstanding his worldly prosperity, few would envy him. He might have been feared and flattered, but he could not have been beloved or respected, by his contemporaries; and his name, contrasted with those of Fortescue and Markham, was long used as an impersonation of the most hollow, deceitful, and selfish qualities which can disgrace mankind.

# CHAPTER IV.

## JOHN FITZJAMES.

Of obscure birth, and not brilliant talents, Sir John Fitzjames made his fortune by his great good humor, and by being at college with Cardinal Wolsey. It is said that Fitzjames, who was a Somersetshire man, kept up an intimacy with Wolsey when the latter had become a village parson in that county; and that he was actually in the brawl at the fair when his reverence, having got drunk, was set in the stocks by Sir Amyas Paulet.

While Wolsey tried his luck in the church, with little hope of promotion, Fitzjames was keeping his terms in the inns of court; but he chiefly distinguished himself on gaudy days, by dancing before the judges, playing the part of "Abbot of Misrule," and swearing strange oaths — especially by *St. Gillian*, his tutelary saint. His agreeable manners made him popular with the "readers" and "benchers;" and through their favor, although very deficient in "moots" and "bolts," he was called to the outer bar. Clients, however, he had none, and he was in deep despair, when his former chum — having insinuated himself into the good graces of the stern and wary old man, Henry VII., and those of the gay and licentious youth, Henry VIII. — was rapidly advancing to greatness. Wolsey, while almoner, and holding subordinate offices about the court, took notice of Fitzjames, advised him to stick to the profession, and was able to throw some business in his way in the court of Wards and Liveries —

> "Lofty and sour to them that lov'd him not:
> But to those men that sought him, sweet as summer."

Fitzjames was devotedly of this second class, and was even suspected to assist his patron in pursuits which drew upon him Queen Catharine's censure: —

> "Of his own body he was ill, and gave
> The clergy ill example."

For these or other services, the cardinal, not long after he wrested the great seal from Archbishop Wareham, and had all legal patronage conferred upon him, boldly made Fitzjames attorney general, notwithstanding loud complaints from competitors of his inexperience and incapacity.

The only state trial which he had to conduct was that of the unfortunate Stafford, Duke of Buckingham, who, having quarrelled with Wolsey, and called him a "butcher's cur," was prosecuted for high treason before the lord high chancellor and Court of Peers, on very frivolous grounds. Fitzjames had little difficulty in procuring a conviction; and although the manner in which he pressed the case seems shocking to us, he probably was not considered to have exceeded the line of his duty: and Shakspeare makes Buckingham, returning from Westminster Hall to the Tower, exclaim —

> "I had my trial,
> And, must needs say, a noble one; which makes me
> A little happier than my wretched father."

The result was, at all events, highly satisfactory to Wolsey, who, in the beginning of the following year, created Fitzjames a puisne judge of the Court of King's Bench, with a promise of being raised to be chief justice as soon as there should be a vacancy. Sir John Fineux, turned of eighty, was expected to drop every term, but held on four years longer. As soon as he expired, Fitzjames was appointed his successor. Wolsey still zealously supported him, although thereby incurring considerable obloquy. It was generally thought that the new chief was not only wanting in gravity of moral character, but that he had not sufficient professional knowledge for such a situation. His highest quality was discretion, which generally enabled him to conceal his ignorance, and to disarm opposition. Fortunately for him, the question which then agitated the country respecting the validity of the king's marriage with Catharine of Arragon, was considered to depend entirely on the canon law, and he was not called upon to give any opinion upon it. He thus quietly discharged the duties of his office till Wolsey's fall. But he then experienced much perplexity. Was he to desert his patron, or to sacrifice his place? He had an exaggerated notion of the king's vengeful feelings. The cardinal having been not only deprived of the great seal, but banished to Esher, and robbed of almost the whole of his property under process of *præmunire*, while an impeachment for treason was still threatened against him, the chief justice concluded that his utter destruction was resolved upon, and that no one could show him any sympathy without sharing his fate. Therefore, instead of going privately to visit him, as some old friends did, he joined in the cry against him, and assisted his enemies to the utmost. Wolsey readily surrendered all his private property, but wished, for the benefit of his successors, to save the palace at Whitehall, which belonged to the see of York, being the gift of a former archbishop. A reference was then made to the judges, "whether it was not forfeited to the crown;" when the chief justice suggested the fraudulent expedient of a fictitious recovery in the Court of Common Pleas, whereby it should be adjudged to the king under a superior title. He had not the courage to show himself in the presence of the man to whom he owed every thing; and Shelley, a puisne judge, was deputed to make the proposal to him in the king's name. "Master Shelley," said the cardinal, "ye shall make report to his highness that I am his obedient subject, and faithful chaplain and bondsman, whose royal commandment and request I will in no wise disobey, but most gladly fulfil and accomplish his princely will and pleasure in all things, and in especial in this matter, inasmuch as the fathers of the law all say that I may lawfully do it. Therefore I charge your conscience, and discharge mine. Howbeit, I pray you show his majesty from me that I most humbly desire his highness to call to his most gracious remembrance that there is both heaven and hell."

This answer was, no doubt, reported by Shelley to his brethren assembled in the Exchequer Chamber, although, probably, not to the king; but it excited no remorse in the breast of Chief Justice Fitzjames, who perfected the machinery by which the town residence of the Archbishops of York henceforth was annexed to the crown, and declared his readiness to concur in any proceedings by which the proud ecclesiastic, who had ventured to sneer at the reverend sages of the law, might be brought to condign punishment.

Accordingly, when Parliament met, and a select committee of the House of Lords was appointed to draw up articles of impeachment against Wolsey, Chief Justice Fitzjames, although only summoned, like the other judges, as an assessor, was actually made a member of the committee, joined in their deliberations, and signed their report.

The authority of the chief justice gave such weight to the articles that they were agreed to by the lords, *nemine contradicente;* but his ingratitude and tergiversation caused much scandal out of doors, and he had the mortification to find that he might have acted an honorable and friendly part without any risk to himself, as the king, retaining a hankering kindness for his old favorite, not only praised the fidelity of Cavendish and the cardinal's other dependants who stuck by him in adversity, but took Cromwell into favor, and advanced him to the highest dignities, pleased with his gallant defence of his old master: thus the articles of impeachment (on which, probably, Fitzjames had founded hopes of the great seal for himself) were ignominiously rejected in the House of Commons.

The recreant chief justice must have been much alarmed by the report that Wolsey, whom he had abandoned, if not betrayed, was likely to be restored to power, and he must have been considerably relieved by the certain intelligence of the sad scene at Leicester Abbey in the following autumn, which secured him forever against the fear of being upbraided or punished in this world according to his deserts. However, he had now lost all dignity of character, and henceforth he was used as a vile instrument to apply the criminal law for the pleasure of the tyrant on the throne, whose relish for blood soon began to display itself, and became more eager the more it was gratified.

Henry retaining all the doctrines of the Roman Catholic religion which we Protestants consider most objectionable, but making himself pope in England in place of the Bishop of Rome, laws were enacted subjecting to the penalties of treason all who denied his *supremacy;* * and many of these offenders were tried and condemned by Lord Chief Justice Fitzjames, although he was suspected of being in his heart adverse to all innovation in religion.

I must confine myself to the two most illustrious victims sacrificed by him — Fisher, Bishop of Rochester, and Sir Thomas More. Henry, not contented with having them attainted of *misprision of treason*, for which they were suffering the sentence of forfeiture of all their property and imprisonment during life, was determined to bring them both to the block, and for this purpose issued a special commission to try them on the capital charge of having denied his supremacy. The lord chancellor was first commissioner; but it was intended that the responsibility and the odium should chiefly rest on the Lord Chief Justice Fitzjames, who was joined in the commission along with several other common law judges of inferior rank.

The case against the Bishop of Rochester rested on the evidence of Rich, the solicitor general, who swore he had heard the prisoner say, "I believe in my conscience, and by my learning I assuredly know, that the king neither is, nor by right can be, supreme head of the church of England;" but admitted that this was in a confidential conversation, which he had introduced by declaring that "he came from the king to ask what the bishop's opinion was upon this question, and by assuring him that it never should be mentioned to any one except the king, and that the king had promised

* The recent claim set up in America for legislative supremacy over conscience — a claim contended for by so many of our leading lawyers and divines — is not less blasphemous and outrageous than this claim of Henry VIII., and belongs to the same category. — *Ed.*

he never should be drawn into question for it afterwards." The prisoner contending that he was not guilty of the capital crime charged for words so spoken, the matter was referred to the judges.

"Lord Chief Justice Fitzjames, in their names, declared 'that this message or promise from the king to the prisoner neither did nor could, by rigor of law, discharge him; but in so declaring of his mind and conscience against the *supremacy* — yea, though it were at the king's own request or commandment — he committed treason by the statute, and nothing can discharge him from death but the king's pardon.'"

*Bishop of Rochester.* — "Yet I pray you, my lords, consider that by all equity, justice, worldly honesty, and courteous dealing, I cannot, as the case standeth, be directly charged therewith as with treason, though I had spoken the words indeed, the same not being spoken maliciously, but in the way of advice or counsel, when it was required of me by the king himself; and that favor the very words of the statute do give me, being made only against such as shall '*maliciously* gainsay the king's supremacy,' and none other; wherefore, although by rigor of law you may take occasion thus to condemn me, yet I hope you cannot find law, except you add rigor to that law, to cast me down, which herein I have not deserved."

*Fitzjames, C. J.* — "All my brethren are agreed that '*maliciously*' is a term of art and an inference of law, not a qualification of fact. In truth, it is a superfluous and void word; for if a man speak against the king's supremacy by any manner of means, that speaking is to be understood and taken in law as *malicious*."

*Bishop of Rochester.* — "If the law be so, then it is a hard exposition, and (as I take it) contrary to the meaning of them that made the law, as well as of ordinary persons who read it. But then, my lords, what says your wisdom to this question, 'Whether a single testimony may be admitted to prove me guilty of treason; and may it not be answered by my negative?' Often have I heard it said, that to overcome the presumption from the oath of allegiance to the king's majesty, and to guard against the dire consequences of the penalties for treason falling on the head of an innocent man, none shall be convicted thereof save on the evidence of two witnesses at the least."

*Fitzjames, C. J.* — "This being the king's case, it rests much in the conscience and discretion of the jury; and as they upon the evidence shall find it, you are either to be acquitted or else to be condemned."

The report says that "the bishop answered with many more words, both wisely and profoundly uttered, and that with a mervailous, couragious, and rare constancy, insomuch as many of his hearers — yea, some of the judges — lamented so grievously, that their inward sorrow was expressed by the outward teares in their eyes, to perceive such a famous and reverend man in danger to be condemned to a cruell death upon so weake evidence, given by such an accuser, contrary to all faith, and the promise of the king himself."

A packed jury, being left to their conscience and discretion, found a verdict of guilty; and Henry was able to make good his saying, when he was told that the pope intended to send Bishop Fisher a cardinal's hat — "'Fore God, then, he shall wear it on his shoulders, for I will have his head off."

The conduct of the chief justice at the trial of Sir Thomas More was not less atrocious. After the case for the crown had been closed, the prisoner, in an able address to the jury, clearly proved that there was no evidence whatever to support the charge, and that he was entitled to an acquittal; when Rich, the solicitor general, was permitted to present himself in the witness box, and to swear falsely, that "having observed, in a private conversation with the prisoner in the Tower, 'No Parliament could make a law that God should not be God,' * Sir Thomas replied, 'No more can the Parliament make the king supreme head of the church.'"

A verdict of guilty was pronounced against the prisoner, notwithstanding his solemn denial of ever having spoken these words. He then moved, in arrest of judgment, that the indictment was insufficient, as it did not properly follow the words of the statute which made it high treason to deny the king's supremacy, even supposing that Parliament had power to pass such a statute. The lord chancellor, whose duty it was, as head of the commission, to pass the sentence — "not willing," says the report, "to take the whole load of his condemnation on himself, asked in open court the advice of Sir John Fitzjames, the lord chief justice of England, whether the indictment was valid or no."

*Fitzjames, C. J.* — "My lords all, by St. Gillian, (for that was always his oath,) I must needs confess that if the act of Parliament be not unlawful, then the indictment is not, in my conscience, invalid."

*Lord Chancellor.* — "*Quid adhuc desideramus, testimonium? Reus est mortis.* (What more do we need? He is worthy of death.) Sir Thomas More, you being, by the opinion of that reverend judge, the chief justice of England, and of all

* This would hardly be allowed by some of our American juridical deniers and deriders of the "higher law." It is hard to distinguish a law (such as the fugitive slave act) which sets the moral sentiment at defiance, from a law that God shall not be God. — *Ed.*

his brethren, duly convicted of high treason, this court doth adjudge that you be carried back to the Tower of London, and that you be thence drawn on a hurdle to Tyburn, where you are to be hanged till you are half dead, and then being cut down alive and embowelled, and your bowels burnt before your face, you are to be beheaded and quartered, your four quarters being set up over the four gates of the city, and your head upon London Bridge."

No one can deny that Lord Chief Justice Fitzjames was an accessory to this atrocious murder.

The next occasion of his attracting the notice of the public was when he presided at the trials of Smeaton and the other supposed gallants of Anne Boleyn. Luckily for him, no particulars of these trials have come down to us, and we remain ignorant of the arts by which a conviction was obtained, and even a *confession* — although there is every reason to believe that the parties were innocent. According to the rules of evidence which then prevailed, the convictions and confessions of the gallants were to be given in evidence to establish the guilt of the unhappy queen, for whose death Henry was now as impatient as he had once been to make her his wife.

When the lord high steward and the peers assembled for her trial, Fitzjames and the other judges attended, merely as assessors, to advise on any point of law which might arise. I do not find that they were consulted till the verdict of guilty had been recorded, and sentence was to be pronounced. *Burning* was the death which the law appointed for a woman attainted of treason; yet as Anne had been Queen of England, some peers suggested that it might be left to the king to determine whether she should die such a cruel and ignominious death, or be *beheaded*, a punishment supposed to be attended with less pain and less disgrace. But then a difficulty arose whether, although the king might remit all the atrocities of the sentence on a man for treason, except beheading, which is part of it, he could order a person to be beheaded who was sentenced to be burnt. A solution was proposed, that she should be sentenced by the lord high steward to be "burnt or beheaded at the king's pleasure;" and the opinion of the judges was asked, "whether such a sentence could be lawfully pronounced."

*Fitzjames, C. J.* — "My lords, neither myself nor any of my learned brothers have ever known or found in the records, or read in the books, or known or heard of, a sentence of death in the alternative or disjunctive, and incline to think that it would be bad for uncertainty. The law delights in certainty. Where a choice is given, by what means is the choice to be exercised? And if the sheriff receives no special directions, what is he to do? Is sentence to be stayed till special directions are given by the king? and if no special directions are given, is the prisoner, being attainted, to escape all punishment? Prudent antiquity advises you *stare super antiquas vias;* and that which is without precedent is without safety."

After due deliberation, it was held that an absolute sentence of beheading would be lawful, and it was pronounced accordingly; the court being greatly comforted by recollecting that no writ of error lay, and that their judgment could not be reversed.

Fitzjames died in the year 1539, before this judgment served as a precedent for that upon the unfortunate Queen Catharine Howard; and he was much missed when the bloody statute of the Six Articles brought so many, both of the old and of the reformed faith, on capital charges, before the Court of King's Bench.

# CHAPTER V.

## THOMAS FLEMING.

The greatest part of my readers never before read or heard of the name of Thomas Fleming; yet, starting in the profession of the law with Francis Bacon, he was not only preferred to him by attorneys, but by prime ministers, and he had the highest professional honors showered upon him, while the immortal philosopher, orator, and fine writer continued to languish at the bar without any advancement, notwithstanding all his merits and all his intrigues. But Fleming had superior good fortune, and enjoyed temporary consequences, because he was a mere lawyer — because he harbored no idea or aspirations beyond the routine of Westminster Hall — because he did not mortify the vanity of the witty, or alarm the jealousy of the ambitious.

He was the younger son of a gentleman of small estate in the Isle of Wight. I do not find any account of his early education, and very little interest can now be felt respecting it; although we catch so eagerly at any trait of the boyhood of his rival, whom he despised. Soon after he was called to the bar, by unwearied drudgery he got into considerable practice; and it was remarked that he always tried how much labor he could bestow upon every case intrusted to him, while his more lively competitors tried with how little labor they could creditably perform their duty.

In the end of the year 1594, he was called to the degree of serjeant, along with eight others, and was thought to be the most deeply versed in the law of real actions of the whole batch. It happened that, soon after, there was a vacancy in the office of solicitor general, on the promotion of Sir Edward Coke to be attorney general. Bacon moved heaven and earth that he himself might succeed to it. He wrote to his uncle, Lord Treasurer Burleigh, saying, "I hope you will think I am no unlikely piece of wood to shape you a true servant of." He wrote to the Queen Elizabeth, saying, "I affect myself to a place of my profession, such as I do see divers younger in proceeding to myself, and men of no great note, do without blame aspire unto; but if your majesty like others better, I shall, with the Lacedemonian, be glad that there is such choice of abler men than myself." He accompanied this letter with a valuable jewel, to show off her beauty. He did what he thought would be still more serviceable, and, indeed, conclusive; he prevailed upon the young Earl of Essex, then in the highest favor with the aged queen, earnestly to press his suit. But the appointment was left with the lord treasurer, and he decided immediately against his nephew, who was reported to be no lawyer, from giving up his time to profane learning — who had lately made an indiscreet, although very eloquent, speech in the House of Commons — and who, if promoted, might be a dangerous rival to his cousin, Robert Cecil, then entering public life, and destined by his sire to be prime minister. The cunning old fox then inquired who would be a competent person to do the queen's business in her courts, and would give no uneasiness elsewhere; and he was told by several black-letter judges whom he consulted that "Serjeant Fleming was the man for him." After the office had been kept vacant by these intrigues above a year, Serjeant Fleming was actually appointed. Bacon's anguish was exasperated by comparing himself with the new solicitor; and in writing to Essex, after enumerating his own pretensions, he says, "When I add hereunto the obscureness and many exceptions to my competitor, I cannot but conclude with myself that no man ever had a more exquisite disgrace." He resolved at first to shut himself up for the rest of his days in a cloister at Cambridge. A soothing message from the queen induced him to remain at the bar; but he had the mortification to see the man whom he utterly despised much higher in the law than himself, during the remainder of this and a considerable part of the succeeding reign.

Fleming, immediately upon his promotion, gave up his serjeantship, and practised in the Court of Queen's Bench. He was found very useful in doing the official business, and gave entire satisfaction to his employers.

At the calling of a new Parliament, in the autumn of 1601, he was returned to the House of Commons for a Cornish borough; and, according to the usual practice at that time, he ought, as solicitor general, to have been elected speaker; but his manner was too "lawyer-like and ungenteel" for the chair, and Serjeant Croke, who was more presentable, was substituted for him.

He opened his mouth in the house only once, and then he broke down. This was in the great debate on the grievance of monopolies. He undertook to defend the system of granting to individuals the exclusive right of dealing in particular commodities; but when he had described the manner in which patents passed through the different offices before the great seal is put to them, he lost his recollection and resumed his seat.

Bacon, now member for Middlesex, to show what a valuable

solicitor general the government had lost, made a very gallant speech, in which he maintained that "the queen, as she is our sovereign, hath both an enlarging and restraining power: for, by her prerogative, she may, 1st, set at liberty things restrained by statute law or otherwise; and 2dly, by her prerogative she may restrain things which be at liberty." He concluded by expressing the utmost horror of introducing any bill to meddle with the powers of the crown upon the subject, and protesting that "the only lawful course was to leave it to her majesty of her own free will to correct any hardships, if any had arisen in the exercise of her just rights, as the arbitress of trade and commerce in the realm."

This pleased her exceedingly, and even softened her ministers, insomuch that a promise was given to promote Fleming as soon as possible, and to appoint Bacon in his place. In those days there never existed the remotest notion of dismissing an attorney or solicitor general, any more than a judge; for, though they all alike held *during pleasure*, till the accession of the house of Stuart the tenure of all of them was practically secure. An attempt was made to induce Fleming to accept the appointment of queen's serjeant, which would have given him precedence over the attorney general; but this failed, for he would thereby have been considered as put upon the shelf, instead of being on the highway to promotion.

Elizabeth died, leaving Bacon with no higher rank than that of queen's counsel; and on the accession of James I., Fleming was reappointed solicitor general.

The event justified his firmness in resisting the attempt to shelve him, for in the following year, on the death of Sir William Peryam, he was appointed chief baron of the Exchequer. While he held this office, he sat along with Lord Chief

Justice Popham on the trial of Guy Fawkes and the gunpowder conspirators; but he followed the useful advice for subordinate judges on such an occasion — "to look wise, and to say nothing."

His most memorable judgment as chief baron was in what is called "The Great Case of Impositions." This was, in truth, fully as important as Hampden's case of ship money, but did not acquire such celebrity in history, because it was long acquiesced in, to the destruction of public liberty, whereas the other immediately produced the civil war. After an act of Parliament had passed at the commencement of James's reign, by which an import duty of 2*s.* 6*d.* per cwt. was imposed upon currants, he by his own authority laid on an additional duty of 7*s.* 6*d.*, making 10*s.* per cwt. Bates, a Levant merchant, who had imported a cargo of currants from Venice, very readily paid the parliamentary duty of 2*s.* 3*d.* upon it, but refused to pay more; thereupon the attorney general filed an information in the Court of Exchequer, to compel him to pay the additional duty of 7*s.* 6*d.*; so the question arose, whether he was by law compellable to do so. After arguments at the bar which lasted many days, —

*Fleming, C. B.*, said: "The defendant's plea in this case is without precedent or example, for he alleges that the imposition which the king has laid is '*indebitè, injustè, et contra leges Angliæ imposita*, and, therefore, he refused to pay it.' The king, as is commonly said in our books, *cannot do wrong;* and if the king seize any land without cause, I ought to sue to him in humble manner (*humillime supplicavit*, &c.), and not in terms of opposition. The matter of the plea first regards the prerogative, and to derogate from that is a part most undutiful in any subject. Next it concerns the transport of commodities into and out of the realm, the due regulation of which is left to the king for the public good. The imposition is properly upon currants, and not upon the defendant, for upon him no imposition shall be but by Parliament. (!) The things are currants, a foreign commodity. The king may restrain the person of a subject in leaving or coming into the realm, and *a fortiori*, may impose conditions on the importation or exportation of his goods. To the king is committed the government of the realm; and Bracton says, 'that for his discharge of his office God hath given him the power to govern.' This power is double — ordinary and absolute. The ordinary is for the profit of particular subjects — the determination of civil justice; that is nominated by civilians *jus privatum*, and it cannot be changed without Parliament. The absolute power of the king is applied for the general benefit of the people; it is most properly named *policy*, and it varieth with the time, according to the wisdom of the king, for the common good. If this imposition is matter of state, it is to be ruled by the rules of policy, and the king hath done well, instead of 'unduly, unjustly, and contrary to the laws of England.' All commerce and dealings with foreigners, like war and peace and public treaties, are regulated and determined by the absolute power of the king. No importation or exportation can be but at the king's ports. They are his gates, which he may open or close when and on what conditions he pleases. He guards them with bulwarks and fortresses, and he protects ships coming hither from pirates at sea; and if his subjects are wronged by foreign princes, he sees that they are righted. Ought he not, then, by the custom he imposes, to enable himself to perform these duties? The impost to the merchant is nothing, for those who wish for his commodities must buy them subject to the charge; and, in most cases, it shall be paid by the foreign grower, and not by the English consumer. As to the argument that the currants are *victual*, they are rather a delicacy, and are no more necessary than wine, on which the king lays what customs seemeth him good. For the amount of the imposition it is not unreasonable, seeing that it is only four times as much as it was before. The wisdom and providence of the king must not be disputed by the subject; by intendment they cannot be severed from his person. And to argue *a posse ad actum*, because by his power he may do ill, is no argument to be used in this place. If it be objected that no reason is assigned for the rise, I answer it is not reasonable that the king should express the cause and consideration of his actions; these are *arcana regis*, and it is for the benefit of every subject that the king's treasure should be increased."

He then at enormous length went over all the authorities and acts of Parliament, contending that they all prove the king's power to lay what taxes he pleases on goods imported, and he concluded by giving judgment for the crown.

Historians take no notice of this decision, although it might have influenced the destinies of the country much more than many of the battles and sieges with which they fill their pages. Had our foreign commerce then approached its present magnitude, Parliaments would never more have met in England, — duties on tea, sugar, timber, tobacco, and corn, imposed by royal proclamation, being sufficient to fill the exchequer, — and the experiment of ship money would never have been necessary. The chief baron most certainly misquotes, misrepresents, and mystifies exceedingly; but, however fallacious his reasoning, the judgment ought not to be passed over in silence by those who pretend to narrate our annals, for it was pronounced by a court of competent jurisdiction, and it was acted upon for years as settling the law and constitution of the country.*

King James declared that Chief Baron Fleming was a judge to his heart's content. He had been somewhat afraid when he came to England that he might hear such unpalatable doctrines as had excited his indignation in Buchanan's treatise, "*De Jure Regni apud Scotis*," and he expressed great joy in the solemn recognition that he was an absolute sovereign. Our indignation should be diverted from him and his unfortunate son, to the base sycophants, legal and ecclesiastical, who misled them.

On the death of Popham, no one was thought so fit to succeed him as Fleming, of whom it was always said that, "*though slow, he was sure;*" and he became chief justice of England the very same day on which Francis Bacon mounted the first step of the political ladder, receiving the comparatively humble appointment of solicitor general.

Lord Chief Justice Fleming remained at the head of the common law rather more than six years. During that time the only case of general interest which arose in Westminster Hall was that of the Postnati. As might be expected, to please the king, he joined cordially in what I consider the illegal decision, that persons born in Scotland after the accession of James to the throne of England, were entitled to all the privileges of natural born subjects in England, although it

* One striking instance, among a thousand, both old and new, how little the so much vaunted decisions of courts virtually amount to. Decisions that are to stand, can only stand upon their own inherent rectitude and reasonableness, and not upon the authority of those who make them. — *Ed.*

was allowed that Scotland was an entirely separate and independent kingdom. Luckily, the question is never likely again to arise since the severance of the crown of Hanover from that of Great Britain; but if it should, I do not think that Calvin's case could by any means be considered a conclusive authority, being founded upon such reasoning as that "if our king conquer a Christian country, its laws remain till duly altered; whereas if he conquer an infidel country, the laws are *ipso facto* extinct, and he may massacre all the inhabitants."

Lord Chief Justice Fleming took the lead in the prosecution of the Countess of Shrewsbury before the Privy Council, on the charge of having refused to be examined respecting the part she had acted in bringing about a clandestine marriage, in the Tower of London, between the Lady Arabella Stuart, the king's cousin, and Sir William Somerset, afterwards Duke of Somerset. He laid it down for law, that "it was a high misdemeanor to marry, or to connive at the marriage of any relation of the king without his consent, and that the countess's refusal to be examined was 'a contempt of the king, his crown and dignity, which, if it were to go unpunished, might lead to many dangerous enterprises against the state.' He therefore gave it as his opinion that she should be fined £10,000 and confined during the king's pleasure."

While this poor creature presided in the King's Bench, he was no doubt told by his officers and dependants that he was the greatest chief justice that had appeared there since the days of Gascoigne and Fortescue; but he was considered a very small man by all the rest of the world, and he was completely eclipsed by Sir Edward Coke, who at the same time was chief justice of the Common Pleas, and who, to a much more vigorous intellect and deeper learning, added respect for constitutional liberty and resolution at every hazard to maintain judicial independence. From the growing resistance in the nation to the absolute maxims of government professed by the king and sanctioned by almost all his judges, there was a general desire that the only one who stood up for law against prerogative should be placed in a position which might give greater weight to his efforts on the popular side; but of this there seemed no prospect, for the subservient Fleming was still a young man, and likely to continue many years the tool of the government.

In the midst of these gloomy anticipations, on the 15th day of October, 1613, the joyful news was spread of his sudden death. I do not know, and I have taken no pains to ascertain, where he was buried, or whether he left any descendants. In private life he is said to have been virtuous and amiable, and the discredit of his incompetency in high office ought to be imputed to those who placed him there, instead of allowing him to prose on as a drowsy serjeant at the bar of the Common Pleas, the position for which nature had intended him.

* Some of our American judges who have of late attained a very unenviable public character have also the reputation of being virtuous and amiable in private life. — *Ed.*

# CHAPTER VI.

## NICHOLAS HYDE.

AFTER the abrupt dissolution of the second Parliament of Charles I. without the grant of a supply, all redress of grievances being refused, the plan was deliberately formed of discontinuing entirely the use of popular assemblies in England, and of ruling merely by prerogative. For this purpose it was indispensably necessary that the king should have the power of imposing taxes, and the power of arbitrary imprisonment. He began to exercise both these powers by assessing sums which all persons of substance were called upon to contribute to the revenue according to their supposed ability, and by issuing warrants for committing to jail those who resisted the demand. But these measures could not be rendered effectual without the aid of the judges; for hitherto in England the validity of any fiscal imposition might be contested in a court of justice; and any man deprived of his liberty might, by suing out a writ of *habeas corpus*, have a deliberate judgment upon the question "whether he was lawfully detained in custody or not." Sir Thomas Darnel, Sir Edmund Hampden, and other public-spirited men, having peremptorily refused to pay the sums assessed upon them, had been cast into prison, and were about to seek legal redress for their wrongs.

In the coming legal contest, almost every thing would depend upon the chief justice of the King's Bench. According to a well-known fashion which prevailed in those times, the attorney general, by order of the government, sounded Sir Randolph Crewe, then holding that office, to which he had been appointed hardly two years before, respecting his opinions on the agitated points, and was shocked to hear a positive declaration from him that by the law of England, no tax or talliage, under whatever name or disguise, can be laid upon the people without the authority of Parliament, and that the king cannot imprison any of his subjects without a warrant specifying the offence with which they are charged. This being reported to the cabinet, Sir Randolph Crewe was immediately dismissed from his office; and, in a few weeks after, Sir Nicholas Hyde was made chief justice in his stead. He was the uncle of the great Lord Clarendon. They were sprung from the ancient family of "*Hyde of that ilk*" in the county palatine of Chester; their branch of it having migrated, in the sixteenth century, into the west of England. The chief justice was the fourth son of Lawrence Hyde, of Gussage St. Michael, in the county of Dorset.

Before being selected as a fit tool of an arbitrary government, he had held no office whatever; but he had gained the reputation of a sound lawyer, and he was a man of unexceptionable character in private life. He was known to be always a stanch stickler for prerogative; but this was supposed to arise rather from the sincere opinion he had formed of what the English constitution was, or ought to be, than from a desire to recommend himself for promotion. He is thus good naturedly introduced by Rushworth:—

"Sir Randolf Crewe, showing no zeal for the advancement of the loan, was removed from his place of lord chief justice, and Sir Nicholas Hyde succeeded in his room — a person who, for his parts and abilities, was thought worthy of that preferment; yet, nevertheless, came to the same with a prejudice, coming in the place of one so well-beloved, and so suddenly removed."

Whether he was actuated by mistaken principle or by profligate ambition, he fully justified the confidence reposed in him by his employers. Soon after he took his seat in the Court of King's Bench, Sir Thomas Darnel and several others, committed under the same circumstances, were brought up before him on a writ of *habeas corpus;* and the question arose whether the King of England, by *lettre de cachet,* had the power of perpetual imprisonment without assigning any cause. The return of the jailer, being read, was found to set out, as the only reason for Sir Thomas Darnel's detention, a warrant, signed by two privy councillors, in these words: —

"Whereas, therefore, the body of Sir Thomas Darnel hath been committed to your custody, these are to require you still to detain him, and to let you know that he was and is committed BY THE SPECIAL COMMAND OF HIS MAJESTY."

Lord Chief Justice Hyde proceeded with great temper and seeming respect for the law, observing, "Whether the commitment be by the king or others, this court is a place where the king doth sit in person, and we have power to examine it; and if any man hath injury or wrong by his imprisonment, we have power to deliver and discharge him; if otherwise, he is to be remanded by us to prison again."

Selden, Noy,* and the other counsel for the prisoners, encouraged by this intimation, argued boldly that the warrant was bad on the face of it, *per speciale mandatum domini regis* being too general, without specifying an offence for

* Noy at this time was of the popular party. He afterwards went over to the court, and was made attorney general. — *Ed.*

which a person was liable to be detained without bail; that the warrant should not only state the authority to imprison, but the cause of the imprisonment; and that if this return were held good, there would be a power of shutting up, till a liberation by death, any subject of the king, without trial and without accusation. After going over all the common law cases and the acts of Parliament upon the subject, from MAGNA CHARTA downwards, they concluded with the *dictum* of Paul the apostle, "It is against reason to send a man to prison without showing a cause."

*Hyde, C. J.* — "This is a case of very great weight and great expectation. I am sure you look for justice from hence, and God forbid we should sit here but to do justice to all men, according to our best skill and knowledge; for it is our oaths and duties so to do. We are sworn to maintain all prerogatives of the king: that is one branch of our oath; but there is another — to administer justice equally to all people. That which is now to be judged by us is this: 'Whether, where one is committed by the king's authority, and by cause declared of his commitment, we ought to deliver him by bail, or to remand him.'"

From such a fair beginning,* there must have been a general anticipation of a just judgment; but, alas! his lordship, without combating the arguments, statutes, or texts of Scripture relied upon, said, "The court must be governed by precedents;" † and then going over all the precedents which had

* Similar pretences of respect for law and popular rights often serve as preface here in America to judgments as atrocious as that of Chief Justice Hyde. — *Ed.*

† This is the universal excuse for all sins, whether of omission or commission, on the part of courts who pay but little regard to Bishop Burnet's sensible observation that a precedent against reason "signifies no more but that the like injustice has been done before." — *Ed.*

been cited, he declared that there was not one where, there being a warrant *per speciale mandatum domini regis*, the judges had interfered and held it insufficient. He said he had found a resolution of all the judges in the reign of Queen Elizabeth, that if a man be committed by the commandment of the king, he is not to be delivered by a *habeas corpus* in this court, "for we know not the cause of the commitment." Thus he concluded: —

"What can we do but walk in the steps of our forefathers? Mr. Attorney hath told you the king has done it for cause sufficient, and we trust him in great matters. He is bound by law, and he bids us proceed by law; we are sworn so to do, and so is the king. We make no doubt the king, he knowing the cause why you are imprisoned, will have mercy. On these grounds we cannot deliver you, but you must be remanded." *

This judgment was violently attacked in both houses of Parliament. In the House of Lords the judges were summoned, and required to give their reasons for it. Sir Nicholas Hyde endeavored to excuse himself and his brethren from this task by representing it as a thing they ought not to do without warrant from the king. Lord Say observed, "If the judges will not declare themselves, we must take into con-

* Though the lawyers, both in England and America, have long since abandoned the pretence, so impudently maintained by Hyde, of a right in the executive authorities to imprison for contempt, into the ground and nature of which the courts had no right to inquire, they still claim for themselves and for one another — at least in Pennsylvania — a like right, and insist with the same unction upon the absolute necessity of trusting "the courts" in these matters, and of relying upon their "mercy." See, in the Appendix, No. 3, the opinion of the Supreme Court of Pennsylvania, as delivered by Judge Black, of which the insolent conclusion was evidently borrowed from the above opinion of Chief Justice Hyde. — *Ed.*

sideration the point of our privilege." To soothe the dangerous spirit which disclosed itself, Buckingham obtained leave from the king that the judges should give their reasons, and Sir Nicholas Hyde again went over all the authorities which had been cited in the King's Bench in support of the prerogative. These were not considered by any means satisfactory; but, as the chief justice could no longer be deemed contumacious, he escaped the commitment with which he had been threatened. Sir Edward Coke,* and the patriots in the House of Commons, were not so easily appeased, and they for some time threatened Lord Chief Justice Hyde and his brethren with an impeachment; but it was hoped that all danger to liberty would be effectually guarded against for the future by compelling the reluctant king to agree to the PETITION OF RIGHT. Before Charles would give the royal assent to it — meaning not to be bound by it himself, but afraid that the judges would afterwards put limits to his power of arbitrary imprisonment — he sent for Chief Justice Hyde and Chief Justice Richardson, of the Common Pleas, to Whitehall, and directed them to return to him the answer of themselves and their brethren to this question, "Whether in no case whatsoever the king may commit a subject without showing cause." The answer shows that they had been daunted by the denunciations of Sir Edward Coke, and that they were driven to equivocate: "We are of opinion that, by the general rule of law, the cause of commitment by his majesty ought to be shown; yet some cases may require such secrecy that the

* This celebrated lawyer, who had succeeded Fleming as chief justice of the King's Bench, had been, as well as Crewe, turned out of office after holding the place for three years, because he would not allow the government to interfere with his administration of justice. He was now the leader of the popular party in the House of Commons. — *Ed.*

king may commit a subject without showing the cause, for a convenient time." Charles then delivered to them a second question, and desired them to keep it very secret, "Whether, if to a *habeas corpus* there be returned a warrant from the king without any special cause, the judges ought to liberate him before they understand from the king what the cause is." They answered, "If no cause be assigned in the warrant, the party ought, by the general rule of law, to be liberated; but, if the case requireth secrecy, and may not presently be disclosed, the court, in its discretion, may forbear to liberate the prisoner for a convenient time, till they are advertised of the truth thereof." He then came to the point with his third question, "Whether, if the king grant the Commons' PETITION, he doth not thereby exclude himself from committing or restraining a subject without showing a cause." Hyde reported this response: "Every law, after it is made, hath its exposition, which is to be left to the courts of justice to determine; and, although the PETITION be granted, there is no fear of conclusion, as is intimated in the question."

The judges having thus pledged themselves to repeal the act for him by misconstruing it,* he allowed it to be added to the statute book. No sooner was the Parliament that passed it abruptly dissolved than it was flagrantly violated, and Selden, Sir John Eliot, and other members of the House of Commons, were arrested for the speeches they had delivered, and for requiring the speaker to put from the chair a motion which had been made and seconded. This proceeding was more alarming to public liberty than any thing that had

* We have had recent striking instances in America of the same thing in some of the "misconstructions" placed by judges on the laws in restraint of drunkenness and liquor selling. — *Ed.*

been before attempted by the crown; if it succeeded, there was no longer the hope of any redress in Parliament for the corrupt decisions of the common law courts.

To make all sure by an extrajudicial opinion,* Lord Chief Justice Hyde and the other judges were assembled at Serjeants' Inn, and, by the king's command, certain questions were put to them by the attorney general. The answers to these, given by the mouth of the chief justice, if acted upon, would forever have extinguished the privilege and the independence of the House of Commons: "That a Parliament man committing an offence against the king in Parliament, not in a parliamentary course, may be punished after the Parliament is ended; for, though regularly he cannot be compelled out of Parliament to answer things done in Parliament in a parliamentary course, it is otherwise where things are done exorbitantly;" and "that by false slanders to bring the lords of the council and the judges, not in a parliamentary way, into the hatred of the people, and the government into contempt, was punishable out of Parliament, in the Star Chamber, as an offence committed in Parliament beyond the office, and besides the duty, of a Parliament man."

The parties committed were brought up by *habeas corpus*, and, the public being much scandalized, an offer was made that they might be bailed; but, they refusing to give bail, which they said would be compromising the privileges of the House of Commons, Lord Chief Justice Hyde remanded them to jail.

The attorney general having then filed an ex-officio information against them for their misconduct in Parliament,

* Like those given by several federal judges in support of the fugitive slave act. — *Ed.*

they pleaded to the jurisdiction of the court "because these offences, being supposed to be done in Parliament, ought not to be punished in this court, or elsewhere than in Parliament."

Chief Justice Hyde tried at once to put an end to the case by saying that "all the judges had already resolved with one voice, that an offence committed in Parliament, criminally or contemptuously, the Parliament being ended, rests punishable in the Court of King's Bench, in which the king by intendment sitteth."

The counsel for the defendants, however, would be heard, and were heard in vain; for Chief Justice Hyde treated their arguments with scorn, and concluded by observing, "As to what was said, that 'an inferior court cannot meddle with matters done in a superior,' true it is that an inferior court cannot meddle with the *judgments* of a superior court; but if particular members of a superior court offend, they are ofttimes punishable in an inferior court — as if a judge shall commit a capital offence in this court, he may be arraigned thereof at Newgate. The behavior of Parliament men ought to be parliamentary. Parliament is a higher court than this, but every member of Parliament is not a court, and if he commit an offence we may punish him. The information charges that the defendants acted *unlawfully*, and they could have no privilege to violate the law. No outrageous speeches have been made against a great minister of state in Parliament that have not been punished." The plea being overruled, the defendants were sentenced to be imprisoned during the king's pleasure, and to be fined, Sir John Eliot in £2000, and the others in smaller sums.

This judgment was severely condemned by the House of Commons at the meeting of the Long Parliament, and was afterwards reversed, on a writ of error, by the House of Lords. But Lord Chief Justice Hyde escaped the fate of his predecessor, Chief Justice Tresilian, who was hanged for promulgating similar doctrines, for he was carried off by disease when he had disgraced his office four years and nine months. He died at his house in Hampshire, on the 25th of August, 1631.

In justice to the memory of Sir Nicholas Hyde, I ought to mention that he was much respected and lauded by true courtiers. Sir George Croke describes him as "a grave, religious, discreet man, and of great learning and piety." Oldmixon pronounces him to have been "a very worthy magistrate," and highly applauds his judgment in favor of the power of the crown to imprison and prosecute Parliament men for what they have done in the House of Commons.

# CHAPTER VII.

## JOHN BRAMPSTON.

On the vacancy in the office of chief justice of the King's Bench, created by the death of Sir Thomas Richardson, A. D. 1635, the king and his ministers were exceedingly anxious to select a lawyer fitted to be his successor. Resolved to raise taxes without the authority of Parliament, they had launched their grand scheme of ship money, and they knew that its validity would speedily be questioned. To lead the opinions of the judges, and to make a favorable impression on the public, they required a chief on whose servility they could rely, and who, at the same time, should have a great reputation as a lawyer, and should be possessed of a tolerable character for honesty. Such a man was Mr. Serjeant Brampston.

He was born at Maldon, in Essex, of a family founded there in the reign of Richard II. by a citizen of London, who had made a fortune in trade and had served the office of sheriff. When very young, he was sent to the university of Cambridge; and there he gained high renown by his skill in disputation, which induced his father to breed him to the bar. Accordingly, he was transferred to the Middle Temple, and studied law there for seven years with unwearied assiduity. At the end of this period, he was called to the bar, having then amassed a store of law sufficient to qualify him at once to step upon the bench. Different public bodies strove to have the benefit of his advice; and very soon he was standing counsel for his own university, and likewise for the city of London, with an annual fee *pro concilio impenso et impendendo*, (for counsel given and to be given.) Having been some years an "apprentice," he took the degree of serjeant at law.

According to a practice very common in our profession, he had, in the language of Mr. Gurney, the famous stenographer, "started in the sedition line," that is, defending persons prosecuted for political offences by the government. He was counsel for almost all the patriots who, in the end of the reign of James I. and the beginning of the reign of Charles I., were imprisoned for their refractory conduct in the House of Commons; and one of the finest arguments to be found in our books is one delivered by him in Sir Thomas Darnel's case, to prove that a warrant of commitment by order of the king, without specifying the offence, is illegal.

He refused a seat in the House of Commons, as it suited him better to plead for those who were in the Tower than to be sent thither himself. By and by, the desire of obtaining the honors of the profession waxed strong within him, and he conveyed an intimation, by a friend, to the lord keeper that it would be much more agreeable to him to be retained for the government than to be always against it. The offer was accepted; he was taken into the counsels of Noy, the attorney general, and he gave his assistance in defending all stretches of prerogative. Promotions were now showered down upon him; he was made chief justice of Ely, attorney general to the queen, king's serjeant, and a knight. Although very zealous for the crown, and really unscrupulous, he was anxious to observe decency of deportment, and to appear never to trangress the line of professional duty.

Noy* would have been the man to be appointed chief justice of the King's Bench to carry through his tax by a judicial decision in its favor, but he had suddenly died soon after the ship money writs were issued; and, after him, Sir John Brampston was deemed the fittest person to place at the head of the common law judges. On the 18th of April, 1635, his installation took place, which was, no doubt, very splendid; but we have no account of it except the following by Sir George Croke: —

"First, the lord keeper made a grave and long speech, signifying the king's pleasure for his choice, and the duties of his place; to which, after he had answered at the bar, returning his thanks to the king, and promising his endeavor of due performance of his duty in his place, he came from the bar into court, and there kneeling, took the oaths of supremacy and allegiance: then standing, he took the oath of judge: then he was appointed to come up to the bench, and then his patent (which was only a writ) being read, the lord keeper delivered it to him. But Sir William Jones (the senior puisne judge) said the patent ought to have been read before he came up to the bench." †

In quiet times, Lord Chief Justice Brampston would have

* Noy had begun, like Brampston, a flaming patriot, but, like him and so many other lawyers, had been bought over to the side of power by the hope of promotion, and being made attorney general, had advised the issue of the writs for ship money. — *Ed.*

† Cro. Car. 403. These forms are no longer used. The chief justice is now sworn in privately before the chancellor; and without any speechifying he enters the court and takes his place on the bench with the other judges. But in Scotland they still subject the new judge to trials of his sufficiency; while these are going on he is called lord probationer; and he might undoubtedly be plucked if the court should think fit.

been respected as an excellent judge. He was above all suspicion of bribery, and his decisions in private causes were sound as well as upright. But, unhappily, he by no means disappointed the expectations of the government.*

Soon after his elevation, he was instructed to take the opinion privately of all the judges on the two celebrated questions:—

"1. Whether, in cases of danger to the good and safety of the kingdom, the king may not impose ship money for its defence and safeguard, and by law compel payment from those who refuse? 2. Whether the king be not the sole judge both of the danger, and when and how it is to be prevented?"

There is reason to think that he himself was taken in by the craft of Lord Keeper Coventry, who represented that the opinion of the twelve judges was wanted merely for the king's private satisfaction, and that no other use would be made of it. At a meeting of all the judges in Serjeant's Inn Hall, Lord Chief Justice Brampston produced an answer to both questions in the affirmative, signed by himself. Nine other judges, without any hesitation, signed it after him; but two, Croke and Hutton, declared that they thought the king of England never had such a power, and that, if he ever had, it was taken away by the act *De Tallagio non concedendo*, the Petition of Right, and other statutes; but they were induced to sign the paper upon a representation that their signature was a mere formality.

The unscrupulous lord keeper, having got the paper into

* This is exactly the sort of judges from whom we in America have so much to fear.— *Ed.*

his possession, immediately published it to the world as the unanimous and solemn decision of all the judges of England; and payment of ship money was refused by John Hampden alone.

His refusal brought on the grand trial, in the Exchequer Chamber, upon the validity of the imposition. Lord Chief Justice Brampston, in a very long judgment, adhered to the opinion he had before given for the legality of the tax, although he characteristically expressed doubt as to the regularity of the proceeding on technical grounds. Croke and Hutton manfully insisted that the tax was illegal; but, all the other judges being in favor of the crown, Hampden was ordered to pay his 20*s*.

Soon after, the same point arose in the Court of King's Bench in the case of the Lord Say, who, envying the glory which Hampden had acquired, allowed his oxen to be taken as a distress for the ship money assessed upon him, and brought an action of trespass for taking them. But Banks, the attorney general, moved that counsel might not be permitted to argue against what had been decided in the Exchequer Chamber; and Lord Chief Justice Brampston said, "Such a judgment should be allowed to stand until it were reversed in Parliament, and none ought to be suffered to dispute against it." *

The crown lawyers were thrown into much perplexity by the freak of the Rev. Thomas Harrison, a country parson, who can hardly be considered a fair specimen of his order at that time, and must either have been a little deranged in his

* We have seen in America similar attempts to stop counsel from exposing the unsoundness of judicial opinions given in support of the fugitive slave act. — *Ed.*

intellect, or animated by an extraordinary eagerness for ecclesiastical promotion. Having heard that Mr. Justice Hutton, while on the circuit, had expressed an opinion unfavorable to ship money, he followed him to London, and, while this reverend sage of the law was seated with his brethren on the bench of the Court of Common Pleas, and Westminster Hall was crowded with lawyers, suitors, and idlers, marched up to him, and making proclamation, "*Oyez! Oyez! Oyez!*" said with a loud voice, "Mr. Justice Hutton, you have denied the king's supremacy, and I hereby charge you with being guilty of high treason." The attorney general, however much he might secretly honor such an ebullition of loyalty, was obliged to treat it as an outrage, and an *ex officio* information was filed against the delinquent for the insult he had offered to the administration of justice. At the trial the reverend defendant confessed the speaking of the words, and gloried in what he had done, saying,—

"I confess that judges are to be honored and revered as sacred persons so long as they do their duty; but having taken the oath of supremacy many times, I am bound to maintain it, and when it is assailed, as by the denying of ship money, it is time for every loyal subject to strike in." *Brampston, C. J.*—The denying of ship money may be, and I think is, very wrong; but is it against the king's supremacy?" *Harrison.*—"As a loyal subject, I did labor the defence of his majesty, and how can I be guilty of a crime? I say again that Mr. Justice Hutton has committed treason, for upon his charge the people of the country do now deny ship money. His offence being openly committed, I conceived it not amiss to make an open accusation. The king will not give his judges leave to speak treason, nor have they power to make or pronounce laws against his prerogative. We are not to question the king's actions; they are only between God and his own conscience. '*Sufficit regi, quod Deus est.*' This thesis I will stand to — that whatsoever the king in his conscience thinketh he may require, we ought to yield." *

The defendant having been allowed to go on in this strain for a long time, laying down doctrines new in courts of justice, although in those days often heard from the pulpit, the chief justice at last interposed, and said, —

"Mr. Harrison, if you have any thing to say in your own defence, proceed; but this raving must not be suffered. Do you not think that the king may govern his people by law?" *Harrison.* — "Yes, and by something else too. If I have offended his majesty in this, I do submit to his majesty, and crave his pardon." *Brampston, C. J.* — "Your 'If' will be very ill taken by his majesty; nor can this be considered a submission."

The defendant, being found guilty, was ordered to pay a fine to the king of £5000, and to be imprisoned — without prejudice to the remedy of Mr. Justice Hutton by action. Such an action was accordingly brought, and so popular was Mr. Justice Hutton, that he recovered £10,000 damages; whereas it was said that, if the chief justice had been the plaintiff in an action for defamation, he need not have expected more than a Norfolk groat.

Lord Chief Justice Brampston's services were likewise required in the Star Chamber. He there zealously assisted Archbishop Laud in persecuting Williams, Bishop of Lincoln,

* This is the very doctrine lately revived, in a little different shape, by some of our American divines — that whatsoever the legislative power in its conscience thinks it may require, we ought to yield. — *Ed.*

ex-keeper of the great seal. When the sentence was to be passed on this unfortunate prelate, ostensibly for tampering with the witnesses who were to give evidence against him on a former accusation, which had been abandoned as untenable, but in reality for opposing Laud's Popish innovations in religious ceremonies, Brampston declaimed bitterly against the right reverend defendant, saying, —

"I find my Lord Bishop of Lincoln much to blame in persuading, threatening, and directing of witnesses — a foul fault in any, but in him most gross who hath *curam animarum* throughout all his diocese. To destroy men's souls is most odious, and to be severely punished. I do hold him not fit to have the cure of souls, and therefore I do censure him to be suspended *tam ab officio quam a beneficio,* to pay a fine of £10,000, and to be imprisoned during the king's pleasure."

This sentence, although rigorously executed, did not satiate the vengeance of the archbishop; and the bishop, while lying a prisoner in the Tower, having received some letters from one of the masters of Westminster School, using disrespectful language towards the archbishop, and calling him "a little great man," a new information was filed against the bishop for not having disclosed these letters to a magistrate, that the writer might have been immediately brought to justice. Of course he was found guilty; and when the deliberation arose about the punishment, thus spoke Lord Chief Justice Brampston: —

"The concealing of the libel doth by no means clear my Lord Bishop of Lincoln, for there is a difference between a letter which concerns a private person and a public officer. If a libellous letter concern a private person, he that receives it may conceal it in his pocket or burn it; but if it concern a public person, he ought to reveal it to some public officer or magistrate. Why should my Lord of Lincoln keep these letters by him, but to the end to publish them, and to have them at all times in readiness to be published? I agree in the proposed sentence, that, in addition to a fine of £5000 to the king, he do pay a fine of £3000 to the archbishop, seeing the offence is against so honorable a person, and there is not the least cause of any grievance or wrong that he hath done to my Lord of Lincoln. For his being degraded, I leave it to those of the Ecclesiastical Court to whom it doth belong. As to the pillory, I am very sorry and unwilling to give such a sentence upon any man of his calling and degree. But when I consider the quality of the person, and how much it doth aggravate the offence, I cannot tell how to spare him; for the consideration that should mitigate the punishment adds to the enormity of the offence."

As no clerical crime had been committed for which degradation could be inflicted, and as it was thought not altogether decent that a bishop, wearing his lawn sleeves, his rochet, and his mitre, should stand on the pillory, to be pelted with brickbats and rotten eggs, the lord chief justice was overruled respecting this last suggestion, and the sentence was limited to the two fines, with perpetual imprisonment. The defendant was kept in durance under it till the meeting of the Long Parliament, when he was liberated; and, becoming an archbishop, he saw his persecutor take his place in the Tower, while he himself was placed at the head of the Church of England.

Now came the time when Lord Chief Justice Brampston himself was to tremble. The first grievance taken up was ship money; and both houses resolved that the tax was illegal, and that the judgment against Hampden for refusing to pay it ought to be set aside. Brampston was much alarmed when he saw Strafford and Laud arrested on a charge of high treason, and Lord Keeper Finch obliged to fly beyond the seas.

The next impeachment voted was against Brampston himself and five of his brethren; but they were more leniently dealt with, for they were only charged with "high crimes and misdemeanors;" and happening to be in the House of Lords when Mr. Waller brought up the impeachment, it was ordered "that the said judges for the present should enter into recognizances of £10,000 each to abide the censure of Parliament." This being done, they enjoyed their liberty, and continued in the exercise of their judicial functions; but Mr. Justice Berkeley, who had made himself particularly obnoxious by his indiscreet invectives against the Puritans,* was arrested while sitting on his tribunal in Westminster Hall, and committed a close prisoner to Newgate.

Chief Justice Brampston tried to mitigate the indignation of the dominant powers by giving judgment in the case of *Chambers* v. *Sir Edward Brunfield, Mayor of London,* against the legality of ship money. To an action of trespass and false imprisonment, the defendant justified by his plea under "a writ for not paying of money assessed upon the plaintiff towards the finding of a ship." There was a demurrer to the plea, so that the legality of the writ came directly in issue. The counsel for the defendant rose to cite Hampden's case and Lord Say's case, in which all their lordships had

* Some of our American federal judges are in the habit of declaiming much in the same style against abolitionists — who, indeed, may be considered as occupying a position in our present affairs in many respects parallel to that of the English Puritans in the times of Charles I. — *Ed.*

concurred, as being decisive in his favor; but Brampston, C. J., said,—

"We cannot now hear this case argued. It hath been voted and resolved in the upper House of Parliament and in the House of Commons, *nullo contradicente*, that the said writ, and what was done by color thereof, was illegal. Therefore, without further dispute thereof, the court gives judgment for the plaintiff." *

The Commons were much pleased with this submissive conduct, but *pro forma* they exhibited articles of impeachment against the chief justice. To the article founded on ship money he answered, "that at the conference of the judges he had given it as his opinion that the king could only impose the charge in case of necessity, and only during the continuance of that necessity."

The impeachment was allowed to drop; and the chief justice seems to have coquetted a good deal with the parliamentary leaders, for, after the king had taken the field, he continued to sit in his court at Westminster, and to act as an attendant to the small number of peers who assembled there, constituting the House of Lords.

But when a battle was expected, Charles, being told that the chief justice of England was chief coroner, and, by virtue of his office, on view of the body of a rebel slain in battle, had authority to pronounce judgment of attainder upon him, so as to work corruption of blood and forfeiture of lands and goods, thought it would be very convenient to have such an officer in the camp, and summoned Lord Chief Justice

* Having once refused to hear counsel against ship money, he now undertook to square the account by refusing to hear counsel for it. — *Ed.*

Brampston to appear at head quarters in Yorkshire. The Lords were asked to give him leave of absence, to obey the king's summons, but they commanded him to attend them day by day at his peril. He therefore sent his two sons to make his excuse to the king. His majesty was highly incensed by his asking leave of the Lords, and — considering another apology that he made, about the infirmity of his health and the difficulty of travelling in the disturbed state of the country, a mere pretence — by a *supersedeas* under the great seal dismissed him from his office, and immediately appointed Sir Robert Heath to be chief justice of England in his stead.

Brampston must now have given in his full adhesion to the parliamentary party, for in such favor was he with them, that, when the treaty of Uxbridge was proceeding, they made it one of their conditions that he should be reappointed lord chief justice of the Court of King's Bench.

Having withdrawn entirely from public life, he spent the remainder of his days at his country house in Essex. There he expired, on the 2d of September, 1654, in the 78th year of his age. If courage and principle had been added to his very considerable talents and acquirements, he might have gained a great name in the national struggle which he witnessed; but, from his vacillation, he fell into contempt with both parties; and, although free from the imputation of serious crimes, there is no respect entertained for his memory.

# CHAPTER VIII.

## ROBERT HEATH.

We must now attend to Sir Robert Heath, who was the last chief justice of Charles I., and was appointed by him to pass judgment, not on the living, but on the dead. If we cannot defend all his proceedings, we must allow him the merit — which successful members of our profession can so seldom claim — of perfect consistency; for he started as a high prerogative lawyer, and a high prerogative lawyer he continued to the day of his death.

He was of a respectable family of small fortune, in Kent, and was born at Etonbridge in that county. He received his early education at Tonbridge School, and was sent from thence to St. John's College, Cambridge. His course of study there is not known; but when he was transferred to the Inner Temple, we are told that he read law and history with the preconceived conviction that the King of England was an absolute sovereign; and so enthusiastic was he that he converted all he met with into arguments to support his theory. One most convenient doctrine solved many difficulties which would otherwise have perplexed him: he maintained that Parliament had no power to curtail the essential prerogatives of the crown, and that all acts of Parliament for such a purpose were *ultra vices* and void. There is no absurdity in this doctrine, for a legislative assembly may have only a limited power, like the Congress of the United States of America; and it was by no means so startling then as now, when the omnipotence of Parliament has passed into a maxim. He had no respect whatever for the House of Commons or any of its privileges, being of opinion that it had been called into existence by the crown only to assist in raising the revenue, and that, if it refused necessary supplies, the king, as *Pater Patriæ*, must provide for the defence of the realm in the same manner as before it had existence. He himself several times refused a seat in that assembly, which he said was "only fit for a pitiful Puritan or a pretending patriot;" and he expressed a resolution to get on in his profession without beginning, as many of his brethren did, by herding with the seditious, and trying to undermine the powers which for the public good the crown had immemorially exercised and inalienably possessed. To enable him to defend these with proper skill and effect, he was constantly perusing the old records; and, from the Conquest downwards, they were as familiar to him as the cases in the last number of the periodical reports are to a modern practitioner. Upon all questions of prerogative law which could arise he was complete master of all the authorities to be cited for the crown, and of the answers to be given to all that could be cited against him.

As he would neither go into Parliament nor make a splash in Westminster Hall in the "sedition line," his friends were apprehensive that his great acquirements as a lawyer never would be known; but it happened that, in the year 1619, he was appointed "reader" for the Inner Temple, and he delivered a series of lectures, explaining his views on constitutional subjects, which forever established his reputation.

On the first vacancy which afterwards occurred in the office of solicitor general, he was appointed to fill it; and Sir Thomas Coventry, the attorney general, expressed high satisfaction at having him for a colleague. Very important proceedings soon after followed, upon the impeachment of Lord Bacon and the punishment of the monopolists; but, as these were all in Parliament, he made no conspicuous figure during the remainder of the reign of James I.

Soon after the commencement of the reign of Charles I., he was promoted to the office of attorney general; and then, upon various important occasions, he delivered arguments in support of the unlimited power of the crown to imprison and to impose taxes, which cannot now be read without admiration of the learning and ingenuity which they display.

The first of these was when Sir Thomas Darnel and his patriotic associates were brought by *habeas corpus* before the Court of King's Bench, having been committed in reality for refusing to contribute to the forced loan, but upon a warrant by the king and council which did not specify any offence. I have already mentioned the speeches of their counsel.* "To these pleadings for liberty," says Hallam, "Heath, the attorney general, replied in a speech of considerable ability, full of those high principles of prerogative which, trampling as it were on all statute and precedent, seemed to tell the judges that they were placed there to obey rather than to determine."

"This commitment," he said, "is not in a legal and ordinary way, but by the special command of our lord the king, which implies not only the fact done, but so extraordinarily done, that it is notoriously his majesty's immediate act, and he wills that it should be so. Shall we make inquiries whether his commands are lawful? Who shall call in question the

* See life of Hyde, ante, p. 97.

justice of the king's actions? Is he to be called upon to give an account of them?"

After arguing very confidently on the legal maxim that "the king can do no wrong," * the constitutional interpretation of which had not yet been settled, he goes on to show how *de facto* the power of imprisonment had recently been exercised by the detention in custody, for years, of Popish and other state prisoners, without any question or doubt being raised. "Some," he observed, "there are in the Tower who were put in it when very young: should they bring a *habeas corpus*, would the court deliver them?" He then dwelt at great length upon the resolution of the judges in the 34th of Elizabeth in favor of a general commitment by the king, and went over all the precedents and statutes cited on the other side, contending that they were either inapplicable or contrary to law. He carried the court with him, and the prisoners were remanded without any considerable public scandal being then created.

During the stormy session in which the "Petition of Right" was passed, Heath, not being a member of the House of Commons, had very little trouble; but once, while it was pending, he was heard against it as counsel for the king before a joint committee of Lords and Commons. Upon this occasion he occupied two whole days in pouring forth his learning to prove that the proposed measure was an infringement of the ancient, essential, and inalienable prerogatives of the crown. He was patiently listened to, but he made no impression on Lords or Commons; and the king, after receiving an assurance

* This supposed inability of the king to do wrong has in America among a certain class been transferred to the federal government, which represents the royal authority of the English. — *Ed.*

from the judges that they would effectually do away with the statute when it came before them for interpretation, was obliged to go through the form of giving the royal assent to it.

As soon as the Parliament was dissolved, Heath was called into full activity; and he now carried every thing his own way, for the extent of the royal prerogative was to be declared by the Court of King's Bench and the Star Chamber. Sir John Eliot, Stroud, Selden, and the other leaders of the country party who had been the most active in carrying the "Petition of Right," were immediately thrown into prison, and the attorney general having assembled the judges, they were as good as their word, by declaring that they had cognizance of all that happened in Parliament, and that they had a right to punish whatsoever was done there by Parliament men in an unparliamentary manner.

The imprisoned patriots having sued out writs of *habeas corpus*, it appeared that they were detained under warrants signed by the king, "for notable contempts committed against ourself and our government, and for stirring up sedition against us." Their counsel argued that a commitment by the king is invalid, as he must act by responsible officers; and that warrants in this general form were in direct violation of the "Petition of Right," so recently become law. But Heath still boldly argued for the unimpaired power of arbitrary imprisonment, pretending that the "Petition of Right" was not a binding statute. "A petition in Parliament," said he, "is no law, yet it is for the honor and dignity of the king to observe it faithfully; but it is the duty of the people not to stretch beyond the words and intention of the king, and no other construction can be made of the 'Petition' than that it is a confirmation of the ancient rights and liberties of the subject. So that now the case remains in the same quality and degree as it was before the 'Petition.'" He proceeded to turn into ridicule the whole proceedings of the late Parliament, and he again went over the bead-roll of his precedents to prove that one committed by command of the king or Privy Council is not bailable. The prisoners were remanded to custody.

In answer to the *information*, it was pleaded that a court of common law had no jurisdiction to take cognizance of speeches made in the House of Commons; that the judges had often declared themselves incompetent to give an opinion upon such subjects; that the words imputed to Sir John Eliot were an accusation against the ministers of the crown, which the representatives of the people had a right to prefer; that no one would venture to complain of grievances in Parliament if he should be subjected to punishment at the discretion of an inferior tribunal; that the alleged precedents were mere acts of power which no attempt had hitherto been made to sanction; and that, although part of the supposed offences had occurred immediately before the dissolution, so that they could not have been punished by the last Parliament, they might be punished in a future Parliament. But

"*Heath, A. G.*, replied that the king was not bound to wait for another Parliament; and, moreover, that the House of Commons was not a court of justice, nor had any power to proceed criminally, except by imprisoning its own members. He admitted that the judges had sometimes declined to give their judgment upon matters of privilege; but contended that such cases had happened during the session of Parliament, and that it did not follow that an offence committed in the house might not be questioned after a dissolution.

The judges unanimously held that, although the alleged offences had been committed in Parliament, the defendants were bound to answer in the Court of King's Bench, in which all offences against the crown were cognizable. The parties refusing to put in any other plea, they were convicted, and the attorney general praying judgment, they were sentenced to pay heavy fines, and to be imprisoned during the king's pleasure.

Heath remained attorney general two years longer. The only difficulty which the government now had was to raise money without calling a Parliament; and he did his best to surmount it. By his advice, a new tax was laid on cards, and all who refused to pay it he mercilessly prosecuted in the Court of Exchequer, where his will was law. All monopolies had been put down at the conclusion of the last reign, with the exception of new inventions. Under pretence of some novelty, he granted patents, vested in particular individuals or companies the exclusive right of dealing in soap, leather, salt, linen rags, and various other commodities, although, of £200,000 thereby levied on the people, scarcely £1500 came into the royal coffers. His grand expedient was to compel all who had a landed estate of £40 a year to submit to knighthood, and to pay a heavy fee; or, on refusal, to pay a heavy fine. This caused a tremendous outcry, and was at first resisted; but the question being brought before the Court of Exchequer, he delivered an argument in support of the claim, in which he traced knighthood from the ancient Germans down to the reigns of the Stuarts, showing that the prince had always the right of conferring it upon all who held of him *in capite* — receiving a reasonable compliment in return. In this instance, Mr. Attorney not only had the decision of the court, but the law on his side. Blackstone says, "The prerogative of compelling the king's vassals to be knighted, or to pay a fine, was expressly recognized in Parliament by the statute *de Militibus*, 1 Ed. II., but yet was the occasion of heavy murmurs when exerted by Charles I., among whose many misfortunes it was, that neither himself nor his people seemed able to distinguish between the arbitrary stretch and the legal exertion of prerogative."*

All these expedients for filling the exchequer proving unproductive, the last hopes of despotism rested upon Noy, who, having been a patriot, was eager to be the slave of the court, and proposed his ship money. If this should be supported by the judges, and endured by the people, Parliaments for ever after would have been unnecessary. Heath was willing enough to defend it; but the inventor was unwilling to share the glory or the profit of it with another. Luckily, at that very time, a vacancy occurred in the office of chief justice of the Common Pleas; and there being an extreme eagerness to get rid of Heath, notwithstanding his very zealous services to the crown, he was "put upon the cushion," and Noy succeeded him as attorney general.

To qualify him to be a judge, it was necessary that he should first become a serjeant; and, according to ancient custom, he distributed rings, choosing a motto which indicated his intention still to put the king above the law — "*Lex Regis, vis Legis.*" On the 25th of October, 1631, he came in his

* 2 Bl. Com. 69. Compulsory knighthood was abolished by the Long Parliament, 16 Car. I. c. 20.

parti-colored robes to the Common Pleas, and performed his ceremonies as serjeant, and the same day kept his feast in Serjeants' Inn; and afterwards, on the 27th of October, he was sworn in chief justice.

In the four years during which he held this office, no case of public interest occurred in his own court; but he took an active part in the Star Chamber, and, having prosecuted the Recorder of Salisbury for breaking a painted window without the bishop's consent, he now sentenced him for the offence. The grand scheme of ship money, which had been long in preparation, was ready to be brought forward, when, to the astonishment of the world, Heath was removed from his office. It has been said that the government was afraid of his opinion of ship money, and wished to prefer Finch, — the most profligate of men, — on whom they could entirely rely. The truth seems to be, that he continued to enjoy the favor and confidence of the government, but that a charge had been brought against him of taking bribes, which was so strongly supported by evidence that it could not be overlooked, although no Parliament was sitting, or ever likely to sit, and that the most discreet proceeding, even for himself, was to remove him quietly from his office. The removal of judges had, under the Stuarts, become so common, that no great sensation was created by a new instance of it, and people merely supposed that some secret displeasure had been given to the king.

Heath presented a petition to the king, setting forth his services as attorney general in supporting the royal right to imprison and to tax the subject, as well as the good will he had manifested while he sat on the bench, and expressing a hope that, as he had been severely punished for his fault, he might not be utterly ruined, but might be permitted to practise at the bar. To this the king, by advice of the Privy Council, consented, on condition that he should be put at the bottom of the list of serjeants, and should not plead against the crown in the Star Chamber.

Accordingly, he took his place at the bar of the Court of Common Pleas, as junior, where he had presided as chief, and speedily got into considerable business. He very soon again insinuated himself into the favor of the government, and assisted Sir John Banks, the attorney general, in state prosecutions. He first addressed the jury for the crown in the famous case of Thomas Harrison, indicted for insulting Mr. Justice Hutton in open court; leaving the attorney general to sum up the evidence.

Not having been on the bench when the judges gave the extrajudicial opinion in favor of ship money, nor when Hampden's trial came on, he escaped impeachment at the meeting of the Long Parliament; and on the removal of those who were impeached, he was made a puisne judge of the Court of King's Bench.

When hostilities were about to commence, he happened to be judge of assize at York, where the king lay. He always protested that he was innocent of any plot to make himself chief justice of the King's Bench; yet, knowing that, from bodily infirmity and lukewarmness in the royal cause, Brampston would not come to York when summoned by the king, there is strong reason to suspect that he suggested the propriety of this summons, on the pretence that the chief justice of England might, as chief coroner, declare an attainder of rebels slain in battle, which would subject their lands and goods to forfeiture. Brampston was ordered to come to York, and not making his appearance, he was removed from his office; and Sir Robert Heath was created chief justice of England, that he might attaint the slaughtered rebels. Sir John Brampston, the autobiographer, son of the judge whom Heath superseded, says, "When Sir Robert Heath had that place, that opinion vanished, and nothing of that nature was ever put in practice."

But in the autumn of the year 1643, the royalists having gained an ascendency in the west of England, a scheme was formed to outlaw, for high treason, the leaders on the Parliament side — as well those who were directing military operations in the field, as the non-combatants who were conducting the government at Westminster. A commission passed the great seal, at Oxford, directed to Lord Chief Justice Heath and three other judges who had taken the king's side, to hold a court of oyer and terminer at Salisbury. Accordingly, they took their seats on the bench, and swore in a grand jury, whom Heath addressed, explaining the law of high treason, showing that flagrant overt acts had been committed by conspiring the king's death and levying war against him, and proving by authorities that all who aided and assisted by furnishing supplies, or giving orders or advice to the rebels, were as guilty as those who fought against his majesty with deadly weapons in their hands. Bills of indictment were then preferred against the Earls of Northumberland, Pembroke, and Salisbury, and divers members of the House of Commons. The grand jury, however, — probably without having read Grotius and the writers on public law, who say that when there is a civil war in a country the opposite parties must treat each other as if they were belligerents belonging to two independent nations, but actuated by a sense of the injustice and impolicy of treating as common malefactors those who, seeking to reform abuses and vindicate the liberties of their fellow-citizens, were commanding armies and enacting laws,—returned all the bills *ignoramus;* and there could neither be any trial nor process of outlawry.

This rash attempt only served to produce irritation, and to render the parliamentarians more suspicious and revengeful when negotiations were afterwards opened which might have led to a satisfactory accommodation.

In the summer of the following year, Chief Justice Heath held assizes at Exeter, and there actually obtained the conviction of Captain Turpine, a parliamentary officer, who had been taken in arms against the king, and was produced as a prisoner at the bar. The sheriff appears to have refused to carry the sentence into execution; but the unfortunate gentleman was hanged by Sir John Berkeley, Governor of Exeter. The Parliament, having heard of their partisan being thus put to death in cold blood, ordered that the judges who condemned him might be impeached of high treason; but they were afterwards satisfied with passing an ordinance to remove Heath, and his brethren who had sat with him on this occasion, from their judicial offices, and to disable them from acting as judges in all time to come.

Sir Robert Heath never ventured to take his seat as chief justice of the Court of King's Bench at Westminster; but, after travelling about for some time with the king, fixed himself at Oxford, where he was made a doctor of the civil law, and attended as a judge when Charles's Parliament was held there.

When Oxford was at last obliged to surrender, and the royalists could no longer make head in any part of England,

Heath found it necessary to fly for safety to the continent. The parliamentary leaders said that they would not have molested him if he had confined himself to the discharge of his judicial duties; or even if, like Lord Keeper Littleton and other lawyers, he had carried arms for the king; but as, contrary to the law of nations, he had proceeded against several of those who bore a commission which the Parliament had granted to them in the king's name, they were determined to make an example of him. Therefore, when an ordinance was passed, granting an indemnity to the royalists who submitted, he was excepted from it by name. After suffering great privations, he died at Caen, in Normandy, in the month of August, 1649.

He had, from his professional gains, purchased a large landed estate, which was sequestrated by the Parliament, but afterwards was restored by Charles II. to his son. He had never tried to make his peace with the dominant party by any concession, and he declared that "he would rather suffer all the ills of exile than submit to the rule of those who had first fought their sovereign in the field, and then had murdered him on the scaffold." With the exception of his bribery, which was never properly inquired into, and does not seem to have injured him much in the opinion of his contemporaries, no grievous stain is attached to his memory; and we must feel respect for the constancy with which he adhered to his political principles, although we cannot defend them.

# CHAPTER IX.

## ROBERT FOSTER.

At the restoration of Charles II. it was considered necessary to sweep away the whole of the judges from Westminster Hall, although, generally speaking, they were very learned and respectable, and they had administered justice very impartially and satisfactorily.* Immense difficulty was found in replacing them. Clarendon was sincerely desirous to select the fittest men that could be found, but from his long exile he was himself entirely unacquainted with the state of the legal profession, and, upon making inquiries, hardly any could be pointed out, whose political principles, juridical acquirements, past conduct, and present position entitled them to high preferment. The most eminent barristers on the royalist side had retired from practice when the civil war began, and the new generation which had sprung up had taken an oath to be faithful to the commonwealth. One individual was discovered — Sir Orlando Bridgman — eminent both for law and for loyalty. Early distinguished as a rising advocate, he had sacrificed his profits that he might assist the royal cause by carrying arms; and, refusing to profess allegiance to those whom he considered rebels, he had spent years in seclusion, — still devoting himself to professional studies, in which he

* Their decisions are still of as much authority on legal questions as those of courts sitting under a commission from the crown; and they were published with the sanction of the chancellor and all the judges in the reigns of Charles II. and James II.

took the highest delight. At first, however, it was thought that he could not properly be placed in a higher judicial office than that of chief baron of the Exchequer; and the chiefships of the King's Bench and Common Pleas were allowed to remain vacant some months, *puisnies* being appointed in each court to carry on the routine business.

At last a chief justice of England was announced — Sir Robert Foster; and his obscurity testified the perplexity into which the government had been thrown in making a decent choice. He was one of the very few survivors of the old school of lawyers, which had flourished before the troubles began; he had been called to the degree of serjeant at law so long ago as the 30th of May, 1636, at a time when Charles I., with Strafford for his minister, was ruling with absolute sway, was imposing taxes by his own authority, was changing the law by proclamation, and hoped never again to be molested by Parliaments. This system was condemned and opposed by the most eminent men at the English bar, but was applauded and supported by some who conscientiously thought that all popular institutions were mischievous, and by more who thought that court favor gave them the best chance of rising in the world. Foster is supposed to have defended ship money, the cruel sentences of the Star Chamber, the billeting of soldiers to live at free quarters, and other flagrant abuses, as well from a sincere love of despotism as from a desire to recommend himself to those in power.*

At the time when tyranny had reached its culminating point, he was appointed a puisne judge of the Court of

* It is doubtless a like mixture of motives that prompts just now the conduct of some of our American lawyers. — *Ed.*

Common Pleas. Luckily for him, Hampden's case had been decided before his appointment, and he was not impeached by the Long Parliament. When the civil war broke out, he followed the king; and afterwards assisted in attempting to hold a Court of Common Pleas at Oxford, but sat alone, and his tribunal was without advocates or suitors. An ordinance passed the House of Commons for removing him from his office, and on account of his excessive zeal in the royal cause, he was obliged to compound for his estate by paying a very large fine.

After the king's death, he continued in retirement till the Restoration. He is said to have had a small chamber in the Temple, and like Sir Orlando Bridgman and Sir Jeffery Pelman, to have practised as a chamber counsel, chiefly addicting himself to conveyancing.

The first act of the government of Charles II. was to reinstate Foster in his old office. There was a strong desire to reward his constancy with fresh honors; but he was thought unfit to be raised higher, and the office of chief justice of the King's Bench could not be satisfactorily filled up.

Only six common law judges had been appointed when the trials of the regicides came on. Foster, being one of them, distinguished himself for his zeal; and when they were over, all scruples as to his fitness having vanished, he, who a few months before, shut up in his chamber that he might escape the notice of the Roundheads, never expected any thing better than to receive a broad piece for preparing a conveyance according to the recently invented expedient of "lease and release," was constituted the highest criminal judge in the kingdom.

He presided in the Court of King's Bench for two years.

Being a deep black letter lawyer, he satisfactorily disposed of the private cases which came before him, although he was much perplexed by the improved rules of practice introduced while he was in retirement, and he was disposed to sneer at the decisions of Chief Justice Rolle, a man in all respects much superior to himself. In state prosecutions he showed himself as intemperate and as arbitrary as any of the judges who had been impeached at the meeting of the Long Parliament.

To him chiefly is to be imputed the disgraceful execution as a traitor, of one who had disapproved of the late king's trial; who was included in the present king's promise of indemnity from Breda; * in whose favor a petition had been presented by the Convention Parliament; who was supposed to be expressly pardoned by the answer to that petition; † but who had incurred the inextinguishable hatred of the Cavaliers by the part he had taken in bringing about the conviction of the Earl of Strafford. Sir Henry Vane the younger, ‡ after lying two years in prison, during which the shame of putting him to death was too strong to be overcome, was at last arraigned for high treason at the King's Bench bar. As

* Charles II., in his *Declaration* from Breda, had promised that he should "proceed only against the immediate murderers of his royal father."

† In answer to the address of the two Houses of the Convention Parliament to spare the lives of Vane and Lambert, the lord chancellor reported, "His majesty grants the desire of the said petition;" — the ancient form of passing acts of Parliament. The ultra Cavalier House of Commons which followed desired Vane's death, but could not alter the law or abrogate the royal promise.

‡ In his younger days, before the civil war, Sir Henry Vane had been among the early emigrants to Massachusetts, and as governor of that colony had borne a part in some remarkable transactions there. — See Hildreth's *History of the United States*, vol. i. ch. ix

he had actually tried to save the life of Charles I., the treason charged upon him was for conspiring the death of Charles II., whose life he would have been equally willing to defend. The indictment alleged this overt act, "that he did take upon him the government of the forces of this nation by sea and land, and appointed colonels, captains, and officers." The crown lawyers admitted that the prisoner had not meditated any attempt upon the natural life of Charles II., but insisted that, by acting under the authority of the commonwealth, he had assisted in preventing the true heir of the monarchy from obtaining possession of the government, and thereby, in point of law, had conspired his death, and had committed high treason. Unassisted by counsel, and browbeaten by Lord Chief Justice Foster, he made a gallant defence; and besides pointing out the bad faith of the proceeding, after the promises of indemnity and pardon held out to him, contended that, in point of law, he was not guilty, on the ground that Charles II. had never been in possession of the government as king during any part of the period in question: that the supreme power of the state was then vested in the Parliament, whose orders he had obeyed; that he was in the same relation to the exiled heir as if there had been another king upon the throne; and that the statute of Henry VII., which was only declaratory of the common law and of common sense, expressly provided that no one should ever be called in question for obeying, or defending by force of arms, a king *de facto*, although he had usurped the throne. He concluded by observing that the whole English nation might be included in the impeachment.

*Foster, C. J.*—"Had there been another king on the throne, though a usurper, you might have been exempted by the statute from the penalties of treason. But the authority you recognized was called by the rebels either 'Commonwealth' or 'Protector,' and the statute takes no notice of any such names or things. From the moment that the martyred sovereign expired, our lord the king that now is must be considered as entitled to our allegiance, and the law declares that he has ever since occupied his ancestral throne. Therefore, obedience to any usurped authority was treason to him. You talk of the sovereign power of Parliament, but the law knows of no sovereign power except the power of our sovereign lord the king. With respect to the number against whom the law shall be put in force, that must depend upon his majesty's clemency and sense of justice. To those who truly repent he is merciful; but the punishment of those who repent not is a duty we owe both to God and to our fellow-men."

A verdict of guilty being returned, the usual sentence was pronounced; but the king, out of regard to his own reputation, if not to the dictates of justice and mercy, was very reluctant to sanction the execution of it, till Chief Justice Foster, going the following day to Hampton Court to give him an account of the trial, represented the line of defence taken by the prisoner as inconsistent with the principles of monarchical government, and said that the supposed promises of pardon were by no means binding, "for God, though ofttimes promising mercy, yet intends his mercy only for the penitent." The king, thus wrought on, notwithstanding his engagement to the contrary, signed the death-warrant, and Vane was beheaded on Tower Hill, saying with his last breath, "I value my life less in a good cause than the king does his promise." Mr. Fox, and other historians, consider this execution "a gross instance of tyranny," but have allowed Chief Justice Foster, who is mainly responsible for it, to escape without censure.

The arbitrary disposition of this chief justice was strongly manifested soon after, when John Crook, and several other very loyal Quakers, were brought before him at the Old Bailey for refusing to take the oath of allegiance.

*Foster, C. J.*—"John Crook, when did you take the oath of allegiance?" *Crook.*—"Answering this question in the negative is to accuse myself, which you ought not to put me upon. '*Nemo debet seipsum prodere.*' I am an Englishman, and I ought not to be taken, nor imprisoned, nor called in question, nor put to answer, but according to the law of the land." *Foster, C. J.*—"You are here required to take the oath of allegiance, and when you have done that, you shall be heard." *Crook.*—"You that are judges on the bench ought to be my counsel, not my accusers." *Foster, C. J.*—"We are here to do justice, and are upon our oaths; and we are to tell you what is law, not you us. Therefore, sirrah, you are too bold." *Crook.*—"*Sirrah* is not a word becoming a judge. If I speak loud, it is my zeal for the truth and for the name of the Lord. Mine innocency makes me bold." *Foster, C. J.*—"It is an evil zeal." *Crook.*—"No, I am bold in the name of the Lord God Almighty, the everlasting Jehovah, to assert the truth and stand as a witness for it. Let my accuser be brought forth." *Foster, C. J.*—"Sirrah, you are to take the oath, and here we tender it you." *Crook.*—"Let me be cleared of my imprisonment, and then I will answer to what is charged against me. I keep a conscience void of offence, both towards God and towards man." *Foster, C. J.*—"Sirrah, leave your canting." *Crook.*—"Is this canting, to speak the words of the Scripture?" *Foster, C. J.*—"It is canting in your mouth, though they are St. Paul's words. Your first denial to take the oath shall be recorded; and on a second denial, you bear the penalties of a *præmunire*, which is the forfeiture of all your estate, if you have any, and imprisonment during life." *Crook.*—"I owe dutiful allegiance to the king, but cannot *swear* without breaking my allegiance to the King of Kings. We dare not break Christ's commandments, who hath said, *Swear not at all;* and the apostle James says, 'Above all things, my brethren, *swear not.*'"

Crook, in his account of the trial, says, "The chief justice thereupon interrupting, called upon the executioner to stop my mouth, which he did accordingly with a dirty cloth and a gag." The other Quakers following Crook's example, they were all indicted for having a second time refused to take the oath of allegiance; and being found guilty, the court gave judgment against them of forfeiture, imprisonment for life, and moreover, that they were "out of the king's protection;" whereby they carried about with them *caput lupinum*, (a wolf's head,) and might be put to death by any one as noxious vermin.

The last trial of importance at which Chief Justice Foster presided was that of Thomas Tonge and others, charged with a plot to assassinate the king. General Ludlow says that this was got up by the government to divert the nation from their ill humor, caused by the sale of Dunkirk;* the invention being, "that divers thousands of ill-affected persons were ready under his command to seize the Tower and the city

* A fortress on the south shore of the English Channel, taken by Cromwell from the Spaniards, and by Charles II. sold at this time to Louis XIV. of France.

of London, then to march directly to Whitehall, in order to kill the king and Monk, with a resolution to give no quarter; and after that to declare for a commonwealth." The case was proved by the evidence of supposed accomplices, which was held to be sufficient without any corroboration. The chief justice seems to have been very infirm and exhausted; for thus he summed up,—

"My masters of the jury, I cannot speak loud to you; you understand this business, such as I think you have not had the like in your time; my speech will not give me leave to discourse of it. The witnesses may satisfy all honest men: it is clear that they all agreed to subvert the government, and to destroy his majesty. What can you have more. The prisoners are in themselves inconsiderable; they are only the out-boughs; but if such fellows are not met withal, they are the fittest instruments to set up a Jack Straw and a Wat Tyler; therefore you must lop them off, as they will encourage others. I leave the evidence to you; go together."

The prisoners being all found guilty, the chief justice thus passed sentence upon them,—

"You have committed the greatest crime against God, our king, and your country, and against every good body that is in this land; for that capital sin of high treason is a sin inexpiable, and, indeed, hath no equal sin as to this world. Meddling with them that are given to change hath brought too much mischief already to this nation; and if you will commit the same sin, you must receive the same punishment, for happy is he who by other men's harms takes heed."

They were all executed, protesting their innocence.

The chief justice went a circuit after this trial, in the hope that country air would revive him. However, he became weaker and weaker, and, although much assisted by his brother judge, he with great difficulty got to the last assize town. From thence he travelled by slow stages to his house in London, where, after languishing for a few weeks, he expired, full of days, and little blamed for any part of his conduct as a judge, however reprehensible it may appear to us, trying it by a standard which he would have thought only fit to be proposed by rebels.

# CHAPTER X.

## ROBERT HYDE.

On the death of Sir Robert Foster, Lord Clarendon thought that he might fairly do a job for an aged kinsman, of respectable, if not brilliant reputation; and he appointed Sir Robert Hyde chief justice of the King's Bench. They were cousins-german, being grandsons of Lawrence Hyde, of West Hatch, in the county of Wilts, and nephews of Sir Nicholas Hyde, chief justice of the King's Bench in the commencement of the reign of Charles I. The Hydes were the most distinguished race of the robe in the 17th century. Robert's father was likewise a lawyer of renown, being attorney general to Anne of Denmark, queen of James I., and he had twelve sons, most of whom followed their father's profession. Robert seems to have been a very quiet man, and to have got on by family interest and by plodding. Although Edward, the future chancellor, played such a distinguished part during the troubles, — first as a moderate patriot, and then as a liberal conservative, — Robert, the future chief justice, was not in the House of Commons, nor did he enlist under the banner of either party in the field. Just before the civil war broke out, he was called to the degree of serjeant at law, and he continued obscurely to carry on his profession during all the vicissitudes of the twenty eventful years between 1640 and 1660.

At the Restoration, he was made a puisne judge of the Common Pleas, and, acting under Chief Justice Bridgman, he acquitted himself creditably.

When he was installed chief justice of the King's Bench, Lord Chancellor Clarendon himself attended in court, and thus addressed him: —

"It's a sign the troubles have been long, that there are so few judges left, only yourself; and after so long suffering of the law and lawyers, the king thought fit to call men of the best reputation and learning, to renew the reverence due and used to the law and lawyers; and the king, as soon as the late chief justice was dead, full of days and of honors, did resolve on you as the ancientest judge left; and your education in this court gives you advantage here above others, as you are the son of an eminent lawyer as any in his days, whose felicity was to see twelve sons, and you one of the youngest a serjeant, and who left you enough, able to live without the help of an elder brother. For your integrity to the crown, you come to sit here. The king and the kingdom do expect great reformation from your activity. For this reason, the king, when I told him Chief Justice Foster was dead, made choice of you. Courage in a judge is necessary as in a general;* therefore you must not want this to punish sturdy offenders. The genteel wickedness of duelling I beseech you inquire into; the carriers of challenges, and fighters, however they escape death, the fining and imprisoning of them will make them more dread this court than the day of judgment."

*Hyde, C. J.* — "I had ever thought of the advice of the wise man, 'not to seek to be a judge, nor ask to sit in the seat

* So Bacon, better at precept than at practice, in his advice to Sir George Villars, requires in judges these three attributes — they must be men of courage, fearing God, and hating covetousness: an ignorant man cannot, a *coward* dare not be a good judge. On the American bench we have too many cowards. — *Ed.*

of honor,' being conscious of my own defects and small learning. But, seeing his majesty's grace, I shall humbly submit, and serve him with my life, with all alacrity and duty. Sins of infirmity I hope his majesty will pardon, and for wilful and corrupt dealings I shall not ask it. I attended in Coke's time as a reporter here; and as he said when he was made chief justice I say now — 'I will behave myself with all diligence and honesty.' "

This chief justice was much celebrated in his day for checking the licentiousness of the press. A printer named John Twyn, having printed a book containing passages which were said to reflect upon the king, was arraigned before him at the Old Bailey on an indictment for high treason. The prisoner being asked how he would be tried, said, "I desire to be tried in the presence of that God who is the searcher of all hearts, and the disposer of all things."

*Hyde, L. C. J.* — "God Almighty is present here, but you must be tried by him and your peers, that is, your country, or twelve honest men." *Prisoner.* — "I desire to be tried by God alone." *Hyde, L. C. J.* — "God Almighty looks down, and beholds what we do here, and we shall answer severely if we do you any wrong. We are careful of our souls as you can be of yours. You must answer in the words of the law." *Prisoner.* — "By God and my country."

It was proved clearly enough that he had printed the book, and some passages of it might have been considered libellous; but there was no other evidence against him, and he averred that he had unconsciously printed the book in the way of his trade.

*Hyde, L. C. J.* — "There is here as much villany and slander as it is possible for devil or man to invent. To rob the king of the love of his subjects, is to destroy him in his person. You are here in the presence of Almighty God, as you desired; and the best you can now do towards amends for your wickedness is by discovering the author of this villanous book. If not, you must not expect — and, indeed, God forbid — there should be any mercy shown you." *Prisoner.* — "I never knew the author of it." *Hyde, L. C. J.* — "Then we must not trouble ourselves. You of the jury, there can be no doubt that publishing such a book as this is as high treason as can be committed, and my brothers will declare the same if you doubt."

The jury having found a verdict of guilty,* the usual sentence was pronounced by Lord Chief Justice Hyde, and the printer was drawn, hanged, and quartered accordingly.

The next trials before his lordship, although the charge was not made capital, (as he said it might have been,) were equally discreditable to him. Several booksellers were indicted for publishing a book which contained a simple and true account of the trial of the regicides, with their speeches and prayers.

*Hyde, L. C. J.* — "To publish such a book is to fill all the king's subjects with the justification of that horrid murder. I will be bold to say no such horrid villany has been done upon the face of the earth since the crucifying of our Savior. To print and publish this is sedition. He that prints a libel against me as Sir Robert Hyde, and he that sets him at work,

* The following dialogue occurred after the verdict: —

*Prisoner.* — I most humbly beseech your lordship to remember my condition, (he had before stated himself to be the father of nine small children,) and intercede for me.

*Lord Hyde.* — I would not intercede for my own father in this case, if he were alive.

must answer it; much more when against the king and the state. *Dying men's words,* indeed! If men are as villanous at their death as in their lives, may what they say be published as the words of dying men? God forbid! It is the king's great mercy that the charge is not for high treason."

The defendants, being found guilty, were sentenced to be fined, to stand several hours in the pillory, and to be imprisoned for life.

[In October, 1664, Chief Justice Hyde caused John Keach to be indicted for libel, which indictment he proceeded forthwith to try, in a manner denounced by Mr. Dunning, in one of his speeches in the House of Commons (Dec. 6, 1770,) as "cruel, brutal, and illegal."

Keach had written a little book called The Child's Instructor; or a new and easy Primer, in which were contained several things contrary to the doctrine and ceremonies of the Church of England. Keach taught that infants ought not to be baptized; that laymen may preach the gospel; that Christ shall reign personally on the earth in the latter day, &c. He had no sooner received a few copies from London, where the book was printed, than a justice of the peace, who had heard of it, entered his house with a constable, seized several of the books, and bound Keach over to answer for it at the next assizes at Aylsbury.

Chief Justice Hyde presiding, Keach was called to the bar, when the following dialogue ensued: —

*Hyde.* — Did you write this book? (Holding out one of the primers.) *

* This practice of putting questions to the prisoner intended to intimidate him, to involve him in contradictions, or to elicit from him some indiscreet admission, had ceased during the Commonwealth, but was revived by the new royal judges.

*Keach.* — I writ most of it.

*Hyde.* — What have you to do to take other men's trades out of their hands? I believe you can preach as well as write books. Thus it is to let you and such as you are have the Scripture to wrest to your own destruction. You have made in your book a new creed. I have seen three creeds before, but I never saw a fourth till you made one.

*Keach.* — I have not made a creed, but a confession of the Christian faith.

*Hyde.* — Well, that is a creed, then.

*Keach.* — Your lordship said you had never seen but three creeds, but thousands of Christians have made a confession of their faith.

The chief justice having denounced several things contained in the book as contrary to the liturgy of the church of England, and so a breach of the test of uniformity —

*Keach.* — My lord, as to those things —

*Hyde.* — You shall not preach here, nor give the reasons of your damnable doctrine, to seduce and infect his majesty's subjects. These are not things for such as you to meddle with, and to pretend to write books of divinity; but I will try you for it before I sleep.

He then directed an indictment to be drawn up, and thus addressed the grand jury: —

"Gentlemen of the grand jury: I shall send you presently a bill against one that hath taken upon him to write a new primer for the instruction of your children. He is a base and dangerous fellow; and if this be suffered, children by learning of it will become such as he is; and therefore I hope you will do your duty."

A long indictment having been found, in which divers

passages from the book were set forth as damnable, seditious, wicked, and contrary to the statute in that case made and provided, Keach was called upon to plead to it. He asked for a copy, and liberty to confer with counsel, and to put in his exceptions before pleading. But Chief Justice Hyde compelled him to plead before he would give him a copy, and then would allow him only an hour's time to consider it, which, as not long enough to be of any benefit, Keach declined to accept.

The evidence was, that thirty copies of the book had been seized at Keach's house by the justice and constable, and that Keach on his examination before the justice had confessed himself the author, and that he had received from London about forty copies, of which he had dispersed about twelve. Hyde then caused the passages contained in the indictment to be read, remarking on each to show that it was contrary to the Book of Common Prayer. This done, the prisoner began to speak in his defence.

*Keach.* — As to the doctrines —

*Hyde.* — You shall not speak here except to the matter of fact; that is to say, whether you writ this book or not.*

*Keach.* — I desire liberty to speak to the particulars of my indictment, and those things that have —

*Hyde.* — You shall not be suffered to give the reasons for your damnable doctrine here to seduce the king's subjects.

*Keach.* — Is my religion so bad that I may not be allowed to speak?

*Hyde.* — I know your religion; you are a Fifth Monarchy man; and you can preach as well as write books; and you

* This was the same doctrine afterwards attempted to be maintained by Lord Mansfield, but overruled by a declaratory act of Parliament.

would preach here if I would let you; but I shall take such order as you shall do no more mischief.*

After some altercation between the judge and the prisoner as to the facts and the evidence, Hyde summed up and charged the jury; but after an absence of several hours one of the officers came in with a message that they could not agree.

*Hyde.* — But they must agree.

*Officer.* — They desire to know whether one of them may not come and speak to your lordship about something whereof they are in doubt.

*Hyde.* — Yes, privately; (and then ordered one to come to him on the bench.)

The officer then called one, and he was set upon the clerk's table, and the judge and he whispered together a great while. It was observed that the judge, having his hands upon his shoulders, would frequently shake him as he spoke to him. Upon this person's returning, the whole jury soon came in, and by their foreman delivered a verdict of guilty in part.

*Clerk.* — Of what part?

*Foreman.* — There is something contained in the indictment which is not in the book.

*Clerk.* — What is that?

*Foreman.* — In the indictment he is charged with these words: "When the thousand years shall be expired, then shall all the rest of the church be raised;" but in the book it is, "Then shall the rest of the dead be raised."

*Clerk.* — Is he guilty of all the rest of the indictment, that sentence excepted?

* An American specimen of this style of judicial decision may be found in Judge Grier's way of speaking on the bench about Abolitionists. — *Ed.*

*One of the Jury.* — I cannot in conscience find him guilty, because the words in the indictment and the book do not agree.

*Hyde.* — That is only through a mistake of the clerk's, and in that sentence only; and you may find him guilty of all, that sentence excepted; but why did you come in before you were agreed?

*Foreman.* — We thought we had been agreed.

*Hyde.* — You must go out again and agree; and as for you that say you cannot in conscience find him guilty, if you say so again, without giving reasons for it, I *shall take an order with you.**

We shall find an explanation of this last threat (which soon produced a verdict in accordance with the wishes of the chief justice) in Hale's Pleas of the Crown,† where it is stated that while Hyde was acting as a judge of *nisi prius*, he introduced the illegal practice of fining juries for not rendering verdicts satisfactory to him. "I have seen," says Hale, "arbitrary practice still go from one thing to another. The fines set upon grand inquests began; then they set fines upon the petit jurors for not finding according to the direction of the court; then afterwards the judges of *nisi prius* proceeded to fine jurors in civil causes if they gave not a verdict according to direction, even in points of fact. This was done by a judge of assize [Justice Hyde, at Oxford, Vaugh. 145] in Oxfordshire, and the fine estreated; but I, by advice of most of the judges of England, stayed process upon that fine. [Hale was at this time chief baron of the Court of Exchequer.] The like was done by the same judge in a case of

* 6 State Trials, 701–709.

† 2 Hale, P. C. 158.

burglary. The fine was estreated into the exchequer; but by the like advice I stayed process; and in the case of Wagstaff, [Vaugh. 153,] and other jurors fined at the Old Bayley for giving a verdict contrary to direction, by advice of all the judges of England, (only one dissenting,) it was ruled to be against law."] *

In the fervor of loyalty which still prevailed, such doctrines were by no means unpopular; and while Chief Justice Hyde was cried up as an eminent judge by the triumphant Cavaliers, the dejected Roundheads hardly ventured to whisper a complaint against him. To the great grief of the one party, and, no doubt, to the secret joy of the other, who interpreted his fate as a judgment, his career was suddenly cut short. On the 1st of May, 1665, as he was placing himself on the bench to try a dissenter who had published a book recommending the "comprehension," that had been promised by the King's Declaration from Breda, while apparently in the enjoyment of perfect health, he dropped down dead.

* The above passage enclosed in brackets has been added by the editor. Our American judges, more subtle than their predecessors, instead of fining juries for not rendering verdicts according to directions, have introduced the practice of questioning jurors beforehand, and not allowing them to sit unless they pass a satisfactory examination. — *Ed.*

## CHAPTER XI.

### JOHN KELYNGE.

AFTER the sudden death of Sir Robert Hyde, Lord Chancellor Clarendon was again thrown into distress by the difficulty of filling up the office of chief justice of the King's Bench, and he allowed it to remain vacant seven months. Only five years had elapsed since the Restoration, and no loyal lawyer of eminence had sprung up. At last the Chancellor thought he could not do better than promote Sir John Kelynge, then a *puisne*, to be the head of the court. The appointment was considered a very bad one; and some accounted for it by supposing that a liberal contribution had been made towards the expense of erecting "Dunkirk House,"* which was exciting the admiration and envy of the town; while others asserted that the collar of S. S.† had been put around the neck of the new legal dignitary by the Duchess of Cleveland. I believe that judicial patronage had not yet been drawn into the vortex of venality, and that Clarendon, left to the freedom of his own will, preferred him whom he considered the least ineligible candidate. But we

* This was an expensive residence built by Clarendon, to which the populace gave that name, under the unfounded idea that the expense of it was defrayed out of bribes received for consenting to the sale of Dunkirk. — *Ed.*

† This has been from great antiquity the decoration of the English chief justices. Dugdale says it is derived from the name of St. Simplicius, a Christian judge, who suffered martyrdom under the Emperor Diocletian. — *Ed.*

cannot wonder at the suspicions which were generally entertained, for Sir John Kelynge's friends could only say in his favor that he was a "violent Cavalier," and his enemies observed that "however fit he might have been to *charge* the Roundheads under Prince Rupert, he was very unfit to *charge* a jury in Westminster Hall."

I can find nothing of his origin, or of his career, prior to the Restoration; and I am unable to say whether, like some loyal lawyers, he actually had carried arms for the king, or, like others, had continued obscurely to practise his profession in London. The first notice I find of him is by himself, in the account which he has left us of the conferences of the judges at Serjeants' Inn, preparatory to the trial of the regicides, when he says he attended that service as junior counsel for the crown. He might have been employed from a notion that he would be useful in solving the knotty points likely to arise,* or, (what is quite as likely,) without any professional reputation, he might have got a brief by favor, in a case which was to draw the eyes of the whole world upon all engaged in it.

When the trials came on, he was very busy and bustling, and eagerly improved every opportunity of bringing himself forward. Before they were over, he took upon himself the degree of serjeant at law, and, to his unspeakable delight, he was actually intrusted with the task of conducting the

* Among these was, "whether the act of severing the head of Charles I. from his body could be alleged to have been committed in his own lifetime," and "whether it should be laid as against the peace of the late or of the present king." Judge Mallet made the confusion more confounded by maintaining that by the law of England a day is indivisible; and that, as Charles II. certainly was our lawful king during a part of that day, no part of it had been in the reign of Charles I.

prosecution against Colonel Hacker, who had commanded the guard during the king's trial and at his execution. He learnedly expounded to the jury that the treason consisted in "compassing and imagining the king's death," and that the overt acts charged of *condemning him* and *executing him* were only to be considered evidence of the evil intention. He then stated the facts which would be proved by the witnesses, and concluded by observing, —

"Thus did he keep the king a prisoner, to bring him before that Mock Court of Injustice; and was so highly trusted by all those miscreants who thirsted for the king's blood, that the bloody warrant was directed to him to see execution done. Nay, gentlemen, he was on the scaffold, and had the axe in his hand." *Hacker.* — "My lords, to save your lordships trouble, I confess that I was upon the guard, and had a warrant to keep the king for his execution." (The original warrant being shown to him, he admitted it.) *Kelynge.* — "After you had that warrant brought to you, did you, by virtue of it, direct another warrant for the execution of the king, and take his sacred majesty's person from the custody of Colonel Tomlinson?" *Hacker.* — "No, sir." *Kelynge.* — "We shall prove it."

Colonel Tomlinson was then examined, and detailed the circumstances of the execution, showing that Colonel Hacker had conducted the king to the scaffold under the original warrant — what had been taken for a fresh warrant being a letter written by him to Cromwell, then engaged in prayer for the king's deliverance with General Fairfax.

*Kelynge.* — "We have other witnesses, but the prisoner hath confessed enough. We have proved that he had the king in custody, and that at the time of the execution he was there to manage it. What do you say for yourself?" *Hacker.* — "Truly, my lord, I have no more to say for myself but that I was a soldier and under command. In obedience to those set over me I did act. My desire hath ever been for the welfare of my country." *L. C. Baron.* — "This is all you have to say for yourself?" *Hacker.* — "Yes, my lord." *L. C. Baron.* — "Then, Colonel Hacker, for that which you say for yourself that you did it by command, you must understand that no power on earth could authorize such a thing. Either he is guilty of compassing the death of the king, or no man can be said to be guilty."

Of course he was convicted and executed.

Serjeant Kelynge was soon after promoted to be a king's serjeant; and in that capacity took a prominent part in the trial of Sir Henry Vane, who, not being concerned in the late king's death, was tried for what he had subsequently done in obedience to the Parliament, then possessed of the supreme power of the state. To the plea that his acts could not be said to be against the peace of Charles II., who was then in exile, Kelynge admitted that if another sovereign, although a usurper, had mounted the throne, the defence would have been sufficient; but urged that the throne must always be full, and that Charles II., in legal contemplation, occupied it while *de facto* he was wandering in foreign lands, and ambassadors from all the states of Europe were accredited to Oliver, the Lord Protector.

Kelynge having suggested this reasoning, which was adopted by the court, and on which Vane was executed as a traitor, he was, on the next vacancy, made a puisne judge of the King's Bench.

While Kelynge was a puisne judge, he made up, by loyal

zeal and subserviency, for his want of learning and sound sense; but, from a knowledge of his incompetency, there was a great reluctance to promote him on the death of Lord Chief Justice Hyde. Sir Matthew Hale was pointed out as the fittest person to be placed at the head of the common law; but Lord Clarendon had not the liberality to raise to the highest dignity one who had sworn allegiance to the Protector, and there being no better man whom he could select, who was free from the suspicion of republican taint, he fixed upon the "violent Cavalier."

Luckily there were no speeches at his installation. On account of the dreadful plague which was then depopulating London, the courts were adjourned to Oxford. "There Kelynge, puisne judge, was made chief justice, and being sworn at the chancellor's lodging, came up privily and took his place in the logic school, where the Court of King's Bench sat. The business was only motions — to prevent any concourse of people. In London died the week before, 7165 of the plague, besides Papists and Quakers."

The new chief justice even exceeded public expectation by the violent, fantastical, and ludicrous manner in which he comported himself. His vicious and foolish propensities broke out without any restraint, and, at a time when there was little disposition to question any who were clothed with authority, he drew down upon himself the contempt of the public and the censure of Parliament.

He was unspeakably proud of the collar which he wore as chief justice, this alone distinguishing him externally from the puisnies, a class on whom he now looked down very haughtily. In his own report of the resolutions of the judges prior to the trial of Lord Morley for murder, before the House of Lords, he considers the following as most important, —

"We did all, *una voce*, resolve that we were to attend at the trial in our scarlet robes, and the chief judges in their collars of S. S. — *which I did accordingly*."

There having been a tumult in an attempt by some apprentices to put down certain disorderly houses in Moorfields, which were a great nuisance to the neighborhood, and cries that no such houses should be tolerated, Chief Justice Kelynge, considering this "an *accroachment* of royal authority," directed those concerned in it to be indicted for HIGH TREASON; and the trial coming on before him at the Old Bailey, he thus laid down the law to the jury, —

"The prisoners are indicted for levying war against the king. By levying war is not only meant when a body is gathered together as in army, but if a company of people will go about any public reformation, this is high treason. These people do pretend their design was against brothels; now, for men to go about to pull down brothels, with a captain, and an ensign, and weapons, — if this thing be endured, *who is safe?* It is high treason because it doth betray the peace of the nation, and every subject is as much wronged as the king; for if every man may reform what he will, no man is safe; therefore the thing is of desperate consequence, and we must make this for a public example. There is reason we should be very cautious; we are but newly delivered from rebellion, and we know that that rebellion first began under the pretence of religion and the law; for the devil hath always this vizard upon it. We have great reason to be very wary that we fall not again into the same error. Apprentices in future shall not go on in this manner. It is proved that Beasely went as their captain with his sword, and flourished it over his head, and that Messenger walked about Moorfields with a green apron on the top of a pole. What was done by one was done by all; in high treason, all concerned are principals."

So the prisoners were all convicted of high treason; and I am ashamed to say that all the judges concurred in the propriety of the conviction except Lord Chief Baron Hale, who, as might be expected, delivered his opinion that there was no treason in the case, and treated it merely as a misdemeanor. Such a proceeding had not the palliation that it ruined a personal enemy, or crushed a rival party in the state, or brought great forfeitures into the exchequer; it was a mere fantastic trick played before high heaven to make the angels weep.*

* This case, thus characterized by Lord Campbell, served as foundation for the remarkable attempt recently made among us to convert opposition to the fugitive slave act into high treason. This bloody idea was first started by George T. Curtis, a slave-catching commissioner of Massachusetts, in his telegraphic despatch to Mr. Webster, giving an account of the rescue at Boston, by a number of colored men, from the hands of the U. S. marshal, of a man named Shadrach, who had been seized on one of Commissioner Curtis's warrants as a fugitive slave.

Not long after, in September, 1851, a Maryland slaveholder named Gorsuch obtained from the notorious Edward D. Ingraham, the Philadelphia slave-catching commissioner, warrants against four alleged fugitive slaves. He proceeded with an armed party and a deputy marshal to Christiana, and besieged a house in which the slaves were said to have taken refuge. Intelligence had been received of the approach of the party, and the slaves manfully resolved to defend themselves, and, if possible, to achieve their freedom. Some of their colored friends gallantly came to their aid and generously shared their danger. Gorsuch, the slave-hunter, and the marshal entered the house, but were repulsed, each party firing at the other, but, as appears, without effect. The besiegers called for assistance, and meeting Caspar Hanway, a white man, on horseback, the marshal, as authorized by the fugitive law, commanded his aid in arresting the slaves. Mr. Hanway, as became a republican and a Christian, refused obedience to the infamous mandate. In the mean time the negroes made, it would seem, a sortie, advancing on the enemy. Hanway called to them *not to fire.* His

When Chief Justice Kelynge was upon the circuit, being without any check or restraint, he threw aside all regard to moderation and to decency. He compelled the grand jury of Somersetshire to find a true bill contrary to their consciences — reproaching Sir Hugh Wyndham, the foreman, as the head of a faction, and telling them "that they were all his servants, and that he would make the best in England stoop."

exhortation was unheeded. Gorsuch was shot dead, another was wounded, and the residue of the slave-catchers sought safety in flight.

At the next meeting of the United States District Court for the Eastern District of Pennsylvania, this case was brought to the notice of the grand jury by Judge Kane.

After reciting the facts as they appeared in the newspapers, he added, that it was reported "that for some months back, gatherings of people, strangers as well as citizens, have been held from time to time in the vicinity of the place of the recent outrage, at which exhortations are made and pledges interchanged to hold the law for the recovery of fugitive slaves as of no validity, and to defy its execution." In other words, anti-slavery meetings had been held in Lancaster county, as in other parts of the free states, and in these meetings one of the most detestable acts of modern legislation had been denounced as cruel and unjust, and the people in attendance had expressed their determination not to participate in slave hunts.

"If," said the judge, "the circumstances to which I have adverted [viz: the riot at Christiana and the anti-slavery meetings] have in fact taken place, they involve the highest crime known to the law." And what crime is that? Treason. And what is treason? The judge answers, "Levying war against the United States." And what had the affair at Christiana to do with war against the United States? Again the judge replies, "Any combination forcibly to prevent or oppose the execution or enforcement of a provision of the Constitution or of a public statute, if accompanied by an act of forcible opposition in pursuance of such combination," is embraced in the expression "levying war against the United States," as used in the constitutional definition of treason. Hence, four negroes combining to maintain their newly-recovered liberty by forcibly resisting the efforts of a slave-catcher, are guilty of levying war against the United States.

But the judge's patriotic zeal against traitors did not confine itself to the enemies of the United States actively engaged in the Christiana campaign. Here, indeed, he went far beyond even the infamous Judge

Some persons were indicted before him for attending a conventicle; and, although it was proved that they had assembled on the Lord's day with Bibles in their hands, *without Prayer Books*, they were acquitted. He thereupon fined the jury one hundred marks apiece, and imprisoned them till the fines were paid. Again, on the trial of a man for murder, who was suspected of being a dissenter, and whom he had a great desire to hang, he fined and imprisoned all the jury

Kelynge. "It is not necessary," so he told the grand jury, "to prove that the individual accused was a direct personal actor in the violence, nor is even his personal presence indispensable. Though he be absent at the actual perpetration, yet if he directed the act, devised, or knowingly furnished the means for carrying it into effect, or instigated others to perform it, he shared their guilt. In treason, there are no accessories." From all this the grand jury were to understand that anti-slavery men, by their doctrines of human rights and their denunciations of the fugitive act, instigated fugitive slaves to defend themselves; hence, as, in treason, all are principals, however remotely and indirectly concerned, these abolition instigators had also levied war, were traitors, and might be legally hung. To strengthen this intended impression on the minds of the jury, the judge launched out into an invective against the abolitionists, concluding with the very significant and smart admonition, "While he (the abolitionist) remains within our borders he is to remember that successfully to instigate treason is to commit it."

What is still more astonishing than even this charge, the grand jury, to whom it was delivered, showed themselves such ready receivers of its infamous and atrocious doctrines as to bring into court thirty bills for high treason, against as many different individuals, founded upon it.

Of these thirty indictments, the only one brought to trial was that against Caspar Hanway, above mentioned. The only acts proved against this man, in support of the charge of having "traitorously levied war against the United States," were, 1. having declined to assist the marshal in arresting the fugitives; and 2. in calling to the negroes and urging them *not* to fire.

Judge Grier presided on the trial, and notwithstanding his vulgar invectives against the abolitionists, found himself compelled to charge the jury, even in the presence of Judge Kane, that "a number of fugitive slaves may infest a neighborhood, and may be encouraged by their neighbors in combining to resist with force and arms their master, or the public officer who may come to arrest them; they may murder or rob them; they are guilty of felony and liable to punishment, but not as traitors." The prisoner was because, contrary to his direction, they brought in a verdict of *manslaughter*.* Upon another occasion, (repeating a coarse jest of one whom he professed to hold in great abhorrence,) when he was committing a man in a very arbitrary manner, the famous declaration in Magna Charta being cited to him, that "no freeman shall be imprisoned except by the judgment of his peers, or the law of the land," the only answer given by my lord chief justice of England was to repeat, with a loud voice, Cromwell's rhyme, "Magna Charta — Magna F——a!!!"

At last, the scandal was so great that complaints against him were brought by petition before the House of Commons, and were referred to the grand committee of justice. After witnesses had been examined, and he himself had been heard in his defence, the committee reported the following resolutions: —

"1. That the proceedings of the lord chief justice in the cases referred to us are innovations in the trial of men for their lives and liberties, and that he hath used an arbitrary and illegal power which is of dangerous consequence to the lives and liberties of the people of England.

"2. That in the place of judicature, the lord chief justice hath undervalued, vilified, and condemned Magna Charta, the great preserver of our lives, freedom, and property.

of course acquitted, and all the other indictments abandoned; and thus ended in shame and ridicule Judge Kane's ingenious device for hanging all who resisted the fugitive slave law. Yet this same man, at a Kossuth meeting at Philadelphia, made a rampant fillibustering speech in behalf of oppressed nations, quoting with exultation the words of Vattel, "When a people from good reasons take up arms against an oppressor, justice and generosity require that brave men should be assisted in the defence of their liberties."— *Ed.*

* See ante, pp. 150, 151.

"3. That the lord chief justice be brought to trial, in order to condign punishment in such manner as the House shall judge most fit and requisite."

The matter assuming this serious aspect, he petitioned to be heard at the bar of the House in his own defence. Lord Chief Baron Atkyns, who was then present, says, "he did it with that great humility and reverence, that those of his own profession and others were so far his advocates that the House desisted from any farther prosecution." His demeanor seems now to have been as abject as it had before been insolent, and he escaped punishment only by the generous intercession of lawyers whom he had been in the habit of browbeating in the King's Bench.

He was abundantly tame for the rest of his days; but he fell into utter contempt, and the business of the court was done by Twisden, a very learned judge, and much respected, although very passionate. Kelynge's collar of S. S. ceased to have any charms for him; he drooped and languished for some terms, and on the 9th of May, 1671, he expired, to the great relief of all who had any regard for the due administration of justice. No interest can be felt respecting the place of his interment, his marriages, or his descendants.

I ought to mention, among his other vanities, that he had the ambition to be an author; and he compiled a folio volume of decisions in criminal cases, which are of no value whatever except to make us laugh at some of the silly egotisms with which they abound.*

* And yet it is upon the authority of these worthless reports that some important American decisions have been based. See 13 *Mass. Reports*, 356, Commonwealth *v.* Bowen; also the preceding note. — *Ed.*

# CHAPTER XII.

## WILLIAM SCROGGS.

It was positively asserted in his lifetime, and it has been often repeated since, that Scroggs was the son of a butcher, and that he was so cruel as a judge because he had been himself accustomed to kill calves and lambs when he was a boy. Yet it is quite certain that this solution of Scroggs's taste for blood is a pure fiction, for he was born and bred a gentleman. His father was a squire, of respectable family and good estate, in Oxfordshire. Young Scroggs was several years at a grammar school, and he took a degree with some credit in the University of Oxford, having studied first at Oriel, and then at Pembroke College. He was intended for the church, and, in quiet times, might have died respected as a painstaking curate, or as Archbishop of Canterbury. But, the civil war breaking out while he was still under age, he enlisted in the king's cause, and afterwards commanded a troop of horse, which did good service in several severe skirmishes. Unfortunately, his morals did not escape the taint which distinguished both men and officers on the Cavalier side. The dissolute habits he had contracted unfitted him entirely for the ecclesiastical profession, and he was advised to try his luck in the law. He had a quick conception, a bold manner, and an enterprising mind ; and prophecies were uttered of his great success if he should exchange the cuirass for the long robe. He was entered as a student at Gray's Inn, and he showed that he was capable, by short fits, of keen application; but his love of profligacy and of expense still continued, and both his health and his finances suffered accordingly.

However, he contrived to be called to the bar; and some of his pot companions being attorneys, they occasionally employed him in causes likely to be won by a loud voice and an unscrupulous appeal to the prejudices of the jury. He practised in the King's Bench, where, although he now and then made a splashy speech, his business by no means increased in the same ratio as his debts. "He was," says Roger North, "a great voluptuary, his debaucheries egregious, and his life loose; which made the Lord Chief Justice Hale detest him." Thinking that he might have a better chance in the Court of Common Pleas, where the men in business were very old and dull, he took the degree of the coif, and he was soon after made a King's Serjeant. Still, however, he kept company with Ken, Guy, and the high-court rakes, and his clients could not depend upon him. His visage being comely, and his speech witty and bold, he was a favorite with juries, and sometimes carried off wonderful verdicts; but, when he ought to have been consulting his chamber in Serjeants' Inn, he was in a tavern or gaming house, or worse place, near St. James's Palace. Thus his gains were unsteady, and the fees which he received were speedily spent in dissipation, so that he fell into a state of great pecuniary embarrassment. On one occasion, he was arrested by a creditor in Westminster Hall as he was about to enter his coach. The process being out of the King's Bench, he complained to that court of a breach of his privileges as a serjeant; but Lord Chief Justice Hale refused to discharge him.

Meanwhile, Serjeant Scroggs was in high favor with Lord Shaftesbury's enemies, who, on the commitment of that turbulent leader to the Tower for breach of privilege, had gained a temporary advantage over him. Through the agency of Chiffinch, superintendent of the secret intrigues of every description which were carried on at Whitehall,* he had been introduced to Charles II., and the merry monarch took pleasure in his licentious conversation. What was of more importance to his advancement, he was recommended to the Earl of Danby, the reigning prime minister, as a man that might be useful to the government if he were made a judge. In consequence, on the 23d of October, 1676, he was knighted, and sworn in a justice of the Court of Common Pleas. Sir Allan Broderick, in a letter to "the Honorable Lawrence Hyde," written a few days after, says, "Sir William Scroggs, on Monday, being admitted judge, made so excellent a speech that my Lord Northampton, then present, went from Westminster to Whitehall immediately, and told the king he had, since his happy restoration, caused many hundred sermons to be printed, and which together taught not the people half so much loyalty; therefore, as a sermon, desired his command to have it printed and published in all the market towns in England."

Mr. Justice Scroggs gave himself little trouble with law business that came before the court; but, in addressing grand juries on the circuit, he was loud and eloquent against the proceedings of the "country party," and he still continued to be frequently in the circle at Whitehall, where he took opportunities not only to celebrate his own zeal, but to sneer

* For an account of Chiffinch, see the Life of Jeffrey, p. 278.

at Sir John Raynsford, the chief justice of the King's Bench, whose place he was desirous to fill. Chiffinch, and his other patrons of the back-stairs, were in the habit of sounding his praise, and asserting that he was the only man who, as head of the King's Bench, could effectually cope with the manœuvres of Shaftesbury. This unconquerable intriguer, having been discharged from custody, was again plotting against the government, was preparing to set up the legitimacy of Monmouth, and was asserting that the Duke of York should be set aside from the succession to the throne and prosecuted as a Popish recusant.

The immediate cause of Raynsford's removal was the desire of the government to have a chief justice of the King's Bench on whose vigor and subserviency reliance could be placed, to counteract the apprehended machinations of Shaftesbury.

On the 31st of May, 1678, Sir William Scroggs was sworn into the office, and he remained in it for a period of three years. How he conducted himself in civil suits is never once mentioned, for the attention of mankind was entirely absorbed by his scandalous misbehavior as a criminal judge. He is looked to with more loathing, if not with more indignation, than Jeffreys, for in his abominable cruelties he was the sordid tool of others, and in his subsequent career he had not the feeble excuse of gratifying his own passions or advancing his own interests.

Although quite indifferent with regard to religion, and ready to have declared himself a Papist, or a Puritan, or a Mahometan, according to the prompting of his superiors, finding that the policy of the government was to outbid Shaftesbury in zeal for Protestantism, he professed an implicit belief in all the wonders revealed by Titus Oates, in the murder of Sir

Edmondbury Godfrey by Papists, and in the absolute necessity for cutting off without pity all those who were engaged in the nefarious design to assassinate the king, to burn London, and to extinguish the flames with the blood of Protestants. He thought himself to be in the singularly felicitous situation of pleasing the government while he received shouts of applause from the mob. Burnet, speaking of his appointment, says, "It was a melancholy thing to see so bad, so ignorant, and so poor a man raised up to that great post. Yet he, now seeing how the stream ran, went into it with so much zeal and heartiness that he was become the favorite of the people." *

* Our recent American history presents a curious parallel to the English Popish plot delusion and the use made of it by the unscrupulous politicians of that age. The basis of that delusion was the well-founded horror which the English people entertained for the Popish religion as hostile to their liberties. The immediate allegation upon which it rested was, that the Papists had formed a conspiracy to assassinate Charles II., and so to open the way to the throne for the Duke of York, (afterwards James II.,) a professed Papist.

The suggestion of this plot, founded merely on vague suspicions, — (if indeed it was not, as some writers think, purposely started for political objects,) — was taken hold of by the unprincipled Shaftesbury, who from having been an ultra courtier, had become the leader of the country party. He sought to use it to stimulate the people against the court, and to prepare the way for his project of excluding the Duke of York from succession to the throne. He expected that the court would oppose this delusion, and so would make itself still more unpopular. But Charles II., no less unprincipled than Shaftesbury, was quite as ready as he to play at any dangerous game; and that he might gain credit for Protestantism, (though all the while secretly a Papist,) he resolved to humor the delusion to the utmost, and to allow it full play against its unfortunate victims.

So here in America, the democrats, (so called, but in fact slavery extenders,) taking advantage of the very strong and well-founded popular sentiment in favor of the Union, and seeking to recommend themselves to favor as a national party, hit upon the similar expedient of accusing the abolitionists of a plot to dissolve the Union, part of the odium of which they hoped to throw upon their political opponents, the so-called whigs, by accusing them as screeners and favorers of the abolitionists. The

The first of the Popish plot judicial murders — which are more disgraceful to England than the massacre of St. Bartholomew's is to France — was that of Stayly, the Roman Catholic banker. Being tried at the bar of the Court of King's Bench, Scroggs, according to the old fashion, which had gone out during the Commonwealth, repeatedly put questions to the prisoner, attempting to intimidate him, or to involve him in contradictions, or to elicit from him some indiscreet admission of facts. A witness having stated that "he had often heard the prisoner say he would lose his blood for the king, and speak as loyally as man could speak," Scroggs exclaimed, "*That is, when he spoke to a Protestant!*" In summing up, having run himself out of breath by the violence with which he declaimed against the Pope and the Jesuits, he thus apologised to the jury: —

"Excuse me, gentlemen, if I am a little warm, when perils are so many, murders so secret. When things are transacted so closely, and our king is in great danger, and religion is at stake, I may be excused for being a little warm. You may think it better, gentlemen, to be warm here than in Smithfield. Discharge your consciences as you ought to do. If guilty, let the prisoner take the reward of his crime, for perchance it may be a terror to the rest. I hope I shall never go to that heaven where men are made saints for killing kings."

whigs, however, in imitation of the policy of Charles II., and under the leadership of the late Daniel Webster, sought to turn this pretended plot to their own advantage, by coming out still more furious Union-savers than even the democrats, and denouncing the abolitionists with still greater fury — thus working up the public mind into a terror at the imaginary danger of the Union, much like that of the English people at the time of the Popish plot. We, too, have had our trials for treason, (see ante, p. 158–161;) and if we have had no bloody executions, it has not been for want of Scroggses, both on and off the bench. — *Ed.*

The verdict of *guilty* being recorded, *Scroggs, C. J.*, said, "Now, you may die a Roman Catholic; and, when you come to die, I doubt you will be found a priest too. The matter, manner, and all the circumstances of the case, make it plain; you may harden your heart as much as you will, and lift up your eyes, but you seem, instead of being sorrowful, to be obstinate. Between God and your conscience be it; I have nothing to do with that; my duty is only to pronounce judgment upon you according to law — you shall be drawn to the place of execution, where you shall be hanged by the neck, cut down alive," &c. &c.

The unhappy convict's friends were allowed to give him decent burial; * but, because they said a mass for his soul, his body was, by order of Lord Chief Justice Scroggs, taken out of the grave, his quarters were fixed upon the gates of the city, and his head, at the top of a pole, was set on London Bridge. So proud was Scroggs of this exploit, that he had an account of it written, for which he granted an IMPRIMATUR, signed with his own name.

I must not run the risk of disgusting my readers by a detailed account of Scroggs's enormities on the trials of Coleman, Ireland, Whitebeard, Langhord, and the other victims whom he sacrificed to the popular fury under pretence that they were implicated in the Popish plot. Whether sitting in his own court at Westminster, or at the Old Bailey in the city of London, as long as he believed that government favored the prosecutions, by a display of all the unworthy arts of cajoling and intimidation he secured convictions. A modern historian, himself a Roman Catholic priest, says, with

* For this he probably received a good sum of money.

temper and discrimination, "The Chief Justice Scroggs, a lawyer of profligate habits and inferior acquirements, acted the part of prosecutor rather than of judge. To the informers he behaved with kindness, even with deference, suggesting to them explanations, excusing their contradictions, and repelling the imputation on their characters; but the prisoners were repeatedly interrupted and insulted; their witnesses were browbeaten from the bench, and their condemnation was generally hailed with acclamations, which the court rather encouraged than repressed."

Meanwhile the chief justice went the circuit; and although the Popish plot did not extend into the provinces, it may be curious to see how he demeaned himself there. Andrew Bromwich being tried before him capitally, for having administered the sacrament of the Lord's supper according to the rites of the church of Rome, thus the dialogue between them proceeded: —

*Prisoner.* — "I desire your lordship will take notice of one thing, that I have taken the oaths of allegiance and supremacy, and have not refused any thing which might testify my loyalty." *Scroggs, C. J.* — "That will not serve your turn; you priests have many tricks. What is that to giving a woman the sacrament several times?" *Prisoner.* — "My lord, it was no sacrament unless I be a priest, of which there is no proof." *Scroggs.* — "What! you expect we should prove you a priest by witnesses who saw you ordained? We know too much of your religion; no one gives the sacrament in a wafer, except he be a Popish priest: you gave that woman the sacrament in a wafer: *ergo*, you are a Popish priest." Thus he summed up: "Gentlemen of the jury, I leave it upon your consciences whether you will let priests escape, who are the very pests of church and state; you had better be rid of one priest than three felons; so, gentlemen, I leave it to you."

After a verdict of guilty, the chief justice said, "Gentlemen, you have found a good verdict, and if I had been one of you I should have found the same myself." He then pronounced sentence of death, describing what seemed to be his own notion of the divine Being, while he imputed this blasphemy to the prisoner: "You act as if God Almighty were some omnipotent mischief, that delighted and would be served with the sacrifice of human blood."

Scroggs was more and more eager, and "ranted on that side more impetuously," when he observed that Lord Shaftesbury, who, although himself too shrewd to believe in the Popish plot, had been working it furiously for his own purposes, was taken into office on the formation of Sir William Temple's new scheme of administration, and was actually made president of the council. But he began to entertain a suspicion that the king had been acting a part against his inclination and his judgment, and, having ascertained the real truth upon this point, he showed himself equally versatile and violent by suddenly going over to the opposite faction. Roger North gives the following racy account of his conversion: —

"It fell out that when the Earl of Shaftesbury had sat some short time in the council, and seemed to rule the roast, yet Scroggs had some qualms in his political conscience; and coming from Windsor in the Lord Chief Justice North's coach, he took the opportunity and desired his lordship to tell him seriously if my Lord Shaftesbury had really so great power with the king as he was thought to have. His lordship answered quick, 'No, my lord, no more than your footman hath with you.' Upon that the other hung his head, and, considering the matter, said nothing for a good while, and then passed to other discourse. After that time he turned as fierce against Oates and his plot as ever before he had ranted for it."

The first Popish plot case which came on after this conversion was the trial of Sir George Wakeman, the queen's physician, against whom Oates and Bedloe swore as stoutly as ever; making out a case which implicated, to a certain degree, the queen herself. But Chief Justice Scroggs now sneered at the marvellous memory or imagination of Oates; and, taking very little notice, in his summing up, of the evidence of Bedloe, thus concluded: —

"If you are unsatisfied upon these things put together, and, well weighing, you think the witnesses have not said true, you will do well to acquit." *Bedloe.* — "My lord, my evidence is not right summed up." *Scroggs, C. J.* — "I know not by what authority this man speaks. Gentlemen, consider of your verdict."

An acquittal taking place, not only were Oates and Bedloe in a furious rage, but the mob were greatly disappointed, for their belief in the plot was still unshaken, and Scroggs, who had been their idol a few hours ago,* was in danger of being torn in pieces by them. Although he contrived to escape in safety to his house, he was assailed next morning by broadsides, ballads sung in the streets, and libels in every imaginable shape.

On the first day of the following term, he bound over in

* "By his zeal in the Protestant cause he gained for a while a universal applause throughout the whole nation." — *Athenæ*, iv. 116.

open court the authors, printers, and signers of some of the worst of them, and made the following speech: —

"I would have all men know that I am not so revengeful in my nature, nor so nettled with this aspersion, that I could not have passed by this and more; but the many scandalous libels that are abroad, and reflect on public justice as well as upon my private self, make it the duty of my place to defend the one, and the duty I owe to my reputation to vindicate the other. This is the properest occasion for both. If once our courts of justice come to be awed or swayed by vulgar noise,* it is falsely said that men are tried for their lives or fortunes; they live by chance, and enjoy what they have as the wind blows, and with the same certainty. Such a base, fearful compliance made Felix, willing to please the people, leave Paul bound. The people ought to be pleased with public justice, and not justice seek to please the people. Justice should flow like a mighty stream; and if the rabble, like an unruly wind, blow against it, the stream they made rough will keep its course. I do not think that we yet live in so corrupt an age that a man may not with safety be just, and follow his conscience; if it be otherwise, we must hazard our safety to preserve our integrity. As to Sir George Wakeman's trial, I am neither afraid nor ashamed to mention it. I will appeal to all sober and understanding men, and to the long robe more especially, who are the best and properest judges in such cases, for the fairness and equality of my carriage on that occasion. For those hireling scribblers who traduce me, — who write to eat and lie for bread, — I intend to

* This profession of contempt for "vulgar noise" has lately been repeated in America by a judge whose manner and bearing on the bench come as near those of Scroggs as the present times will bear. — *Ed.*

meet with them another way, for, like vermin, they are only safe while they are secret. And let those vipers, those printers and booksellers by whom they vend their false and braided ware, look to it; they shall know that the law wants not power to punish a libellous and licentious press, nor I resolution to put the law in force. And this is all the answer fit to be given (besides a whip) to those hackney writers and dull observators that go as they are hired or spurred, and perform as they are fed. If there be any sober and good men that are misled by false reports, or by subtlety deceived into any misapprehensions concerning that trial or myself, I should account it the highest pride and the most scornful thing in the world if I did not endeavor to undeceive them. To such men, therefore, I do solemnly declare in the seat of justice, where I would no more lie or equivocate than I would to God at the holy altar, I followed my conscience according to the best of my understanding in all that trial, without fear, favor, or reward, *without the gift of one shilling, or the value of it directly or indirectly, and without any promise or expectation whatsoever.** Do any think it an even wager, whether I am the greatest villain in the world or not — one that would sell the life of the king, my religion, and country, to Papists for money? He that says great places have great temptations, has a little if not a false heart himself. Let us pursue the discovery of the plot in God's name, and not balk any thing where there is suspicion on reasonable grounds; but do not pretend to find what is not, nor count him a turncoat that will not betray his conscience, nor believe incredible things. Those

* From this asseveration a suspicion arises of pecuniary corruption; but I believe that Scroggs was swayed in this instance by a disinterested love of rascality.

are foolish men who think that an acquittal must be wrong, and that there can be no justice without an execution."

Many were bound over; but not more than one prosecution was brought to trial — that against Richard Radley, who was convicted of speaking scandalous words of the Lord Chief Justice Scroggs, and fined £200.

When the Earl of Castlemaine — the complaisant husband of the king's mistress — was brought to trial for being concerned in the plot, Scroggs was eager to get him off, still despising popular clamor. Bedloe being utterly ruined in reputation, Dangerfield was now marched up, as the second witness, to support Oates. He had been sixteen times convicted of infamous offences; and, to render him competent, a pardon under the great seal was produced. But the chief justice was very severe upon him, saying, in summing up to the jury, "Whether this man be of a sudden become a saint because he has become a witness, I leave that to you to consider. Now I must tell you, though they have produced two witnesses, if you believe but one, this is insufficient. In treason, there being two witnesses, the one believed, the other disbelieved, may there be a conviction? I say, no. Let us deal fairly and aboveboard, and so preserve men who are accused and not guilty." The defendant being acquitted, the chief justice was again condemned as a renegade.

He further made himself obnoxious to the charge of having gone over to the Papists, by his conduct on the trial of Mrs. Elizabeth Cellier, who, if she had been prosecuted while he believed that the government wished the plot to be considered real, would unquestionably have been burned alive for high treason, but now was the object of his especial protection and favor. The second witness against her was Dangerfield, who, when he was put into the box, before any evidence had been given to discredit him, was thus saluted by Chief Justice Scroggs: —

"We will not hoodwink ourselves against such a fellow as this, that is guilty of such notorious crimes. A man of modesty, after he hath been in the pillory, would not look a man in the face. Such fellows as you are, sirrah, shall know we are not afraid of you. It is notorious enough what a fellow this is. I will shake all such fellows before I have done with them." *Dangerfield.* — "My lord, this is enough to discourage a man from ever entering into an honest principle." *Scroggs, C. J.* — "What! Do you, with all the mischief that hell hath in you, think to have it in a court of justice? I wonder at your impudence, that you dare look a court of justice in the face, after having been made appear so notorious a villain. Come, gentlemen of the jury, this is a plain case; here is but one witness in a case of treason; therefore lay your heads together, and say *not guilty.*"

Mrs. Cellier was set at liberty, and Dangerfield was committed to occupy her cell in Newgate.

When holding assizes in the country, he took every opportunity of proclaiming his slavish doctrines. Going the Oxford circuit with Lord Chief Baron Atkyns, he told the grand jury that a petition from the lord mayor and citizens of London to the king, for calling a Parliament, was high treason. Atkyns, on the contrary, affirmed "that the people might petition the king, and, so that it was done without tumult, it was lawful." Scroggs, having peremptorily denied this, went on to say "that the king might prevent printing and publishing whatever he chose by proclamation." Atkyns mildly remarked, "that such matters were fitter for Parliament, and that, if the king could do this work of Parliament, we were never like to have Parliaments any more." Scroggs, highly indignant, sent off a despatch to the king, stating the unconstitutional and treasonable language of Chief Baron Atkyns. This virtuous judge was in consequence superseded, and remained in a private station till he was reinstated in his office after the revolution.

Before Scroggs was himself prosecuted and dismissed from his office with disgrace, he swelled the number of his delinquencies by an attack on the liberty of the press, which was more violent than any that had ever been attempted by the Star Chamber, and which, if it had been acquiesced in, would have effectually established despotism in this country. Here he was directly prompted by the government, and it is surprising that this proceeding should so little have attracted the notice of historians who have dwelt upon the arbitrary measures of the reign of Charles II. The object was to put down all free discussions, and all complaints against misrule, by having, in addition to a licenser, a process of *injunction* against printing — to be summarily enforced, without the intervention of a jury, by fine, imprisonment, pillory, and whipping. There was then in extensive circulation a newspaper called "The Weekly Pacquet of Advice from Rome, or the History of Papacy," which reflected severely upon the religion now openly professed by the Duke of York and secretly embraced by the king himself. In Trinity term, 1680, an application being made to the Court of King's Bench, on the ground that this newspaper was libellous, Scroggs, with the assent of his brother judges, granted a rule absolute in the first instance, forbidding the publication of it in future. The editor and printer being served with the rule, the journal was suppressed till the matter was taken up in the House of Commons, and Scroggs was impeached.

The same term he gave the crowning proof of his servility and contempt of law and of decency. Shaftesbury, to pave the way for the exclusion bill, resolved to prosecute the Duke of York as a "Popish recusant." The heir presumptive to the throne was clearly liable to this proceeding and to all the penalties, forfeitures, and disqualifications which it threatened, for he had been educated a Protestant, and, having lately returned from torturing the Covenanters in Scotland, he was in the habit of ostentatiously celebrating the rites of the Romish religion in his chapel in London. An indictment against him was prepared in due form, and this was laid before the grand jury for the county of Middlesex by Lord Shaftesbury, along with Lord Russell, Lord Cavendish, Lord Grey de Werke, and other members of the country party. This alarming news being brought to Scroggs while sitting on the bench, he instantly ordered the grand jury to attend in court. The bailiff found them examining the first witness in support of the indictment; but they obeyed orders. As soon as they had entered the court, the chief justice said to them, "Gentlemen of the grand jury, you are discharged, and the country is much obliged to you for your services."

There were two classes whom he had offended, of very different character and power — the witnesses in support of the Popish plot, and the exclusionist leaders. The first began by preferring articles against him to the king in council, which alleged, among other things, that at the trial of Sir George Wakeman "he did browbeat and curb Dr. Titus Oates and Captain Bedloe, two of the principal witnesses for the king, and encourage the jury impanelled to try the malefactors to disbelieve the said witnesses, by speaking of them slightingly and abusively, and by omitting material parts of their evidence; that the said chief jnstice, to manifest his slighting opinion of the evidence of the said Dr. Titus Oates and Captain Bedloe in the presence of his most sacred majesty and the lords of his majesty's most honorable Privy Council, did dare to say that Dr. Titus Oates and Captain Bedloe always had an accusation ready against any body; that the said lord chief justice is very much addicted to swearing and cursing in his common discourse, and to drink to excess, to the great disparagement of the dignity and gravity of his office."

It seems surprising that such charges, from such a quarter, against so high a magistrate, should have been entertained, although he held his office during the pleasure of the crown. The probability is that, being in favor with the government, it was considered to be the most dexterous course to give him the opportunity of being tried before a tribunal by which he was sure of being acquitted, in the hope that his acquittal would save him from the fangs of an enraged House of Commons.

He was required to put in an answer to the articles, and a day was appointed for hearing the case. When it came on, to give great *éclat* to the certain triumph of the accused, the king presided in person. Oates and Bedloe were heard, but they and their witnesses were constantly interrupted and stopped, on the ground that they were stating what was not evidence, or what was irrelevant; and, after a very eloquent and witty speech from the chief justice, in the course of which he caused much merriment by comments on his supposed immoralities, judgment was given that the complaints against him were false and frivolous.

But Shaftesbury was not so easily to be diverted from his

revenge. On the meeting of Parliament he caused a motion to be made in the House of Commons for an inquiry into the conduct of Lord Chief Justice Scroggs in discharging the Middlesex grand jury and in other matters. A committee was accordingly appointed, which presented a report recommending that he should be impeached. The report was adopted by a large majority, and articles of impeachment were voted against him. These were *eight* in number. The *first* charged in general terms " that the said William Scroggs, chief justice of the King's Bench, had traitorously and wickedly endeavored to subvert the fundamental laws and the established religion and government of the kingdom of England." The *second* was for illegally discharging the grand jury, " whereby the course of justice was stopped maliciously and designedly — the presentments of many Papists and other offenders were obstructed — and in particular a bill of indictment against James, Duke of York, which was then before them, was prevented from being proceeded upon." The *third* was founded on the illegal order for suppressing the Weekly Pacquet newspaper. The three following articles were for granting general warrants, for imposing arbitrary fines, and for illegally refusing bail. The *seventh* charged him with defaming and scandalizing the witnesses who proved the Popish plot. The *last* was in these words: " VIII. Whereas the said Sir William Scroggs, being advanced to be chief justice of the Court of King's Bench, ought, by a sober, grave, and virtuous conversation, to have given a good example to the king's liege people, and to demean himself answerably to the dignity of so eminent a station; yet, on the contrary thereof, he doth, by his frequent and notorious excesses and debaucheries, and his profane and atheistical discourses, daily affront Almighty God, dishonor his majesty, give countenance and encouragement to all manner of vice and wickedness, and bring the highest scandal on the public justice of the kingdom."

These articles were carried to the House of Peers by Lord Cavendish, who there, in the name of all the Commons of England, impeached Chief Justice Scroggs for "high treason, and other high crimes and misdemeanors."

The articles being read, the accused, who was present, sitting on the judge's woolsack, was ordered to withdraw. A motion was then made, that he be *committed;* but the previous question was moved and carried, and a motion for an address to suspend him from his office till his trial should be over, was got rid of in the same manner. He was then called in, and ordered to find his bail in £10,000, to answer the articles of impeachment, and to prepare for his trial.

Luckily for him, at the end of three days the Parliament was abruptly dissolved. It would have been difficult to make out that any of the charges amounted to *high treason;* but in those days men were not at all nice about such distinctions, and a dangerous but convenient doctrine prevailed, that, upon an impeachment, the two Houses of Parliament might retrospectively declare any thing to be treason, according to their discretion, and punish it capitally. At any rate, considering that the influence of Shaftesbury in the Upper House was so great, and that Halifax and the respectable anti-exclusionists could not have defended or palliated the infamous conduct of Scroggs, had his case come to a hearing, he could not have got off without some very severe and degrading punishment.

Although he escaped a judicial sentence, his character was so blown upon, and juries regarded him with such horror, and were so much inclined to go against his direction, that the government found that he would obstruct instead of facilitating their designs against the whig leaders, and that it was necessary to get rid of him. After the dissolution of the Oxford Parliament the court was completely triumphant, and, being possessed for a time of absolute power, had only to consider the most expedient means of perpetuating despotism, and wreaking vengeance on the friends of freedom. Before long, Russell, Sydney, and Shaftesbury were to be brought to trial, that their heads might pay the penalty of the Exclusion Bill; but if Scroggs should be their judge, any jury, whether inclined to Protestantism or to Popery, would probably acquit them.

Accordingly, in the beginning of April, to make room for one who, it was hoped, would have more influence with juries, and make the proceedings meditated against the city of London and other corporations pass off with less discredit, while he might be equally subservient, Sir William Scroggs was removed from his office of chief justice of the King's Bench. So low had he fallen, that little regard was paid to his feelings, even by those for whom he had sacrificed his character and his peace of mind; and, instead of a "resignation on account of declining health," it was abruptly announced to him that a *supersedeas* had issued, and that Sir FRANCIS PEMBERTON, who had been a puisne judge under him, was to succeed him as chief justice.

His disgrace caused general joy in Westminster Hall, and over all England; for, as Jeffreys had not yet been clothed in ermine, the name of Scroggs was the by-word to express all that could be considered loathsome and odious in a judge.

He was allowed a small pension, or retired allowance, which

he did not long enjoy. When cashiered, finding no sympathy from his own profession, or from any class of the community, he retired to a country house which he had purchased, called Wealde Hall, near Brentwood, in Essex. Even here, his evil fame caused him to be shunned. He was considered by the gentry to be without religion and without honor; while the peasantry, who had heard some vague rumors of his having put people to death, believed that he was a murderer, whispered stories of his having dealings with evil spirits, and took special care never to run the risk of meeting him after dark. His constitution was undermined by his dissolute habits; and, in old age, he was still a solitary selfish bachelor. After languishing, in great misery, till the 25th day of October, 1683, he then expired, without a relation or friend to close his eyes. He was buried in the parish church of South Wealde; the undertaker, the sexton, and the parson of the parish, alone attending the funeral. He left no descendants; and he must either have been the last of his race, or his collateral relations, ashamed of their connection with him, had changed their name; for, since his death, there has been no Scroggs in Great Britain or Ireland. The word was long used by nurses to frighten children; and as long as our history is studied, or our language is spoken or read, it will call up the image of a base and bloody-minded villain. With honorable principles, and steady application, he might have been respected in his lifetime, and left an historical reputation behind him. "He was a person of very excellent and nimble parts," and he could both speak and write our language better than any lawyer of the seventeenth century, Francis Bacon alone excepted. He seems to have been little aware of the light in which his judicial conduct would be viewed; for it is a curious fact that the published reports of the State Trials at which he presided were all revised and retouched by himself; and his speeches, which fill us with amazement and horror, he expected would be regarded as proofs of his spirit and his genius. He had excellent natural abilities, and might have made a great figure in his profession; but was profligate in his habits, brutal in his manners, with only one rule to guide him — a regard to what he considered his own interest — without a touch of humanity, wholly impenetrable to remorse.

## CHAPTER XIII.

### FRANCIS NORTH.

WE now come to one of the most contemptible of men — Francis North, known by the title of Lord Keeper Guilford. He had not courage to commit great crimes; but — selfish, cunning, sneaking, and unprincipled — his only restraint was a regard to his own personal safety, and throughout his whole life he sought and obtained advancement by the meanest arts.

Our hero, although he himself ascribed his success to his poverty, was of noble birth. The founder of his family was Edward North, a serjeant at law, chancellor of the Augmentations, and created a baron by writ in the reign of Henry VIII. Dudley, the third baron, "having consumed the greatest part of his estate in the gallantries of King James's court, or, rather, his son Prince Henry's," retired and spent the rest of his days at his seat in Cambridgeshire. When the civil war broke out, he sided with the Parliament, and on rare occasions coming to London, he is said to have sat on the trial of Laud, and to have voted for his death. Having reached extreme old age, he died in the year 1666.

Dudley, his heir, who, at the age of sixty-three, stood on the steps of the throne in the House of Lords as "the eldest son of a peer," was a great traveller in his youth, and served with distinction in the Low Countries under Sir Francis Vere. Yet he never would put on his hat, nor sit down in the presence of his father, unless by the old peer's express commands.

Being returned to the Long Parliament for the county of Cambridge, he strenuously opposed the Court, and signed the Solemn League and Covenant; but, adhering to the Presbyterian party, he was turned out by *Pride's purge*, and lived in retirement till the Restoration. He married Anne, one of the daughters and coheirs of Sir Charles Montagu, brother of the Earl of Manchester, by whom he had a very numerous family.

The subject of this memoir was their second son, and was born on the 22d of October, 1637. Though he turned out such a zealous royalist and high churchman, his early training began among republicans and fanatics. As soon as he left the nursery, he was sent to a preparatory school at Isleworth, the master of which was a rigid Presbyterian. His wife was a furious Independent, and she ruled the household. "She used to instruct her babes in the gift of praying by the Spirit, and all the scholars were made to kneel by a bedside and pray; but this petit spark was too small for that posture, and was set upon a bed to kneel, with his face to a pillow."

His family becoming disgusted with the extravagance of the ruling powers, and beginning to look to royalty as the only cure for the evils the nation was suffering, he was removed from Isleworth, and put to a grammar school at Bury St. Edmunds, under a cavalier master.

In 1653, he was admitted a fellow commoner at St. John's College, Cambridge. He is said to have remained there two or three years, applying diligently to the studies of the place; but he seems to have devoted much of his time to the bass-viol, and he left the university without a degree.

He was then transferred to the Middle Temple. His father bought him a very small set of chambers, in which he shut himself up, and dedicated himself to the study of the law. He early learned and often repeated this saying of the citizens to their apprentices, "Keep your shop, and your shop will keep you." He did not frequent riding schools, or dancing schools, or playhouses, or gaming houses — so dangerous to youth at the Inns of Court. Though he could "make one at gammon, gleek, piquet, or even the merry-main, he had ever a notable regard to his purse to keep that from oversetting, like a vessel at sea that hath too much sail and too little ballast."

While a student, he paid frequent and long visits to his grandfather, who seems to have become a most singularly tyrannical and capricious old man. Frank exerted himself to the utmost to comply with all his humors, being allowed by him £20 a year. He was always industrious during these visits, though he could not altogether avoid bowling, fishing, hunting, visiting, and billiards; he spent the greater part of his time in reading and commonplacing the law books brought down to him by the carrier.

While in town, he always dined in the hall — twelve at noon being the hour of dinner — and supped there again at six; after which "case-putting" began in the cloister walks; and he acquired the character of a great "put-case." He kept a commonplace book, which seems to have been almost as massive as Brooke's "Abridgment of the Law." He made himself well acquainted with the Year Books, although not altogether so passionately attached to them as Serjeant Maynard, who, when he was taking an airing in his coach, always carried a volume of them along with him, which, he said, amused him more than a comedy. He attended all famous legal arguments, particularly those of Sir Heneage Finch, and taking notes in the morning in law French, he employed himself at night in making out in English a report of the cases he had heard.

By way of relaxation he would go to music meetings, or to hear Hugh Peters preach. Nothing places him in such an amiable point of view as the delight he is said to have taken, on rare occasions, in "a petit supper and a bottle," when there really seems to have been a short oblivion of anxiety about his rise in the world; but, to show his constitutional caution, his brother Roger assures us that, "whenever he was a little overtaken, it was a warning to him to take better care afterwards."

Long before he was called to the bar, "he undertook the practice of court-keeping;" that is, he was appointed the steward of a great many manors by his grandfather and other friends, and he did all the work in person, writing all his court-rolls, and making out his copies with his own hand. I am afraid he now began his violation of the rights and liberties of his fellow-subjects by practising some petty extortions upon the bumpkins who came before him. "His grandfather," says Roger,* with inimitable simplicity, "had a venerable old steward, careful by nature and faithful to his lord, employing all his thoughts and time to manage for supply of his house and upholding his rents, — in short, one of a race of human kind heretofore frequent, but now utterly extinct, — affectionate as well as faithful, and diligent rather for love than self-interest. This old gentleman, with his boot-hose and beard, used to accompany his young master to his court-

* Roger North, whose curious life of his brother is largely quoted in this memoir. — *Ed.*

keeping, and *observing him reasoning the country people out of their pence for essoines, &c.*, he commended him, saying, 'If you will be contented, Master Frank, to be a great while getting a little, you will be a little while getting a great deal;' wherein he was no false prophet."

Having been the requisite time on the books of the society of the Middle Temple, and performed all his moots, (upon which he bestowed great labor,) Francis was called to the bar.

The allowance of sixty pounds a year which he had hitherto received from his father was now reduced to fifty, in respect of the pence he collected by court-keeping and the expected profits of his practice. He highly disapproved of this reduction, and wrote many letters to his father to remonstrate against it. At last he received an answer which he hoped was favorable, but which contained only these words, "Frank, I suppose by this time, having vented all your discontent, you are satisfied with what I have done." The reduced allowance, however, was continued to him as long as his father lived, who said "he would not discourage industry by rewarding it when successful with loss."

The young barrister was now hard put to it. He took "a practising chamber" on a first floor in Elm Court, "a dismal hole — dark next the court, and on the other side a high building of the Inner Temple standing within five or six yards of the windows." He was able to fill his shelves with all useful books of the law from the produce of certain legacies and gifts collected for him by his mother,* and he seems

* At that time not more than fifty volumes were required. Now, unfortunately, a law library is "*multorum camelorum onus*," (a load for many camels.)

still to have had a small pecuniary help from his grandfather. For some time he had great difficulty in keeping free from debt; but he often declared that "if he had been sure of a hundred pounds a year to live upon, he had never been a lawyer."

He is much praised by his brother, because it is said "he did not, (as seems to have been common,) for the sake of pushing himself, begin by bustling about town and obtruding himself upon attorneys, or bargaining for business, but was contented if chance or a friend brought him a motion, as he was standing at the bar taking notes." These, however, came so rarely that he fell into a very dejected and hypochondriacal state. Thinking himself dying, he carried a list of his ailments to a celebrated physician, Dr. Beckenham of Bury, who laughed at him and sent him away, prescribing fresh air and amusement.

He was in danger of utterly sinking in the slough of despond, when he was suddenly taken by the hand by the great lawyer, Sir Jeffrey Palmer, who was made attorney general on the restoration of Charles II., and who if he had lived must have been lord chancellor. His son Edward, a very promising young man, lately called to the bar, died about this time in the arms of Francis North, who had been at college with him, and had shown him great attention during his illness.

All the business destined for young Palmer now somehow found its way to his surviving friend. His powerful protector, the attorney general, rapidly brought him forward by employing him in government prosecutions, and even when he himself was confined by illness, by giving him his briefs in smaller matters to hold for him in court. North, we may be sure, was most devotedly assiduous in making a suitable return for this kindness, and in flattering his patron. Instead of the sentiments he had imbibed from his family in his early days, he now loudly expressed those of an ultra prerogative lawyer, exalting the power of the king both over the church and the Parliament.

Being considered a rising man, his private friends and near relations came to consult him. He was once asked if he took fees from them. "Yes," said he; "they no doubt come to do me a kindness; and what kindness have I if I refuse their money?"

Soon after he was called to the bar, he went the Norfolk circuit, where his family interest lay; but here again he chiefly relied upon his grand resource of flattering his superiors and accommodating himself to their humors. "He was exceeding careful to keep fair with the cocks of the circuit, and particularly with Serjeant Earl, who had almost a monopoly. The Serjeant was a very covetous man, and when none would starve with him in journeys, this young gentleman kept him company." They once rode together from Cambridge to Norwich without drawing bit, to escape the expense of baiting at an inn; and North would have been famished, if the serjeant's man, knowing his master's habits, had not privately furnished him with a cake. He asked the serjeant, out of compliment to his riches, how he kept his accounts, "for you have," said he, "lands, securities, and great comings in of all kinds." "Accounts, boy!" exclaimed the serjeant, "I get as much as I can, and I spend as little as I can; and there is all the account I keep." In these journeys the serjeant talked so agreeably of law, and tricks, and purchases, and management, that North's hunger was beguiled, and he thought only of the useful knowledge he was acquiring, and the advantage to be derived from the countenance of a man so looked up to.

Lord Chief Justice Hyde generally rode the Norfolk circuit, and so completely had North taken the measure of his foot, that my lord called him "cousin" in open court, "which was a declaration that he would take it for a respect to himself to bring him causes." The biographer to whom we are so much indebted lays it down that there is no harm in a judge letting it be known "that a particular counsel will be easily heard before him, and that his errors and lapses, when they happen, will not offend his lordship or hurt the cause." The morality of the bar in those days will be better understood by the following observations of simple Roger: "In circuit practice there is need of an exquisite knowledge of the judge's humor, as well as his learning and ability to try causes; and he, North, was a wonderful artist at watching a judge's tendency, to make it serve his turn, and yet never failed to pay the greatest regard and deference to his opinion; for so they get credit; because *the judge for the most part thinks that person the best lawyer that respects most his opinion.* I have heard his lordship say, that sometimes he hath been forced to give up a cause to the judge's opinion when he (the judge) was plainly in the wrong, and when more contradiction had but made him more positive; and, besides, that in so doing he himself had weakened his own credit with the judge, thereby been less able to set him right when he was inclined to it. A good opinion so gained often helps at another time to good purpose, and sometimes to ill purpose; as I heard it credibly reported of Serjeant Maynard that, being the leading counsel in a small feed cause, he would give it up to the judge's mistake, and not contend to set him right, that he might gain credit to mislead him in some other cause in which he was well feed." These gentlemen of the long robe ought to have changed places in court with the highwaymen they were retained to prosecute.*

There was no nonsense, however arrant, a silly judge might speak in deciding for North, which he would not back. Thus a certain Mr. Justice Archer, who seems to have been the laughing stock of the profession, having, to the amusement of the juniors, "noted a difference between a renunciation of an executorship upon record and *in pais*," North said, "Ay, my lord; just so, my lord;" upon which his lordship became as fierce as a lion, and would not hear the argument on the other side. But even such a learned and sensible judge as Chief Justice Hale, North could win by an affectation of modesty, diffidence, and profound veneration. Early in his career, when he found it difficult to get to his place in a very crowded court, Sir Matthew said from the bench, "Good people, make way for this little gentleman; he will soon make way for himself."

His consultations were enormously long, and he gained vast applause at them by his care and dexterity in probing the cause, starting objections, inventing points, foretelling what would be said by the opposite counsel and by the judge, and showing how the verdict might be lost or was to be secured; but, to make security doubly sure, after mastering the record and perusing the deeds to be given in evidence, he himself

* This sort of practice on the weakness of judges, keeping them in good humor by flattery and complaisance, may possibly, as the text implies, be abandoned in England, but in America it is still sufficiently common. — *Ed.*

examined the witnesses, and thus had an opportunity of presenting the facts properly to their minds.

Need we wonder that from an humble beginner, rejoicing in a cause that came to him, he soon became "cock of the circuit" — all who had trials rejoicing to have him on their side?

I shall give one specimen of his conduct as a leader. He was counsel for the defendant in an action tried before his friend Judge Archer, for not setting out tithes — in which the treble value was to be recovered. Finding that he had not a leg to stand upon, he manœuvred to get his client off with the single value; so he told his lordship that this was a cause to try a right of a very intricate nature, which would require the reading a long series of records and ancient writings, and that it ought not to be treated as a penal action; wherefore, they should agree upon the single value of the tithes, for which the verdict should be taken conditionally, and then proceed fairly to try the merits. The judge insisted on this course being adopted; and the other side, not to irritate him, acquiesced in North's proposal. "Then did he open a long history of matters upon record, of bulls, monasteries, orders, greater and lesser houses, surrenders, patents, and a great deal more, *very proper if it had been true*, while the counsel on the other side stared at him; and having done, they bid him go to his evidence. He leaned back, as speaking to the attorney, and then, '*My lord*,' said he, '*we are very unhappy in this cause. The attorney tells me they forgot to examine their copies with the originals at the Tower*;' and (so folding up his brief,) '*My lord*,' said he, '*they must have the verdict, and we must come better prepared another time*.' So, notwithstanding all the mooting the other side could make, the judge held them to it, and they were choused of the treble value."

While North had such success on the circuit, he was equally flourishing in Westminster Hall. By answering cases and preparing legal arguments for Sir Jeffrey Palmer, and by flouting at parliamentary privilege, he was still higher than ever in favor with that potential functionary. It happened that in the year 1668, after the fall of the Earl of Clarendon, a writ of error was brought in the House of Lords by Denzil Hollis, now Lord Hollis, the only defendant surviving, upon the judgment of the Court of King's Bench in the great case of *The King* v. *Sir John Elliot, Denzil Hollis, and Others*, decided in the fifth year of the reign of Charles I. This had been a prosecution by the king against five members of the House of Commons, for what had been done in the House on the last day of the session, when Sir John Finch was held in the chair while certain resolutions alleged to be seditious had been voted, and one of the defendants had said "that the Council and judges had all conspired to trample under foot the liberties of the subject." They had pleaded to the jurisdiction of the Court of King's Bench, "that the supposed offences were committed in Parliament, and ought not to be punished or inquired of in this court, or elsewhere than in Parliament." But their plea had been overruled, and they were all sentenced to heavy fine and imprisonment.

Although there had been resolutions of the House of Commons, on the meeting of the Long Parliament, condemning this judgment, it still stood on record, and Lord Hollis thought it was a duty he owed to his country, before he died, to have it reversed.

Sir Jeffrey Palmer, as attorney general, pleaded *in nullo*

*est erratum;* but having returned his writ of summons to the House of Lords, and being in the habit of sitting there on the woolsack, as one of the assessors to the peers, he could not himself argue the case as counsel at the bar. The king's serjeants declined to do so out of respect to the House of Commons. Francis North, thinking this a most favorable opportunity to make himself known at court as an anti-parliamentarian lawyer, volunteered to support the judgment, and his services were accepted. He says himself "he was satisfied he argued on the right side, and that on the record the law was for the king." Accordingly, on the appointed day he boldly contended that, as the information averred that the offences were committed *against the peace*, as privilege of Parliament does not extend to offences in breach of the peace, as they had not been punished in the Parliament in which they were committed, and as no subsequent Parliament could take notice of them, they were properly cognizable in a court of common law. The judgment was reversed, but North's fortune was made. The Duke of York was pleased to inquire "who that young gentleman was who had argued so well." Being told that "he was the younger son of the Lord North, and, what was rare among young lawyers at that time, of loyal principles," his royal highness undertook to encourage him by getting the king to appoint him one of his majesty's counsel. North was much gratified by receiving a message to this effect, but was alarmed lest the Lord Keeper Bridgeman, who by his place was to superintend preferments in the law, might conceive a grudge against him for this interference with his patronage. The lord keeper acquitted him of all blame, wished him joy, and with peculiar civility desired him to take his place within the bar.

Things went on very smoothly with him now till the death of Sir Jeffrey Palmer, when Sir Heneage Finch being promoted to be attorney general, the solicitor's place was vacant. North, being the only king's counsel, and having been long employed in crown business, had a fair claim to succeed, and he was warmly supported by the lord keeper, as well as the new attorney general, who was desirous of having him for a colleague; but the Duke of Buckingham, at this time considered prime minister, preferred Sir William Jones, who was North's chief competitor in the King's Bench, and over whose head he had been put when he received his silk gown.*

To terminate the difference they were both set aside, and the office of solicitor general was given to Sir Edward Turner, speaker of the House of Commons, who held it for a twelvemonth, at the end of which he was made chief baron of the Exchequer, in the room of Sir Matthew Hale, promoted to be chief justice of the Common Pleas.

Buckingham's influence had greatly declined, and North was made solicitor general without difficulty, Jones being solaced with a silk gown, and the promise of further promotion on the next vacancy.

The Cabal was now in its full ascendancy; and as the leaders did not take any inferior members of the government into their councils, and contrived to prevent the meeting of Parliament for nearly two years, the new solicitor had only to attend to his profession. Of course, he gave up

* The distinguishing badge worn by the king's counsel. The barristers wear stuff gowns. The serjeants, (the highest rank of practitioners,) enjoying a monopoly of the practice of the Court of Common Pleas, which originally had exclusive cognizance of all civil actions, have or had, as their badges, a coif, or black velvet cap, (for which a wig was about this time substituted,) and parti-colored robes. — *Ed.*

the circuit, and he set the example, generally followed for one hundred and fifty years, of making the Court of Chancery his principal place of practice, on being promoted to be a law officer of the crown; henceforth going to other courts only in cases in which the crown was concerned, or which were of very great magnitude. To keep up his law, when he could be spared from the Court of Chancery, he stepped across the hall and seated himself in the Court of King's Bench, "with his note book in his hand, reporting as the students about the court did, and during the whole time of his practice every Christmas he read over Littleton's Tenures." He had hitherto practised conveyancing to a considerable extent; but he now turned over this business to Siderfin the reporter, whom he appointed to serve him in the capacity of "devil," as he himself had served Sir Jeffrey Palmer. He was on very decent terms with Sir Heneage Finch, who had much assisted his promotion; but he showed his characteristic cunning by an expedient he adopted to get the largest share of the patent business. Then, as now, all patents of dignity belong exclusively to the attorney general; but the warrants for all other patents might be carried either to the attorney or solicitor. North, with much dexterity, took into his employment a clerk of Sir Jeffrey Palmer, who was reputed to have a magazine of the best precedents, and who had great interest among the attorneys, whereby many patents came to his chambers which otherwise would have gone to the attorney general's.

But if he was eager to get money, he spent it freely. He was now appointed "autumn reader" of the Middle Temple, and though the festivity was not honored with the presence of royalty, like Finch's, in the Inner Temple, it was conducted sumptuously, and cost him above a thousand pounds. He took for his subject "The Statute of Fines," which he treated very learnedly, and the arguers against him, the best lawyers of the society, did their part very stoutly. On the "Grand Day" all the king's chief ministers attended, and the profusion of the best provisions and wine led to such debauchery, disorder, tumult, and waste, that this was the last public reading in the Inns of Court, the lectures being discontinued and the banqueting commuted for a fine.

I must not pass over his loves, although they were not very romantic or chivalrous. He was desirous of being married, among other reasons, because he was tired of dining in the hall and eating "a costelet and salad at Chastelin's in the evening with a friend;" and he wished to enjoy the pleasures of domestic life. One would have thought that the younger son of a peer, of great reputation at the bar, solicitor general at thirty-one, and rising to the highest offices in the law, might have had no difficulty in matching to his mind; but he met with various rebuffs and disappointments. Above all, he required wealth, which it seems was not then easily to be obtained without the display of a long rent roll. He first addressed the daughter of an old usurer in Gray's Inn, who speedily put an end to the suit by asking him "what estate his father intended to settle upon him for present maintenance, jointure, and provision for children." He could not satisfy this requisition by an "abstract" of his "profitable rood of ground in Westminster Hall." He then paid court to a coquettish young widow; but after showing him some favor, she jilted him for a jolly old knight of good estate. The next proposition was made by him to a city alderman, the father of many daughters, who, it was given out, were to have each a portion of six thousand pounds. North dined with the alderman, and liked one of them very much; but coming to treat, the fortune shrank to five thousand pounds. He immediately took his leave. The alderman ran after him, and offered him to boot five hundred pounds on the birth of the first child, but he would not bate a farthing of the six thousand.

At last his mother found him a match to his mind in the Lady Frances Pope, one of the three daughters and coheirs of the Earl of Down, who lived at Wroxton, in Oxfordshire, with fortunes of fourteen thousand pounds apiece. We are surprised to find that, with all his circuit and Westminster Hall earnings, he was obliged to borrow six hundred pounds from a friend before he could compass six thousand pounds to be settled upon her. He then ventured down with grand equipage and attendance, and in less than a fortnight obtained the young lady's consent, and the writings being sealed, the lovers were happily married. The feasting and jollities in the country lasted three weeks, and Mr. Solicitor, heartily tired of them, was very impatient to get back to his briefs. However, he seems always to have treated his wife, while she lived, with all due tenderness. He took a house in Chancery Lane, near Serjeants' Inn, and acquired huge glory by constructing a drain for the use of the neighborhood — a refinement never before heard of in that quarter. This was the happiest period of his life.

In the beginning of 1673, the meeting of Parliament could be deferred no longer, and it was considered necessary that the solicitor general should have a seat in the House of Commons.

He remained member for Lynn till he was made chief justice of the Common Pleas, in January, 1675; but I can hardly find any trace of his ever having spoken in the House of Commons.

Shaftesbury was at last turned out, the great seal was given to Sir Heneage Finch, and North became attorney general. He had for his colleague as solicitor his old rival, Sir William Jones, who seems to have been a considerable man, who afterwards had the virtue voluntarily to give up office that he might join the popular party, and who, if not cut off by an early death, would probably have acted the part of Lord Somers at the Revolution, and left a great name in history.

Parliament met in a few weeks after North's promotion. We are told that "little or nothing of the king's business in the House of Commons leaned upon him, because Mr. Secretary Coventry was there, who managed for the court." North once or twice spoke a few words, "in resolving the fallacies of the country party," but did not venture beyond an opinion upon a point of law which incidentally arose.

"He could not attend the house constantly, but took the liberty of pursuing his practice in Westminster Hall."* There he was easily the first; and the quantity of business which he got through in Chancery ("his home") and the other courts where he went *special* seems to have been enormous. His mode of preparation was (like Lord Erskine's) to have a consultation in the evening before reading his brief, when "he was informed of the history of the cause, and where the pinch was." Next morning at four he was called by a trusty boy, who never failed, winter or summer, to come into his chamber

* The hours then kept must have been very inconvenient for lawyers in Parliament, as all the courts and both houses met at eight in the morning and sat till noon.

at that hour,* and by the sitting of the court he had gone through his brief, and was ready to do ample justice to his clients.

Fees now flowed in upon him so fast that he hardly knew how to dispose of them. He seems to have taken them from his clients with his own hand. At one time he had had a fancy, for his health, to wear a sort of skullcap. He now routed out three of these, which he placed on the table before him, and into these he distributed the cash as it was paid to him. "One had the gold, another the crowns and half crowns, and another the smaller money." When these vessels were full, they were committed to his brother Roger, who told out the pieces and put them into bags, which he carried to Child's, the goldsmith, at Temple Bar.†

But still Mr. Attorney was dissatisfied with his position. He could not but be mortified by his insignificance in the House of Commons. The country party there was rapidly gaining strength, and although it was not then usual for the crown to turn out its law officers on a change of ministers, he began to be very much frightened by threats of impeachment uttered against all who were instrumental in executing the measures of the government. Shaftesbury was in furious opposition. While only at the head of a small minority in the House of Lords, the House of Commons was more and more under his influence. North was exceedingly timid, always conjuring up imaginary dangers, and exaggerating such as he had to encounter. He now exceedingly longed to

* This early rising rendered it necessary for him to take "a short turn in the other world after dinner."

† Roger assures us he did not purloin any part of the treasure, for which he takes infinite credit to himself.

lay his head on "the cushion of the Common Pleas," instead of running the risk of its being laid on the block on Tower Hill.

Vaughan, the chief justice of that court, died, and North's wishes were accomplished, notwithstanding some intrigues to elevate Sir William Jones or Sir William Montagu. When it came to the pinch, North was rather shocked to think of the sacrifice of profit which he was making, "for the attorney's place was (with his practice) near seven thousand pounds per annum, and the cushion of the Common Pleas not above four thousand. But accepting, he accounted himself enfranchised from the court brigues and attendances at the price of the difference."

North held the office of chief justice of the Common Pleas nearly eight years, which may be divided into two periods — 1st. From his appointment till the formation of the Council of Thirty, on the recommendation of Sir William Temple, in the year 1679; 2dly. From thence till he received the great seal, in the end of the year 1682. During the former he mixed little in politics, and devoting himself to his juridical duties, he discharged them creditably.

At this time, and for long after, the emoluments of the judges in Westminster Hall depended chiefly upon fees, and there was a great competition between the different courts for business. The King's Bench, originally instituted for criminal proceedings, had, by a dexterous use of their writ of "*latitat*," tricked the Common Pleas of almost all civil actions; and when the new chief justice took his seat, he found his court a desert. There was hardly sufficient business to countenance his coming every day in term to Westminster Hall, while the serjeants and officers were repining and starving. But he was soon up with the King's Bench, by a new and more dexterous use of the "*capias*," the ancient writ of that court — applying it to all personal actions.

At this time, a judge, when appointed, selected a circuit, to which he steadily adhered, till another, which he preferred, became vacant. Chief Justice North for several years "rode the western;" and in his charges to juries, as well as in his conversation with the country gentlemen, he strongly inculcated the most slavish church-and-king doctrines, insomuch that the Cavaliers called him "*Deliciæ Occidentis*," or "The Darling of the West."

The chief justice afterwards went the northern circuit, attended by his brother Roger, who gives a most entertaining account of his travels, and who seems to have thought the natives of Northumberland and Cumberland as distant, as little known, and as barbarous, as we should now think the Esquimaux or the aborigines of New Zealand.

Till the Popish plot broke out, Chief Justice North had no political trials before him; and the only cases which gave him much anxiety were charges of witchcraft. He does not appear, like Chief Justice Hale, to have been a believer in the black art; but, with his characteristic timidity, he was afraid to combat the popular prejudice, lest the countrymen should cry, "This judge hath no religion; he doth not believe witches." Therefore he avoided trying witches himself as much as possible, and turned them over to his brother judge, Mr. Justice Raymond, whom he allowed to hang them. He was once forced to try a wizard; but the fraud of a young girl, whom the prisoner was supposed to have enchanted and made to spit pins, was so clearly exposed by the witnesses, that the chief justice had the boldness to direct an acquittal.

The Popish plot he treated as he did witchcraft. He disbelieved it from the beginning, but was afraid openly to express a doubt of its reality. He thought it might be exposed by the press, and he got a man to publish an anonymous pamphlet against it, to which he contributed; but sitting along with Chief Justice Scroggs, who presided at the trial of those charged with being implicated in it, he never attempted to restrain this "butcher's son and butcher" from slaughtering the victims.

So on the trial of Lord Stafford, though he privately affected severely to condemn the proceeding, he would not venture to save Lord Nottingham,* the high steward, from the disgrace of assisting in that murder; and he dryly gave his own opinion that two witnesses were not necessary to each overt act of treason.

We have still more flagrant proof of his baseness on the trial of Reading, prosecuted by order of the House of Commons for trying to suppress evidence of the plot. North himself now presided, and having procured a conviction, in sentencing the defendant to fine, imprisonment, and pillory, he said, "I will tell you your offence is so great, and hath such a relation to that which the whole nation is concerned in, because it was an attempt to baffle the evidence of that conspiracy, which, if it had not been, by the mercy of God,

* This was the title taken by Finch on promotion to the great seal. Nottingham is greatly lauded by Blackstone and other writers on jurisprudence as a "consummate lawyer," and as the father of the modern English equity system. His abilities were unquestionable, but his political career, like that of so many other "consummate lawyers," has some very black spots. — *Ed.*

detected, God knows what might have befallen us all by this time."

We now come to present North on the political stage, where he continued to act a very conspicuous and disreputable part down to the time of his death. In the year 1679, when the king adopted his new plan of government by a Council of Thirty, of which Shaftesbury was made president, and into which Lord Russell and several of the popular leaders were introduced, it was thought fit to balance them by some determined ultra-royalists; and the lord chief justice of the Common Pleas, who had acquired himself the reputation of being the most eminent of that class, was selected, although he had not hitherto been a privy councillor. At first he seldom openly gave any opinion in council, but he secretly engaged in the intrigues which ended in the abrupt prorogation and dissolution of the Parliament, in the dismissal of Shaftesbury, and the resignation of Lord Russell and the whigs. The scheme of government was then altered, and a cabinet, consisting of a small number of privy councillors, was formed, North being one of them. To his opinion on legal and constitutional questions the government was now disposed to show more respect than to that of Lord Chancellor Nottingham.

There being much talk against the court in the London coffee houses, it was wished to suppress them by proclamation; and our chief justice, being consulted on the subject, gave this response — that "though retailing of coffee may, under certain circumstances, be an innocent trade, yet as it is used at present in the nature of a common assembly to discourse of matters of state, news, and great persons, it becomes unlawful; and as the coffee houses are nurseries of idleness and pragmaticalness, and hinder the consumption of our native provisions, they may be treated as common nuisances." Accordingly, a proclamation was issued for shutting up all coffee houses, and forbidding the sale of coffee in the metropolis; but this caused such a general murmur, not only among politicians and idlers, but among the industrious classes connected with foreign and colonial trade, that it was speedily recalled.

The meeting of the new Parliament summoned in the end of 1679 having been repeatedly postponed, there arose the opposite factions of "Petitioners" and "Abhorrers"—the former *petitioning* the king that Parliament might be speedily assembled for the redress of grievances, and the latter, in their addresses to the king, expressing their *abhorrence* of such seditious sentiments. The "Petitioners," however, were much more numerous and active, and a council was called to consider how their proceedings might be stopped or punished. Our chief justice recommended a proclamation, which the king approved of, and ordered the attorney general, Sir Creswell Levinz, to draw. Mr. Attorney, alarmed by considering how he might be questioned for such an act on the meeting of Parliament, said, "I do not well understand what my lord chief justice means, and I humbly pray of your majesty that his lordship may himself draw the proclamation." *King.*—"My lord, I think then you must draw this proclamation." *Chief Justice.*—"Sire, it is the office of your majesty's attorney general to prepare all royal proclamations, and it is not proper for any one else to do it. I beg that your majesty's affairs may go on in their due course; but if in this matter Mr. Attorney doubts any thing, and will give himself the trouble to call upon me, I will give him the best assistance I can."

Sir Creswell, having written on a sheet of paper the formal commencement and conclusion of a royal proclamation, carried it to the chief justice, who filled up the blank with a recital that, "for spurious ends and purposes relating to the public, persons were going about to collect and procure the subscriptions of multitudes of his majesty's subjects to petitions to his majesty; which proceedings were contrary to the known laws of this realm, and ought not to go unpunished;" and a mandate to all his majesty's loving subjects, of what rank or degree soever, "that they presume not to agitate or promote any such subscriptions, nor in any wise join in any petition in that manner to be preferred to his majesty, upon pain of the utmost rigor of the law, and that all magistrates and other officers should take effectual care that all such offenders against the laws be prosecuted and punished according to their demerits."*

Parliament at last met, and strong measures were taken against the "Abhorrers," who had obstructed the right of petitioning. An inquiry was instituted respecting the proclamation. Sir Creswell Levinz was placed at the bar, and asked by whose advice or assistance he had prepared it. He several times refused to answer; but being hard pressed, and afraid of commitment to the Tower, he named the Lord Chief Justice North, against whom there had been a strong suspicion, but no proof. A hot debate arose, which ended in the resolution, "That the evidence this day given to this house against Sir Francis North, chief justice of the Common Pleas, is sufficient ground for this house to proceed

* Here we have one of many English precedents of assault upon the right of petition — a thing by no means unknown in our American politics. — *Ed.*

upon an impeachment against him for high crimes and misdemeanors."

He was a good deal alarmed by the vote of impeachment,* but it raised him still higher in favor at court. Next day, presiding in the House of Lords as speaker, in the absence of the lord chancellor, and seeming very much dejected, King Charles (according to his manner) "came and clapped himself down close by him on the woolsack, and 'My lord,' said he, 'be of good comfort; I will never forsake my friends, as my father did.'" His majesty, without waiting for a reply, then walked off to another part of the house.

A committee was appointed to draw up the articles of impeachment against the chief justice; but before they made any report, this Parliament too was dissolved.

Soon after the summoning of Charles's last Parliament, North was obliged to set off upon the spring circuit; and notwithstanding his best efforts to finish the business rapidly, he could not arrive at Oxford till the two houses had assembled.

He was one of the small junto to whom was intrusted the secret of immediate dissolution. The moment the deed was done, he set off for London, pretending to be afraid of what he called "the positive armament against the king, which manifestly showed itself at Oxford."

As soon as the Cabinet met at Whitehall, North advised the issuing of a Declaration to justify the dissolution of the three last Parliaments which had met respectively at Westminster and Oxford, and himself drew an elaborate one, which was adopted. This state paper certainly puts the

* The same Parliament had already impeached Scroggs. See ante, p. 180.

popular party in the wrong upon the "exclusion question" and other matters with considerable dexterity, and it was supposed to have contributed materially to the reaction going on in favor of the government.

So far his conduct was legitimate, and in the fair exercise of his functions as a privy councillor; but I am sorry to say that he now sullied his ermine by a flagrant disregard of his duties as a judge. The grand jury for the city of London having very properly thrown out the bill of indictment against Stephen College, "the Protestant joiner," it was resolved to try him at Oxford; and for this purpose a special commission was issued, at the head of which was placed Lord Chief Justice North. Burnet says mildly, "North's behavior in that whole matter was such that, probably, if he had lived to see an impeaching Parliament, he might have felt the ill effects of it." After perusing the trial, I must say that his misconduct upon it was most atrocious. The prisoner, being a violent enemy to Popery, had attended the city members to Oxford as one of their guard, with "No Popery" flags and cockades, using strong language against the Papists and their supporters, but without any thought of using force. Yet the chief justice was determined that he should be found guilty of compassing and imagining the king's death, and levying war against him in his realm.* College's papers, which he was to use in his defence, were forcibly taken from him, on the ground that they had been written by some other persons, who gave him hints what he was to say. They were in reality prepared by his legal advisers, Mr. Aaron Smith and Mr

* Here again is the old pretence of "levying war," under which it has been attempted with us to convert hostility to the fugitive slave act into treason. See ante, p. 158. — *Ed.*

West. The prisoner was checked and browbeaten as often as he put a question or made an observation. His defence was much more able than could have been expected from a person in his station of life, but of course he was convicted. The chief justice, in passing sentence, observed, "Look you, Mr. College; because you say you are innocent, it is necessary for me to say something in vindication of the verdict, which I think the court were all well satisfied with. I thought it was a case that, as you made your own defence, small proof would serve the turn to make any one believe you guilty. For, as you defend yourself by pretending to be a Protestant, I did wonder, I must confess, when you called so many witnesses to your religion and reputation, that none of them gave an account that they saw you receive the sacrament within these many years, or any of them particularly had seen you at church in many years, or what kind of Protestant you were. But crying aloud against the Papists, it was proved here who you called Papists. You had the boldness to say the king was a Papist, the bishops were Papists, and the church of England were Papists. If these be the Papists you cry out against, what kind of Protestant you are I know not — I am sure you can be no good one. How it came into your head, that were but a private man, to go to guard the Parliament, I much wonder. Suppose all men of your condition should have gone to have guarded the Parliament, what an assembly had there been! And though you say you are no man of quality, nor likely to do any thing upon the king's guards or the king's person, yet if all your quality had gone upon the same design, what ill consequences might have followed! We see what has been done by Massaniello, a mean man, in another country — what by Wat Tyler and Jack

Straw in this kingdom." College asked him to fix the day of his death, but he answered that that depended on the king; adding, in a tone of great humanity, "that he should have due notice of it to prepare, by repenting of his crimes." College's innocence was so manifest, that even Hume, eager to palliate all the atrocities of this reign, says, "that his whole conduct and demeanor prove him to have been governed by an honest but indiscreet zeal for his country and his religion." On the 31st of August, 1681, the sentence, with all its savage barbarities, was carried into execution. "Sir Francis North," observes Roger Coke, "was a man cut out, to all intents and purposes, for such a work."

He was next called upon to assist at the immolation of a nobler victim, who escaped from the horns of the altar. Shaftesbury had been for some time very careful never to open his mouth on politics out of the city of London and county of Middlesex, and during the Oxford Parliament had touched on no public topic except in the House of Lords. It was resolved at all hazards to bring him to trial; but this could only be done by an indictment to be found at the Old Bailey. There did North attend when the indictment was to be preferred, and resolutely assist Lord Chief Justice Pemberton in perverting the law,* by examining the witnesses in open court, and by trying to intimidate and mislead the grand jury; but he was punished by being present at the shout, which lasted an hour, when "*Ignoramus*" was returned.

He next zealously lent himself to the scheme of the court for upsetting the municipal privileges of the city of London,

* Pemberton, though well aware that, to justify the grand jury in finding an indictment, a *prima facie* case of guilt must be made out, instructed them that "a probable ground of accusation" was sufficient. — *Ed.*

and of obtaining sheriffs for London and Middlesex who would return juries at the will of the government. The lord mayor having been gained over, and the stratagem devised of creating a sheriff by the lord mayor drinking to him, instead of by the election of his fellow-citizens, the difficulty was to find any freeman of fair character who would incur all the odium and risk of being so introduced to the shrievalty. It so happened that at that time there returned to England a brother of the chief justice, Mr. Dudley, afterwards Sir Dudley North, who was free of the city from having been apprenticed there to a merchant, and who had amassed considerable wealth by a long residence in Turkey. It being suggested at court that this was the very man for their sheriff, "the king very much approved of the person, but was very dubious whether the chief justice, with his much caution and wisdom, would advise his brother to stand in a litigious post. But yet he resolved to try; and one day he spoke to Sir Francis with a world of tenderness, and desired to know if it would be too much to ask his brother Dudley to hold sheriff on my lord mayor's drinking." The wily chief justice immediately saw the advantage this proposal might bring to the whole family, and returned a favorable answer. "For matter of title," says Roger, "he thought there was more squeak than wool; for whatever people thought was at the bottom, if a citizen be called upon an office by the government of the city, and obeys, where is the crime? But then such a terrible fear was artificially raised up in the city as if this service was the greatest hazard in the world." Sir Francis gently broke the matter to his brother, saying "that there was an opportunity which preferred itself whereby he might make a fortune if he wanted it, and much enlarge what he had, besides great reputation to be gained, which would make him all the days of his life very considerable, laying open the case of the lord mayor's right very clear and plain, against which in common sense there was no reply." Dudley, however, made many objections, and talked of the terrible expense to which he should be exposed. The chief justice urged that if he served, the obligation was so transcendent, that there could be no employment by commission from the crown which would not fall to his share, "and as for the charge," said he, "here, brother, take a thousand pounds to help make good your account, and if you never have an opportunity by pensions or employments to reimburse you and me, I will lose my share; else I shall be content to receive this thousand pounds out of one half of your pensions when they come in, and otherwise not at all." The merchant yielded; and under this pure bargain, proposed by the judge before whom the validity of the appointment might come to be decided, when his health was given by the lord mayor as sheriff of London and Middlesex, he agreed to accept the office.

But the old sheriffs insisted on holding a common hall for the election of their successors, according to ancient usage, on Midsummer day; when Lord Chief Justice North had the extreme meanness, at the king's request, to go into the city and take post in a house near Guildhall, belonging to Sir George Jeffreys, "who had no small share in the conduct of this affair, to the end that if any incident required immediate advice, or if the spirits of the lord mayor should droop, which in outward appearance were but faint, there might be a ready recourse." It is true the opposite faction had the Lord Grey de Werke and other leaders from the west end of the town, to advise and countenance them; but this could be no excuse for a judge so degrading himself. The poll going for the popular candidates, the lord mayor, by Chief Justice North's advice, under pretence of a riot, attempted to adjourn the election; but the sheriffs required that the polling should continue, and declared Papillon and Dubois duly elected.

This causing great consternation at Whitehall, a council was called, to which the lord mayor and aldermen were summoned. Lord Chief Justice North, by the king's command, addressed them, saying, "that the proceedings of the sheriffs at the common hall after the adjournment were not only utterly null and void, but the persons were guilty of an audacious riot and contempt of lawful authority, for which by due course of law they would be severely punished; but in the mean time it was the lord mayor's duty and his majesty's pleasure that they should go back to the city and summon the common hall, and make election of sheriffs for the year ensuing." The lord mayor, having been told that the courtiers would bamboozle him and leave him in the lurch, when North had concluded, said, "My lord, will your lordship be pleased to give me this under your hand?" The king and all the councillors were much tickled to see the wily chief justice thus nailed, "expecting some turn of wit to fetch himself off, and thinking to have sport in seeing how woodenly he would excuse himself." But to their utter astonishment, for once in his life Francis North was bold and straightforward, and cheating them all, he answered, without any hesitation, "Yes, and you shall have it presently." Then seizing a pen, he wrote, "I am of opinion that it is in the lord mayor's power to call, adjourn, and dissolve the common hall at his pleasure, and that all acts done there, as of the common hall, during such adjournment, are mere nullities, and have no legal effect." This he signed and handed to the lord mayor, who then promised obedience.

Accordingly, another common hall was called, at which it was pretended that Sir Dudley North and Rich were elected, and they were actually installed in the office of sheriff. By the contrivance of Lord Chief Justice North, the office of lord mayor for the ensuing year was likewise filled by a thorough passive-obedience tool of the court. Gould, the liberal candidate, had a majority of legal votes on the poll, but under a pretended scrutiny, Pritchard was declared duly elected, and Sir John More, the renegade mayor, willingly transferred to him the insignia of chief magistrate, so that the king had now the city authorities completely at his devotion. Shaftesbury fled to Holland; and it was for the court to determine when the blow should be struck against the popular leaders who remained.

Such were the services of Lord Chief Justice North, which all plainly saw would ere long be rewarded by higher promotion. The health of Lord Nottingham, the chancellor, was rapidly declining, and the court had already designated his successor. Lord Craven, famous for wishing to appear intimate with rising men, in the circle at Whitehall, now seized Lord Chief Justice North by the arm and whispered in his ear; and the foreign ambassadors so distinctly saw the shadow of the coming event that they treated him with as great respect as if he had been prime minister, "and when any of them looked towards him and thought he perceived it, they very formally bowed."

We are told that in many things North acted as "co-chancellor" with Nottingham; and for the first time the office of chancellor seems to have been like that of sheriff of Middlesex, one in its nature, but filled by two officers of equal authority. It is said that "the *aspirant* dealt with all imaginable kindness and candor to the *declinant*, and that never were predecessor and successor such cordial friends to each other, and in every respect mutually assistant, as those two were."

While the lord chancellor was languishing, the chief justice being at Windsor, the king plainly intimated to him that when the fatal event, which must be shortly looked for, had taken place, the great seal would be put into his hands. He modestly represented himself to his majesty as unfit for the place, and affected by all his art and skill to decline it. In truth, he really wished to convey to the king's mind the impression that he did not desire it, although he had been working so foully for it — as he knew it would be pressed upon him, there being no competitor so knowing and so pliant, and he had an important stipulation to make for a pension before he would accept it. When he came back to London, and confidentially mentioned what had passed between him and the king, he pretended to be annoyed, and said "that if the seal were offered to him he was determined to refuse it;" but it is quite clear that he was highly gratified to see himself so near the great object of his ambition, and that his only anxiety now was, that he might drive a good bargain when he should consent to give up "the cushion of the Common Pleas."

Lord Nottingham having died about four o'clock in the afternoon of Monday, the 18th of December, 1682, the great seal was carried next morning from his house, in Great Queen Street, to the king at Windsor. The following day his majesty brought it with him to Whitehall, and in the evening sent for the lord chief justice of the Common Pleas, to offer it to him.

When North arrived, he found Lord Rochester, the treasurer, and several other ministers, closeted with Charles. As yet there was no distinction between the funds to be applied to the king's private expenses and to the public service — the exchequer being now very empty, and the resolution being taken never more to summon a Parliament for supplies — it was considered an object that the keeper of the great seal should be contented with the fees of his office, without any allowance or pension from the crown. Charles himself was careless about such matters, but the treasurer had inculcated upon him the importance of this piece of economy. As soon as North entered, his majesty offered him the seal, and the ministers began to congratulate the new lord keeper; but, with many acknowledgments for his majesty's gracious intentions, he begged leave to suggest the necessity, for his majesty's honor, that a pension * should be assigned to him, as it had been to his predecessor, for otherwise the dignity of this high office could not be supported. Rochester interposed, pointing out the necessity, in times like these, for all his majesty's servants to be ready to make some sacrifices; that the emoluments of the great seal were considerable; and that it would be more becoming to trust to his majesty's bounty than to seek to drive a hard bargain with him. But Sir George Jeffreys being yet only a bustling city officer, who could not with any decency have been put at the head of the law; the attorney and solicitor general not being considered men of mark or likelihood; Sir Harbottle Grimston, the master of the rolls, being at death's door, and no other common law

* By this word "pension," I conceive we are to understand *salary* while the lord keeper was in office, and not, as might be supposed, an allowance on his retirement.

judge besides himself being produceable, the little gentleman was firm, and positively declared that he would not touch the great seal without a pension. After much haggling, a compromise took place, by which he was to have two thousand pounds a year instead of the four thousand pounds a year assigned to his predecessor. The king then lifted up the purse containing the seal, and putting it into his hand, said, "Here, my lord, take it; you will find it heavy." "Thus," says Roger North, "his majesty acted the *prophet* as well as the *king;* for, shortly before his lordship's death, he declared that, *since he had the seal, he had not enjoyed one easy and contented minute.*"

When the new lord keeper came home at night from Whitehall to his house in Chancery Lane, bringing the great seal with him, and attended by the officers of the Court of Chancery, instead of appearing much gratified, as was expected by his brother and his friends, who were waiting to welcome him, he was in a great rage — disappointed that he had not been able to make a better bargain, and, perhaps, a little mortified that he had only the title of "lord keeper" instead of the more sounding one of "lord chancellor." Recriminating on those with whom he had been so keenly acting the chapman, he exclaimed, "To be haggled with about a pension, as at the purchase of a horse or an ox! After I had declared that I would not accept without a pension, to think I was so frivolous as to insist and desist all in a moment! As if I were to be wheedled and charmed by their insignificant tropes! To think me worthy of so great a trust, and withal so little and mean as to endure such usage! It is disobliging, inconsistent, and insufferable. What have I done that may give them cause to think of me so poor a spirit as to be thus trifled with?" It might have been answered that, though the king and the courtiers made use of him for their own ends, they had seen his actions, understood his character, and had no great respect for him. Till Jeffreys was a little further advanced, they could not run the risk of breaking with him; but then he was subjected to all sorts of mortifications and insults.

On the first day of the following Hilary term he took his place in the Court of Chancery. By this time he was in possession of his predecessor's house in Great Queen Street, Lincoln's Inn Fields, and he had a grand procession from thence to Westminster Hall, attended by the Duke of Ormond, the Earls of Craven and Rochester, the great officers of state, and the judges. He took the oaths, the master of the rolls holding the book. He does not appear to hâve delivered any inaugural address. The attendant lords staid and heard a motion or two, and then departed, leaving the lord keeper in court.

They might have been well amused if they had remained. For the crooked purposes of the government, with a view to the disfranchising of the city of London by the *quo warranto* defending against it, Pemberton * was this day to be removed from being chief justice of the King's Bench to be chief justice of the Common Pleas, and Edmund Saunders was to be at once raised from wearing a stuff gown at the bar to be chief justice of the King's Bench. This keen but unscrupulous lawyer was previously to be made a serjeant, that he might be qualified to be a judge, and, coming into the Court

* Pemberton had been appointed to succeed Scroggs as chief justice of the King's Bench, but not being found quite serviceable enough, was now removed into another court. — *Ed.*

of Chancery, he presented the lord keeper with a ring for himself, and another for the king, inscribed with the courtly motto, "*Principi sic placuit.*" The lord keeper then accompanied him into court where he was to preside, called him to the bench, and made him a speech on the duties of his office. The ceremonies of the day were concluded by his lordship afterwards going to his old court, the Common Pleas, and there swearing in Pemberton as his successor, whom he congratulated upon "the ease with dignity" which he was now to enjoy.

Parasites and preferment-hunters crowded the levee of the new lord keeper. He was immediately waited upon by the courtly Evelyn, who discovered in him a thousand good qualities.*

In the midst of these blandishments he applied himself with laudable diligence to the discharge of his judicial duties. He declared that he was shocked by many abuses in the Court of Chancery, and he found fault with the manner in which his two predecessors, Bridgeman and Nottingham, had allowed the practice of the court to lead to delay and expense.

North's conduct as a law reformer was extremely characteristic. He talked much of issuing a new set of "rules and orders" to remedy all abuses, but he was afraid "that it would give so great alarm to the bar and officers, with the solicitors, as would make them confederate and demur, and, by making a tumult and disturbance, endeavor to hinder the

* "Sir F. North being made lord keeper on the death of the Earl of Nottingham, the lord chancellor, I went to congratulate him. He is a most knowing, learned, and ingenious person; and, besides having an excellent person, of an ingenuous and sweet disposition, very skilful in music, painting, the new philosophy, and political studies." — *Mem.* i. 513. Judge Kane is said to be quite an accomplished person. — *Ed.*

doing any thing of that kind which they would apprehend to be very prejudicial to their interests." * Then, when he wished to simplify the practice and to speed causes to a hearing and final decree, he considered that he was not only to regard the suitors, but that "there was a justice due as well to the crown, which had advantage growing by the disposition of places, profits, by process of all sorts, as also the judges and their servants, and counsel at the bar, and solicitors, who were all in possession of their advantages, and by public encouragement to spend their youth to make them fit for them, and had no other means generally to provide for themselves and their families, and had a right to their reasonable profits, if not strictly by law, yet through long connivance."

I think we must say that his alleged merit as a chancery reformer consists chiefly in the profession of good intentions; that he allowed the practice of the court to remain pretty much as he found it; and that if he saw and approved what was right, he followed what was wrong — aggravating his errors by disregarding the strong dictates of his conscience.

Nevertheless, he applied himself very assiduously to the business of his court, which, from his experience at the bar, and from his having often sat for his predecessor, was quite familiar to him; and he seems to have disposed of it satisfactorily. He was not led into temptation by having to decide in equity any political case; and no serious charge was preferred against him of bribery or undue influence. Till the meeting of Parliament in the reign of James, and the failure of his health, he prevented the accumulation of arrears; and, upon the whole, as an Equity judge, he is to be praised rather than censured.

* The principal obstacle to law reform in America is the pecuniary interest which the lawyers think they have in keeping up old abuses. — *Ed.*

I wish as much could be said of his political conduct while he held the great seal. He may have *wished* "to bring the king to rule wholly by law, and to do nothing which, by any reasonable construction, might argue the contrary;" but for this purpose he would make feeble efforts, and no sacrifice; and all the measures of the court, however profligate, when resolved upon, he strenuously assisted in carrying into execution.

The ministers who now bore sway, and who were on several points opposed to each other, were Halifax, Sunderland, and Rochester. The Duke of York, restored to the office of lord high admiral and to the Privy Council, in direct violation of the "test act," had so much influence, that it was said that "to spite those who wished to prevent him from reigning at the king's death, he was permitted to reign during the king's life." The Duchess of Portsmouth was likewise at the head of a party at court, although Mrs. Gwin, her Protestant rival, did not interfere with politics. With none of these would the lord keeper combine. His policy was to study the peculiar humors of the king — to do whatever would be most agreeable personally to him — to pass for "the king's friend" — and to be "*solus cum solo*."

Charles, although aware of his cunning and his selfishness, was well pleased with the slavish doctrines he laid down, and with the devoted zeal he expressed for the royal prerogative; and till Jeffrey's superior vigor, dexterity, and power of pleasing gained the ascendancy, usually treated him with decent consideration.

He never would give any opinion on foreign affairs, nor attend a committee of council summoned specially to consider them, professing himself, for want of a fit education and study, incompetent to judge at all of these matters, and declaring, like a true courtier, that "King Charles II. understood foreign affairs better than all his councils and councillors put together." But he regularly attended all other cabinet meetings, and when there was any business of a judicial nature to be done at the council-table, he always presided there, "the lord president not having the art of examining into and developing cases of intricacy."

The first of these in which he had to display his powers, was the disfranchisement of the city of London. Saunders, counsel in the *quo warranto*, having been appointed chief justice, to decide in favor of the sufficiency of the pleadings which he himself had drawn, the opinion of the Court of King's Bench had been pronounced for the crown, "that all the city charters were forfeited." Formal judgment was not yet entered on the record, to give an opportunity to the mayor, aldermen and citizens, to make their submission and to accept terms which might henceforth annihilate their privileges and make them the slaves of the government. They accordingly did prepare a petition to the king, imploring his princely compassion and grace, which they presented to him at a council held at Windsor on the 18th of June, 1683. The petition being read, they were ordered to withdraw, and when they were again called in, the lord keeper thus addressed them, disclosing somewhat indiscreetly the real motives for the *quo warranto:* "My lord mayor, I am by the king's command to tell you that he hath considered the humble petition of the city of London, where so many of the present magistrates and other eminent citizens are of undoubted loyalty and affection to his service; that for their sakes his majesty will show the city all the favor they can reasonably desire. It was very long before his majesty took resolutions to question their charter; it was not the seditious discourses of the coffee-houses, the treasonable pamphlets and libels daily published and dispersed thence into all parts of the kingdom, the outrageous tumults in the streets, nor the affronts to his courts of justice, could provoke him to it. His majesty had patience until disorders were grown to that height, that nothing less seemed to be designed than a ruin to the government both of church and state." After pointing out the mischief of having factious magistrates, he adds: "It was high time to put a stop to this growing evil. This made it necessary for his majesty to inquire into the abuses of franchises, that it might be in his power to make a regulation sufficient to restore the city to its former good government." He then stated the regulations to which they were required to assent, among which were — "That no lord mayor, sheriff, or other officer should be appointed without the king's consent; that the king might cashier them at his pleasure; that if the king disapproved of the sheriffs elected, he might appoint others by his own authority; and that the king should appoint all magistrates in the city by his commission, instead of their being elected as hitherto."

The citizens refused to comply with these terms, and judgment was entered up. Thus, on the most frivolous pretexts, and by a scandalous perversion of the forms of law, was the city of London robbed of the free institutions which it had enjoyed, and under which it had flourished for many ages. The proceeding was less appalling to the public than the trial and execution of eminent patriots, but was a more dangerous blow to civil liberty. London remained disfranchised, and governed by the agents of the crown, during the rest of this reign, and till the expected invasion of the Prince of Orange near the conclusion of the next — when, too late, an offer was made to restore its charters with all its ancient privileges. Immediately after the revolution, they were irrevocably confirmed by act of Parliament.

The lord keeper's conduct in this affair gave such high satisfaction at court, that, as a reward for it, he was raised to the peerage by the title of Baron Guilford. His brother says that he did not seek the elevation from vanity, but that he might be protected against the attacks which might hereafter be made upon him in the House of Commons. He obtained it on the recommendation of the Duke of York, who overlooked his dislike of Popery in respect of his steady hatred to public liberty.

To show his gratitude, the new peer directed similar proceedings to be commenced against many other corporations, which ended in the forfeiture or surrender of the charters of most of the towns in England in which the liberal party had enjoyed an ascendancy.

Gilbert Burnet,* about this time appointed preacher at the rolls, thought he had secured a protector in the lord keeper; but as soon as this whig divine had incurred the displeasure of the court, his lordship wrote to the master of the rolls that the king considered the chapel of the rolls as one of his own chapels, and that Dr. Burnet must be dismissed as one disaffected to the government. In consequence, he was obliged to go beyond seas, and to remain in exile, till he returned with King William.

Soon after followed the disgraceful trials for high treason, which arose out of the discovery of the rye-house plot. The

* Bishop Burnet, the historian.

lord keeper did not preside at these; but having directed them — superintending the general administration of justice, and especially bound to see that the convictions had been obtained on legal evidence — he is deeply responsible for the blood that was shed. He must have known that if, in point of law, the witnesses made out a case to be submitted to the jury against Lord Russell, that virtuous nobleman was really prosecuted for his support of the exclusion bill; and he must have seen that against Algernon Sydney no case had been made out to be submitted to the jury, as there was only one witness that swore to any thing which could be construed into an overt act of treason, and the attempt to supply the defect by a MS. containing a speculative essay on government, which was found in his study, and had been written many years before, was futile and flagitious. Yet did he sign the death-warrants of both these men, whose names have been honored, while his has been execrated in all succeeding times.

It is edifying and consolatory to think that he was outdone by his own arts, and that the rest of his career was attended by almost constant mortification, humiliation, and wretchedness. Saunders enjoyed the office of chief justice of the king's bench only for a few months, being carried off by an apoplexy soon after the decision of the great London *quo warranto* cause. An intrigue was immediately set on foot to procure the appointment for Jeffreys, who had more than ever recommended himself to the court by his zeal on the trial of Lord Russell, in which he had eclipsed the attorney and solicitor general; and he was anxiously wanted to preside at the trial of Sydney, against whom the case was known to be so slender, but who was particularly obnoxious on account of his late quarrel with the Duke of York, and his sworn enmity to despotism.* The pretensions of Jeffreys were supported by Sunderland, probably out of ill will to the lord keeper, who had intuitively shown a great jealousy of the new favorite. But the proposal produced great opposition and bickerings among different sections of courtiers. The lord keeper of course resisted it *totis viribus*, representing to the king that the office, according to ancient and salutary usage, ought to be offered to the attorney and solicitor general, who had been irregularly passed over on the appointment of the late chief justice, to gain an object of such magnitude as the forfeiture of the city charters; that Saunders was a man of immense learning, which countenanced *his* sudden elevation; but that Jeffreys, though gifted with a fluency of speech, was known to be unequal to so high an office; and that the whole profession of the law, and the public, would condemn an act so arbitrary and capricious. Charles was, or pretended to be, impressed by these arguments, which he repeated to Sunderland, and the office was kept vacant for three months after the death of Saunders. But on the 29th of September, the lord keeper had the mortification to put the great seal to the writ constituting Jeffreys "chief justice of England," and on the first day of the following Michaelmas term to make a speech, publicly congratulating him on his rise to the supreme seat of criminal justice, so well merited by his learning, his abilities, and his services.

What was worse, the new lord chief justice was not only sworn a privy councillor, but, in a few weeks, was admitted into the cabinet, where he, from the first, set himself to oppose the opinions, and to discredit the reputation, of him who, he knew, had opposed his appointment, and whom (his ambition

* See beyond, life of Jeffreys, p. 302.

being still unsatiated) he was resolved, in due time, to supplant.

Jeffreys began with interfering very offensively in the appointment of puisne judges, which of right belonged to the lord keeper. At first he was contented with the reputation of power in this department.

He next resolved to make a judge, by his own authority, of a man almost as worthless as himself. This was Sir Robert Wright, who had never had any law, who had spent his patrimony in debauchery, and who, being in great distress, had lately sworn a false affidavit to enable him to commit a fraud upon his own mortgagee.*

Jeffreys was not satisfied with his triumph without proclaiming it to all Westminster Hall. "Being there that same morning, while the Court of Chancery was sitting, he beckoned to Wright to come to him, and giving him a slap on the shoulder, and whispering in his ear, he flung him off, holding out his arms towards the lord keeper. This was a public declaration *that, in spite of that man above there, Wright should be a judge.* His lordship saw all this as it was intended he should, and it caused some melancholy." But he found it convenient to pocket the insult: he put the great seal to Wright's patent, and assisted at the ceremony of his installation. There is no trace of the lord keeper's speech on this occasion, so that we do not know in what terms he complimented the new judge on his profound skill in the law, his spotless integrity, and his universal fitness to adorn the judgment seat.

* An account of Guilford's unavailing attempt to prevent this appointment will be found in the life of Wright, chap. xix. — *Ed.*

When heated with liquor, Jeffreys could not now conceal his contempt for the lord keeper, even in the king's presence. It is related that, upon the hearing of a matter before the council, arising out of a controversy for jurisdiction between two sets of magistrates, Guilford proposed some sort of compromise between them, when the lord chief justice, "flaming drunk," came from the lower to the upper end of the board, and "talking and staring like a madman," bitterly inveighed against "trimmers," and told the king "he had *trimmers* in his court, and he never would be easy till all the *trimmers* were sent about their business." "The lord keeper, knowing that these darts were aimed at him,* moved the king that the whole business should be referred to the lord chief justice, and that he should make a report to his majesty in council of what should be fit to be done." This was ordered, and Guilford seems to have entertained a hope that Jeffreys, from the state of intoxication he was in, would entirely forget the reference, and so might fall into disgrace.†

But the most serious difference between them in Charles's time was on the return of Jeffreys from the northern circuit in the autumn of 1684, when, backed by the Duke of York, he had a deliberate purpose of immediately grasping the great seal. At a cabinet council, held on a Sunday evening, he stood up, and addressing the king while he held in his hands the rolls of the recusants in the north of England — "Sir,"

* It is curious that Roger gravely states that "he was dropped from the tory list and turned trimmer." — *Life*, i. 404.

† Life, ii. 179. It should be recollected that, at this time, the council met in the afternoon, between two and three — dinner having taken place soon after twelve, and a little elevation from wine was not more discreditable at that hour than in our time between eleven and twelve o'clock at night.

said he, "I have a business to lay before your majesty which I took notice of in the north, and which well deserves your majesty's royal commiseration. It is the case of numberless members of your good subjects that are imprisoned for recusancy: * I have the list of them here to justify what I say. They are so many that the great jails cannot hold them without their lying one upon another." After tropes and figures about "rotting and stinking in prison," he concluded with a motion to his majesty "that he would, by his pardon, discharge all the convictions for recusancy, and thereby restore air and liberty to these poor men." This was a deep-laid scheme, for besides pleasing the royal brothers, one of whom was a secret, and the other an avowed Papist, he expected that Guilford must either be turned out for refusing to put the great seal to the pardon, or that he would make himself most obnoxious to the public, and afterwards to Parliament, by compliance. A general silence prevailed, and the expectation was that Halifax or Rochester, who were strong Protestants, would have stoutly objected. The lord keeper, alarmed lest the motion should be carried, and seeing the dilemma to which he might be reduced, plucked up courage and said, "Sir, I humbly entreat your majesty that my lord chief justice may declare whether all the persons named in these rolls are actually in prison or not?" *Chief Justice.* — "No fair man could suspect my meaning to be that all these are actual prisoners; for all the jails in England would not hold them.

* James and Jeffreys setting themselves up as the special advocates of toleration, (with a view to the introduction of Popery,) is like our American slaveholders putting themselves forward as advocates of the rights of property and as special democrats, for the purpose of upholding slavery, based as slavery is on principles at war with the fundamental idea of property and democracy. — *Ed.*

But if they are not in prison, their case is little better; for they lie under sentence of commitment, and are obnoxious to be taken up by every peevish sheriff or magistrate, and are made to redeem their liberty with gross fees, which is a cruel oppression to them and their families." *Lord Keeper.* — "Sir, I beg your majesty will consider what little reason there is to grant such a general pardon at this time. For they are not all Roman Catholics that lie under sentence of recusancy, but sectaries of all kinds and denominations; perhaps as many, or more, who are all professed enemies to your majesty and your government in church and state. They are a turbulent people, and always stirring up sedition. What will they not do when your majesty gives them a discharge at once? Is it not better that your enemies should live under some disadvantages, and be obnoxious to your majesty's pleasure, so that, if they are turbulent or troublesome, you may inflict the penalties of the law upon them? If there be any Roman Catholics whom you wish to favor, grant to them a particular and express pardon, but do not by a universal measure set your enemies as well as your friends at ease. The ill uses that would be made of such a step to the prejudice of your majesty's interests and affairs are obvious and endless." * The king was much struck with these observations, urged with a boldness so unusual in the lord keeper. The other lords wondered, and the motion was dropped.

The lord keeper, not without reason, boasted of this as the most brilliant passage of his life. When he came home at night, he broke out in exclamations — "What can be their meaning? Are they all stark mad?" And before he went to bed, as a memorial of his exploit, he wrote in his

* Life, ii. 150, 153, 334.

almanack, opposite to the day of the month, "Motion *cui solus obstiti*."

By such an extraordinary exhibition of courage, to which he was driven by the instinct of self-preservation, he escaped the peril which Jeffreys had planned for him, and he retained the great seal till the king's death.

In the morning of Monday, the 2d of February, 1685, he was sent for to Whitehall, by a messenger announcing that his majesty had had an apoplectic seizure. According to the ancient custom and supposed law when the sovereign is dangerously distempered, the Privy Council was immediately assembled; and the lord keeper examined the king's physicians.* "Their discourse ran upon indefinites — what they observed, their method intended, and success hoped. He said to them, *that these matters were little satisfactory to the council, unless they would declare, in the main, what they judged of the king's case; whether his majesty was like to recover or not?* But they would never be brought to that; *all lay in hopes*."

With short intervals the council continued to sit day and night. After a time, the physicians came into the council chamber, smiling, and saying they had good news, for the

* Lord Coke lays down, that upon such an occasion there ought to be a warrant by advice of the Privy Council, as in 32 H. 8, to certain physicians and surgeons named, authorizing them to administer to the royal patient "potiones, syrupos, confectiones, laxitivas medicinas, clysteria, suppositoria, capitis purgea, capitis rasuram, fomentationes, embrocationes, emplastra," &c.; still, that no medicine should be given to the king but by the advice of his council; that no physic should be administered except that which is set down in writing, and that it is not to be prepared by any apothecary, but by the surgeons named in the warrant. — 4 *Inst.* 251. These were the precautions of times when no eminent person died suddenly without suspicion of poison. Even Charles II. was at first said to have been cut off to make way for a Popish successor, although, when the truth came out, it appeared that he had himself been reconciled to the Roman Catholic church.

king had a fever. *Lord Keeper.* — "Gentlemen, what do you mean? Can any thing be worse?" *First Physician.* — "Now we know what to do." *Lord Keeper.* — "What is that?" *Second Physician.* — "To give him the cortex." The exhibition of Jesuits' bark was sanctioned by the council, but proved fatal, and being continued, while the poor king grew weaker and weaker, at the end of four days he expired. The lord keeper and the council were kept in ignorance of the fact that Chiffinch (accustomed to be employed on royal errands of a different sort) had been sent for a Roman Catholic priest, to receive his confession and administer the sacraments to him, when he had declined the spiritual assistance of a bishop of the church of England.

The council was still sitting when the news was brought that Charles was no more. After a short interval, James, who, leaving the death-bed of his brother, had decently engaged in a devotional exercise in his own closet, entered the apartment in which the councillors were assembled, and all kneeling down, they saluted him as their sovereign. When he had seated himself in the chair of state, and delivered his declaration, which, with very gracious expressions, smacked of the arbitrary principles so soon acted upon, Lord Guilford surrendered the great seal into his hands, and again received it from him with the former title of lord keeper. James would, no doubt, have been much better pleased to have transferred it to Jeffreys; but it was his policy, at the commencement of his reign, to make no change in the administration, and he desired all present to retain the several charges which they held under his deceased brother, assuring them that he earnestly wished to imitate the good and gracious sovereign whose loss they deplored.

Jeffreys, though continued a member of the cabinet, was probably a good deal disappointed, and he resolved to leave nothing undone to mortify the man who stood between him and his object, and to strike him down as soon as possible.

The first question upon which James consulted the council was respecting the levying of the duties of customs and excise, which had been granted by Parliament only during the life of the late king. The lord keeper intimating a clear conviction that Parliament would continue the grant as from the demise of the crown, recommended a proclamation requiring that the duties should be collected and paid into the exchequer, and that the officers should keep the product separate from other revenues till the next session of Parliament, in order to be disposed of as his majesty and the two houses should think fit. But the lord chief justice represented this advice as low and trimming, and he moved that "his majesty should cause his royal proclamation to issue, commanding all officers to collect, and the subjects to pay, these duties for his majesty's use, as part of the royal revenue." The lord keeper ventured humbly to ask his majesty to consider whether such a proclamation would be for his service, as it might give a handle to his majesty's enemies to say that his majesty, at the very entrance upon his government, levied money of the subject without the authority of Parliament. The chief justice's advice was far more palatable. The proclamation which he recommended was therefore ordered to be drawn up, and was immediately issued. The lord keeper had the baseness to affix the great seal to this proclamation, thinking as he did of its expediency and legality. But rather than resign or be turned out of his office, he was ready to concur in any outrage on the constitution, or to submit to any personal indignity.

A Parliament was found indispensable; and, counting on the very loyal disposition manifested by the nation, writs for calling one were issued, returnable the 19th of May.

As that day approached, the lord keeper began to write the speech which he expected to deliver in the presence of the king to the two houses on their assembling. He was much pleased with this performance, on which he had taken uncommon pains, and when finished, he read it to his brother and his officers, who highly applauded it. But what was his consternation when he was told that he was not to be allowed to open his mouth upon the occasion! *

Parliament meeting, the course was adopted which has been followed ever since. Instead of having on the first day of the session, before the choice of a speaker by the Commons, one speech from the king, and another from the lord chancellor or lord keeper, to explain the causes of the summons, the Commons being sent for by the black rod, the lord keeper merely desired them to retire to their own chamber and choose a speaker, and to present him at an hour which was named, for his majesty's approbation. The speaker being chosen and approved of, and having demanded and obtained a recognition of the privileges of the Commons, on the following day the king himself made a speech from the throne, and immediately withdrew.

But this speech was not in modern fashion settled at the cabinet; nor was it read the evening before at the Cockpit, or to the chief supporters of the government in both houses at the dinner-table of the two leaders respectively; nor was

* See the speech at full length. Life, ii. 192. There is nothing in it very good or very bad.

it to be treated as the speech of the minister. "At least the lord keeper had no hand in it; for he was not so much as consulted about either the matter or expressions the king intended to use, as one might well judge by the unguarded tenor of it."

Yet he still was mean enough to cling to office, and to do what he could for a government impatient to get rid of him. He had been very active in the elections; and by his influence had procured the return of a good many zealous church-and-king members. "And to make the attendance easy to these gentlemen, whose concerns were in the country, he took divers of them to rack and manger in his family, where they were entertained while the Parliament sat." But nothing which he could do would mitigate the hostility of those who had vowed his destruction.

At the meeting of Parliament, Jeffreys was made a peer, that he might have the better opportunity to thwart and insult the lord keeper; although there had been no previous instance of raising a common-law judge to the peerage.

There were several appeals from decrees of the lord keeper speedily brought to a hearing. "Jeffreys affected to let fly at them, to have it thought that he was fitter to be chancellor." He attended, neglecting all other business; and during the argument, and in giving his opinion, took every opportunity of disparaging the lord keeper's law, preparatory to moving reversals. He was particularly outrageous in the case of *Howard* v. *The Duke of Norfolk*, being emboldened to talk confidently on matters with which he was not much acquainted, by having to rest on the reputation of Lord Nottingham. That great equity lawyer, contrary to the opinion of the two chief justices and the chief baron, whom he had called in to assist him, had held that an equitable estate tail might be created in a term of years; but his successor had reversed his decree, and the decree of reversal was now under appeal. "Lord Chief Justice Jeffreys, by means of some encouragement he had met with, took upon him the part of slighting and insulting his lordship on all occasions that proffered. And here he had a rare opportunity; for, in his rude way of talking, and others of a party after him, he battered the poor decree; not without the most indecent affronts to his lordship that in such an assembly ever were heard." The courtesy now prevailing between law lords of opposite political parties was not then known between colleagues sitting in the same cabinet; and the poor lord keeper was assailed by the coarsest vituperation, and the most cutting ridicule. The second Earl of Nottingham, son of the chancellor, "who hated him because he had endeavored to detract from his father's memory," likewise took this opportunity to attack him, and got together many instances of his ill administration of justice, and greatly exposed him. He was not roused into retaliation or resistance; and he contented himself with a dry legal argument. The decree was reversed; and when he announced that the *contents had it*, he must have felt as if he had been sounding his own death knell. The lay lords who voted could have known nothing of the merits of such a nice question; and must have been guided by favor or enmity to the lord keeper or the lord chief justice. What rendered the defeat and contemptuous usage the more galling was the presence of the king; for James, like his brother, attended in the House of Lords when any thing interesting was coming on; and walked about the house, or stood by the fire, or sat in his chair of state or on the woolsack, as suited his fancy.

"Having opened this scene," says Roger, "we are not to expect other than opposition, contempt, and brutal usage, of that chief towards his lordship while he lived."

There were few debates in the House of Lords during this short session; but, even in going through the common forms of the House, Jeffreys found opportunities publicly to testify his contempt for the lord keeper; and in the cabinet, in discussing the dispensation to be granted to Catholic officers to serve in the army, and other subjects, he constantly laid traps for him, with a view of either making him obnoxious to the king, or odious to the public — who considered him the author of every declaration or dispensation which passed the great seal.

Sunderland and other members of the cabinet openly joined in this persecution, and "he was little less than derided by them. Being soon to be laid aside, he was not relied upon in any thing, but was truly a seal-keeper rather than a minister of state, and kept on for despatch of the formularies, rather than for advice or trust." Why did he not resign? It is difficult to understand the reasoning of his brother, who thus accounts for his continuing to bear such insults: — "His lordship was so ill used at court by the Earl of Sunderland, Jeffreys, and their sub-sycophants, that I am persuaded if he had had less pride of heart, he had been tempted to have delivered up the seal in full health. But he cared not to gratify, by that, such disingenuous enemies. He cared not to humor these barkers, or to quit his place before he might do it with safety to his dignity. He intended to stay till the king would bear him no longer, and then make it his majesty's own act to remove him."

He felt keenly a sense of the insignificance and disfavor

into which he had fallen; and the anticipation of "the worse remaining behind," when he was to be finally kicked out, preyed upon his spirits. No longer was he ear-wigged by the Lord Cravens, who worship a favorite; no more did the foreign ambassadors bow low when they thought that he observed them: his levee was now deserted; he seemed to himself to discover a sneer on every countenance at Whitehall; and he suspected that the bar, the officers of the court, and the bystanders in chancery, looked at him as if they were sure of his coming disgrace. To shade himself from observation, while he sat on the bench he held a large nosegay before his face.

Dreadfully dejected, he lost his appetite and his strength. He could not even get through the business of the court; and *remanets* multiplying upon him kept him awake at night, or haunted him in his sleep. He drooped so much, that for some time he seemed quite heart-broken. At last, he had an attack of fever, which confined him to his bed.

The coronation was approaching, and it was important that he should sit in the "Court of Claims." Having recovered a little by the use of Jesuits' bark, he presided there, though still extremely weak; and he walked at the coronation "as a ghost with the visage of death upon him, such a sunk and spiritless countenance he had."

While he was in this wretched state, news arrived that the Duke of Monmouth had landed in the west of England and raised the standard of rebellion. The Parliament, having come to a number of loyal votes, having attainted the duke, and granted a supply, was adjourned, that the members might assist in preserving tranquillity in their several districts.

The lord keeper talked of resigning, and wrote a letter to

the Earl of Rochester, to ask leave to go into the country for the recovery of his health, saying, "I have put myself into the hands of a doctor, who assures me of a speedy cure by entering into a course of physic." Leave was given, and he proceeded to Wroxton, in Oxfordshire, the seat which belonged to him in right of his wife.

Here he languished while the battle of Sedgemoor was fought — Monmouth, after in vain trying to melt the heart of his obdurate uncle, was executed on Tower Hill under his parliamentary attainder, and the inhuman Jeffreys, armed with civil and military authority, set out on his celebrated "campaign." Roger North would make us believe that the dying Guilford was horrified by the effusion of blood which was now *incarnardining* the western counties by command of the lord general chief justice, and that he actually interposed to stay it: — "Upon the news returned of his violent proceedings, his lordship saw the king would be a great sufferer thereby, and went directly to the king, and moved him to put a stop to the fury, which was in no respect for his service; but in many respects for the contrary. For though the executions were by law just, yet never were the deluded people all capitally punished; and it would be accounted a carnage and not law or justice; and thereupon orders went to mitigate the proceeding. I am sure of his lordship's intercession to the king on this occasion, being told it at the very time by himself." It is painful to doubt the supposed exertion of mercy and firmness by the lord keeper; but an attention to dates, of which this biographer is always so inconceivably negligent, shows the story to be impossible. Jeffreys did not open his campaign by the slaughter of the Lady Lisle, at Winchester, till the 27th of August, and he carried it on with increased cruelty till the very end of September. On the 5th of September died Lord Keeper Guilford, at Wroxton, after having been for some weeks in a state of such debility and exhaustion that, able only to attend to his spiritual concerns, he thought no more of domestic treason or foreign levy than if he had already slept in the grave. For a short time after his arrival there, he rallied, by the use of mineral waters, but he soon had a relapse, and he could with difficulty sign his will. He was peevish and fretful during his sickness, but calmly met his end. "He advised his friends not to mourn for him, yet commended an old maid-servant for her good will that said, '*As long as there is life there is hope.*' At length, having strove a little to rise, he said, '*It will not do;*' and then, with patience and resignation, lay down for good and all, and expired."

He was buried in Wroxton Church, in a vault belonging to his wife's family, the Earls of Down.

"He was a crafty and designing man," says Bishop Burnet. "He had no mind to part with the great seal, and yet he saw he could not hold it without an entire compliance with the pleasure of the court. Nothing but his successor made him be remembered with regret. He had not the virtues of his predecessor; but he had parts far beyond him. They were turned to craft; so that whereas the former (Lord Nottingham) seemed to mean well even when he did ill, this man was believed to mean ill even when he did well." I accede to this character, with the exception of the estimate of North's "parts," which I think are greatly overrated. He was sharp and shrewd, but of no imagination, of no depth, of no grasp of intellect, any more than generosity of sentiment. Cunning, industry, and opportunity may make such a man at any time. A Nottingham does not arise above once in a century.

Guilford had as much law as he could contain, but he was incapable of taking an enlarged and commanding view of any subject. In equity, he did nothing to rear up the system of which the foundations had been so admirably laid by his predecessor. His industry was commendable; and I think he may be fairly acquitted of corruption, notwithstanding his indiscreet acceptance of a present of one thousand pounds from the six clerks, when they had a dispute with the sixty, on which he was to adjudicate. Where he was not under the apprehension of personal responsibility, there was nothing which he would not say or do to exalt the prerogative and please his patrons. I shall add only one instance. Sir Thomas Armstrong was outlawed for high treason while beyond the seas unless he surrendered within a year. Being sent over a prisoner from Holland within a year, he insisted that he was entitled to a writ of error to reverse the outlawry and to be admitted to make his defence; but the lord keeper refused him his writ of error, first, on the pretence that there was no fiat for it by the attorney general, and then, that he had no right to reverse his outlawry, as he was present by compulsion. Thus the unhappy victim was sent to instant execution without trial.

So zealous a conservative was Guilford, that "he thought the taking away of the tenures" (*i. e.* the abolition of wardship and the other oppressive feudal burdens introduced at the conquest) "a desperate wound to the liberties of the people."

The court wags made great sport of him, the Earl of Sunderland taking the lead, and giving out the signal, while

Jeffreys was always ready to join in the laugh. I may offer as an example "the story of the rhinoceros." My lord keeper went one day into the city, accompanied by his brother Sir Dudley, to see a rhinoceros of enormous size lately imported, and about to be exhibited as a show.* Next morning, at Whitehall, a rumor was industriously spread that the lord keeper had been riding on the rhinoceros, "and soon after dinner some lords and others came to his lordship to know the truth from himself; for the setters of the lie affirmed it positively, as of their own knowledge. That did not give his lordship much disturbance, for he expected no better from his adversaries. But that his friends, intelligent persons, who must know him to be far from guilty of any childish levity, should believe it, was what *roiled* him extremely, and much more when they had the face to come to him to know if it were true. So it passed; and the Earl of Sunderland, with Jeffreys and others of that crew, never blushed at the lie of their own making, but valued themselves upon it as a very good jest."

To try how far his compliance with the humors of the court would go, they next persuaded his own brother-in-law (that he might not suspect the hoax) to wait upon him, and in strict confidence, and with great seriousness, to advise him to keep a mistress, "otherwise he would lose all his interest with the king; for it was well understood that he was ill looked upon for want of doing so, because he seemed continually to reprehend them by not falling in with the general custom; and the messenger added, that if his lordship pleased

* Evelyn tells us that this was the first rhinoceros ever introduced into England, and that it sold for two thousand pounds.

he would help him to one." He declined the offer — with much politeness, however, lest he should give offence. But with his familiar friends "he made wonderfully merry with this state policy, especially the procuring part, and said, that if he were to entertain a madam, it would be one of his own choosing, and not one of their stale trumpery."

Although he never aimed at oratory, it is said that he meditated a "history of his own times." He might have transmitted to us many curious anecdotes, but the performance must have been without literary merit; for some of his notes which he had written as materials are in the most wretched style, and show that he was unacquainted with the first principles of English composition, and even with the common rules of grammar. He did publish two or three short tracts "on music" and other subjects, which were soon forgotten. He was well versed in music, conversed with Sir Peter Lely about painting, speculated with natural philosophers on the use of the bladder of fishes, and learned several of the continental languages; but he seems never to have looked into a classical writer after he left college, and to have had the same taste for the *belles lettres* as his brother Roger, who, placing them all in the same category, talks with equal contempt of "departed quacks, *poets*, and almanack makers." Although his two immediate predecessors were libelled and lauded by popular verses in the mouths of every one, I can find no allusion in any fine writer either of the court or country party to North; and it may be doubtful whether he knew anything of the works of Butler, of Dryden, of Waller, or of Cowley, beyond the snatches of them he may have heard repeated in the merry circle at Whitehall.

He lived very hospitably, receiving those who retailed the

gossip of the day in his house in Great Queen Street, Lincoln's Inn Fields, then the fashionable quarter of the town for the great nobility as well as for eminent lawyers. The nobility and chief gentry coming to London frequently dined with him. The dinner was at a very early hour, and did not last long. "After a solemn service of tea in a withdrawing room, the company usually left him." He had a court room fitted up on the ground floor, which he then entered, and there he continued hearing causes and exceptions, sometimes to what was considered a late hour. About eight o'clock came supper, which he took with a few private friends, and relished as the most agreeable and refreshing meal of the day.

In the vacations, when he could be spared from London, he retired to his seat at Wroxton. For some years he likewise rented a villa at Hammersmith, but this he gave up soon after his wife's death. He had the misfortune to lose her after they had been married only a few years. She seems to have been a very amiable person. She found out when her husband had any trouble upon his spirits, and she would say, "Come, Sir Francis, (as she always styled him,) you shall not think; we must talk and be merry, and you shall not look on the fire as you do. I know something troubles you; and I will not have it so." He would never marry again, which in his last illness he repented, for "he fancied that in the night human heat was friendly."

He was extremely amiable in all the relations of domestic life. Nothing can be more touching than the account we have of the warm and steady affection subsisting between him and his brother, who survived to be his biographer.

The lord keeper was a little but handsome man, and is said to have had "an ingenuous aspect."

He left behind him Francis, his son and heir, the second Baron Guilford, father of Francis, the third Baron Guilford, on whom descended the barony of North, by failure of the elder branch of the family, and who, in 1752, was created Earl of Guilford, and was the father of Lord North, the prime minister, so celebrated for his polished oratory, his refined wit, and amiable manners.*

When we estimate what the lord keeper achieved, we should bear in mind that he died at *forty-eight*, an age considerably more advanced than that reached by his immediate successor; yet under that at which other lord chancellors and lord keepers began to look for promotion. He was in truth solicitor general at *thirty-four*, attorney general at *thirty-seven*, chief justice of the Common Pleas at *thirty-eight*, and lord keeper and a peer at *forty-five*. It is probably well for his memory that his career was not prolonged. He might have made a respectable judge when the constitution was settled; but he was wholly unfit for the times in which he lived.

I ought not to conclude this memoir without acknowledging my obligations to "Roger North s Life of the Lord Keeper;" which, like "Boswell's Life of Johnson," interests us highly, without giving us a very exalted notion of the author. Notwithstanding its extravagant praise of the hero of the tale, its inaccuracies, and its want of method, it is a most valuable piece of biography, and with Roger's lives of his brothers "Dudley and John," and his "Examen," ought to be studied by every one who wishes to understand the history and the manners of the reign of Charles II.

* We may add — for his tory principles, and for the loss of America to the British crown. — *Ed.*

# CHAPTER XIV.

## EDMUND SAUNDERS.

THERE never was a more flagrant abuse of the prerogative of the crown than the appointment of a chief justice of the King's Bench for the undisguised purpose of giving judgment for the destruction of the charters of the city of London, as a step to the establishment of despotism over the land. Sir Edmund Saunders accomplished this task effectually, and would, without scruple or remorse, have given any other illegal judgment required of him by a corrupt government. Yet I feel inclined to treat his failings with lenience, and those who become acquainted with his character are apt to have a lurking kindness for him. From the disadvantages of his birth and breeding, he had little moral discipline; and he not only showed wonderful talents, but very amiable social qualities. His rise was most extraordinary, and he may be considered as our *legal Whittington.*

"He was at first," says Roger North, "no better than a poor beggar-boy, if not a parish foundling, without known parents or relations." There can be no doubt that, when a boy, he was discovered wandering about the streets of London in the most destitute condition — penniless, friendless, without having learned any trade, without having received any education. But although his parentage was unknown to the contemporaries with whom he lived when he had advanced himself in the world, recent inquiries have ascertained that he was born in the parish of Barnwood, close by the city of

Gloucester; and his father, who was above the lowest rank of life, died when he was an infant, and that his mother took for her second husband a man of the name of Gregory, to whom she bore several children. We know nothing more respecting him, with certainty, till he presented himself in the metropolis; and we are left to imagine that he might have been driven to roam abroad for subsistence, by reason of his mother's cottage being levelled to the ground during the siege of Gloucester; or that, being hardly used by his step-father, he had run away, and had accompanied the broad-wheeled wagon to London, where he had heard that riches and plenty abounded.

The little fugitive found shelter in Clement's Inn, where "he lived by obsequiousness, and courting the attorneys' clerks for scraps." He began as an errand boy, and his remarkable diligence and obliging disposition created a general interest in his favor. Expressing an eager ambition to learn to write, one of the attorneys of the Inn got a board knocked up at a window on the top of a staircase. This was his desk, and, sitting here, he not only learned the *running hand* of the time, but *court hand*, *black letter*, and *engrossing*, and made himself "an expert entering clerk." In winter, while at work, he covered his shoulders with a blanket, tied hay bands round his legs, and made the blood circulate through his fingers by rubbing them when they grew stiff. His next step was to copy deeds and law papers, at so much a folio or page, by which he was enabled to procure for himself wholesome food and decent clothes. Meanwhile he not only picked up a knowledge of Norman French and law Latin, but, by borrowing books, acquired a deep insight into the principles of conveyancing and special pleading. By and by the friends he had acquired enabled him to take a small chamber, to furnish it, and to begin business on his own account as a conveyancer and special pleader. But it was in the latter department that he took greatest delight and was the most skilful — insomuch that he gained the reputation of being familiarly acquainted with all its mysteries; and although the order of "special pleaders under the bar" was not established till many years after, he was much resorted to by attorneys who wished by a sham plea to get over the term, or by a subtle replication to take an undue advantage of the defendant.

It has been untruly said of him, as of Jeffreys, that he began to practise as a barrister without ever having been called to the bar. In truth, the attorneys who consulted him having observed to him that they should like to have his assistance to maintain in court the astute devices which he recommended, and which duller men did not comprehend, or were ashamed of, he rather unwillingly listened to their suggestion that he should be entered of an Inn of Court, for he never cared much for great profits or high offices; and having money enough to buy beer and tobacco, the only luxuries in which he wished to indulge, he would have preferred to continue the huggermugger life which he now led. He was domesticated in the family of a tailor in Butcher Row, near Temple Bar, and was supposed to be rather too intimate with the mistress of the house. However, without giving up his lodging here, to which he resolutely stuck till he was made lord chief justice of England, he was prevailed upon to enter as a member of the Middle Temple. Accordingly, on the 4th of July, 1660, he was admitted there by the description of "Mr. Edward Saunders, of the county of the city of Gloucester, gentleman." The omission to mention the name of his father might have given rise to the report that he was a foundling; but a statement of parentage on such occasions, though usual, was not absolutely required, as it now is.

He henceforth attended "moots," and excited great admiration by his readiness in putting cases and taking of objections. By his extraordinary good humor and joviality, he likewise stood high in the favor of his brother templars. The term of study was then seven years, liable to be abridged on proof of proficiency; and the benchers of the Middle Temple had the discernment and the liberality to call Saunders to the bar when his name had been on their books little more than four years.

We have a striking proof of the rapidity with which he rushed into full business. He compiled reports of the decisions of the Court of King's Bench, beginning with Michaelmas term, 18 Charles II., A. D. 1666, when he had only been two years at the bar. These he continued till Easter term, 24 Charles II., A. D. 1672. They contain all the cases of the slightest importance which came before the court during that period; and he was counsel in every one of them.

His "hold of business" appears the more wonderful when we consider that his *liaison* with the tailor's wife was well known, and might have been expected to damage him even in those profligate times; and that he occasionally indulged to great excess in drinking, so that he must often have come into court very little acquainted with his "breviat," and must have trusted to his quickness in finding out the questions to be argued, and to his storehouses of learning for the apposite authorities.

But when we peruse his "reports," the mystery is solved.

There is no such treat for a common lawyer. Lord Mansfield called him the "Terence of reporters," and he certainly supports the forensic dialogue with exquisite art, displaying infinite skill himself in the points which he makes, and the manner in which he defends them; doing ample justice at the same time to the ingenuity and learning of his antagonist. Considering the barbarous dialect in which he wrote, (for the Norman French was restored with Charles II.,) it is marvellous to observe what a clear, terse, and epigrammatic style he uses on the most abstruse juridical topics.

He labored under the imputation of being fond of sharp practice, and he was several times rebuked by the court for being "*trop subtile*," or "going too near the wind;" but he was said by his admirers to be fond of his craft only *in meliori sensu*, or in the good sense of the word, and that, in entrapping the opposite party, he was actuated by a love of fun rather than a love of fraud. Thus is he characterized, as a practitioner, by Roger North: —

"Wit and repartee in an affected rusticity were natural to him. He was ever ready, and never at a loss, and none came so near as he to be a match for Serjeant Maynard. His great dexterity was in the art of special pleading, and he would lay snares that often caught his superiors, who were not aware of his traps. And he was so fond of success for his clients that, rather than fail, he would set the court hard with a trick; for which he met sometimes with a reprimand, which he would wittily ward off, so that no one was much offended with him. But Hale could not bear his irregularity of life; and for that, and suspicion of his tricks, used to bear hard upon him in the court. But no ill usage from the bench was too hard for his hold of business, being such as scarce any could do but himself."

He did not, like Scroggs and Jeffreys, intrigue for advancement. He neither sought favor with the popular leaders in the city, nor tried to be introduced into Chiffinch's "spie office" at Whitehall. "In no time did he lean to faction, but did his business without offence to any. He put off officious talk of government and politics with jests, and so made his wit a catholicon or shield to cover all his weak places and infirmities." He was in the habit of laughing both at Cavaliers and Roundheads; and, though nothing of a Puritan himself, the semi-Popish high-churchmen were often the objects of his satire.

His professional, or rather his special pleading, reputation forced on him the advancement which he did not covet. Towards the end of the reign of Charles II., when the courts of justice were turned into instruments of tyranny, (or, as it was mildly said, "the court fell into a steady course of using the law against all kinds of offenders,") Saunders had a general retainer from the crown, and was specially employed in drawing indictments against Whigs, and *quo warrantos* against whiggish corporations. In crown cases he really considered the king as his client, and was as eager to gain the day for him, by all sorts of manœuvres, as he had ever been for a roguish Clement's Inn attorney. He it was that suggested the mode of proceeding against Lord Shaftesbury for high treason; on his recommendation the experiment was made of examining the witnesses before the grand jury in open court, and he suggested the subtlety that "the usual secresy observed being for the king's benefit, it might be waived by the king at his pleasure." When the important day arrived, he himself interrogated very artfully Mr. Blathwayt, the clerk of the council, who was called to produce the papers which had been seized at Lord Shaftesbury's house in Aldersgate street, and gave a treasonable tinge to all that passed. The *ignoramus* of his indictment must have been a heavy disappointment to him; but the effort which he made gave high satisfaction to the king, who knighted him on the occasion, and from that time looked forward to him as a worthy chief justice.

Upon the dissolution of the Oxford Parliament and the rout of the Whig party, it being resolved to hang Fitzharris, Saunders argued with uncommon zeal against the prisoner's plea, that there was an impeachment depending for the same offence, and concluded his legal argument in a manner which seems to us very inconsistent with the calmness of a dry legal argument — "Let him plead guilty or not guilty; I rather hope that he is not guilty than he is guilty; but if he be guilty, it is the most horrid, venomous treason ever spread abroad in any age, and for that reason your lordships will not give countenance to any delay."

I find him several times retained as counsel against the crown; but upon these occasions the government wished for an acquittal. He defended the persons who were prosecuted for attempting to throw discredit on the Popish Plot, he was assigned as one of the counsel for Lord Viscount Stafford, and he supported the application made by the Earl of Danby to be discharged out of custody. On this last occasion he got into a violent altercation with Lord Chief Justice Pemberton. The report says that "Mr. Saunders had hardly begun to speak when the Lord Chief Justice Pemberton did reprimand the said Mr. Saunders for having offered to impose upon the court. To all which Mr. Saunders replied, that he humbly begged his lordship's pardon, but he did believe that the rest of his brethren understood the matter as he did." The Earl of Danby supported this statement, and Saunders had a complete triumph over the chief justice.

Pemberton was soon removed from the office of chief justice of the King's Bench, and Saunders sat in his place.

In spite of the victory which the king had gained over the Whigs at the dissolution of his last Parliament, he found one obstacle remain to the perpetuation of his despotic sway in the franchises of the city of London. The citizens (among whom were then included all the great merchants and some of the nobility and gentry) were still empowered to elect their own magistrates; they were entitled to hold public meetings; and they could rely upon the pure administration of justice by impartial juries, should they be prosecuted by the government. The attorney and solicitor general, being consulted, acknowledged that it passed their skill to find a remedy; but a case being laid before Saunders, he advised that something should be discovered which might be set up as a forfeiture of the city charters, and that a *quo warranto* should be brought against the citizens, calling upon them to show by what authority they presumed to act as a corporation. Nothing bearing the color even of irregularity could be suggested against them, except that, on the rebuilding and enlarging of the markets after the great fire, a by-law had been made, requiring those who exposed cattle and goods to contribute to the expense of the improvements by the payment of a small toll; and that the lord mayor, aldermen, and commonalty of the city had, in the year 1679, presented a petition to the king lamenting the prorogation of Parliament in the following terms: "Your petitioners are greatly surprised at the late prorogation, whereby the prosecution of the public justice of the kingdom, and the making of necessary provisions for the preservation of your majesty and your Protestant subjects, have received interruption."

Saunders allowed that these grounds of forfeiture were rather scanty, but undertook to make out the by-law to be the usurpation of a power to impose taxes without authority of Parliament, and the petition a seditious interference with the just prerogative of the crown.*

Accordingly, the *quo warranto* was sued out, and, to the plea setting forth the charters under which the citizens of London exercised their privileges as a corporation, he drew an ingenious replication, averring that the citizens had forfeited their charters by usurping a power to impose taxes without authority of Parliament, and by seditiously interfering with the just prerogative of the crown. The written pleadings ended in a demurrer, by which the sufficiency of the replication was referred, as a question of law, to the judgment of the Court of King's Bench.

Saunders was preparing himself to argue the case as counsel for the crown, when, to his utter astonishment, he received a letter from the lord keeper announcing his majesty's pleasure that he should be chief justice. He not only never had intrigued for the office, but his appointment to it had never entered his imagination; and he declared, probably with sincerity, that he would much sooner have remained at the bar, as he doubted whether he could continue to live with the tailor in Butcher Row, and he was afraid that all his favorite habits would be dislocated. This arrangement must have been suggested by cunning lawyers, who were distrustful of Pemberton,

* Saunders was very ingenious; but in the invention of charges to serve the turn of tyranny he has his match in some of our American lawyers. — *Ed.*

and were sure that Saunders might be relied upon. But Roger North ascribed it to Charles himself; not attempting, however, to disguise the corrupt motive for it. "The king," says he, "observing him to be of a free disposition, loyal, friendly, and without greediness or guile, thought of him to be chief justice of the King's Bench *at that nice time.* And the ministry could not but approve of it. So great a weight was then at stake as could not be trusted to men of doubtful principles, or such as any thing might tempt to desert them."

On the 23d of January, being the first day of Hilary term, 1683, Sir Edmund Saunders appeared at the bar of the Court of Chancery, in obedience to a writ requiring him to take upon himself the degree of serjeant at law, and distributed the usual number of gold rings, of the accustomed weight and fineness, with the courtly motto, "*Principi sic placuit.*" He then had his coif put on, and proceeded to the bar of the Common Pleas, where he went through the form of pleading a sham cause as a serjeant. Next he was marched to the bar of the King's Bench, where he saw the lord keeper on the bench, who made him a flowery oration, pretending "that Sir Francis Pemberton, at his own request, had been allowed to resign the office of chief justice of that court, and that his majesty, looking only to the good of his subjects, had selected as a successor him who was allowed to be the fittest, not only for learning, but for every other qualification." The new chief justice, who often expressed a sincere dislike of *palaver*, contented himself with repeating the motto on his rings, "*Principi sic placuit;*" and having taken the oaths, was placed on the bench, and at once began the business of the court.

In a few days afterwards came on to be argued the great case of *The King* v. *the Mayor and Commonalty of the City of London.* Fitch, the solicitor general, appeared for the crown; and Treby, the recorder of London, for the defendants. The former was heard very favorably; but the latter having contended that, even if the by-law and the petition were illegal, they must be considered only as the acts of the individuals who had concurred in them, and could not affect the privileges of the body corporate, — an *ens legis,* without a soul, and without the capacity of sinning, — Lord Chief Justice Saunders exclaimed, —

"According to your notion, never was one corporate act done by them; certainly, whatsoever the Common Council does, binds the whole; otherwise it is impossible for you to do any corporate act; for you never do, and never can, convene all the citizens. Then you say your petition is no reflection on the king, but it says that by the prorogation public justice was interrupted. If so, by whom was public justice interrupted? Why, by the king! And is it no reflection on the king that, instead of distributing justice to his people, he prevents them from obtaining justice? You must allow that the accusation is either true or false. But, supposing it true that the king did amiss in prorogating the Parliament, the Common Council of London, neither by charter nor prescription, had any right to control him. If the matter were not true, (as it is not,) the petition is a mere calumny. But if you could justify the presenting of the petition, how can you justify the printing of it, whereby the mayor, aldermen, and citizens of London do let all the nation know that the king, by the prorogation of Parliament, hath given the public justice of the nation an interruption? Pray, by what law, or custom, or charter, is this privilege of censure exercised? You stand forth as 'chartered libertines.' As for the *impeccability* of the corporation, and your doctrine that nothing which it does can affect its being, strange would be the result if that which the corporation does is not the act of the corporation, and if, the act being unlawful and wicked, the corporation shall be dispunishable. I tell you, I deliver no opinion now; I only mention some points worthy of consideration. Let the case be argued again next term."

In the ensuing term the case was again argued by Sawyer, the attorney general, for the crown, and Pollexfen for the city, when Lord Chief Justice Saunders said, "We shall take time to be advised of our opinion, but I cannot help now saying what a grievous thing it would be if a corporation cannot be forfeited or dissolved for any crime whatsoever. Then it is plain that you oust the king of his *quo warranto*, and that, as many corporations as there are, so many independent commonwealths are established in England. We shall look into the precedents, and give judgment next term."

When next term arrived, the Lord Chief Justice Saunders was on his death-bed. His course of life was so different from what it had been, and his diet and exercise so changed, that the constitution of his body could not sustain it, and he fell into an apoplexy and palsy from which he never recovered. But before his illness he had secured the votes of his brethren.

The judgment of the court was pronounced by Mr. Justice Jones,* the senior puisne judge, who said, —

* This is not the William Jones mentioned in the life of Lord North, but a person of a different character, one Edward Jones. — *Ed.*

"Several times have we met and had conference about this matter, and we have waited on my Lord Saunders during his sickness often; and upon deliberation, we are unanimously of opinion that a corporation aggregate, such as the city of London, may be forfeited and seized into the king's hands, on a breach of the trust reposed in it for the good government of the king's subjects; that to assume the power of making by-laws to levy money is a just cause of forfeiture; and that the petition in the pleadings mentioned is so scandalous to the king and his government that it is a just cause of forfeiture. Therefore, this court doth award that the liberties and franchises of the city of London be seized into the king's hand."

This judgment was considered a prodigious triumph, but it led directly to the misgovernment which in little more than five years brought about the Revolution and the establishment of a new dynasty. To guard against similar attempts in all time to come, the charters, liberties, and customs of the city of London were then confirmed, and for ever established, by act of Parliament.

Saunders was chief justice so short a time, and this was so completely occupied with the great *Quo Warranto* case, that I have little more to say of him as a judge. We are told that "while he sat in the Court of King's Bench he gave the rule to the general satisfaction of the lawyers."

We have the account of only one trial before him at *nisi prius*, that of *Pilkington, Lord Grey de Werke, and others*, for a riot. Before the city of London was taken by a regular siege, an attempt had been made upon it by a *coup de main*. The scheme was to prevent the regular election of sheriffs, and to force upon the city the two court candidates, who had only a small minority of electors in their favor. In spite of violence used on their behalf, the poll was going in favor of the liberal candidates, when the lord mayor, who had been gained over by the government, pretended to adjourn the election to a future day. The existing sheriffs, who were the proper officers to preside, continued the poll, and declared the liberal candidates duly elected. Nevertheless, the court candidates were sworn in as sheriffs, and those who had insisted on continuing the election after the pretended adjournment by the lord mayor were prosecuted for a riot.* They pleaded not guilty, and a jury to try them having been summoned by the new sheriffs, the trial came on at Guildhall before Lord Chief Justice Saunders. He was then much enfeebled in health, and the excitement produced by it was supposed to have been the cause of the fatal malady by which he was struck a few days after.

The jury being called, the counsel for the defendants put in *a challenge to the array*, on the ground that the supposed sheriffs, by whom the jury had been returned, were not the lawful sheriffs of the city of London, and had an interest in the question.

*L. C. J. Saunders.* — "Gentlemen, I am sorry you should have so bad an opinion of me, and think me so little of a lawyer, as not to know that this is but trifling, and has nothing in it. Pray, gentlemen, do not put these things upon me." *Mr. Thompson.* — "I desire it may be read, my lord." *L. C. J. Saunders.* — "You would not have done this before another judge; you would not have done it if Sir Matthew Hale had been here. There is no law in it." *Mr. Thompson.* — "We

* So we have lately seen five inhabitants of Philadelphia prosecuted for a riot, for aiding to give effect to a statute of that state abolishing negro slavery. — *Ed.*

desire it may be read." *L. C. J. Saunders.* — "This is only to tickle the people." The challenge, however, was read. *Jeffreys.* — "Here is a tale of a tub indeed!" *L. C. J. Saunders.* — "Ay, it is nothing else, and I wonder that lawyers should put such a thing upon me." *Mr. Thompson.* — "My lord, we desire this challenge should be allowed." *L. C. J. Saunders.* — "No, indeed, won't I. There is no color for it." *Mr. Thompson.* — "My lord, is the fact true or false? If it be insufficient in point of law, let them demur." *Jeffreys.* — "'Robin Hood on Greendale stood'!!! I pray for the king that it may be overruled." *Mr. Thompson.* — "My lord, I say where a sheriff is interested in point of title, he is no person in law to return a jury. The very title to the office is here in question." *L. C. J. Saunders.* — "Mr. Thompson, methinks you have found out an invention, that the king should never have power to try it even so long as the world stands. Who would you have the process go to?" *Mr. Thompson.* — "To the coroner." *L. C. J. Saunders.* — "My speech is but bad; let me know what objection is made, and if I can but retain it in my memory, I don't question but to give you satisfaction. The sheriffs who returned the jury are sheriffs *de facto*, and their title cannot thus be inquired into. Wherever the defendant thinks it may go hard with him, are we to have a trial whether the sheriffs be sheriffs or no? What you are doing may be done in every cause that may be trying." *Mr. Thompson.* — "My lord, we pray a bill of exceptions." *Jeffreys.* — "This discourse is only for discourse sake. Swear the jury." *L. C. J. Saunders.* — "Ay, swear the jury."

So far, he was right in point of law; but, when the trial proceeded upon the merits, to suit the purposes of the government and to obtain a conviction he laid down doctrines which he must well have known to be indefensible respecting the power of the lord mayor to interrupt the poll by an adjournment, and the supposed offence of the electors in still continuing the election, they believing that they were exercising a lawful franchise. Finally, in summing up to the jury, he observed, —

"But they pretend that the sheriffs were the men, and that the lord mayor was nobody; that shows that it was somewhat of the Commonwealth seed that was like to grow up among the good corn." [Here the report says, *the people hummed and interrupted my lord.* He thus continued.] "Pray, gentlemen, that is a very indecent thing; you put an indignity upon the king. Pray, gentlemen, forbear; such demeanor does not become a court of justice. When things were topsy turvy I can't tell what was done, and I would be loth to have it raked up now. These defendants tell you that they believed they were acting according to law; but ignorance of the law is now no excuse, and you will consider whether they did not in a tumultuary way make a riot to set up a magistracy by the power of the people? Gentlemen, it hath been a long trial, and it may be I have not taken it well; my memory is bad, and I am but weak. I don't question but your memories are better than mine. Consider your verdict, and find as many guilty as you think fit."

The jury having been carefully packed, the defendants were all found guilty, and they were heavily fined; but after the Revolution this judgment was reversed by the legislature.

During Lord Chief Justice Saunders's last illness, the Ryehouse Plot was discovered, and it was a heavy disappointment to the government that no further aid could be expected from him in the measures still contemplated for cutting off the Whig leaders and depressing the Whig party. His hopeless condition being ascertained, he was deserted and neglected by all his Whitehall patrons, who had lately been so attentive to him, and he received kindness only from humble dependents and some young lawyers, who, notwithstanding all his faults, had been attached to him from his singular good humor.

A few minutes after ten o'clock in the forenoon of Tuesday, the 19th of June, 1683, he expired in a house at Parson's Green, to which he had unwillingly transferred himself from Butcher Row when promoted to be chief justice. His exact age was not known, but he was not supposed to be much turned of fifty, although a stranger who saw him for the first time would have taken him to be considerably more advanced in life. Of his appearance, his manners, and his habits, we have, from one who knew him intimately, the following graphic account, which it would be a sin to abridge or to alter, —

"As to his person, he was very corpulent and beastly — a mere lump of morbid flesh. He used to say, 'by his *troggs*, (such a humorous way of talking he affected,) none could say he wanted issue of his body, for he had nine in his back.' He was a fetid mass that offended his neighbors at the bar in the sharpest degree. Those whose ill fortune it was to stand near him were confessors, and in summer time almost martyrs. This hateful decay of his carcass came upon him by continual sottishness; for, to say nothing of brandy, he was seldom without a pot of ale at his nose or near him. That exercise was all he used; the rest of his life was sitting at his desk or piping at home; and that *home* was a tailor's house, in Butcher Row, called his lodging, and the man's wife was his nurse or worse; but by virtue of his money, of which he made little account, though he got a great deal, he soon became master of the family; and being no changeling, he never removed, but was true to his friends and they to him to the last hour of his life. With all this, he had a goodness of nature and disposition in so great a degree that he may be deservedly styled a *philanthrope*. He was a very Silenus to the boys, as in this place I may term the students of the law, to make them merry whenever they had a mind to it. He had nothing of rigid or austere in him. If any near him at the bar grumbled at his stench, he ever converted the complaint into content and laughing with the abundance of his wit. As to his ordinary dealing, he was as honest as the driven snow was white; and why not, having no regard for money or desire to be rich? And for good nature and condescension, there was not his fellow. I have seen him, for hours and half hours together, before the court sat, stand at the bar, with an audience of students over against him, putting of cases, and debating so as suited their capacities and encouraged their industry. And so in the temple, he seldom moved without a parcel of youths hanging about him, and he merry and jesting with them. Once, after he was in the king's business, he dined with the lord keeper, and there he showed another qualification he had acquired, and that was to play jigs upon a harpsichord, having taught himself with the opportunity of an old virginal of his landlady's; but in such a manner, not for defect but figure, as to see him was a jest."

23

His Reports are entertaining as well as instructive.* Notwithstanding his carelessness about money, he left considerable property behind him.

* The editions of these Reports by the late Serjeant Williams, and by the present most learned judges, Mr. Justice Patteson and Mr. Justice Vaughan Williams, illustrated by admirable notes, may be said to embody the whole common law of England, scattered about, I must confess, rather immethodically.

# CHAPTER XV.

## GEORGE JEFFREYS.*

George Jeffreys was a younger son of John Jeffreys, Esq., of Acton, near Wrexham, in Denbighshire, a gentleman of a respectable Welsh family, and of small fortune. His mother was a daughter of Sir Thomas Ireland, Knight, of the County Palatine of Lancaster. Never was child so unlike parents; for they were both quiet, sedate, thrifty, unambitious persons, who aspired not higher than to be well reputed in the parish in which they lived, and decently to rear their numerous offspring. Some imputed to the father a niggardly and covetous disposition; but he appears only to have exercised a becoming economy, and to have lived at home with his consort in peace and happiness till he was made more anxious than pleased by the irregular advancement of his boy George. It is said that he had an early presentiment that this son would come to a violent end; and was particularly desirous that he should be brought up to some steady trade, in which he might be secured from temptation and peril.

He was born in his father's lowly dwelling at Acton in the year 1648. He showed, from early infancy, the lively parts, the active temperament, the outward good humor, and the

* The name is spelt no fewer than eight different ways — "Jeffries," "Jefferies," "Jefferys," "Jeffereys," "Jefferyes," "Jeffrys," "Jeffryes," and "Jeffreys," and he himself spelt it differently at different times of his life; but the last spelling is that which is found in his patent of peerage, and which he always used afterwards.

overbearing disposition which distinguished him through life. He acquired an ascendancy among his companions in his native village by coaxing some and intimidating others, and making those most opposed to each other believe that he favored both. At marbles and leap-frog he was known to take undue advantages; and nevertheless, he contrived, notwithstanding secret murmurs, to be acknowledged as "master of the revels."

While still young, he was put to the free school at the town of Shrewsbury, which was then considered a sort of metropolis for North Wales. Here he continued for two or three years; but we have no account how he demeaned himself. At the end of this time his father, though resolved to bind him apprentice to a shopkeeper in Wales, sent him for a short time to St. Paul's School, in the city of London. The sight of the metropolis had a most extraordinary effect upon the mind of this ardent youth, and exceedingly disgusted him with the notion of returning into Denbighshire, to pass his life in a small provincial town as a mercer. On the first Sunday in every term he saw the judges and the serjeants come in grand procession to St. Paul's Cathedral, and afterwards go to dine with the lord mayor — appearing little inferior to this great sovereign of the city in power and splendor. He heard that some of them had been poor boys like himself, who had pushed themselves on without fortune or friends; and though he was not so presumptuous as to hope, like another Whittington, to rise to be lord mayor, he was resolved that he would be lord chief justice or lord chancellor.

Now it was that he acquired whatever scholarship he ever possessed. Jeffreys applied with considerable diligence to Greek and Latin, though occasionally flogged for idleness and insolence. He at last ventured to disclose his scheme of becoming a great lawyer to his father, who violently opposed it, as wild and romantic and impossible, and who inwardly dreaded that, from involving him in want and distress, it might lead to some fatal catastrophe. He wrote back to his son, pointing out the inability of the family to give him a university education, or to maintain him at the inns of court till he should have a chance of getting into practice — his utter want of connections in London, and the hopelessness of his entering into a contest in an overstocked profession with so many who had the advantage of superior education, wealth, and patronage. Although the aspirant professed himself unconvinced by these arguments, and still tried to show the certainty of his success at the bar, he must have stood a crop-eared apprentice behind a counter in Denbigh, Ruthyn, or Flint, if it had not been for his maternal grandmother, who was pleased to see the blood of the Irelands break out, and who, having a small jointure, offered to contribute a part of it for his support. The university was still beyond their means ; but it was thought this might be better dispensed with if he should be for some time at one of the great schools of royal foundation, where he might form acquaintances afterwards to be useful to him. The father reluctantly consented, in the hope that his son would soon return to his sober senses, and that the project would be abandoned with the general concurrence of the family. Meanwhile young George was transferred to Westminster School, then under the rule of the celebrated Busby.

There is reason to fear that the zeal for improvement which he had exhibited at St. Paul's soon left him, and that he here began to acquire those habits of intemperance which afterwards proved so fatal to him. His father hearing of these had all his fears revived, and when the boy was at Acton during the holidays, again tried in vain to induce him to become a tradesman. But finding all dissuasions unavailing, the old gentleman withdrew his opposition, giving him a gentle pat on the back, accompanied by these words — "Ah, George, George, I fear thou wilt die with thy shoes and stockings on!"

Yet the wayward youth, while at Westminster, had fits of application, and carried away from thence a sufficient stock of learning to prevent him from appearing in after-life grossly deficient when any question of grammar arose. He was fond of reminding the world of the great master under whom he had studied.

His confidence in his own powers was so great, that, without conforming to ordinary rules, he expected to overcome every obstacle. Being now in the neighborhood of Westminster Hall, his ambition to be a great lawyer was inflamed by seeing the grand processions on the first day of term, and by occasionally peeping into the courts when an important trial was going forward. When he was actually lord chancellor, he used to relate that, while a boy at Westminster School, he had a dream, in which a gipsy read his fortune, foretelling "that he should be the chief scholar there, and should afterwards enrich himself by study and industry, and that he should come to be the second man in the kingdom, but in conclusion should fall into disgrace and misery."

He was now sixteen, an age after which it was not usual to remain at school in those days. A family council was called at Acton, and as George still sanguinely adhered to the law, it was settled that, the university being quite beyond their reach, he should immediately be entered at an inn of court; that, to support him there, his grandmother should allow him forty pounds a year, and that his father should add ten pounds a year for decent clothing.

On the 19th of May, 1663, to his great joy, he was admitted a member of the Inner Temple. He got a small and gloomy chamber, in which, with much energy, he began his legal studies. He not only had a natural boldness of eloquence, but an excellent head for law. With steadiness of application he would have greatly excelled Lord Keeper Guilford, and in the mastery of this science would have rivalled Lord Hale and Lord Nottingham. But he could not long resist the temptations of bad company. Having laid in a very slender stock for a counsel or a judge, he forsook Littleton and Plowden, "moots and readings," for the tavern, where was his chief delight. He seems to have escaped the ruinous and irreclaimable vice of gaming, but to have fallen into all others to which reckless templars were prone. Nevertheless, he had ever a keen eye to his own interest; and in these scenes of dissipation he assiduously cultivated the acquaintance of young attorneys and their clerks, who might afterwards be useful to him. When they met over a bowl of punch at the Devil tavern, or some worse place, he charmed them with songs and jokes, and took care to bring out before them, opportunely, any scrap of law which he had picked up, to impress them with the notion that, when he put on his gown and applied to business, he should be able to win all the causes in which he might be retained. He was exceedingly popular, and he had many invitations to dinner; which, to make his way in the world, he thought it better to accept than to waste his time over the midnight oil in acquiring knowledge which it might never be known that he possessed.

After the first fervor of loyalty which burst out at the restoration had passed away, a malcontent party was formed, which gradually gained strength. In this, most of the aspiring young lawyers, not actually employed by the government, were ranged — finding it politic to begin in "the sedition line," that their value might be better appreciated by the court, and a better price might be bid for them. From such reasoning, or perhaps from accidental circumstances, Jeffreys associated himself with the popular leaders, and in the hour of revelry would drink on his knees any toasts to "the good old cause," and to "the immortal memory of old Noll."

He was often put to great shifts from the embarrassed state of his finances, the ten pounds for "decent clothing" for a year being expended in a single suit of cut velvet, and his grandmother's forty pounds being insufficient to pay his tavern bills. But he displayed much address in obtaining prolonged and increased credit from his tradesmen. He borrowed adroitly; and it is said that such an impression was made by his opening talents, that several wealthy men on the popular side voluntarily made him presents of money, in the hope of the important services they were speedily to receive from his support.

It is very much to be regretted that we have not from a Roger North more minute information with respect to the manner in which his character was formed, and his abilities were cultivated. He seems to have been a most precocious young man. While still in his twentieth year, he was not only familiarly acquainted with the town, and completely a man of the world, exciting confident expectations of great future eminence, but he was already received among veteran statesmen as a member of an important party in the state, consulted as to their movements, and regarded as their future leader.

After keeping all his terms, and doing all his exercises, he was regularly called to the bar on the 22d day of November, 1668 — having been on the books of the society five years and six months — the requisite period of probation having been previously, by a general regulation, reduced from seven to the present period of five years.

Although he does not ever appear to have been chosen "reader" or "treasurer" of the society, yet in the year 1678, on being elected recorder of London, he was made a bencher, and he continued to be so till he took the coif, when he necessarily left it for Serjeants' Inn.

During his early career he was involved in difficulties, which could only have been overcome by uncommon energy. Pressed by creditors, and at a loss to provide for the day that was passing over him, he had burdened himself with the expenses of a family. But this arose out of a speculation, which, in the first instance, was very prudent. Being a handsome young fellow, and capable of making himself acceptable to modest women, notwithstanding the bad company which he kept, he resolved to repair his fortunes by marrying an heiress; and he fixed upon the daughter of a country gentleman of large possessions, who, on account of his agreeable qualities, had invited him to his house. The daughter, still very young, was cautiously guarded, and almost always confined to her chamber; but Jeffreys contrived to make a confidant and friend of a poor relation of hers, who was the daughter of a country parson, and lived with her as a companion. Through this agency he had established a correspondence with the heiress, and an interest in her affections, so that on his last visit she had agreed, if her father's consent could not be obtained, to elope with him. What was his disappointment, soon after his return to his dismal chamber in the Inner Temple, which he had hoped soon to exchange for a sumptuous manor-house, to receive a letter from the *companion*, informing him "that his correspondence with the *heiress* had been discovered by the old father, who was in such a rage, that locking up her cousin, he had instantly turned herself out of doors, and that having taken shelter in the house of an acquaintance in Holborn, she was there in a state of great destitution and distraction, afraid to return to her father, or to inform him of what had happened." The conduct of Jeffreys on this occasion may be truly considered the brightest passage in his history. He went to her, found her in tears, and considering that he had been the means of ruining her prospects in life, (to say nothing of her being much handsomer than her rich cousin,) he offered her his hand. She consented. Her father, notwithstanding the character and circumstances of his proposed son-in-law, out of regard to his daughter's reputation, sanctioned their union, and to the surprise of all parties, gave her a fortune of three hundred pounds.

She made an excellent wife, and I do not find any complaint of his having used her ill till near the time of her death, a few years after, when he had cast his affections upon the lady who became the second Mrs. Jeffreys. Meanwhile he left her at her father's, occasionally visiting her; and he continued to carry on his former pursuits, and to strengthen his connections in London, with a view to his success at the bar, on which he resolutely calculated with unabated confidence.

He was not disappointed. Never had a young lawyer risen so rapidly into practice. But he cut out a new line for himself. Instead of attending in Westminster Hall to take notes in law French of the long-winded arguments of serjeants and eminent counsel, where he would have had little chance of employment, he did not go near any of the superior courts for some years, but confined himself to the Old Bailey, the London Sessions, and Hicks's Hall. There he was soon "the cock of the walk."

Some of his pot companions were now of great use to him in bringing him briefs, and recommending him to business. All this pushing would have been of little avail if he had not fully equalled expectation by the forensic abilities which he displayed. He had a very sweet and powerful voice, having something in its tone which immediately fixed the attention, so that his audience always were compelled to listen to him, irrespective of what he said. "He was of bold aspect, and cared not for the countenance of any man." He was extremely voluble, but always perspicuous and forcible, making use of idiomatic, and familiar, and colloquial, and sometimes of coarse language. He never spared any assertion that was likely to serve his client. He could get up a point of law so as to argue it with great ability, and with the justices, as well as with juries, his influence was unbounded. He was particularly famous for his talent in cross-examination, indulging in ribaldry and banter to a degree which would not now be permitted. The audience being ever ready to take part with the persecuted witness, the laugh was sometimes turned against him. It is related that, about this time, beginning to cross-examine a witness in *a leathern doublet*, who had made out a complete case against his client, he bawled forth — "You fellow in the leathern doublet, pray what have you for swearing?" The man looked steadily at him, and "Truly, sir," said he, "if you have no more for lying than I have for swearing, you might wear a leathern doublet as well as I." This blunt reply got to the west end of the town, and was remembered among the courtiers against Jeffreys when he grew to be a great man.

While a trial was going on, he was devotedly earnest in it; but when it was over, he would recklessly get drunk, as if he never were to have another to conduct. Coming so much in contact with the aldermen, he ingratiated himself with them very much, and he was particularly patronized by a namesake (though no relation) of his own — Jeffreys, alderman of Bread Street Ward, who was very wealthy, a great smoker, (an accomplishment in which the lawyer could rival him, as well as in drinking,) and who had immense influence with the livery.

Pushed by him, or rising rapidly by his own buoyancy, our hero, before he had been two years and a half at the bar, and while only twenty-three years of age, was elected common serjeant of the city of London — an office which has raised a Denman as well as a Jeffreys to be chief justice of England. This first step of his elevation he obtained on the 17th of March, 1671.

But his ambition was only inflamed by this promotion, which disqualified him for a considerable part of his bar practice, and he resolved entirely to change the field of his operations, making a dash at Westminster Hall. He knew well that he could not be employed to draw declarations and pleas, or to argue demurrers or special verdicts; but he hoped his talent for examining witnesses and for speaking might avail him. At any rate, this was the only road to high distinction in his profession, and he spurned the idea of spending his life in trying petty larcenies, and dining with the city companies.

Hard drinking was again his grand resource. He could now afford to invite the great city attorneys to his house as well as carouse with them at taverns, and they were pleased with the attentions of a rising barrister as well as charmed with the pleasantry of the most jovial of companions. He likewise began to cultivate fashionable society, and to consider how he might contrive to get an introduction at court. "He put himself into all companies, for which he was qualified by using himself to drink hard." Now was the time when men got forward in life by showing their hatred of puritanism, their devotion to church and king, and an affectation of vice, even if actually free from it.

Yet such was the versatility of Jeffreys, that for the nonce he could appear sanctimonious, and even puritanical. Thus he deceived the religious, the moral, the immaculate Sir Matthew Hale, then chief justice of the King's Bench. Roger North, in drawing the character of this extraordinary man, says, — "Although he was very grave in his own person, he loved the most bizarre and irregular wits in the practice of the law before him most extravagantly. So Sir George Jeffreys gained as great an ascendant in practice over him as ever counsel had over a judge."

As a King's Bench practitioner, Jeffreys was first employed at Nisi Prius in actions for assaults and defamation; but before long the city attorneys gave him briefs in commercial causes tried at Guildhall, and though in *banc* he could not well stand up against regularly-bred lawyers, like Sir Francis North, Sir William Jones, Sir Creswell Levinz, and Heneage Finch, the son of the Lord Chancellor Nottingham, he was generally equal to them before a jury, and he rapidly trod upon their heels.

He anxiously asked himself how he was to climb to high office. He had started with the disaffected party, and they had been of essential use to him; but though they were growing in strength, no chance existed of their being able to make attorney generals, chief justices, or chancellors. At the same time he did not like yet to break with those who might still serve him — particularly in obtaining the recordership, which he coveted as a stepping stone to something better. He resolved so to manage as to be a favorite of both parties till he could devote himself entirely, and exclusively, and openly to the one which should be dominant; and he again succeeded.

From his well-known influence in the city he found no difficulty in making the acquaintance of Will Chiffinch, "the trusty page of the back stairs," who, besides other employments of a still more confidential nature, was intrusted by Charles II. to get at the secrets of all men of any consequence in every department of life. "This Mr. Chiffinch," says Roger North, "was a true secretary as well as page, for he had a lodging at the back stairs, which might have been properly termed 'the Spy Office,' where the king spoke with particular persons about intrigues of all kinds; and all little informers, projectors, &c., were carried to Chiffinch's lodging. He was a most impetuous drinker, and in that capacity an admirable spy; for he let none part with him sober, if it were possible to get them drunk, and his great artifice was pushing idolatrous healths of his good master, and being always in haste; *for the king is coming;* which was his word. Being an Hercules well breathed at the sport himself, he commonly had the better, and so fished out many secrets, and discovered men's characters, which the king could never have obtained the knowledge of by any other means. It is likely that Jeffreys, being a pretender to main feats with the citizens, might forward himself, and be entertained by Will Chiffinch, and that which at first was mere spying turn to acquaintance, if not friendship, such as is apt to grow up between immense drinkers, and from thence might spring recommendations of him to the king, as the most useful man that could be found to serve his majesty in London."

Thus, while Mr. Common Serjeant was caballing in the city with Lord Shaftesbury, who had established himself in Aldersgate Street, and talked of becoming lord mayor, he had secretly got a footing at court, and by assurances of future services disposed the government to assist him in all his jobs. His opposition friends were a little startled by hearing that he had been made solicitor to the Duke of York; but he assured them that this was merely a professional employment, unconnected with politics, which, according to professional etiquette, he could not decline; and when he was knighted as a mark of royal favor, with which he was silly enough to be much tickled, he said that he was obliged reluctantly to submit to the degradation as a consequence of his employment.

By some mischance, which is not explained, he missed the office of recorder on the vacancy occasioned by the resignation of Sir John Howel, who so outraged public decency on the trial of Penn and Mead; but Sir William Dolbein, the successful candidate, being made a judge on the 22d of October, 1678, Jeffreys was then elected his successor. Upon this occasion there were three other candidates; but he was so warmly supported by both parties in politics, that they all withdrew before the day of nomination, and he is said in the city records to have been "freely and unanimously elected."

The new recorder had hardly been sworn in, when feeling that the liberals could do nothing more for him, he utterly cast them off, becoming for the rest of his life the open, avowed, unblushing slave of the court, and the bitter, persecuting, and unappeasable enemy of the principles he had before supported, and of the men he had professed to love.

He entirely forsook Thanet House, in Aldersgate Street, and all the meetings of the Whigs in the city; and instead of secret interviews with Will Chiffinch in the "Spy Office," he went openly to court, and with his usual address, he contrived, by constant assiduities and flatteries, to gain the good graces both of Nell Gwyn and of the Duchess of Portsmouth, who, since the fall of Lady Castlemaine, held divided empire at Whitehall, balancing the Roman Catholic and Protestant parties. To each of these ladies, it would appear from the libels of the day, his rise was attributed.

However, not long after he had openly ratted, an accident happened that had like to have spoiled all his projects; and that was the breaking out of the Popish plot. Although there is no reasonable ground for saying that it was contrived by Shaftesbury, he made such skilful and unscrupulous use of it, that suddenly, from appearing the leader of a small, declining, and despairing party, he had the city and the nation at his beck, and with a majority in both houses of Parliament, there seemed every probability that he would soon force himself upon the king, and have at his disposal all the patronage of the government. Jeffreys was for some time much disconcerted, and thought that once in his life he had made a false move. He was utterly at a loss how to conduct himself, and his craft never was put to so severe a trial.

Being called into council, he recommended that the government should profess to credit the plot, and should outvie the other side in zeal for the Protestant religion, but should contrive to make Shaftesbury answerable for the reality of the conspiracy; so that, if hereafter it should blow up, or the people should get tired of it, all that was done to punish the supposed authors of it might be laid to his account.

He immediately began diligently to work the Popish plot according to his own scheme. Coleman, Whitbread, Ireland, and all whom Oates and Bedloe accused being committed to prison, it was resolved to prosecute them for high treason in having compassed the death of the king, as well as the overthrow of the Protestant religion; and their trials were conducted by the government as state trials, partly at the bar of the Court of King's Bench, and partly at the Old Bailey. In the former Jeffreys acted as a counsel, in the latter as a judge. It is asserted, and not improbably, that he had a real horror of Popery, which, though he could control it in the presence of the Duke of York, and when his interest required, at other times burst out with sincerity as well as fierceness.

Scroggs presided at the Old Bailey, but Jeffreys whetted his fury by telling him that the king was a thorough believer in the plot, and by echoing his expressions; as, when the chief justice said to the jury, "You have done like honest men," he exclaimed in a stage whisper, "They have done like honest men." As mouthpiece of the lord mayor, the head of the commission, after conviction he had the pleasing duty of passing sentence of death by the protracted tortures which the law of treason prescribed.

He had a still greater treat in passing the like sentence on Richard Langhorne, an eminent Catholic barrister, with whom he had been familiarly acquainted. He first addressed generally the whole batch of the prisoners convicted, whom he thus continues to upbraid for trying to root out "the best of religions:" "I call it the best of religions, even for your sakes; for had it not been for the sake of our religion, that teaches us not to make such requitals as yours seems to teach you, you had not had this fair, formal trial, but murder would have been returned to you for the murder you intended to commit both upon the king and most of his people. What a strange sort of religion is that whose doctrine seems to allow them to be the greatest saints in another world who have been the most impudent sinners in this! Murder and the blackest of crimes were the best means among you to get a man to be canonized a saint hereafter." Then he comes to his brother lawyer — "There is one gentleman that stands at the bar whom I am very sorry to see, with all my heart, in this condition, because of some acquaintance I have had with him heretofore. To see that a man who hath understanding in the law, and who hath arrived at so great an eminency in that profession as this gentleman hath done, should not remember that it is not only against the rules of Christianity, but even against the rules of his profession, to attempt any injury against the person of the king! He knows it is against all the rules of law to endeavor to introduce a foreign power into this land. So that you have sinned both against your conscience and your own certain knowledge." Last of all, he offers his friend the assistance of a Protestant divine to prepare him for a speedy departure, and, referring him to the statute whereby the ministration of a Catholic priest is made illegal, he himself, though "a layman," gives him some "pious advice." He had carried the sympathies of his audience along with him, for, when he had concluded with the "quartering," he was greeted with a loud shout of applause.

Thus, by the powerful assistance of the recorder, did the government obtain popularity for prosecuting the plot, till the people at last actually did get tired of it, and Shaftesbury was prevented from deriving any fruit from it beyond the precarious tenure, for a few months, of his office of president of the council.

The recorder was equally zealous, on all other occasions, to do what he thought would be agreeable at court. With the view of repressing public discussion, he laid down for law, as he said, on the authority of all the judges, "that no person whatsoever could expose to the public knowledge any thing that concerned the affairs of the public without license from the king, or from such persons as he may think fit to intrust with that power."

The grand jury having several times returned "*ignoramus*" to an indictment against one Smith for a libel, in respect of a very innocent publication, though they were sent out of court to reconsider the finding, he at last exclaimed, "God bless me from such jurymen. I will see the face of every one of them, and let others see them also." He accordingly cleared the bar, and, calling the jurymen one by one, put the question to them, and made each of them repeat the word "*ignoramus*." He then went on another tack, and addressing the defendant, said, in a coaxing tone, "Come, Mr. Smith, there are two persons besides you whom this jury have brought in *ignoramus;*

but they have been ingenuous enough to confess, and I cannot think to fine them little enough; they shall be fined twopence for their ingenuity in confessing. Well, come, Mr. Smith, we know who hath formerly owned both printing and publishing this book." *Smith.* — "Sir, my ingenuity hath sufficiently experienced the reward of your severity; and, besides, I know no law commands me to accuse myself; neither shall I; and the jury have done like true Englishmen and worthy citizens, and blessed be God for such a jury." Jeffreys was furious, but could only vent his rage by committing the defendant till he gave security for his good behavior.

Such services were not to go unrewarded. It was the wish of the government to put the renegade Jeffreys into the office of chief justice of Chester, so often the price of political apostasy; but Sir Job Charlton, a very old gentleman, who now held it, could not be prevailed upon voluntarily to resign, for he had a considerable estate in the neighborhood, and was loath to be stripped of his dignity. Jeffreys, supported by the Duke of York, pressed the king hard, urging that "a Welshman ought not to judge his countrymen," and a message was sent to Sir Job that he was to be removed. The old gentleman was imperfectly consoled with the place of puisne judge of the Common Pleas, which, in the reign of James II., he was subsequently allowed to exchange for his beloved Chester. Meanwhile he was succeeded by Jeffreys, "more Welshman than himself," who was at the same time made counsel for the crown, at Ludlow, where a court was still held for Wales.

Immediately afterwards, the new chief justice was called to the degree of the coif, and made king's serjeant, whereby he had precedence in Westminster Hall of the attorney and solicitor general. The motto on his rings, with great brevity and point, inculcated the prevailing doctrines of divine right and passive obedience — "*A Deo Rex, a Rege Lex.*" As a further mark of royal favor, there was conferred upon him the hereditary dignity of a baronet. He still retained the recordership of London, and had extensive practice at the bar.

The great prosperity which Jeffreys now enjoyed had not the effect which it ought to have produced upon a good disposition, by making him more courteous and kind to others. When not under the sordid dread of injuring himself by offending superiors, he was universally insolent and overbearing. Being made chief justice of Chester, he thought that all puisne judges were beneath him, and he would not behave to them with decent respect, even when practising before them. At the Kingston assizes, Baron Weston having tried to check his irregularities, he complained that he was not treated like a counsellor, being curbed in the management of his brief. *Weston, B.* — "Sir George, since the king has thrust his favors upon you, and made you chief justice of Chester, you think to run down every body; if you find yourself aggrieved, make your complaint; here's nobody cares for you." *Jeffreys.* — "I have not been used to make complaints, but rather to stop those that are made." *Weston, B.* — "I desire, sir, that you will sit down." He sat down, and is said to have wept with anger. His intemperate habits had so far shaken his nerves, that he shed tears very freely on any strong emotion.

We may be prepared for his playing some fantastic tricks before his countrymen at Chester, where he was subject to no control; but the description of his conduct there by Lord Delamere, (afterwards Earl of Warrington,) in denouncing it in the House of Commons, must surely be overcharged: —

"The county for which I serve is Cheshire, which is a county palatine; and we have two judges peculiarly assigned us by his majesty. Our puisne judge I have nothing to say against; he is a very honest man, for aught I know; but I cannot be silent as to our chief judge; and I will name him, because what I have to say will appear more probable. His name is Sir George Jeffreys, who, I must say, behaved himself more like a jack-pudding than with that gravity which becomes a judge. He was witty upon the prisoners at the bar. He was very full of his jokes upon people that came to give evidence, not suffering them to declare what they had to say in their own way and method, but would interrupt them because they behaved themselves with more gravity than he. But I do not insist upon this, nor upon the late hours he kept up and down our city; it's said he was every night drinking till two o'clock, or beyond that time, and that he went to his chamber drunk; but this I have only by common fame, for I was not in his company; I bless God I am not a man of his principles and behavior; but in the mornings he appeared with the symptoms of a man that overnight had taken a large cup. That which I have to say is the complaint of every man, especially of them that had any lawsuits. Our chief justice has a very arbitrary power in appointing the assize when he pleases, and this man has strained it to the highest point; for whereas we were accustomed to have two assizes, the first about April or May, the latter about September, it was this year the middle (as I remember) of August before we had any assize; and then he despatched business so well that he left half the causes untried; and, to help the matter, has resolved we shall have no more assizes this year."

Being tired of revelling in Chester, he put a sudden end to

his first assize there, that he might pay a visit to his native place; to which I am afraid he was less prompted by a pious wish to embrace his father, who had been so resolutely bent on making him a shopkeeper, and who, from the stories propagated about his conduct as a judge, still expressed some misgivings about him, as to dazzle his old companions with the splendor of his new state. Accordingly he came with such a train that the cider barrels at Acton ran very fast, and the larder was soon exhausted; whereupon the old gentleman, in a great fret, charged his son with a design to ruin him, by bringing a whole county at his heels, and warned him against again attempting the same prodigality.

But a violent political storm now arose, which threatened entirely to overwhelm our hero, and from which he did not escape unhurt. In the struggle which arose from the long delay to assemble Parliament, he had leagued himself strongly with the "Abhorrers" against the "Petitioners," and proceedings were instituted in the House of Commons on this ground, against him along with Chief Justice Scroggs and Chief Justice North.

A petition from the city of London, very numerously signed, having been presented, complaining that the recorder had obstructed the citizens in their attempts to have Parliament assembled for the redress of grievances, a select committee was appointed, who, having heard evidence on the subject, and examined him in person, presented a report, on which the following resolutions were passed: —

"That Sir George Jeffreys, recorder of the city of London, by traducing and obstructing petitioning for the sitting of this Parliament, hath destroyed the right of the subject.

"That an humble address be presented to his majesty, to remove Sir George Jeffreys out of all public offices.

"That the members of this house serving for the city of London do communicate these resolutions to the Court of Aldermen for the said city."

The king was stanch, and returned for answer to the address the civil refusal "that he would consider of it;" * but Jeffreys, who, where he apprehended personal danger, was "none of the intrepids," quailed under the charge, and, afraid of further steps being taken against him, came to an understanding that he should give up the recordership, which his enemies wished to be conferred upon their partisan, Sir George Treby. The king was much chagrined at the loss of such a valuable recorder, and said sarcastically that "he was not Parliament-proof." But he was obliged to acquiesce, and Jeffreys, having been reprimanded on his knees at the bar, was discharged. The address of Speaker Williams was very bitter, and caused deep resentment in the mind of Jeffreys. On the 2d of December he actually did resign his office, and Treby was chosen to succeed him.

In a few days after there was exhibited one of Lord Shaftesbury's famous Protestant processions, on the anniversary of the accession of Queen Elizabeth. In this rode a figure on horseback, to represent the ex-recorder, with his face to the tail, and a label on his back, "I am an Abhorrer." At Temple Bar he was thrown into a bonfire, coupled with the devil; the preceding pair, who suffered the same fate, being Sir Roger L'Estrange † and the Pope of Rome.

* "*Le roy s'avisera*," the royal veto to a bill passed by the two houses.

† Roger L'Estrange was a noted pamphleteer, one of the oracles of the high church and Tory party, and the founder of the first English newspaper. — *Ed.*

However, all these indignities endeared him to the court; and his pusillanimity was forgiven from the recollection of past and the hope of future services. A petition from the city being presented to the king at Hampton Court, he attended as a liveryman, though no longer the mouthpiece of the corporation, when he was treated with marked civility by Charles, and detained to dinner, while the lord mayor and aldermen and the new recorder were sent off with a reprimand.

To oblige the court, and to assist them in their criminal jobs, he accepted the appointment of chairman of the Middlesex sessions at Hicks's Hall, although it was somewhat beneath his dignity, and it deprived him of a portion of his practice. Here the grand jury were sworn in; and as they were returned by sheriffs whom the city of London elected, and who were still of the liberal party, the problem was to have them remodelled, so that they might find bills of indictment against all whom the government wished to prosecute. With this view, Jeffreys declared that none should serve except true church of England men; and he ordered the under-sheriff to return a new panel purged of all sectarians. He had a particular spite against the Presbyterians, who had mainly contributed to his being turned out of the recordership. The under-sheriff disobeying his summons, he ordered the sheriffs to attend next day in person; but in their stead came the new recorder, who urged that, by the privileges of the city of London, they were exempted from attending at Hicks's Hall. He overruled this claim with contempt, and fined the sheriffs one hundred pounds. It was found, however, that while the city retained the power of electing the sheriffs, all these attempts to pervert justice would be fruitless.

Jeffreys remained in a state of painful anxiety during Charles's last Westminster Parliament, and during the few days of the Oxford Parliament. The popular party had such a majority in the House of Commons, and seemed so powerful, that it is said the renegade again expressed deep regret that he had left them; but late at night, on Monday, the 28th day of March, 1681, news arrived in London, that early that morning the king had dissolved the Parliament, and had declared his firm determination never to call another. If Jeffreys was still sober, and got drunk that night, we ought to excuse him.

Now his talents were to be brought into full play. In the conflict, the ranks of the enemy being thrown into disorder, the brigade of the lawyers, who had been kept back as a reserve, was marched up to hang on their broken rear, insulting, and to sweep them from the field.

First came on the trial of Fitzharris for high treason. Jeffreys, as counsel for the crown, argued the demurrer to the plea of the pendency of the impeachment; and then, having assisted the Duchess of Portsmouth to evade the questions which were put to her for the purpose of showing that the prisoner had acted under the king's orders, he addressed the jury with great zeal after the solicitor general, and was mainly instrumental in obtaining the conviction.

Next came the trial of Archbishop Plunkett, the Roman Catholic Primate of Ireland, in which Jeffreys was so intemperate that the attorney general was obliged to check him, that the prisoner might have some show of fair play. But it was on the trial of College, "the Protestant joiner," * that he

* See the account of this trial in the life of North, Lord Guilford, ante, p. 210.

gave the earliest specimen of his characteristic ribaldry, and his talent for jesting in cases of life and death, which shone out so conspicuously when he was lord chief justice of the King's Bench. He began with strongly justifying the act of taking from the prisoner the papers he was to use in his defence, saying, that to allow him to see them would be "assigning counsel to him with a vengeance." A witness having stated that pistols were found in the prisoner's holsters when he was attending the city members at Oxford, he exclaimed with a grin, "I think a *chisel* might have been more proper for a *joiner*."

There was called as a witness, by the prisoner, one Lun, who, being a waiter at the Devil Tavern and a fanatic, had some years before been caught on his knees praying against the Cavaliers, saying, "Scatter them, good Lord! Scatter them!" from whence he had ever after borne the nickname of "Scatter'em." Jeffreys thus begins his cross-examination: "We know you, Mr. Lun; we only ask questions about you that the jury too may know you as well as we." *Lun.* — "I don't care to give evidence of any thing but the truth. I was never on my knees before the Parliament for any thing." *Jeffreys.* — "Nor I neither for much; yet you were once on your knees when you cried, 'Scatter them, good Lord!' Was it not so, Mr. Scatter'em?"

He had next an encounter with the famous Titus Oates, who was called by College, and who, when cross-examined by him, appealed to Sir George Jeffreys's own knowledge of a fact about which he was inquiring. *Jeffreys.* — "Sir George Jeffreys does not intend to be an evidence, I assure you." *Dr. Oates.* — "I do not desire Sir George Jeffreys to be an evidence for me; I had credit in Parliaments, and Sir George had disgrace in one of them." *Jeffreys.* — "Your servant, doctor; you are a witty man and a philosopher." He had his full revenge when the doctor himself was afterwards tried before him.

We may judge of the councillor's general style of treating witnesses by his remark on the trial of Lord Grey de Werke for carrying off the Lady Henrietta Berkeley; when his objection was overruled to the competency of the young lady as a witness for the defendant, although she was not only of high rank and uncommon beauty, but undoubted veracity, he observed, "Truly, my lord, we would prevent perjury if we could."

We now come to transactions which strikingly prove the innate baseness of his nature in the midst of his pretended openness and jolly good humor. He owed every thing in life to the corporation of the city of London. The freemen, in the exercise of their ancient privileges, had raised him from the ground by electing him common serjeant and recorder, and to the influence he was supposed to have in the Court of Common Council and in the Court of Aldermen must be ascribed his introduction to Whitehall and all his political advancement. But when, upon the failure of the prosecution against Lord Shaftesbury, the free municipal constitution of the city became so odious to the government, he heartily entered into the conspiracy to destroy it. It is said that he actually suggested the scheme of having a sheriff nominated by the lord mayor, and he certainly took a very active part in carrying it into execution. On Midsummer day, having planted Lord Chief Justice North in his house in Aldermanbury, that he might be backed by his authority, he himself appeared on the hustings in Guildhall; and when the poll was going against the court candidates, illegally advised the lord mayor to dissolve the hall, and afterwards to declare them duly elected. He did every thing in his power to push on and to assist the great *quo warranto*, by which the city was to be entirely disfranchised.*

When success had crowned these efforts, and Pilkington and Shute, the former sheriffs, with Alderman Cornish and others, were to be tried before a packed jury for a riot at the election, finding that he had the game in his hand, his insolence knew no bounds. The defendants having challenged the array, on the ground that the sheriffs who returned the panel were not lawfully appointed,† as soon as the challenge was read, he exclaimed, "Here's a tale of a tub indeed!" The counsel for the defendants insisted that the challenge was good in law, and at great length argued for its validity.

*Jeffreys.* — "Robin Hood
Upon Greendale stood."

*Thompson, Counsel for the Defendants.* — "If the challenge be not good, there must be a defect in it either in point of law or in point of fact. I pray that the crown may either demur or traverse." *Jeffreys.* — "This discourse is only for discourse sake. I pray the jury may be sworn." *Lord Chief Justice Saunders.* — "Ay, ay, swear the jury." The defendants were, of course, all found guilty; and as there were among them the most eminent of Jeffreys's old city friends, he exerted himself to the utmost not only in gaining a conviction, but in aggravating the sentence.

* See ante, p. 220. † See life of Saunders, ante, p. **261.**

But this was only a case of misdemeanor, in which he could ask for nothing beyond fine and imprisonment. He was soon to be engaged in prosecutions for high treason against the noblest of the land, in which his savage taste for blood might be gratified. The Ryehouse plot broke out, for which there was some foundation; and after the conviction of those who had planned it, Lord Russell was brought to trial at the Old Bailey, on the ground that he had consented to it.

Jeffreys, in the late state trials, had gradually been encroaching on the attorney and solicitor general, Sir Robert Sawyer and Sir Heneage Finch, and in Lord Russell's case, to which the government attached such infinite importance, he almost entirely superseded them. To account for his unexampled zeal, we must remember that the office of chief justice of the King's Bench was still vacant, Saunders having died a few months before, and Lord Keeper North having strongly opposed the appointment of Jeffreys as his successor.

These trials took place before a commission, at the head of which was placed Pemberton, chief justice of the Common Pleas, to whom a chance was thus afforded of earning a reappointment to the chief justiceship of the King's Bench, in which he had been superseded by Saunders.

The case of Colonel Walcot was taken first; and here there was no difficulty, for he had not only joined in planning an insurrection against the government, but was privy to the design of assassinating the king and the Duke of York, and in a letter to the secretary of state he had confessed his complicity, and offered to become a witness for the crown. This trial was meant to prepare the public mind for that of Lord Russell, the great ornament of the Whig party, who had carried the exclusion bill through the House of Commons, and, attended by a great following of Whig members, had delivered it with his own hand to the lord chancellor at the bar of the House of Lords. In proportion to his virtues was the desire to wreak vengeance upon him. But the object was no less difficult than desirable, for he had been kept profoundly ignorant of the intention to offer violence to the royal brothers, from the certainty that he would have rejected it with abhorrence; and although he had been present when there were deliberations respecting the right and the expediency of resistance by force to the government after the system had been established of ruling without Parliaments, he had never concurred in the opinion that there were no longer constitutional means of redress; much less had he concerted an armed insurrection. Notwithstanding all the efforts made to return a prejudiced jury, there were serious apprehensions of an acquittal.

Pemberton, the presiding judge, seems to have been convinced that the evidence against him was insufficient; and although he did not interpose with becoming vigor, by repressing the unfair arts of Jeffreys, who was leading counsel for the crown, and although he did not stop the prosecution, as an independent judge would do in modern times, he cannot be accused of any perversion of law; and, instead of treating the prisoner with brutality, as was wished and expected, he behaved to him with courtesy and seeming kindness.

Lord Russell, on his arraignment at the sitting of the court in the morning, having prayed that the trial should be postponed till the afternoon, as a witness for him was absent, and it had been usual in such case to allow an interval between the arraignment and the trial, Pemberton said, "Why may not this trial be respited till the afternoon?" and the only answer being the insolent exclamation, "Pray call the jury," he mildly added, "My lord, the king's counsel think it not reasonable to put off the trial longer, and we cannot put it off without their consent in this case."

The following dialogue then took place, which introduced the touching display of female tenderness and heroism of the celebrated Rachel, Lady Russell, assisting her martyred husband during his trial — a subject often illustrated both by the pen and the pencil.

*Lord Russell.* — "My lord, may I not have the use of pen, ink, and paper?" *Pemberton.* — "Yes, my lord." *Lord Russell.* — "My lord, may I not make use of any papers I have?" *Pemberton.* — "Yes, by all means." *Lord Russell.* — "May I have somebody write to help my memory?" *Attorney General.* — "Yes, a servant." *Lord Russell.* — "My wife is here, my lord, to do it." *Pemberton.* — "If my lady please to give herself the trouble."

The chief justice admitted Dr. Burnet, Dr. Tillotson, and other witnesses, to speak to the good character and loyal conversation of the prisoner, and gave weight to their testimony, notwithstanding the observation of Jeffreys that "it was easy to express a regard for the king while conspiring to murder him."

Lord Russell had certainly been present at a meeting of the conspirators, when there was a consultation about seizing the king's guards; but he insisted that he came in accidentally, that he had taken no part in the conversation, and that he was not acquainted with their plans. The aspirant chief justice saw clearly where was the pinch of the case, and the attorney general, who was examining Colonel Rumsey, being contented with asking — "Was the prisoner at the debate?" and receiving the answer "Yes," Jeffreys started up, took the witness into his own hands, and calling upon him to draw the inference which was for the jury, pinned the basket by this leading and highly irregular question — "Did you find him averse to it or agreeing to it?" Having got the echoing answer which he suggested, "*Agreeing to it*," he looked round with exultation, and said, "If my Lord Russell now pleases to ask any questions, he may!"

Jeffreys addressed the jury in reply after the solicitor general had finished, and much outdid him in pressing the case against the prisoner, while he disclaimed with horror the endeavor to take away the life of the innocent.

The jury retired, and the courtiers present were in a state of the greatest alarm; for against Algernon Sydney, who was to be tried next, the case was still weaker; and if the two whig chiefs, who were considered already cut off, should recover their liberty, and should renew their agitation, a national cry might be got up for the summoning of Parliament, and a new effort might be made to rescue the country from a Popish successor. These fears were vain. The jury returned a verdict of guilty, and Lord Russell expiated on the scaffold the crime of trying to preserve the religion and liberties of his country.

Jeffreys had all the glory of the verdict of guilty, and as the Lord Chief Justice Pemberton had rather flinched during this trial, and the attorney and solicitor general were thought men who would cry CRAVEN, and as the next case was not less important and still more ticklish, all objections to the proposed elevation of the favorite vanished, and he became chief justice of England, as the only man fit to condemn Algernon Sydney.*

The new chief justice was sworn in on the 29th of September, 1683, and took his seat in the Court of King's Bench on the first day of the following Michaelmas term.

Sydney's case was immediately brought on before him in this court, the indictment being removed by *certiorari* from the Old Bailey, that it might be under his peculiar care. The prisoner wishing to plead some collateral matter, was told by the chief justice that, if overruled, sentence of death would immediately be passed upon him. Though there can be no doubt of the illegality of the conviction, the charge against Jeffreys is unfounded, that he admitted the MS. treatise on government to be read without any evidence of its having been written by the prisoner, beyond "similitude of hands." Two witnesses, who were acquainted with his handwriting from having seen him indorse bills of exchange, swore that they believed it to be his handwriting, and they were corroborated by a third, who, with his privity, had paid notes purporting to be indorsed by him without any complaint ever being made. But the undeniable and ineffaceable atrocity of the case was the lord chief justice's doctrine, that "*scribere est agere*," and that therefore this MS. containing some abstract speculations on different forms of government written many years before, never shown to any human being, and containing nothing beyond the constitutional principles of Locke and Paley, was tantamount to the evidence of a witness to prove an overt act of high treason. "If you believe

* Evelyn, Oct. 4, 1683. "Sir Geo. Jeffreys was advanced, reputed to be most ignorant, but most daring."

that this was Colonel Sydney's book, writ by him, no man can doubt that it is a sufficient evidence that he is guilty of compassing and imagining the death of the king. It fixes the whole power in the Parliament and the people. The king, it says, is responsible to them; the king is but their trustee. Gentlemen, I must tell you I think I ought more than ordinarily to press this upon you, because I know the misfortune of the late unhappy rebellion, and the bringing of the late blessed king to the scaffold, was first begun with such kind of principles. They cried he had betrayed the trust that was delegated to him by the people, so that the case rests not upon two but upon greater evidence than twenty-two witnesses, if you believe this book was writ by him."

The chief justice having had the satisfaction of pronouncing with his own lips the sentence upon Sydney, of death and mutilation, instead of leaving the task as usual to the senior puisne judge, a scene followed which is familiar to every one. *Sydney.* — "Then, O God! O God! I beseech thee to sanctify these sufferings unto me, and impute not my blood to the country; let no inquisition be made for it, but if any, and the shedding of blood that is innocent must be revenged, let the weight of it fall only upon those that maliciously persecute me for righteousness sake." *Lord C. J. Jeffreys.* — "I pray God work in you a temper fit to go unto the other world, for I see you are not fit for this." *Sydney.* — "My lord, feel my pulse [holding out his hand,] and see if I am disordered. I bless God I never was in better temper than I now am." By order of the chief justice, the lieutenant of the tower immediately removed the prisoner.

A very few days after, and while this illustrious patriot was still lying under sentence of death, the Lord Chief Justice

Jeffreys and Mr. Justice Withins, who sat as his brother judge on the trial, went to a gay city wedding, where the lord mayor and other grandees were present. Evelyn, who was of the party, tells us that the chief and the puisne both "danced with the bride and were exceeding merry." He adds, "These great men spent the rest of the afternoon until eleven at night in drinking healths, taking tobacco, and talking much beneath the gravity of judges, who had but a day or two before condemned Mr. Algernon Sydney."

The next exhibition in the court of King's Bench which particularly pleased Jeffreys and horrified the public, was the condemnation of Sir Thomas Armstrong. This gentleman was outlawed while beyond the seas, and being sent from Holland within the year, sought, according to his clear right in law, to reverse the outlawry.* I have had occasion to reprobate the conduct of Lord Keeper North in refusing him his writ of error, and suffering his execution; but Jeffreys may be considered the executioner. When brought up to the King's Bench bar, Armstrong was attended by his daughter, a most beautiful and interesting young woman, who, when the chief justice had illegally overruled the plea, and pronounced judgment of death under the outlawry, exclaimed, "My lord, I hope you will not murder my father." *Chief Justice Jeffreys.* — "Who is this woman? Marshal, take her into custody. Why, how now? Because your relative is attainted for high treason, must you take upon you to tax the courts of justice for murder when we grant execution according to law? Take her away." *Daughter.* — "God Almigh-

* Stat. 6 Ed. 6 enacted that if any outlaw yielded himself to the chief justice, &c., within a year, he should be discharged of the outlawry, and entitled to a jury.

ty's judgments light upon you." *Chief Justice Jeffreys.* — "God Almighty's judgments will light upon those that are guilty of high treason." *Daughter.* — "Amen. I pray God." *Chief Justice Jeffreys.* — "So say I. I thank God I am clamor proof." [The daughter is committed to prison, and carried off in custody.] *Sir Thomas Armstrong.* — "I ought to have the benefit of the law, and I demand no more." *Chief Justice Jeffreys.* — "That you shall have, by the grace of God. See that execution be done on Friday next, according to law. You shall have the full benefit of the law!" Armstrong was hanged, embowelled, beheaded, and quartered accordingly.

When Jeffreys came to the king at Windsor soon after this trial, "the king took a ring of good value from his finger and gave it to him for these services. The ring upon that was called his *blood stone*." * In the reign of William and Mary, Armstrong's attainder was reversed. Jeffreys was then out of reach of process, but for the share which Sir Robert Sawyer had in it as attorney general, he was expelled the House of Commons.

Jeffreys had now the satisfaction of causing an information to be filed against Sir William Williams for having, as Speaker of the House of Commons, under the orders of the House, directed the printing of "Dangerfield's Narrative," † the vengeful tyrant thus dealing a blow at once to an old enemy who had reprimanded him on his knees, and to the privileges

* Burn. Own Times, i. 580. "The king accompanied the gift with a piece of advice somewhat extraordinary from a king to a judge: — 'My lord, as it is a hot summer, and you are going the circuit, I desire you will not drink too much.' "

† Dangerfield had been a confederate of Oates as one of the false witnesses to the pretended Popish plot. — *Ed.*

of the House, equally the object of his detestation. He was in hopes of deciding the case himself, but he left it as a legacy to his successor, Chief Justice Herbert, who, under his auspices, at once overruled the plea, and fined the defendant ten thousand pounds.

Not only was Jeffreys a privy councillor, but he had become a member of the cabinet, where, from his superior boldness and energy, as well as his more agreeable manners, he had gained a complete victory over Lord Keeper North, whom he denounced as a "trimmer," and the great seal seemed almost within his grasp.* To secure it, he still strove to do every thing he could devise to please the court, as if hitherto nothing base had been done by him. When, to his great joy, final judgment was entered up against the city of London on the *quo warranto*, he undertook to get all the considerable towns in England to surrender their charters on the threat of similar proceedings; and with this view, in the autumn of 1684, he made a "campaign in the north," which was almost as fatal to corporations as that "in the West," the following year, proved to the lives of men. To show to the public the special credit he enjoyed at court, the London Gazette, just before he set out, in reference to the gift bestowed upon him for the judgment against Sir Thomas Armstrong, announced "that his majesty, as a mark of his royal favor, had taken a ring from his own finger and placed it on that of Lord Chief Justice Jeffreys." In consequence, although when on the circuit he forgot the caution against hard drinking, with which the gift had been accompanied, he carried every thing before him, "charters fell like the walls of Jericho," and he returned laden with his hyperborean spoils.

* For the disputes between them, see ante, p. 228–240.

I have already related the clutch at the great seal which he then made, and his temporary disappointment.* He was contented to "bide his time." There were only two other occasions when he had it in his power to pervert the law, for the purpose of pleasing the court, during the present reign. The first was on the trial of Hampden, the grandson of the great Hampden, for a trifling misdemeanor. Although this young gentleman was only heir apparent to a moderate estate, and not in possession of any property, he was sentenced to pay a fine of forty thousand pounds — Jeffreys saying that the clause in Magna Charta, "*Liber homo non amercietur pro magno delicto nisi salvo contenemento suo,*" does not apply to fines imposed by the king's judges. The other was the inquisition in the action of *scan. mag.* brought by the Duke of York against Titus Oates, in which the jury, under his direction, awarded one hundred thousand pounds damages.

Ever since the disfranchisement of the city of London, the ex-recorder had ruled it with a rod of iron. He set up a nominal lord mayor and nominal aldermen; but, as they were entirely dependent upon him, he treated them with continual insolence.

On the sudden death of Charles II., Jeffreys no doubt thought the period was arrived when he must be rewarded for the peculiar zeal with which he had abandoned himself to the service of the successor; but he was at first disappointed, and he had still to "wade through slaughter" to the seat he so much coveted.

Not dismayed, he resolved to act on two principles: 1st, If possible, to outdo himself in pleasing his master, whose arbitrary and cruel disposition became more apparent from

* Ante, p. 230.

the hour that he mounted the throne. 2dly, To leave no effort untried to discredit, disgrace, disgust, and break the heart of the man who stood between him and his object.

Being confirmed in the office of chief justice of the King's Bench, he began with the trial for perjury of Titus Oates, whose veracity he had often maintained, but with whom he had a personal quarrel, and whom he now held up to reprobation — depriving him of all chance of acquittal. The defendant was found guilty on two indictments, and the verdict on both was probably correct; but what is to be said for the sentence — "To pay on each indictment a fine of one thousand marks; to be stript of all his canonical habits; to be imprisoned for life; to stand in the pillory on the following Monday, with a paper over his head, declaring his crime; next day to stand in the pillory at the Royal Exchange, with the same inscription; on the Wednesday to be whipped from Aldgate to Newgate; on the Friday to be whipped from Newgate to Tyburn; upon the 25th of April in every year, during life, to stand in the pillory at Tyburn, opposite the gallows; on the 9th of August in every year to stand in the pillory opposite Westminster Hall gate; on the 10th of August in every year to stand in the pillory at Charing Cross; and the like on the following day at Temple Bar; and the like on the 2d of September, every year, at the Royal Exchange;" — the court expressing deep regret that they could not do more, as they would "not have been unwilling to have given judgment of death upon him." *

* This rigorous sentence was rigorously executed. On the day on which Oates was pilloried in Palace Yard, he was mercilessly pelted, and ran some risk of being pulled in pieces; but in the city his partisans mustered in great force, raised a riot, and upset the pillory. They were, however,

Next came the trial of Richard Baxter, the pious and learned Presbyterian divine, who had actually said, and adhered to the saying, "*Nolo episcopari*," and who was now prosecuted for a libel, because in a book on church government he had reflected on the church of Rome in words which might possibly be applied to the bishops of the church of

unable to rescue their favorite. It was supposed that he would try to escape the horrible doom which awaited him by swallowing poison. All that he ate and drank was therefore carefully inspected. On the following morning he was brought forth to undergo his first flogging. At an early hour an innumerable multitude filled all the streets from Aldgate to the Old Bailey. The hangman laid on the lash with such unusual severity as showed that he had received special instructions. The blood ran down in rivulets. For a time the criminal showed a strange constancy; but at last his stubborn fortitude gave way. His bellowings were frightful to hear. He swooned several times; but the scourge still continued to descend. When he was unbound, it seemed that he had borne as much as the human frame can bear without dissolution. James was entreated to remit the second flogging. His answer was short and clear. "He shall go through with it, if he has breath in his body." An attempt was made to obtain the queen's intercession, but she indignantly refused to say a word in favor of such a wretch. After an interval of only forty-eight hours, Oates was again brought out of his dungeon. He was unable to stand, and it was necessary to drag him to Tyburn on a sledge. He seemed quite insensible, and the tories reported that he had stupefied himself with strong drink. A person who counted the stripes on the second day said that they were seventeen hundred. The bad man escaped with life, but so narrowly that his ignorant and bigoted admirers thought his recovery miraculous, and appealed to it as a proof of his innocence. The doors of the prison closed upon him. During many months he remained ironed in the darkest hole of Newgate. It was said that in his cell he gave himself up to melancholy, and sat whole days uttering deep groans, his arms folded, and his hat pulled over his eyes. It was not in England alone that these events excited strong interest. Millions of Roman Catholics, who knew nothing of our institutions or of our factions, had heard that a persecution of singular barbarity had raged in our island against the professors of the true faith, that many pious men had suffered martyrdom, and that Titus Oates had been the chief murderer. There was, therefore, great joy in distant countries when it was known that the divine justice had overtaken him. Engravings of him, looking out from the pillory, and writhing at the cart's tail, were circulated all over Europe; and epigram-

England. No such reference was intended by him; and he was known not only to be of exemplary private character, but to be warmly attached to monarchy, and always inclined to moderate measures in the differences between the established church and those of his own persuasion.* Yet, when he pleaded *not guilty*, and prayed on account of ill health that his trial might be postponed, Jeffreys exclaimed, "Not a minute more to save his life. We have had to do with other sort of persons, but now we have a saint to deal with; and I know how to deal with saints as well as sinners. Yonder stands Oates in the pillory, [Oates was at that moment suffer-

matists, in many languages, made merry with the doctoral title which he pretended to have received from the university of Salamanca, and remarked that since his forehead could not be made to blush, it was but reasonable that his back should do so.

Horrible as were the sufferings of Oates, they did not equal his crimes. Nevertheless, the punishment which was inflicted upon him cannot be justified. In sentencing him to be stripped of his ecclesiastical habit and imprisoned for life, the judges seem to have exceeded their legal power. They were undoubtedly competent to inflict whipping, nor had the law assigned a limit to the number of stripes; but the spirit of the law clearly was that no misdemeanor should be punished more severely than the most atrocious felonies. The worst felon could only be hanged. The judges, as they believed, sentenced Oates to be scourged to death. That the law was defective, is not a sufficient excuse; for defective laws should be altered by the legislature, and not strained by the tribunals; and least of all should the law be strained for the purpose of inflicting torture and destroying life. That Oates was a bad man is not a sufficient excuse; for the guilty are almost always the first to suffer those hardships which are afterward used as precedents for oppressing the innocent. Thus it was in the present case. Merciless flogging soon became an ordinary punishment for political misdemeanors of no very aggravated kind. Men were sentenced for hasty words spoken against the government to pain so excruciating that they, with unfeigned earnestness, begged to be brought to trial on capital charges, and sent to the gallows. Happily, the progress of this great evil was speedily stopped by the revolution, and by that article of the Bill of Rights which condemns all cruel and unusual punishments. —*Macaulay's History of England.*

* Fox's Hist. James, ii. 96.

ing part of his sentence in Palace Yard, outside the great gate of Westminster Hall,] and he says he suffers for the truth; and so says Baxter; but if Baxter did but stand on the outside of the pillory with him, I would say *two of the greatest rogues and rascals in the kingdom stood there together.*" Having silenced the defendant's counsel by almost incredible rudeness, the defendant himself wished to speak, when the chief justice burst out, "Richard, Richard, thou art an old fellow and an old knave; thou hast written books enough to load a cart; every one is as full of sedition, I might say treason, as an egg is full of meat; hadst thou been whipt out of thy writing trade forty years ago, it had been happy. Thou pretendest to be a preacher of the gospel of peace, and thou hast one foot in the grave; it is time for thee to begin to think what account thou intendest to give; but leave thee to thyself, and I see thou wilt go on as thou hast begun; but, by the grace of God, I'll look after thee. Gentlemen of the jury, he is now modest enough; but time was when no man was so ready at *bind your kings in chains and your nobles in fetters of iron,* crying, *To your tents, O Israel!* Gentlemen, for God's sake do not let us be gulled twice in an age." The defendant was, of course, found guilty, and thought himself lucky to escape with a fine of five hundred pounds, and giving security for his good behavior for seven years.*

* Macaulay gives the following account of this trial:

"When the trial came on at Guildhall, a crowd of those who loved and honored Baxter filled the court. At his side stood Doctor William Bates, one of the most eminent Nonconformist divines. Two Whig barristers of great note, Pollexfen and Wallop, appeared for the defendant. Pollexfen had scarce begun his address to the jury, when the chief justice broke forth — 'Pollexfen, I know you well. I will set a mark on you. You are

The lord chief justice, for his own demerits, and to thrust a thorn into the side of Lord Keeper Guilford, was now raised to the peerage by the title of "Baron Jeffreys of Wem"— the preamble of his patent narrating his former promotions— averring that they were the reward of virtue, and after the statement of his being appointed to preside in the Court of

the patron of the faction. This is an old rogue, a schismatical knave, a hypocritical villain. He hates the liturgy. He would have nothing but long-winded cant without book;' and then his lordship turned up his eyes, clasped his hands, and began to sing through his nose, in imitation of what he supposed to be Baxter's style of praying, 'Lord, we are thy people, thy peculiar people, thy dear people.' Pollexfen gently reminded the court that his late majesty had thought Baxter deserving of a bishopric. 'And what ailed the old blockhead then,' cried Jeffreys, 'that he did not take it?' His fury now rose almost to madness. He called Baxter a dog, and swore that it would be no more than justice to whip such a villain through the whole city.

"Wallop interposed, but fared no better than his leader. 'You are in all these dirty causes, Mr. Wallop,' said the judge. 'Gentlemen of the long robe ought to be ashamed to assist such factious knaves.' The advocate made another attempt to obtain a hearing, but to no purpose. 'If you do not know your duty,' said Jeffreys, 'I will teach it you.'

"Wallop sat down, and Baxter himself attempted to put in a word; but the chief justice drowned all expostulation in a torrent of ribaldry and invective, mingled with scraps of Hudibras. 'My lord,' said the old man, 'I have been much blamed by dissenters for speaking respectfully of bishops.' 'Baxter for bishops!' cried the judge; 'that's a merry conceit indeed. I know what you mean by bishops—rascals like yourself, Kidderminster bishops, factious, snivelling Presbyterians!' Again Baxter essayed to speak, and again Jeffreys bellowed, 'Richard, Richard, dost thou think we will let thee poison the court? Richard, thou art an old knave. Thou hast written books enough to load a cart, and every book as full of sedition as an egg is full of meat. By the grace of God, I'll look after thee. I see a great many of your brotherhood waiting to know what will befall their mighty Don. And there,' he continued, fixing his savage eye on Bates, 'there is a doctor of the party at your elbow. But, by the grace of God Almighty, I will crush you all!'

"Baxter held his peace. But one of the junior counsel for the defence made a last effort, and undertook to show that the words of which complaint was made would not bear the construction put on them by the information. With this view he began to read the context. In a moment

King's Bench, adding, "Where at this very time he is faithfully and boldly doing justice and affording protection to our subjects, according to law, in consequence of which virtues we have thought him fit to be raised to the peerage of this realm." *

He took his seat in the House of Lords on the first day of the meeting of James's only Parliament, along with nineteen others either raised in the peerage or newly created since the dissolution of the Oxford Parliament — the junior being John Lord Churchill, afterwards Duke of Marlborough. The journals show that Lord Jeffreys was very regular in his attendance during the session, and as the house sat daily and still met at the same early hour as the courts of law, he must generally have left the business of the King's Bench to be transacted by the other judges. He was now occupied day and night with plans for pushing the already disgraced lord keeper from the woolsack.

he was roared down. 'You sha'n't turn the court into a conventicle!' The noise of weeping was heard from some of those who surrounded Baxter. 'Snivelling calves!' said the judge.

"Witnesses to character were in attendance, and among them were several clergymen of the established church. But the chief justice would hear nothing. 'Does your lordship think,' said Baxter, 'that any jury will convict a man on such a trial as this?' 'I warrant you, Mr. Baxter,' said Jeffreys. 'Don't trouble yourself about that.' Jeffreys was right. The sheriffs were the tools of the government. The jury, selected by the sheriffs from among the fiercest zealots of the Tory party, conferred for a moment, and returned a verdict of guilty. 'My lord,' said Baxter, as he left the court, 'there was once a chief justice who would have treated me very differently.' He alluded to his learned and virtuous friend, Sir Matthew Hale. 'There is not an honest man in England,' said Jeffreys, 'but looks on thee as a knave.'"

* It is remarkable that the first common law judge, ever as such raised to the peerage, was this infamous Jeffreys. We speak of Lord Coke, Lord Hale, and so of the other chief justices, but they were lords simply by their surnames and by virtue of their office, and not peers. — *Ed.*

I have already, in the life of Lord Guilford, related how these plans were conducted in the cabinet, in the royal circle at Whitehall, and in the House of Lords — particularly the savage treatment which the "staggering statesman" received on the reversal of his decree in *Howard* v. *Duke of Norfolk*, after which he never held up his head more.* The probability is, that although he clung to office so pusillanimously in the midst of all sorts of slights and indignities, he would now have been forcibly ejected if his death had not appeared to be near at hand, and if there had not been a demand for the services of "Judge Jeffreys" in a scene very different from the drowsy tranquillity of the Court of Chancery.

By the month of July, Monmouth's rebellion had been put down, and he himself had been executed upon his parliamentary attainder without the trouble of a trial: but all the jails in the West of England were crowded with his adherents, and, instead of Colonel Kirke doing military execution on more of them than had already suffered from his "lambs," it was resolved that they should all perish by the flaming sword of justice — which, on such an occasion, there was only one man fit to wield.

No assizes had been held this summer on the western circuit; but for all the counties upon it a special commission to try criminals was now appointed, at the head of which Lord Chief Justice Jeffreys was put; and by a second commission, he, singly, was invested with the authority of commander-in-chief over all his majesty's forces within the same limits.

On entering Hampshire he was met by a brigade of soldiers, by whom he was guarded to Winchester. During the rest of his progress he never moved without a military escort;

* Ante, p. 237, *et seq.*

he daily gave the word; orders for going the rounds, and for the general disposal of the troops, were dictated by him — sentinels mounting guard at his lodgings, and the officers on duty sending him their reports.

I desire at once to save my readers from the apprehension that I am about to shock their humane feelings by a detailed statement of the atrocities of this bloody campaign in the west, the character of which is familiar to every Englishman. But, as a specimen of it, I must present a short account of the treatment experienced by Lady Lisle, with whose murder it commenced.

She was the widow of Major Lisle, who had sat in judgment on Charles I., had been a lord commissioner of the great seal under Cromwell, and, flying on the restoration, had been assassinated at Lausanne. She remained in England, and was remarkable for her loyalty as well as piety. Jeffreys's malignant spite against her is wholly inexplicable; for he had never had any personal quarrel with her, she did not stand in the way of his promotion, and the circumstance of her being the widow of a regicide cannot account for his vindictiveness. Perhaps without any personal dislike to the individual, he merely wished to strike terror into the west by his first operation.

The charge against her, which was laid capitally, was that after the battle of Sedgemoor she had harbored in her house one Hickes, who had been in arms with the Duke of Monmouth — *she knowing of his treason.* In truth she had received him into her house, thinking merely that he was persecuted as a non-conformist minister, and the moment she knew whence he came, she (conveying to him a hint that he should escape) sent her servant to a justice of peace to give information concerning him. There was the greatest difficulty even to show that Hickes had been in the rebellion, and the judge was worked up to a pitch of fury by being obliged himself to cross-examine a Presbyterian witness, who had showed a leaning against the prosecution. But the principal traitor had not been convicted, and there was not a particle of evidence to show the *scienter*, *i. e.*, that the supposed accomplice, at the time of the harboring was acquainted with the treason. Not allowed the benefit of counsel, she herself, prompted by natural good sense, took the legal objection that the principal traitor ought first to have been convicted, "because, peradventure, he might afterwards be acquitted as innocent after she had been condemned for harboring him;" and she urged with great force to the jury, "that at the time of the alleged offence she had been entirely ignorant of any suspicion of Hickes having participated in the rebellion; that she had strongly disapproved of it, and that she had sent her only son into the field to fight under the royal banner to suppress it."

It is said by almost all the contemporary authorities, that thrice did the jury refuse to find a verdict of guilty, and thrice did Lord Chief Justice Jeffreys send them back to reconsider their verdict. In the account of the proceeding in the State Trials, which has the appearance of having been taken in short hand, and of being authentic, the repeated sending back of the jury is not mentioned; but enough appears to stamp eternal infamy on Jeffreys, if there were nothing more extant against him. After a most furious summing up, "the jury withdrew, and staying out a while, the Lord Jeffreys expressed a great deal of impatience, and said he wondered that in so plain a case they would go from the bar, and would have sent for them, with an intimation that, if they did not come quickly, he would adjourn, and let them lie by it all night; but, after about half an hour's stay, the jury returned, and the foreman addressed himself to the court thus: 'My lord, we have one thing to beg of your lordship some directions in before we can give our verdict: we have some doubt whether there be sufficient evidence that she knew Hickes to have been in the army.' *L. C. J.*—'There is as full proof as proof can be; but you are judges of the proof; for my part, I thought there was no difficulty in it.' *Foreman.*—'My lord, we are in some doubt of it.' *L. C. J.*—'I cannot help your doubts; was there not proved a discourse of the battle and the army at supper time?' *Foreman.*—'But, my lord, we are not satisfied that she had notice that Hickes was in the army.' *L. C. J.*—'I cannot tell what would satisfy you. Did she not inquire of Dunne whether Hickes had been in the army? and when he told her he did not know, she did not say she would refuse him if he had been there, but ordered him to come by night, by which it is evident she suspected it. . . . . But if there was no such proof, the circumstances and management of the thing is as full a proof as can be. I wonder what it is you doubt of.' *Lady Lisle.*—'My lord, I hope ——.' *L. C. J.*—'You must not speak now.' The jury laid their heads together near a quarter of an hour, and then pronounced a verdict of guilty. *L. C. J.*—'Gentlemen, I did not think I should have had any occasion to speak after your verdict; but finding some hesitancy and doubt among you, I cannot but say I wonder it should come about; for I think in my conscience the evidence was as full and plain as could be, and if I had been among you, and she had been my own mother, I should have found her guilty.'"

He passed sentence upon her with great *sang froid*, and, I

really believe, would have done the same had she been the mother that bore him — "That you be conveyed from hence to the place from whence you came, and from thence you are to be drawn on a hurdle to the place of execution, where your body is to be burnt alive till you be dead. And the Lord have mercy on your soul."

The king refused the most earnest applications to save her life, saying that he had promised Lord Chief Justice Jeffreys not to pardon her; but, by a mild exercise of the prerogative, he changed the punishment of burning into that of beheading, which she actually underwent. After the Revolution, her attainder was reversed by act of Parliament, on the ground that "the verdict was injuriously extorted by the menaces and violence and other illegal practices of George Lord Jeffreys, Baron of Wem, then lord chief justice of the King's Bench."

From Winchester, the "lord general judge" proceeded to Salisbury, where he was obliged to content himself with whippings and imprisonments for indiscreet words, the Wiltshire men not having actually joined in the insurrection. But when he got into Dorsetshire, the county in which Monmouth had landed, and where many had joined his standard, he was fatigued, if not satiated, with shedding blood. Great alarm was excited, and not without reason, by his being seen to laugh in church, both during the prayers and sermon which preceded the commencement of business in the hall — his smile being construed into a sign that he was about "to breathe death like a destroying angel, and to sanguine his very ermine in blood." His charge to the grand jury threw the whole county into a state of consternation; for he said he was determined to exercise the utmost rigor of the law, not only against principal traitors, but all aiders and abettors, who, by any expression, had encouraged the rebellion, or had favored the escape of any engaged in it, however nearly related to them, unless it were the harboring of a husband by a wife, which the wisdom of our ancestors permitted, because she had sworn to obey him.

Bills of indictment for high treason were found by the hundred, often without evidence, the grand jury being afraid that, if they were at all scrupulous, they themselves might be brought in "aiders and abettors." It happened, curiously enough, that as he was about to arraign the prisoners, he received news, by express, that the Lord Keeper Guilford had breathed his last at Wroxton, in Oxfordshire. He had little doubt that he should himself be the successor, and very soon after, by a messenger from Windsor, he received assurances to that effect, with orders "to finish the king's business in the west." Although he had no ground for serious misgivings, he could not but feel a little uneasy at the thought of the intrigues which in his absence might spring up against him in a corrupt court, and he was impatient to take possession of his new dignity. But what a prospect before him, if all the prisoners against whom there might be indictments, here and at other places, should plead not guilty, and *seriatim* take their trials! He resorted to an expedient worthy of his genius by openly proclaiming, in terms of vague promise but certain denunciation, that "if any of those indicted would relent from their conspiracies, and plead guilty, they should find him to be a merciful judge; but that those who put themselves on their trials, (which the law mercifully gave them all in strictness a right to do,) if found guilty, would have very little time to live; and, therefore, that such as were conscious they had no defence, had better spare him the trouble of trying them."

He was at first disappointed. The prisoners knew the sternness of the judge, and had some hope from the mercy of their countrymen on the jury. The result of this boldness is soon told. He began on a Saturday morning, with a batch of thirty. Of these, only one was acquitted for want of evidence, and the same evening he signed a warrant to hang thirteen of those convicted on the Monday morning, and the rest the following day. An impressive defence was made by the constable of Chardstock, charged with supplying the Duke of Monmouth's soldiers with money; whereas they had actually robbed him of a considerable sum which he had in his hands for the use of the militia. The prisoner having objected to the competency of a witness called against him, "Villain! rebel!" exclaimed the judge, "methinks I see thee already with a halter about thy neck." And he was specially ordered to be hanged the first, my lord jeeringly declaring "that if any with a knowledge of the law came in his way, he should take care to *prefer them!*"

On the Monday morning, the court sitting rather late on account of the executions, the judge, on taking his place, found many applications to withdraw the plea of not guilty, and the prisoners pleaded guilty in great numbers; but his ire was kindled, and he would not even affect any semblance of mercy. Two hundred and ninety-two more received judgment to die, and of these seventy-four actually suffered — some being sent to be executed in every town, and almost in every village, for many miles round. While the whole county was covered with the gibbeted quarters of human beings, the towns resounded with the cries of men, and even of women and children, who were cruelly whipped for sedition, on the ground that by words or looks, they had favored the insurrection.

Jeffreys next proceeded to Exeter, where one John Fower-acres, the first prisoner arraigned, had the temerity to plead not guilty, and being speedily convicted, was sent to instant execution. This had the desired effect; for all the others confessed, and his lordship was saved the trouble of trying them. Only thirty-seven suffered capitally in the county of Devon, the rest of the two hundred and forty-three against whom indictments were found being transported, whipped, or imprisoned.

Somersetshire afforded a much finer field for indulging the propensities of the chief justice, as in this county there had not only been a considerable rising of armed men for Monmouth, but processions, in which women and children had joined, carrying ribbons, boughs, and garlands to his honor. There were five hundred prisoners for trial at Taunton alone. Jeffreys said in his charge to the grand jury, "it would not be his fault if he did not purify the place." The first person tried before him here was Simon Hamling, a dissenter of a class to whom the judge bore a particular enmity. In reality, the accused had only come to Taunton, during the rebellion, to warn his son, who resided there, to remain neuter. Conscious of his innocence, he insisted on pleading not guilty; he called witnesses, and made a resolute defence, which was considered great presumption. The committing magistrate, who was sitting on the bench, at last interposed and said, "There must certainly be some mistake about the individual." *Jeffreys.* — "You have brought him here, and, if he be innocent, his blood be upon your head." The prisoner was found guilty, and ordered for execution next morning. Few afterwards gave his lordship the trouble of trying them, and one hundred and forty-three are said here to have been ordered for execution, and two hundred and eighty-four to have been sentenced to transportation for life. He particularly piqued himself upon his *bon mot* in passing sentence on one Hucher, who pleaded, in mitigation, that, though he had joined the Duke of Monmouth, he had sent important information to the king's general, the Earl of Feversham. "You deserve a double death," said the impartial judge; "one for rebelling against your sovereign, and the other for betraying your friends."

He showed great ingenuity in revenging himself upon such as betrayed any disapprobation of his severities. Among these was Lord Stawell, who was so much shocked with what he had heard of the chief justice, that he refused to see him. Immediately after, there came forth an order that Colonel Bovet, of Taunton, a friend to whom this cavalier nobleman had been much attached, should be executed at Cotheleston, close by the house where he and Lady Stawell and his children then resided.

A considerable harvest here arose from compositions levied upon the friends of twenty-six young virgins who presented the invader with colors, which they had embroidered with their own hands. The fund was ostensibly for the benefit of "the queen's maids of honor," but a strong suspicion arose that the chief justice participated in bribes for these as well as other pardons. He thought that his *peculium* was encroached upon by a letter from Lord Sunderland, informing him of "the king's pleasure to bestow one thousand convicts on several courtiers, and one hundred on a favorite of the queen — security being given that the prisoners should be enslaved for ten years in some West India island." In his remonstrance he said that "these convicts would be worth ten or fifteen pounds apiece," and, with a view to his own claim, returned thanks for his majesty's gracious acceptance of his services. However, he was obliged to submit to the royal distribution of the spoil.

Where the king did not personally interfere, Jeffreys was generally inexorable if he did not himself receive the bribe for a pardon. Kiffin, a Nonconformist merchant, had agreed to give three thousand pounds to a courtier for the pardon of two youths, his grandsons, who had been in Monmouth's army; but the chief justice would listen to no circumstances of mitigation, as another was to pocket the price of mercy. Yet, to a buffoon who attended him on the circuit and made sport by his mimicry, in an hour of revelry at Taunton, he tossed the pardon of a rich culprit, expressing a hope "that it might turn to good account."

The jails at Taunton being incapable of containing all the prisoners, it was necessary to adjourn the commission to Wells, where the same horrible scenes were again acted, notwithstanding the humane exertions of that most honorable man, Bishop Ken, who afterwards, having been one of the seven bishops prosecuted by King James, resigned his see at the Revolution, rather than sign the new tests.

The Cornishmen had all remained loyal, and the city of Bristol* only remained to be visited by the commission. There were not many cases of treason here, but Jeffreys had a particular spite against the corporation magistrates, because they were supposed to favor dissenters, and he had them very much in his power by a discovery he made, that they had

* Bristol at this time was next to London in population, wealth, and commerce. — *Ed.*

been in the habit of having in turn assigned to them prisoners charged with felony, whom they sold for their own benefit to be transported to Barbadoes. In addressing the grand jury, (while he complained of a fit of the stone, and was seemingly under the excitement of liquor,) he said,—

"I find a special commission is an unusual thing here, and relishes very ill; nay, the very women storm at it, for fear we should take the upper hand of them too; for by-the-bye, gentlemen, I hear it is much in fashion in this city for the women to govern and bear sway." Having praised the mild and paternal rule of King James, he thus proceeded: "On the other hand, up starts a puppet prince, who seduces the mobile into rebellion, into which they are easily bewitched; for I say rebellion is like the sin of witchcraft. This man, who had as little title to the crown as the least of you, (for I hope you are all legitimate,) being overtaken by justice, and by the goodness of his prince brought to the scaffold, he has the confidence, (good God, that men should be so impudent!) to say that God Almighty did know with what joyfulness he did die, (a traitor!) Great God of heaven and earth! what reason have men to rebel? But, as I told you, rebellion is like the sin of witchcraft: Fear God and honor the king is rejected for no other reason, as I can find, but that it is written in St. Peter. Gentlemen, I must tell you I am afraid that this city hath too many of these people in it, and it is your duty to find them out. Gentlemen, I shall not stand complimenting with you; I shall talk with some of you before you and I part, I tell you; I tell you I have brought a besom, and I will sweep every man's door, whether great or small. Certainly, here are a great many of those men whom they call Trimmers; a Whig is but a mere fool to those; for a Whig is some sort of a subject in comparison of these; for a Trimmer is but a cowardly and base-spirited Whig; for the Whig is but the journeyman prentice that is hired and set over the rebellion, whilst the Trimmer is afraid to appear in the cause." He then opens his charge against the aldermen for the sale of convicts, and thus continues: "Good God! where am I?—in Bristol? This city it seems claims the privilege of hanging and drawing among themselves. I find you have more need of a special commission once a month at least. The very magistrates, that should be the ministers of justice, fall out with one another to that degree they will scarcely dine together; yet I find they can agree for their interest if there be but a *kid* in the case; for I hear the trade of *kidnapping* is much in request in this city. You can discharge a felon or a traitor, provided they will go to Mr. Alderman's plantation in the West Indies. Come, come, I find you stink for want of rubbing. It seems the dissenters and fanatics fare well amongst you, by reason of the favor of the magistrates; for example, if a dissenter who is a notorious and obstinate offender comes before them, one alderman or another stands up and says, *He is a good man*, (though three parts a rebel.) Well, then, for the sake of Mr. Alderman, he shall be fined but five shillings. Then comes another, and up stands another goodman alderman, and says, *I know him to be an honest man*, (though rather worse than the former.) Well, for Mr. Alderman's sake, he shall be fined but half a crown; so *manus manum fricat;* you play the knave for me now, and I will play the knave for you by and by. I am ashamed of these things; but, by God's grace, I will mend them; for, as I have told you, I have brought a brush in my pocket, and I shall be sure to rub the dirt wherever it is, or on whomsoever it sticks." "Thereupon," says Roger North, "he turns to the mayor, accoutred with his scarlet and furs, and gave him all the ill names that scolding eloquence could supply; and so, with rating and staring, as his way was, never left till he made him quit the bench and go down to the criminal's post at the bar; and there he pleaded for himself as a common rogue or thief must have done; and when the mayor hesitated a little, or slackened his pace, he bawled at him,-and stamping, called for his guards, for he was still general by commission. Thus the citizens saw their scarlet chief magistrate at the bar, to their infinite terror and amazement."

Only three were executed for treason at Bristol; but Jeffreys looking at the end of his campaign to the returns of the enemy killed, had the satisfaction to find that they amounted to three hundred and thirty, besides eight hundred prisoners ordered to be transported.*

He now hastened homewards to pounce upon the great seal. In his way through Somersetshire, with a regiment of dragoons as his life-guards, the mayor took the liberty to say that there were two Spokes who had been convicted, and that one of these left for execution was not the one intended to suffer, the other having contrived to make his escape, and that favor might perhaps still be shown to him whom it was intended to pardon. "No!" said the general-judge; "his family owe a life; he shall die for his namesake!" To render such narratives credible, we must recollect that his mind was often greatly disturbed by fits of the stone, and still more by intemperance. Burnet, speaking of his behavior at this

* Macaulay states the number of the transported at eight hundred and forty-one, and of the hanged at three hundred and twenty. — *Ed.*

time, says, "He was perpetually either drunk or in a rage, liker a fury than the zeal of a judge."

I shall conclude my sketch of Jeffreys as a criminal judge with his treatment of a prisoner whom he was eager to hang, but who escaped with life. This was Prideaux, a gentleman of fortune in the west of England, who had been apprehended on the landing of Monmouth, for no other reason than that his father had been attorney general under Cromwell. A reward of five hundred pounds, with a free pardon, was offered to any witnesses who would give evidence against him; but none could be found, and he was discharged. Afterwards, two convicts were prevailed upon to say that they had seen him take some part in the insurrection, and he was again cast into prison. His friends, alarmed for his safety, though convinced of his innocence, tried to procure a pardon for him, when they were told "that nothing could be done for him, as the king had given him to the chief justice," (the familiar phrase for the grant of an estate about to be forfeited.) A negotiation was then opened with Jennings, the avowed agent of Jeffreys for the sale of pardons, and the sum of fifteen thousand pounds was actually paid to him by a banker for the deliverance of a man whose destruction could not be effected by any perversion of the formalities of law.*

There is to be found only one defender of these atrocities. "I have indeed sometimes thought," says the author of A Caveat against the Whigs, "that in Jeffreys's western circuit justice went too far before mercy was remembered, though there was not above a fourth part executed of what were

* He bought with it a large estate, the name of which the people changed to Aceldama, as being bought with innocent blood. — *Ed.*

convicted. But when I consider in what manner several of those lives then spared were afterwards spent, I cannot but think a little more *hemp* might have been usefully employed upon that occasion." *

A great controversy has arisen, "who is chiefly to be blamed — Jeffreys or James?" Sheffield, Duke of Buckingham, declares that "the king never forgave the cruelty of the judge in executing such multitudes in the west against his express orders." And reliance is placed by Hume on the assertion of Roger North, that his brother, the lord keeper, going to the king and moving him "to put a stop to the fury which was in no respect for his service, and would be counted a

* Perhaps this writer had in his eye the case of John Tutchin, a noted political writer, satirized by Pope, a mere boy at the time of the rebellion, and of whose case Macaulay gives the following account: "A still more frightful sentence was passed on a lad named Tutchin, who was tried for seditious words. He was, as usual, interrupted in his defence by ribaldry and scurrility from the judgment seat. 'You are a rebel; and all your family have been rebels since Adam. They tell me that you are a poet. I'll cap verses with you.' The sentence was, that the boy should be imprisoned seven years, and should, during that period, be flogged through every market town in Dorsetshire every year. The women in the galleries burst into tears. The clerk of the arraigns stood up in great disorder. 'My lord,' said he, 'the prisoner is very young. There are many market towns in our county. The sentence amounts to whipping once a fortnight for seven years.' 'If he is a young man,' said Jeffreys, 'he is an old rogue. Ladies, you do not know the villain as well as I do. The punishment is not half bad enough for him. All the interest in England shall not alter it.' Tutchin, in his despair, petitioned, and probably with sincerity, that he might be hanged. Fortunately for him, he was, just at this conjuncture, taken ill of the small pox, and given over. As it seemed highly improbable that the sentence would ever be executed, the chief justice consented to remit it in return for a bribe which reduced the prisoner to poverty. The temper of Tutchin, not originally very mild, was exasperated to madness by what he had undergone. He lived to be known as one of the most acrimonious and pertinacious enemies of the house of Stuart and of the Tory party." — *Ed.*

carnage, not law or justice, orders went to mitigate the proceedings."

I have already demonstrated that this last assertion is a mere invention,* and though it is easy to fix deep guilt on the judge, it is impossible to exculpate the monarch. Burnet says that James "had a particular account of his proceedings writ to him every day, and he took pleasure to relate them in the drawing-room to foreign ministers, and at his table, calling it Jeffreys's campaign; speaking of all he had done in a style that neither became the majesty nor the mercifulness of a great prince." Jeffreys himself, (certainly a very suspicious witness,) when in the Tower, declared to Tutchin that "his instructions were much more severe than the execution of them; and that at his return he was snubbed at court for being too merciful." And to Dr. Scott, the divine who attended him on his death bed, he said, "Whatever I did then I did by express orders; and I have this further to say for myself, that I was not half bloody enough for him who sent me thither." We certainly know from a letter written to him by the Earl of Sunderland at Dorchester, that "the king approved entirely of all his proceedings." And though we cannot believe that he stopped short of any severity which he thought would be of service to himself, there seems no reason to doubt (if that be any palliation) that throughout the whole of these proceedings his object was to please his master, whose disposition was now most vindictive, and who thought that, by such terrible examples, he should secure to himself a long and quiet reign.†

* Ante, p. 000.

† One of the strongest testimonies against James is his own letter to the Prince of Orange, dated Sept. 24, 1685, in which, after giving him a long

The two were equally criminal,* and both had their reward. But in the first instance, and till the consequences of such wickedness and folly began to appear, they met each other with mutual joy and congratulations. Jeffreys returning from the west, by royal command stopped at Windsor Castle. He arrived there on the 28th of September; and after a most gracious reception, the great seal was immediately delivered to him with the title of lord chancellor.

We learn from Evelyn that it had been three weeks in the king's personal custody. "About six o'clock came Sir Dudley North and his brother Roger North, and brought the great seal from my lord keeper, who died the day before. The king went immediately to council, every body guessing who was most likely to succeed this great officer; most believed it would be no other than Lord Chief Justice Jeffreys, who had so rigorously prosecuted the late rebels, and was now gone

account of his fox-hunting, he says, "As for news, there is little stirring, but that the lord chief justice has almost done his campaign. He has already condemned several hundreds, some of which are already executed, some are to be, and the others sent to the plantations."—*Dalrymple's App.* part ii. 165. The only public man who showed any bowels of compassion amidst these horrors was Lord Sunderland. Whig party writers are at great pains to exculpate Pollexfen, the great Whig lawyer, who conducted all these prosecutions as counsel for the crown; but I think he comes in for no small share of the infamy then incurred, and he must be considered as principal *aide de camp* to Jeffreys in the *western campaign.* He ought to have told the jury that there was no case against the Lady Lisle, and when a few examples had been made, he ought to have stopped the prosecutions, or have thrown up his briefs.

* I hope I have not been prejudiced in my estimate of James's character by the consideration that when acting as regent in Scotland he issued an order (afterwards recalled) for the utter suppression of the name of CAMPBELL, "which," says Mackintosh, "would have amounted to a proscription of several noblemen, a considerable body of gentry, and the most numerous and powerful tribe in the kingdom."

the western circuit to punish the rest that were secured in the several counties, and was now near upon his return."

The London Gazette of October 1, 1685, contains the following notice:

"*Windsor, Sept.* 28.

"His majesty taking into his royal consideration the many eminent and faithful services which the Right Honorable George Lord Jeffreys, of Wem, lord chief justice of England, has rendered the crown, as well in the reign of the late king, of ever blessed memory, as since his majesty's accession to the throne, was pleased this day to commit to him the custody of the great seal of England, with the title of lord chancellor."

The new lord chancellor, having brought the great seal with him from Windsor to London, had near a month to prepare for the business of the term.

He had had only a very slender acquaintance with Chancery proceedings, and he was by no means thoroughly grounded in common-law learning; but he now fell to the study of equity pleading and practice, and though exceedingly inferior to his two immediate predecessors in legal acquirements, his natural shrewdness was such that, when entirely sober, he contrived to gloss over his ignorance of technicalities, and to arrive at a right decision. He was seldom led into temptation by the occurrence of cases in which the interests of political parties, or religious sects, were concerned; and, as an equity judge, the multitude rather regarded him with favor.

The public and the profession were much shocked to see such a man at the head of the law; but as soon as he was installed in his office, there were plenty ready enough to gather round him, and, suppressing their real feelings, to load him with flattery and to solicit him for favors.

Evelyn, who upon his appointment as chief justice, describes him as "most ignorant, but most daring," now assiduously cultivated his notice; and, having succeeded in getting an invitation to dine with him, thus speaks of him:

"31*st Oct.*, 1685.

"I dined at our great Lord Chancellor Jeffreys's, who used me with much respect. This was the late chief justice, who had newly been the western circuit to try the Monmouth conspirators, and had formerly done such severe justice amongst the obnoxious in Westminster Hall, for which his majesty dignified him by creating him first a baron, and now lord chancellor; is of an assured and undaunted spirit, and has served the court interest on all hardiest occasions; is of nature civil, and a slave of the court."

The very first measure which James proposed to his new chancellor was, literally, the hanging of an alderman. He was still afraid of the mutinous spirit of the city, which, without some fresh terrors, might again break out, although the charters were destroyed; and no sufficient atonement had yet been made for the hostility constantly manifested by the metropolis to the policy of his family for half a century. His majesty proposed that Alderman Clayton, a very troublesome agitator, should be selected as the victim. The chancellor agreed that "it was very fit an example should be made, as his majesty had graciously proposed; but if it were the same thing to his majesty, he would venture to suggest a different choice. Alderman Clayton was a bad subject, but Alderman Cornish was still more troublesome, and more dangerous." The king readily acquiesced, and Alderman Cornish was immediately brought to trial before a packed jury, and executed on a gibbet erected in Cheapside, on pretence that some years before he had been concerned in the Ryehouse plot. The apologists of Jeffreys say (and as it is the only alleged instance of his gratitude I have met with, I have great pleasure in recording it) that he was induced to save Sir Robert Clayton from recollecting that this alderman had been his pot companion, and had greatly assisted him in obtaining the office of common serjeant.

Monmouth's rebellion in England, and Argyle's in Scotland, being put down, and the city of London reduced to subjection, James expressed an opinion, in which the chancellor concurred, that there was no longer any occasion to disguise the plan of governing by military force, and of violating at pleasure the solemn acts of the legislature. Parliament reassembled on the 9th of November, when Jeffreys took his seat on the woolsack. The king alone (as had been concerted) addressed the two houses, and plainly told them that he could rely upon "nothing but a good force of well disciplined troops in constant pay," and that he was determined to employ "officers in the army, not qualified by the late tests, for their employments."

When the king had withdrawn, Lord Halifax rose, and said, sarcastically, "They had now more reason than ever to give thanks to his majesty, since he had dealt so plainly with them, and discovered what he would be at."

This the chancellor thought fit to take as a serious motion, and immediately put the question, as proposed by a noble lord, "that an humble address be presented to his majesty to thank him for his gracious speech from the throne." No one ventured to offer any remark, and it was immediately carried, *nemine dissentiente.* The king returned a grave answer to the address, "That he was much satisfied to find their lordships were so well pleased with what he said, and that he would never offer any thing to their house that he should not be convinced was for the true interest of the kingdom."

But the lords very soon discovered the false position in which they had placed themselves, and the bishops were particularly scandalized at the thought that they were supposed to have thanked the king for announcing a principle upon which Papists and Dissenters might be introduced into every civil office, and even into ecclesiastical benefices.

Accordingly, Compton, Bishop of London, moved "that a day might be appointed for taking his majesty's speech into consideration," and said "that he spoke the united sentiments of the Episcopal bench when he pronounced the test act the chief security of the established church." This raised a very long and most animated debate, at which King James, to his great mortification, was present. Sunderland, and the popishly inclined ministers, objected to the regularity of the proceeding, urging that, having given thanks for the speech, they must be taken to have already considered it, and precluded themselves from finding fault with any part of it. The lords Halifax, Nottingham, and Mordaunt, on the other side, treated with scorn the notion that the constitution was to be sacrificed to a point of form, and, entering into the merits of the question, showed that if the power which the sovereign now, for the first time, had openly claimed were conceded to him, the rights, privileges, and property of the nation lay at his mercy.

At last the lord chancellor left the woolsack, and not only bitterly attacked the regularity of the motion after a unanimous vote of thanks to the king for his speech, but gallantly insisted on the legality and expediency of the power of the sovereign to dispense with laws for the safety and benefit of the state. No lord chancellor ever made such an unfortunate exhibition. He assumed the same arrogant and overbearing tone with which he had been accustomed from the bench to browbeat juries, counsel, witnesses, and prisoners, and he launched out into the most indecent personalities against his opponents. He was soon taught to know his place, and that frowns, noise, and menaces would not pass for arguments there. While he spoke he was heard with marked disgust by all parts of the house; when he sat down, being required to retract his words by those whom he had assailed, and finding all the sympathies of the House against him, he made to each of them an abject apology, "and he proved by his behavior that insolence, when checked, naturally sinks into meanness and cowardice."

The ministerialists being afraid to divide the House, Monday following, the 23d of November, was fixed for taking the king's speech into consideration. But a similar disposition having been shown by the other House, before that day Parliament was prorogued, and no other national council met till the Convention Parliament, after the landing of King William.

James, far from abandoning his plans, was more resolute to carry them into effect. The Earl of Rochester, his own brother-in-law, and others who had hitherto stood by him, having in vain remonstrated against his madness, resigned their offices; but Jeffreys still recklessly pushed him forward in his headlong career. In open violation of the test act, four Catholic lords were introduced into the cabinet, and one of them, Lord Bellasis, was placed at the head of the treasury in the room of the Protestant Earl of Rochester. Among such colleagues the lord chancellor was contented to sit in council, and the wonder is that he did not follow the example of Sunderland and other renegades, who at this time, to please the king, professed to change their religion, and were reconciled to the church of Rome. Perhaps, with his peculiar sagacity, Jeffreys thought it would be a greater sacrifice in the king's eyes to appear to be daily wounding his conscience by submitting to measures which he must be supposed inwardly to condemn.

As a grand *coup d'état,* he undertook to obtain a solemn decision of the judges in favor of the dispensing power,* and for this purpose a fictitious action was brought against Sir Edward Hales, the lieutenant of the Tower, an avowed Roman Catholic, in the name of his coachman, for holding an office in the army without having taken the oath of supremacy, or received the sacrament according to the rites of the church of England, or signed the declaration against transubstantiation. Jeffreys had put the great seal to letters patent, authorizing him to hold the office without these tests, "*non obstante*" the act of Parliament. This dispensation was pleaded in bar of the action, and upon a demurrer to the plea, after a sham argument by counsel, all the judges except one (Baron Street) held the plea to be sufficient, and pronounced judgment for the defendant. It was now proclaimed at court that the law was not any longer an obstacle to any scheme that might be thought advisable.

* This "dispensing power" claimed by Jeffreys and the English judges for James II. was but a trifle compared to the "dispensing power" recently claimed by some of our American lawyers and judges for acts of Congress. All that was claimed for James was, power to dispense with acts of Parliament, while our American improvers upon this doctrine go so far as to claim for Congress a power to dispense with and supersede the laws of God. — *Ed.*

The Earl of Castlemaine was sent to Rome, regularly commissioned as ambassador to his holiness the pope, a papal nuncio being reciprocally received at St. James's. But assuming that religion was not embraced in the negotiations between the two courts, however impolitic the proceeding might be, I do not think that the king and the chancellor are liable to be blamed, as they have been by recent historians, for having in this instance violated acts of Parliament. If all those are examined which had passed from the commencement of the reformation down to the "Bill of Rights," it will probably be found that none of them can be applied to a mere diplomatic intercourse with the pope, however stringent their provisions may be against receiving bulls or doing any thing in derogation of the king's supremacy.*

There can be no doubt of the illegality of the next measure of the king and the chancellor. The Court of High Commission was revived with some slight modification, although it had been abolished in the reign of Charles I. by an act of Parliament, which forbade the erection of any similar court; and Jeffreys, having deliberately put the great seal to the patent creating this new arbitrary tribunal, undertook to preside in it. The commissioners were vested with unlimited jurisdiction over the church of England, and were empowered, even in cases of suspicion, to proceed inquisitorially, like the abolished court, "*notwithstanding any law or statute to the contrary.*" The object was to have all ecclesiastics under

* Whether diplomatic intercourse with the pope is now forbidden, depends upon the construction to be put upon the words, "shall hold *communion* with the see or church of Rome" in the Bill of Rights. This seems to refer to *spiritual* communion only, or the queen would hold communion with the successor of Mahomet by appointing an ambassador to the sublime porte.

complete control, lest any of them should oppose the intended innovations in religion.*

Jeffreys selected as his first victims, Sharp, rector of St. Giles's, called the "railing parson," who had made himself very obnoxious to the government by inveighing against the errors of Popery — and Compton, Bishop of London, his diocesan, who had raised the storm against the dispensing power in the House of Lords. A mandate was issued to the bishop to suspend the rector, and this being declined on the ground that no man can be lawfully condemned till he has been heard in his defence, both were summoned before the high commission.

The bishop appearing, and being asked by the chancellor why he had not obeyed the king's orders by suspending Dr. Sharp, prayed time to prepare his defence, as his counsel were on the circuit, and he begged to have a copy of the commission. A week's time was given; but as to the commission, he was told "all the coffee-houses had it for a penny." On the eighth day the business was resumed; but the bishop still said he was unprepared, having great difficulty to procure a copy of the commission; when the chancellor made him a bantering apology. "My lord, in telling you our commission was to be seen in every coffee-house, I did not speak with any design to reflect on your lordship, as if you were a haunter of coffee-houses. I abhor the thoughts of it!" A further indulgence of a fortnight was granted.

At the day appointed, the bishop again appeared with four

* The strong analogy between these ecclesiastical commissioners and our recent American slave catching commissioners, both in powers, method of procedure, and object arrived at, has been already referred to, and can hardly fail to strike the reader. — *Ed.*

doctors of the civil law, who were so frightened, that they hardly dared to say a word for him; but he himself firmly, though mildly, argued, "that he had acted *jurisperitorum consilio*, and could not have had any bad motive; that he should not have been justified in obeying an illegal order; that he had privately recommended to Dr. Sharp not to preach; that this advice had been followed, so that the king's wish was complied with; and that if he had committed any fault, he ought to be tried for it before his archbishop and brother bishops."

Several of the commissioners were inclined to let him off with an admonition; but Jeffreys obtained and pronounced sentence of *suspension during the king's pleasure*, both on the bishop and the rector.*

There was another political trial where justice was done to the accused, although Jeffreys presided at it. A charge was brought against Lord Delamere, the head of an ancient family in Cheshire, that he had tried to excite an insurrection in that county in aid of Monmouth's rebellion. An indictment for high treason being found against him, he was brought to trial upon it before Jeffreys, as lord high steward, and thirty peers-triers. The king was present, and was very desirous of a conviction, as Lord Delamere, when a member of the House of Commons, had taken an active part in supporting the exclusion bill.

Jeffreys did his best to gratify this wish. According to

* Judge Kane, in Passmore Williamson's case, went further than that. Because he refused to obey the mandate of Judge Kane to produce in his court certain persons over whom he had no control, with a view to their surrender to slavery, Judge Kane, under the name of a contempt, sentenced him to an indefinite imprisonment. — *Ed.*

the habit he had lately acquired in the west, he at first tried to induce the noble prisoner to confess, in the hope of pardon "from the king's known clemency." "My lord," said he, "if you are conscious to yourself that you are guilty of this heinous crime, give glory to God, make amends to his vicegerent the king, by a plain and full discovery of your guilt, and do not, by an obstinate persisting in the denial of it, provoke the just indignation of your prince, who has made it appear to the world that his inclinations are rather to show mercy than inflict punishment."

Lord Delamere, to ease his mind from the anxiety to know whether the man who so spoke was to pronounce upon his guilt or innocence, said, "I beg your grace would please to satisfy me whether your grace be one of my judges in concurrence with the rest of the lords." *L. H. Steward.* — "No, my lord, I am judge of the court, but I am none of your triers." *

A plea to the jurisdiction being put in, Lord Delamere requested his grace to advise with the other peers upon it, as it was a matter of privilege. *L. H. Steward.* — "Good my lord, I hope you that are a prisoner at the bar are not to give me direction who I should advise with, or how I should demean myself here."

This plea was properly overruled, and not guilty pleaded, when his grace, to prejudice the peers-triers against the noble prisoner as a notorious exclusionist, delivered an inflammatory address to them before any evidence was given.

* When a peer is tried in Parliament before the House of Lords, the lord high steward votes like the rest of the peers, who have all a right to be present; but if the trial be out of Parliament, the lord high steward is only the judge to give direction in point of law, and the verdict is by the lords triers specially summoned.

To create a further prejudice, poor Lord Howard was called to repeat once more his oft-told tale of the ryehouse plot, with which it was not pretended that the prisoner had any connection. The charge in the indictment was only supported by one witness, who himself had been in the rebellion, and who swore that Lord Delamere, at a time and place which he specified, had sent a message by him to Monmouth, asking a supply of money to maintain ten thousand men to be levied in Cheshire against King James. An *alibi* was clearly proved. Yet his grace summed up for a conviction, and took pains, "for the sake of the numerous and great auditory, that a mistake in point of law might not go unrectified, which seemed to be urged with some earnestness by the noble lord at the bar, *that there is a necessity there should be two positive witnesses to convict a man of treason.*"

To the honor of the peerage of England, there was a unanimous verdict of acquittal. James himself even allowed this to be right, wreaking all his vengeance on the witness for not having given better evidence, and swearing that he would have him first convicted of perjury, and then hanged for treason. Jeffreys seems to have struggled hard to behave with moderation on this trial; but his habitual arrogance from time to time broke out, and must have created a disgust among the peers-triers very favorable to the prisoner.

Jeffreys, still pretending to be a strong Protestant, eagerly assisted the king in his mad attempt to open the church and the universities to the intrusion of the Catholics. The fellows of Magdalen College, Oxford, having disobeyed the royal mandate to elect, as head of their college, Anthony Farmer, who was not qualified by the statutes, and was a man of infamous character, and having chosen the pious and learned

Hough, were summoned before the Court of Ecclesiastical Commission. Jeffreys observed that Dr. Fairfax, one of their number, had not signed the answer of the college to the charge of disregarding the king's recommendation. Fairfax asking leave to explain his reasons for declining to sign the answer, Jeffreys thought that he was willing to conform, and exclaimed, "Ay, this looks like a man of sense, and a good subject. Let's hear what he will say." *Fairfax.* — "I don't object to the answer, because it is the vindication of my college: I go further; and as, according to the rules of the ecclesiastical courts, a libel is given to the party that he may know the grounds of his accusation, I demand that libel; for I do not know otherwise wherefore I am called here, and besides, this affair should be discussed in Westminster Hall." *Jeffreys.* — "You are a doctor of *divinity*, not of *law*." — *Fairfax.* — "By what authority do you sit here?" *Jeffreys.* — "Pray, what commission have you to be so impudent in court? This man ought to be kept in a dark room. Why do you suffer him without a guardian? Why did you not bring him to me? Pray let my officers seize him."

Three members of the ecclesiastical commission were sent to Oxford to represent that formidable body, and they annulled the election of Hough, expelled the refractory fellows, and made Magdalen College, for a time, a Popish establishment — the court in London, under the presidency of Jeffreys, confirming all their proceedings.

The lord chancellor next involved the king in the prosecution of the seven bishops, which, more than any other act of misrule during his reign, led to his downfall.* On the 25th

* In James's memoirs, all the blame of this prosecution is thrown upon Jeffreys; but it is more probable that he only recklessly supported his master.

of April, 1688, a new "declaration of indulgence" came out under the great seal; and, that it might be the more generally known and obeyed, an order was sent from the council to all bishops in England, enjoining that it should be read by the clergy in all churches and chapels within their dioceses during divine service. A petition, signed by Sancroft, the archbishop, and six other prelates, was laid before the king, praying in respectful language that the clergy might be excused from reading the declaration; not because they were wanting in duty to the sovereign, or in tenderness to the dissenters, but because it was founded upon the dispensing power, which had often been declared illegal in Parliament, and on that account they could not, in prudence, honor, or conscience, be such parties to it as the reading of it in the church would imply.

Even the Earl of Sunderland and Father Peter represented to the king the danger of arraying the whole church of England against the authority of the crown, and advised him that the bishops should merely be admonished to be more compliant. But with the concurrence of Jeffreys he resolved to visit them with condign punishment, and they were ordered to appear before the council, with a view to obtain evidence against them, as the petition had been privately presented to the king. When they entered the council chamber, Jeffreys said to them, "Do you own the petition?" After some hesitation, the archbishop confessed that he wrote it, and the bishops, that they signed it. *Jeffreys.* — "Did you publish it?" They, thinking he referred to the *printing* of it, of which the king had loudly complained, denied this very resolutely; but they admitted that they had delivered it to the king at Whitehall palace, in the county of Middlesex. This was considered enough to fix them with a publication, in point of law, of the supposed libel; and Jeffreys, after lecturing them on their disloyalty, required them to enter into a recognizance to appear before the Court of King's Bench, and answer the high misdemeanor of which they were guilty. They insisted that, according to the privileges of the House of Peers, of which they were members, they could not lawfully be committed, and were not bound to enter into the required recognizance. Jeffreys threatened to commit them to the Tower as public delinquents. *Archbishop.* — "We are ready to go whithersoever his majesty may be pleased to send us. We hope the King of kings will be our protector and our judge. We fear nought from man; and having acted according to law and our consciences, no punishment shall ever be able to shake our resolutions."

If this struggle could have been foreseen, even Jeffreys would have shrunk from the monstrous impolicy of sending these men to jail, on what would be considered the charge of temperately exercising a constitutional right in defence of the Protestant faith, so dear to the great bulk of the nation; but he thought it was too late to resile. He therefore, with his own hand, drew a warrant for their commitment, which he signed, and handed round the board. It was signed by all the councillors present, except Father Peter, whose signature the king excused, to avoid the awkward appearance of Protestant bishops being sent to jail by a Jesuit.

An account of their trial will be found in the next chapter; but there are some circumstances connected with their acquittal in which Jeffreys personally appears.

Seeing how he had acquired such immense favor, there were other lawyers who tried to undermine him by his own arts. One of the most formidable of these was Sir John Trevor, master of the rolls, who, some authors say, certainly would have got the great seal had James remained longer on the throne, but whom Jeffreys had hitherto kept down by reversing his decrees. The chancellor's alarm was now excited by a report that Sir William Williams (who, from being Speaker of the last Westminster Parliament, and fined ten thousand pounds on the prosecution of the Duke of York, was become the caressed solicitor general to James II.) had a positive promise of the great seal if he could obtain a conviction of the seven bishops.* His brutal conduct to them during the whole trial, which was no doubt reported to Jeffreys, would confirm the rumor and increase his apprehensions. The jury having sat up all night without food, fire, or candle, to consider of their verdict, the lord chancellor had, while they were still enclosed, come down to Westminster Hall next morning, and taken his seat in court. When he heard the immense shout arise which soon made the king tremble on Hounslow Heath, he smiled and hid his face in his nosegay, "as much," observes the relater of the anecdote, "as to say, Mr. Solicitor, I keep my seal."

However, the part he had taken in sending the bishops to the Tower had caused such scandal, that the University of Oxford would not have him for their chancellor, although, in the prospect of a vacancy, he had received many promises of support. The moment the news arrived of the death of the

* The arrangement of counsel in this celebrated case was very whimsical. The bishops were defended by Pemberton, the ex-chief justice, who had presided at several of the late state trials, by Levinz, Sawyer, and Finch, who had conducted them very oppressively for the crown, and by Pollexfen, Treby, and Somers, considered steady Whigs.

old Duke of Ormond, his grandson was elected to succeed him; and next day a mandate coming from court to elect Lord Jeffreys, an answer was returned that an election had already taken place, which could not be revoked.

Suspecting that things were now taking an unfavorable turn, he began privately to censure the measures of the court, and to insinuate that the king had acted against his advice, saying, "It will be found that I have done the part of an honest man, but as for the judges they are most of them rogues."

About this time he was present at an event which was considered more than a counterpoise to recent discomfitures, but which greatly precipitated the crisis by taking away the hope of relief by the rightful succession of a Protestant heir. Being suddenly summoned to Whitehall, he immediately repaired thither, and found that the queen had been taken in labor. Other councillors and many ladies of quality soon arrived, and they were all admitted into her bedchamber. Her majesty seems to have been much annoyed by the presence of the lord chancellor. The king calling for him, he came forward and stood on the step of the bed to show that he was there. She then begged her consort to cover her face with his head and periwig; for she declared "she could not be brought to bed, and have so many men look on her." However, the fright may have shortened her sufferings; for James III., or "the old pretender," very speedily made his appearance, and the midwife having made the concerted signal that the child was of the wished-for sex, the company retreated.

Considering the surmises which had been propagated ever since the queen's pregnancy was announced, that it was feigned, and that a suppositious child was to be palmed upon the world, Jeffreys was lamentably deficient in duty to the king in not having recommended steps to convince the public from the beginning, beyond all possibility of controversy, of the genuineness of the birth. When the story of the "warming-pan" had taken hold of the public mind, many witnesses were examined before the Privy Council to disprove it, but it continued an article of faith with thorough anti-Jacobites during the two succeeding reigns.*

The birth of a son, which the king had so ardently longed for, led to his speedy overthrow. Instead of the intrigues between the discontented at home and the Prince and Princess of Orange, hitherto regarded as his successors, being put an end to, they immediately assumed a far more formidable aspect. William, who had hoped in the course of a few years to wield the energies of Britain against the dangerous ambition of Louis XIV., saw that if he remained quiet he should with difficulty even retain the circumscribed power of Stadtholder of the United Provinces. He therefore gladly listened to the representations of those who had fled to Holland to escape from the tyranny exercised in their native country, or who sent secret emissaries to implore his aid; and he boldly resolved to come to England — not as a military conqueror, but for their deliverance, and to obtain the crown with the assent of the nation. That he and his adherents might be protected against any sudden effort to crush them, a formidable fleet was equipped in the Dutch ports, and a considerable army, which had been assembled professedly for a dif-

* It was pretended by the anti-Jacobites, that is, the enemies of James and the exiled Stuarts, that the infant had been smuggled into the queen's bed in a warming-pan. — *Ed.*

ferent purpose, was ready on a short notice to be embarked in it.

James, who had been amusing himself by making the pope godfather to his son, and had listened with absolute incredulity to the rumors of the coming invasion, suddenly became sensible of his danger, and to avert it was willing to make any sacrifice to please his people. The slender merit of the tardy, forced, and ineffectual concessions which were offered is claimed respectively by the apologists of the king, of Jeffreys, and of the Earl of Sunderland, but seems due to the last of the three. James's infatuation was so transcendent, — he was so struck with judicial blindness, — being doomed to destruction, he was so demented, — that, if let alone, he probably would have trusted with confidence to his divine right and the protection of the Virgin, even when William had landed at Torbay. As far as I can discover, from the time when Jeffreys received the great seal, he never originated any measures, wise or wicked, and without remonstrance, he heartily coöperated in all those suggested by the king, however illegal or mischievous they might be. I do not find the slightest foundation for the assertion that, with all his faults, he had a regard for the Protestant religion, which made him stand up in its defence. The "Declaration of Indulgence," to which he put the great seal, might be imputed to a love of toleration, (to which he was a stranger,) but what can be said of the active part he took in the High Commission Court, and in introducing Roman Catholics into the universities and into the church? The Earl of Sunderland, though utterly unprincipled, was a man of great discernment and courage; he could speak boldly to the king, and he had joined in objecting to the precipitate measures for giving ascendancy to his new religion, which had produced this crisis. His seemingly forced removal from office he himself probably suggested, along with the other steps now taken to appease the people.

Whoever might first propose the altered policy, Jeffreys was the instrument for carrying it into effect, and thereby it lost all its grace and virtue. He took off the suspension of the Bishop of London, and, by a *supersedeas* under the great seal, abolished the High Commission Court. He annulled all the proceedings respecting Magdalen College, and issued the necessary process for reinstating Dr. Hough and the Protestant fellows. He put the great seal to a general pardon.

But the reaction was hoped for, above all, from the restoration of the city charters. On the 2d of October he sent a flattering message to the mayor and aldermen to come to Whitehall in the evening, that they might be presented at court by "their old recorder." Here the king told them that he was mightily concerned for the welfare of their body, and that at a time when invasion threatened the kingdom, he was determined to show them his confidence in their loyalty by restoring the rights of the city to the state in which they were before the unfortunate *quo warranto* proceedings had been instituted in the late reign. Accordingly, on the following day a meeting of the Common Council was called at Guildhall, and the lord chancellor proceeded thither in his state carriage, attended by his purse-bearer, mace-bearer, and other officers, and after a florid speech, delivered them letters patent under the great seal, which waived all forfeitures, revived all charters, and confirmed all liberties the city had ever enjoyed under the king or any of his ancestors. Great joy was manifested; but the citizens could not refrain from showing their abhorrence of the man who brought these glad tidings, and on his return they hissed him and hooted him, and gave him a foretaste of the violence he was soon to experience from an English mob.

The forfeited and surrendered charters were likewise restored to the other corporations in England. These popular acts, however, were generally ascribed to fear, and the coalition of all parties, including the preachers of passive obedience, to obtain a permanent redress of grievances by force, continued resolute and unshaken.

When William landed, the frightful severities of Jeffreys in the west had the effect of preventing the populace from flocking to his standard, but he met with no opposition, and soon persons of great consideration and influence sent in their adhesion to him.

When we read in history of civil commotions and foreign invasions, we are apt to suppose that all the ordinary business of life was suspended. But on inquiry, we find that it went on pretty much as usual, unless where interrupted by actual violence. While the Prince of Orange was advancing to the capital, and James was marching out to give him battle, if his army would have stood true, the Court of Chancery sat regularly to hear "exceptions" and "motions for time to plead;" and on the very day on which the Princess Anne fled to Nottingham, and her unhappy father exclaimed, in the extremity of his agony, "God help me! my own children have forsaken me," the lord chancellor decided that "if an administrator pays a debt due by bond before a debt due by a decree in equity, he is still liable to pay the debt due by the decree.*

* 24th November, 1688. 2 Vernon, 88, *Searle* v. *Lane.* By a reference to the minute books in the registrar's office, it appears that Jeffreys sat again on Monday, Nov. 26, when he decided *Duval* v. *Edwards*, a case on

Change of dynasty was not yet talked of, and the cry was for "a free Parliament." To meet this, the king resolved to call one in his own name; and the last use which Jeffreys made of the great seal was by sealing writs for the election of members of the House of Commons, who were ordered to meet on the 15th of January following.

This movement only infused fresh vigor into the Prince of Orange, who now resolved to bring matters to a crisis; and James, finding himself almost universally deserted, as the most effectual way, in his judgment, of annoying his enemies, very conveniently for them, determined to leave the kingdom. Preparatory to this, he had a parting interview with Jeffreys, to whom he did not confide his secret; but he obtained from him all the parliamentary writs which had not been issued to the sheriffs, amounting to a considerable number, and these, with his own hand, he threw into the fire, so that a lawful Parliament might not be assembled when he was gone. To increase the confusion, he required Jeffreys to surrender the great seal to him, — having laid the plan of destroying it, — in the belief that without it the government could not be conducted.

All things being prepared, and Father Peter and the Earl of Melfort having been informed of his intentions, which he still concealed from Jeffreys, on the night of the 10th of December, James, disguised, left Whitehall, accompanied by Sir Edward Hales, whom he afterwards created Earl of Tenterden. London Bridge (which they durst not cross) being the

exceptions, nine in number, giving a separate judgment on each. He did not sit on the 27th, but he did on the 28th, which was the last day of term. So late as the 8th of December he sat and heard several petitions. In the evening of this day the great seal was taken from him.

only one then over the Thames, they drove in a hackney-coach to the Horse Ferry, Westminster, and as they crossed the river with a pair of oars, the king threw the great seal into the water, and thought he had sunk with it forever the fortunes of the Prince of Orange. At Vauxhall they found horses in readiness for them, and they rode swiftly to Feversham, where they embarked for France.

Instead of narrating the adventures of the monarch, when he was intercepted at Feversham, we must confine ourselves to what befell the unhappy ex-chancellor. He heard early next morning of the royal flight, and was thrown into a state of the greatest consternation. He was afraid of punishment from the new government which was now to be established, and being asked by a courtier if he had heard "what the *heads* of the Prince's declaration were," he answered, "I am sure that *my head* is one, whatever the rest may be." He dreaded still more the fury of the mob, of which the most alarming accounts were soon brought him. In the existing state of anarchy, almost the whole population of the metropolis crowded into the streets in quest of intelligence; the excitement was unexampled; there was an eager desire to prevent the king's evil councillors from escaping along with him; and many bad characters, under a pretence of a regard for the Protestant religion, took the opportunity to gratify their love of violence and plunder.

The first object of vengeance was Father Peter; but it was found that, in consequence of the information of the king's intentions conveyed to him and the Earl of Melfort, they had secretly withdrawn the day before, and were now in safety. The pope's nuncio was rescued from imminent peril by the interposition of the lords of the Council, who had met, and, exercising temporarily the powers of government, were striving to preserve the public tranquillity.

The next victim demanded was Jeffreys, who (no one knowing that the great seal had been taken from him) still went by the name of "the chancellor," and who, of all professing Protestants, was the most obnoxious to the multitude. He retired early in the day from his house in Duke Street to the obscure dwelling of a dependent in Westminster, near the river side, and here, lying concealed, he caused preparations to be made for his escape from the kingdom. It was arranged that a coal ship which had delivered her cargo should clear out at the custom house as for her return to Newcastle, and should land him at Hamburg.

To avoid, as he thought, all chance of being recognised by those who had seen him in ermine or gold-embroidered robes, with a long white band under the chin, his collar of S. S. round his neck, and on his head a full-bottom wig, which had recently become the attribute of judicial dignity, instead of the old-fashioned coif or black velvet cap, — he cut off his bushy eyebrows, wont to inspire such terror, he put on the worn-out dress of a common sailor, and he covered his head with an old tarred hat that seemed to have weathered many a blast.

Thus disguised, as soon as it was dusk he got into a boat; and the state of the tide enabling him to shoot London Bridge without danger, he safely reached the coal ship lying off Wapping. Here he was introduced to the captain and the mate, on whose secrecy he was told he might rely; but, as they could not sail till next day, when he had examined his berth, he went on board another vessel that lay at a little distance, there to pass the night. If he had not taken this precaution, he would have been almost immediately in the power of his enemies. The mate, without waiting to see what became of him, hurried on shore, and treacherously gave information to some persons who had been in pursuit of him, that he was concealed in the Newcastle collier. They applied to justices of the peace in the neighborhood for a warrant to arrest him, which was refused, on the ground that no specific charge was sworn against him. They then went to the lords of the council, whom they found sitting, and who actually gave them a warrant to apprehend him for high treason, under the belief that the safety of the state required his detention. Armed with this, they returned to the coal ship in which he had taken his passage, but he was not there, and the captain, a man of honor, baffled all their inquiries.

He slept securely in the vessel in which he had sought refuge; and had it not been for the most extraordinary imprudence, leading to the belief that he was fated speedily to expiate his crimes, he might have effected his escape. Probably with a view of indulging more freely his habit of intemperance, he next morning came ashore, and made his appearance at a little alehouse bearing the sign of "The Red Cow," in Anchor and Hope Alley, near King Edward's Stairs, Wapping, and called for a pot of ale. When he had nearly finished it, still wearing his sailor's attire, with his hat on his head, he was so rashly confident as to put his head out from an open window to look at the passengers in the street.

I must prepare my readers for the scene which follows by relating, in the words of Roger North, an anecdote of the behavior of Jeffreys to a suitor in the heyday of his power and arrogance. "There was a scrivener of Wapping brought to hearing for relief against a *bummery bond.** The contingency of losing all being showed, the bill was going to be dismissed; † but one of the plaintiff's counsel said that the scrivener was a strange fellow, and sometimes went to church, sometimes to conventicles, and none could tell what to make of him; and it was thought he was a trimmer. At that the chancellor fired; and 'A trimmer!' said he; 'I have heard much of that monster, but never saw one. Come forth, Mr. Trimmer, turn you round, and let us see your shape,' and at that rate talked so long that the poor fellow was ready to drop under him; but at last the bill was dismissed with costs, and he went his way. In the hall one of his friends asked him how he came off. 'Came off,' said he; 'I am escaped from the terrors of that man's face, which I would scarce undergo again to save my life, and I shall certainly have the frightful impression of it as long as I live.' " ‡

It happened, by a most extraordinary coincidence, that this

* "Bottomry bond." This contraction shows the etymology of an elegant English word from "bottom," which Dr. Johnson chooses to derive from the Dutch word "bomme."

† *i. e.* The principal being put in hazard, the interest was not usurious.

‡ The following is from Macaulay's elaborate portraiture of Jeffreys on the bench: "All tenderness for the feelings of others, all self-respect, all sense of the becoming, were obliterated from his mind. He acquired a boundless command of the rhetoric in which the vulgar express hatred and contempt. The profusion of maledictions and vituperative epithets which composed his vocabulary could hardly have been rivalled in the fish-market or the bear-garden. His countenance and his voice must always have been unamiable; but these natural advantages — for such he seems to have thought them — he had improved to such a degree that there were few who, in his paroxysms of rage, could see or hear him without emotion. Impudence and ferocity sat upon his brow. The glare of his eyes had a fascination for the unhappy victim on whom they were fixed; yet his brow and eye were said to be less terrible than the savage lines of his mouth. His yell of fury, as was said by one who had often heard it, sounded like the thunder of the judgment day."

very scrivener was then walking through Anchor and Hope Alley on the opposite side of the way, and immediately looking towards "The Red Cow," thought he recollected the features of the sailor who was gazing across towards him. The conviction then flashed upon his mind that this could be no other than the lord chancellor who had so frightened him out of his wits before pronouncing a decree in his favor about the "*bummery bond*." But hardly believing his own senses, he entered the tap-room of the alehouse to examine the countenance more deliberately. Upon his entrance, Jeffreys must have recognized the "trimmer," for he coughed, turned to the wall, and put the quart pot before his face. An immense multitude of persons were in a few minutes collected round the door by the proclamation of the scrivener that the pretended sailor was indeed the wicked Lord Chancellor Jeffreys. He was now in the greatest jeopardy, for, unlike the usual character of the English mob, who are by no means given to cruelty, the persons here assembled were disposed at first to tear him limb from limb, and he was only saved by the interposition of some of the more considerate, who suggested that the proper course would be to take him before the lord mayor.

The cry was raised, "To the lord mayor's!" but before he could be secured in a carriage to be conveyed thither, they assaulted and pelted him, and might have proceeded to greater extremities if a party of the train-bands had not rescued him from their fury. They still pursued him all the way with whips, and halters, and cries of "Vengeance! justice! justice!" Although he lay back in the coach, he could still be discovered in his blue jacket, and with his sailor's hat flapped down upon his face. The lord mayor, Sir John Chapman, a nervous, timid man, who had stood in tremendous awe of the lord chancellor, could not now see him, disguised as a sailor, without trepidation; and instead of ordering him to stand at the bar of his justice room, with much bowing and scraping, and many apologies for the liberty he was using, requested that his lordship would do him the honor to dine with him, as, it being now past twelve o'clock, he and the lady mayoress were about to sit down to dinner. Jeffreys, though probably with little appetite, was going to accept the invitation, when a gentleman in the room exclaimed, "The lord chancellor is the lord mayor's prisoner, not his guest, and now to harbor him is treason, for which any one, however high, may have to answer with his own blood." The lord mayor swooned away, and died (it is said of apoplexy) soon after.

The numbers and violence of the mob had greatly increased from the delay in examining the culprit, and they loudly threatened to take the law into their own hand. Some were for examining him before an alderman, and leading him out by a back way for that purpose; but he himself showed most prudence by advising that, without any previous examination, he should be committed to the Tower for safe custody, and that two other regiments of the train-bands should be ordered up to conduct him thither. In the confusion, he offered to draw the warrant for his own commitment. This course was followed, but was by no means free from danger, the mob defying the matchlocks and pikes of the soldiers, and pressing round the coach in which the noble prisoner was carried, still flourishing the whips and halters, and expressing their determined resolution to execute summary justice upon him for the many murders he had committed. Seeing the imminent danger to which he was exposed, and possibly conscience struck when he thought he was so near his end, he lost all sense of dignity and all presence of mind. He held up his imploring hands, sometimes on one side of the coach, and sometimes on the other, exclaiming, "For the Lord's sake, keep them off! For the Lord's sake, keep them off!" Oldmixon, who was an eye-witness of this procession, and makes loud professions of compassion for malefactors, declares that he saw these agonizing alarms without pity.

The difficulty was greatest in passing the open space on Tower Hill. But at length the carriage passed the drawbridge, and the portcullis descended. Within all was still. Jeffreys was courteously received by Lord Lucas, recently appointed lieutenant, and in a gloomy apartment, which he never more left, he reflected in solitude on the procession which had just terminated, so different from those to which he had been accustomed for some years on the first day of each returning term, when, attended by the judges and all the grandees of the law, he had moved in state to Westminster Hall, the envy and admiration of all beholders.

A regular warrant for his commitment was the same night made out by the lords of the Council, and the next day a deputation from their body, consisting of Lords North, Grey, Chandos and Ossulston, attended to examine him at the Tower. Four questions were asked him. 1. "What he had done with the great seal of England." He answered "that he had delivered it to the king on the Saturday before at Mr. Cheffnel's, no person being present, and that he had not seen it since." He was next asked, 2. "Whether he had sealed all the writs for the Parliament, and what he had done with them." "To the best of his remembrance," he said, "the writs were all sealed and delivered to the king," (suppressing that he had seen the king throw a great many of them in the fire.) 3. "Had he sealed the several patents for the then ensuing year?" He declared "that he had sealed several patents for the new sheriffs, but that he could not charge his memory with the particulars." Lastly, he was asked "whether he had a license to go out of the kingdom." And to this he replied, "that he had several licenses to go beyond sea, which were all delivered to Sir John Friend." He subscribed these answers with an affirmation that "they were true upon his honor," and the lords withdrew.

But no sympathy did he meet with from any quarter, and he was now reproachfully spoken of even by the king. The news of the outbreak against him coming speedily to Feversham, the fugitive monarch, who then meditated an attempt to remount his throne, thought that his chancellor might possibly be accepted by the nation as a scape-goat, and laid upon him the great errors of his reign. It happened, strangely enough, that the inn to which James had been carried when captured off Sheerness, was kept by a man on whom Jeffreys, for some supposed contempt of court, had imposed a very heavy fine, which had not yet been levied. Complaining of this arbitrary act to his royal guest, — who had admitted him to his presence, and had asked him, in royal fashion, "his name, his age, and his history," — James desired him to draw a discharge as ample as he chose; and, establishing a precedent, which has been often followed since, for writing in a seemingly private and confidential document what is intended afterwards to be communicated to the public, he subjoined to his signature these remarkable words, which were immediately proclaimed in Feversham and transmitted to London: "I am sensible that my lord chancellor hath been a very ill man, and hath done very ill things."

Jeffreys was assailed by the press in a manner which showed how his cruelties had brutalized the public mind. A poetical letter, addressed to him, advising him to cut his own throat, thus concluded: "I am your lordship's obedient servant in any thing of this nature. From the little house over against Tyburn, where the people are almost dead with expectation of you."

This was followed by "a letter from hell from Lord Ch——r Jeffreys to L—— C—— B—— W——d." His "confession," hawked about the streets, contained an exaggerated statement of all the bad measures of the latter part of the preceding and of the present reign. Then came his "last will and testament," commencing, "In the name of Ambition, the only god of our setting and worshipping, together with Cruelty, Perjury, Pride, Insolence, &c., I, George Jeffreys, being in sound and perfect memory, of high commissions, *quo warrantos*, dispensations, pillorizations, floggations, gibitations, barbarity, butchery, &c., do make my last will," &c. Here is the concluding legacy: "Item, I order an ell and a half of fine cambric to be cut into handkerchiefs for drying up all the wet eyes at my funeral; together with half a pint of burnt claret for all the mourners in the kingdom."

When he had been some weeks in confinement, he received a small barrel, marked "Colchester oysters," of which, ever since his arrival in London when a boy, he had been particularly fond. Seeing it, he exclaimed — "Well, I have some friends left still;" but on opening it, the gift was — a halter!

An actual serious petition was received by the lords of the

council of England from "the widows and fatherless children in the west," beginning, "We, to the number of a thousand and more widows and fatherless children of the counties of Dorset, Somerset, and Devon; our dear husbands and tender fathers having been so tyrannously butchered and some transported; our estates sold from us, and our inheritance cut off, by the severe and brutish sentence of George Lord Jeffreys, now we understand in the Tower of London, a prisoner," &c. After enumerating some of his atrocities, and particularly dwelling upon his indecent speech (which I may not copy) to a young lady who asked the life of her lover, convicted before him, the petitioners thus concluded:—"These, with many hundred more tyrannical acts, are ready to be made appear in the said counties by honest and credible persons, and therefore your petitioners desire that the said George Jeffreys, late lord chancellor, the vilest of men, may be brought down to the counties aforesaid, where we the good women of the west shall be glad to see him, and give him another manner of welcome than he had there three years since."

Meanwhile, the great seal, the *clavis regni*, the emblem of sovereign sway, which had been thrown into the Thames that it might never reach the Prince of Orange, was found in the net of a fisherman near Lambeth, and was delivered by him to the lords of the council, who were resolved to place it in the hands of the founder of the new dynasty; and James, after revisiting the capital and enjoying a fleeting moment of popularity, had finally bid adieu to England, and was enjoying the munificent hospitality of Louis at St. Germaine's.

The provisional government, in deference to the public voice, issued an order for the more rigorous confinement of the ex-chancellor in the Tower, and intimated a resolution that he should speedily be brought to trial for his misdeeds; but, amidst the stirring events which rapidly followed, he was allowed quietly to languish out the remainder of his miserable existence. While the elections were proceeding for the Convention Parliament — while the two houses were struggling respecting the "abdication" or "desertion" of the throne — while men were occupied with discussing the "declaration of rights" — while preparations were making for the coronation of the new sovereigns — while curiosity was keenly alive in watching their demeanor, and while alarms were spread by the adherence of Ireland to the exiled king — the national indignation, which at first burst forth so violently against the crimes of Jeffreys, almost entirely subsided, and little desire was evinced to see him punished as he deserved.

However, considerable sensation was excited by the news that he was no more. He breathed his last in the Tower of London, on the 19th of April, 1689, at thirty-five minutes past four in the morning. Those who take a vague impression of events, without attention to dates, may suppose, from the crowded vicissitudes of his career, that he must have passed his grand climacteric, but he was still only in the forty-first year of his age.

On the meeting of the Convention Parliament, attempts were made to attaint the late Chancellor Jeffreys, to prevent his heirs from sitting in Parliament, and to charge his estates with compensation to those whom he had injured; but they all failed, and no mark of public censure was set upon his memory beyond excepting him, with some other judges, from the act of indemnity passed at the commencement of the new reign.

We have no very distinct account of him in domestic life.

Having lost his first wife, whom he had espoused so generously, within three months from her death he again entered the married state. The object of his choice was the widow of a Montgomeryshire gentleman, and daughter of Sir Thomas Bludworth, who had been lord mayor of London, and for many years one of the city representatives. I am sorry to say there was much scandal about the second Lady Jeffreys, and she presented him prematurely with a full-grown child. It is related that he was once disagreeably reminded of this mistake: when cross-examining a flippant female, he said to her, "Madam, you are very quick in your answers." "Quick as I am, Sir George," cried she, "I was not so quick as your lady." Even after the marriage she is still said to have encouraged Sir John Trevor, M. R., and other lovers, while her husband was indulging in his cups.

He had children by both his wives; but of these only one son grew up to manhood, and survived him. This was John, the second Lord Jeffreys, who has acquired celebrity only by having rivalled his father in the power of drinking, and for having, when in a state of intoxication, interrupted the funeral of Dryden, the poet. He was married, as we have seen, to the daughter of the Earl of Pembroke, but dying in 1703, without male issue, the title of Jeffreys happily became extinct. He soon dissipated large estates, which his father, by such unjustifiable means, had acquired in Shropshire, Buckinghamshire, and Leicestershire.

In his person Jeffreys was rather above the middle stature, his complexion (before it was bloated by intemperance) inclining to fair, and he was of a comely appearance. There was great animation in his eye, with a twinkle which might breed a suspicion of insincerity and lurking malice. His brow was commanding, and he managed it with wonderful effect, whether he wished to terrify or to conciliate. There are many portraits of him, all, from his marked features, bearing a great resemblance to each other, and, it may be presumed, to the original.

"He had a set of banterers for the most part near him, as in old time great men kept fools to make them merry. And these fellows, abusing one another and their betters, were a regale to him." But there can be no doubt that he circulated in good society. He was not only much at court, but he exchanged visits with the nobility and persons of distinction in different walks of life. In the social circle, being entirely free from hypocrisy and affectation, from haughtiness and ill-nature, laughing at principle, courting a reputation for profligacy, talking with the utmost freedom of all parties and all men — he disarmed the censure of the world, and, by the fascination of his manners, while he was present, he threw an oblivion over his vices and his crimes.

On one occasion, dining in the city with Alderman Duncomb, the lord treasurer and other great courtiers being of the party, they worked themselves up to such a pitch of loyalty by bumpers to "confusion to the Whigs," that they all stripped to their shirts, and were about to get upon a signpost to drink the king's health, when they were accidentally diverted from their purpose, and the lord chancellor escaped the fate which befell Sir Charles Sedley, of being indicted for indecently exposing his person in the public streets. But this frolic brought upon him a violent fit of the stone, which nearly cost him his life.

As a civil judge he was by no means without high qualifications, and in the absence of any motive to do wrong, he was willing to do right. He had a very quick perception, a vigorous and logical understanding, and an impressive eloquence.

When quite sober, he was particularly good as a Nisi Prius judge. His summing up, in what is called "the Lady Ivy's case" — an ejectment between her and the dean and chapter of St. Paul's to recover a large estate at Shadwell — is most masterly. The evidence was exceedingly complicated, and he gives a beautiful sketch of the whole, both documentary and parol; and, without taking the case from the jury, he makes some admirable observations on certain deeds produced by the Lady Ivy, which led to the conclusion that they were forged, and to a verdict for the dean and chapter.*

Considering the systematic form which equity jurisprudence had assumed under his two immediate predecessors, Jeffreys must have been very poorly furnished for presiding in chancery. He had practised little before these judges, and none of their decisions were yet in print; so that if he had been so inclined, he had not the opportunity to make himself familiar with the established practice and doctrines of the court.

Although he must often have betrayed his ignorance, yet with his characteristic boldness and energy he contrived to get through the business without any signal disgrace, and among all the invectives, satires, and lampoons by which his memory is blackened, I find little said against his decrees. He did not promulgate any body of new orders according to recent custom; but, while he held the great seal, he issued separate orders from time to time, some of which were very useful.

* Down to this time trials at nisi prius had not assumed their present shape. The issue being read to the jury, the evidence was given, and with hardly any speeches from counsel, all seems to have been left to the judge.

He first put an end to a very oppressive practice, by which a plaintiff, having filed a frivolous and vexatious bill, might dismiss it on paying merely twenty shillings costs, and he directed that the defendant should be allowed all the costs he had incurred, to be properly ascertained by an officer of the court. He then checked the abuse of staying actions at law for the examination of witnesses abroad, by requiring, before a commission to examine them issued, an affidavit specifying the names of the witnesses, and the facts they were expected to prove. By subsequent orders which he framed, vexatious applications for re-hearings were guarded against, and an attempt was made to get rid of what has ever been the opprobrium of the court — controversies about settling the minutes of a decree after it has been pronounced.

I have discovered one benevolent opinion of this cruel judge, and strange to say, it is at variance with that of the humane magistrates who have adorned Westminster Hall in the nineteenth century. "The prisoner's convict bill" was condemned and opposed by almost all the judges in the reign of William IV., yet even Jeffreys was struck with the injustice and inequality of the law, which, allowing the accused to defend himself by counsel "for a two-penny trespass," refuses that aid "where life, estate, honor, and all are concerned," and lamented its existence, while he declared himself bound to adhere to it.* The venerable sages who apprehended such multiplied evils from altering the practice must have been greatly relieved by finding that their objections have proved as unfounded as those which were urged against the abolition of "*peine forte et dure;*" and the alarming innovation, so

* 10 State Trials, 267.

long resisted, of allowing witnesses for the prisoner to be examined under the sanction of an oath.

He has been so much abused, that I began my critical examination of his history in the hope and belief that I should find that his misdeeds had been exaggerated, and that I might be able to rescue his memory from some portion of the obloquy under which it labors; but I am sorry to say, that in my matured opinion, although he appears to have been a man of high talents, of singularly agreeable manners, and entirely free from hypocrisy, his cruelty and his political profligacy have not been sufficiently exposed or reprobated; and that he was not redeemed from his vices by one single solid virtue.

# CHAPTER XVI.

## ROBERT WRIGHT.

I NOW come to the last of the profligate chief justices of England; for since the Revolution they have all been men of decent character, and most of them have adorned the seat of justice by their talents and acquirements, as well as by their virtues. Sir Robert Wright, if excelled by some of his predecessors in bold crimes, yields to none in ignorance of his profession, and beats them all in the fraudulent and sordid vices.

He was the son of a respectable gentleman who lived near Thetford, in Suffolk, and was the representative of an ancient family, long seated at Kelverstone, in Norfolk; he enjoyed the opportunity of receiving a good education at Thetford Free Grammar School, and at the University of Cambridge; and he had the advantage of a very handsome person and agreeable manner. But he was by nature volatile, obtuse, intensely selfish, with hardly a particle of shame, and quite destitute of the faculty of distinguishing what was base from what was honorable. Without any maternal spoiling, or the contamination of bad company, he showed the worst faults of childhood, and these ripened, while he was still in early youth, into habits of gaming, drinking, and every sort of debauchery. There was a hope of his reformation when, being still under age, he captivated the affections of one of the daughters of Dr. Wren, Bishop of Ely, and was married to her. But he continued his licentious course of life, and, having wasted her fortune, he treated her with cruelty.

He was supposed to study the law at an Inn of Court, but when he was called to the bar he had not imbibed even the first rudiments of his profession. Nevertheless, taking to the Norfolk Circuit, the extensive influence of his father-in-law, which was exercised unscrupulously in his favor, got him briefs, and for several years he had more business than North, (afterwards Lord Keeper Guilford,) a very industrious lawyer, who joined the circuit at the same time. "But withal," says Roger, the inimitable biographer, "he was so poor a lawyer that he could not give an opinion upon a written case, but used to bring such cases as came to him to his friend, Mr. North, and he wrote the opinion on a paper, and the lawyer copied it and signed under the case as if it had been his own. It run so low with him, that when North was at London, he sent up his cases to him, and had opinions returned by the post; and in the mean time he put off his clients upon pretence of taking more serious consideration."

At last the attorneys found him out so completely that they entirely deserted him, and he was obliged to give up practice. By family interest he obtained the lucrative sinecure of "treasurer to the chest at Chatham," but by his voluptuous and reckless course of life he got deeper and deeper in debt, and he mortgaged his estate to Mr. North for fifteen hundred pounds, the full amount of its value. From some inadvertence, the title deeds were allowed to remain in Wright's hands, and being immediately again in want, he applied to Sir Walter Plummer to lend him five hundred pounds on mortgage, offering the mortgaged estate as a security, and asserting that this would be the first charge upon it. The wary Sir

31 *

Walter thought he would make himself doubly safe by requiring an affidavit that the estate was clear from all incumbrances. This affidavit Wright swore without any hesitation, and he then received the five hundred pounds. But the money being spent, and the fraud being detected, he was in the greatest danger of being sent to jail for debt, and also of being indicted for swindling and perjury.

He had only one resource, and this proved available. Being a clever mimic, he had been introduced into the circle of parasites and buffoons who surrounded Jeffreys, at this time chief justice of the King's Bench, and used to make sport for him and his companions in their drunken orgies by taking off the other judges, as well as the most eminent counsel. One day, being asked why he seemed to be melancholy, he took the opportunity of laying open his destitute condition to his patron, who said to him, "As you seem to be unfit for the bar, or any other honest calling, I see nothing for it but that you should become a judge yourself." Wright naturally supposed that this was a piece of wicked pleasantry, and when Jeffreys had declared that he was never more serious in his life, asked how it could be brought about, for he not only felt himself incompetent for such an office, but he had no interest, and, still more, it so happened, unfortunately, that the Lord Keeper Guilford, who made the judges, was fully aware of the unaccountable lapse of memory into which he had fallen when he swore the affidavit for Sir Walter Plummer, that his estate was clear from all incumbrances, the lord keeper himself being the first mortgagee. *Jeffreys, C. J.*—"Never despair, my boy; leave all that to me."

We know nothing more of the intrigue with certainty, till the following dialogue took place in the royal closet. We can only conjecture that in the meanwhile Jeffreys, who was then much cherished at court, and was impatient to supersede Guilford entirely, had urgently pressed the king that Wright might be elevated to the bench as a devoted friend of the prerogative, and that, as the lord keeper had a prejudice against him, his majesty ought to take the appointment into his own hands. But we certainly know that, a vacancy occurring in the Court of Exchequer, the lord keeper had an audience of his majesty to take his pleasure on the appointment of a new baron, and that he named a gentleman at the bar, in great practice and of good character, as the fittest person to be appointed, thinking that Charles would nod assent with his usual easy indifference, when, to his utter amazement, he was thus interrogated: "My lord, what think you of Mr. Wright? Why may not he be the man?" *Lord Keeper.*—"Because, sir, I know him too well, and he is the most unfit person in England to be made a judge." *King.*—"Then it must not be." Upon this, the lord keeper withdrew, without having received any other notification of the king's pleasure; and the office remained vacant.

Again there is a chasm in the intrigue, and we are driven to guess that Jeffreys had renewed his solicitation, had treated the objections started to Wright as ridiculous, and had advised the cashiering of the lord keeper if he should prove obstinate. The next time that the lord keeper was in the royal presence, the king, opening the subject of his own accord, observed, "Good my lord, why may not Wright be a judge? He is strongly recommended to me; but I would have a due respect paid to you, and I would not make him without your concurrence. Is it impossible, my lord?" *Lord Keeper.*—"Sir, the making of a judge is your majesty's choice, and not my pleasure. I am bound to put the seal as I am commanded, whatever the person may be. It is for your majesty to determine, and me, your servant, to obey. But I must do my duty by informing your majesty of the truth respecting this man, whom I personally know to be a dunce, and no lawyer; who is not worth a groat, having spent his estate by debauched living; who is without honesty, having been guilty of wilful perjury to gain the borrowing of a sum of money. And now, sir, I have done my duty to your majesty, and am ready to obey your majesty's commands in case it be your pleasure that this man be a judge." The king thanked the lord keeper, without saying more, but next day there came a warrant under the sign manual for creating the king's "trusty and well-beloved Robert Wright" a baron of his Exchequer, and orders were given for making out the patent in due form; and the detected swindler, knighted, and clothed in ermine, took his place among the twelve judges of England.

People were exceedingly shocked when they saw the seat of justice so disgraced; but this might be what Jeffreys intended; and one of his first acts, when he himself obtained the great seal, was to promote his *protégé* from being a baron of the Exchequer to be a judge of the Court of King's Bench.

Wright continued to do many things which caused great scandal, and, therefore, was dearer than ever to his patron, who would have discarded him if he had shown any symptoms of reformation. He accompanied General Jeffreys as *aide de camp* in the famous "campaign in the west;" in other words, he was joined in commission with him as a judge in the "bloody assize," and, sitting on the bench with him at the trial of Lady Lisle and the others which followed, concurred in all his atrocities. He came in for very little of the bribery; Jeffreys, who claimed the lion's share, tossing him by way of encouragement one solitary pardon, for which a small sum only was expected.

But on the death of Sir Henry Beddingfield he was made chief justice of the Common Pleas; and very soon afterwards, the unexpected quarrel breaking out between Sir Edward Herbert and the government about martial law and the punishment of deserters,* the object being to find some one who

* The plan was formed of ruling by a standing army. But without a Parliament, how was this army to be kept in a proper state of discipline? In time of war, or during a rebellion, troops in the field were subject to martial law, and they might be punished, by sentence of a court martial, for mutiny or desertion. But the country was now in a state of peace and profound tranquillity; and the common law, which alone prevailed, knew no distinction between citizen and soldier; so that, if a lifeguardsman deserted, he could only be sued for breach of contract, and if he struck his officer, he was only liable to an indictment or an action of battery. While the king's military force consisted of a few regiments of household troops, with high pay, desertion was not to be apprehended, and military offences were sufficiently punished by dismission from the service. But James found it impossible to govern the numerous army which he had collected at Hounslow without the assistance of martial law; and he contended that, without any act of Parliament, he was at all times entitled, by virtue of his prerogative, to put martial law in force against military men, although it could only be put in force against civilians when war or rebellion was raging in the kingdom.

The question first arose at the Old Bailey, before Sir John Holt, then recorder of London, and he decided against the crown, as might have been expected; for, while avoiding keen partisanship in politics, he had been always Whiggishly inclined. James thought he was quite secure by appealing to the ultra Tory, Lord Chief Justice Herbert. To the utter amazement of the king and the courtiers, this honorable, although shallow, magistrate declared that, without an act of Parliament, all laws were equally applicable to all his majesty's subjects, whether wearing red coats or gray. Being taunted with inconsistency in respect of his judgment in favor of the dispensing power, he took this distinction, "that a statute altering the common law might be suspended by the king, who is really the lawgiver, notwithstanding the form that he enacts 'with the *assent* of the lords by no possibility could go against the government, or hesitate about doing any thing required of him, however base or however bloody, Wright was selected as chief justice of the king's bench. Unluckily we have no account of the speeches made at any of his judicial installations, so that we do not know in what terms his learning and purity of conduct were praised, or what were the promises which he gave of impartiality and of rigorous adherence to the laws of the realm.

On the very day on which he took his seat on the bench he gave good earnest of his servile spirit. The attorney general renewed his motion for an order to execute at Plymouth the deserter who had been capitally convicted at Reading for deserting his colors. The new chief justice, without entering into reasons, or explaining how he came to differ from the opinion so strongly expressed by his predecessor, merely said, "Be it so!" The puisnies now nodded assent, and the

spiritual and temporal, and Commons;' but that the common law cannot be altered by the king's sole authority, and that the king can do nothing contrary to the common law, as that must be considered coeval with the monarchy."

James, with the infatuated obstinacy which was now driving him to destruction, set this opinion at defiance; and, encouraged by Jeffreys, caused a soldier to be capitally prosecuted, at the Reading assizes, for deserting his colors. The judges who presided there resorted to some obsolete, inapplicable act of Parliament, and were weak enough to lay down the law in the manner suggested to them by the chancellor, so that a conviction was obtained. To give greater solemnity and *eclat* to the execution, the attorney general moved the Court of King's Bench for an order that it might take place at Plymouth, in sight of the garrison from which the prisoner had run away. But Herbert peremptorily declared that the court had no jurisdiction to make such an order, and prevailed on his brother Wythens to join with him in this opinion. Mr. Attorney took nothing by his motion, but the recreant chief justice and the recreant puisne were both next morning dismissed from their offices, to make way for the most sordid wretches to be picked up in Westminster Hall — Sir Robert Wright and Sir Richard Allibone, a professed Papist.

prisoner was illegally executed at Plymouth under the order so pronounced.

Confidence was entirely lost in the administration of justice in Westminster Hall, for all the three common law courts were at last filled by incompetent and corrupt judges. Pettifogging actions only were brought in them, and men settled their disputes by arbitration, or by taking the opinion of counsel. The reports during the whole reign of James II. hardly show a single question of importance settled by judicial decision. Thus, having no distinct means of appreciating Chief Justice Wright's demerits as a judge in private causes, we must at once follow him in his devious course as a political judge.

The first occasion on which, after his installation, he drew upon himself the eyes of the public was when he was sent down to Magdalene College, Oxford, for the purpose of turning it into a Popish seminary. Upon a vacancy in the office of president, the fellows, in the exercise of their undoubted right, had elected the celebrated Dr. Hough, who had been duly admitted into the office; and the preliminary step to be taken was to annul the election, for the purpose of making way for another candidate, named by the king. There were associated with Wright, in this commission, Cartwright, Bishop of Chester, who was ready to be reconciled to Rome in the hope of higher preferment, and Sir Thomas Jenner, a baron of the Exchequer, a zealous follower in the footsteps of the chief justice of the King's Bench. Nothing could equal the infamy of their object except the insolence of their behavior in trying to accomplish it. They entered Oxford escorted by three troops of cavalry with drawn swords, and, having taken their seats with great parade in the hall of the college, summoned the fellows to attend them. These reverend and gallant divines appeared, headed by their new president, who defended his rights with skill, temper and resolution; steadily maintaining that, by the laws of England, he had a freehold in his office, and in the house and revenues annexed to it. Being asked whether he submitted to this royal visitation, he answered: —

"My lords, I do declare here, in the name of myself and the fellows, that we submit to the visitation as far as it is consistent with the laws of the land and the statutes of the college, and no further." *Wright, C. J.* — "You cannot imagine that we act contrary to the laws of the land; and as to the statutes, the king has dispensed with them. Do you think we come here to break the laws?" *Hough.* — "It does not become me, my lords, to say so; but I will be plain with your lordships. I find that your commission gives you authority to alter the statutes. Now, I have sworn to uphold and obey them; I must admit no alteration of them, and by the grace of God never will." He was asked whether one of the statutes of the founder did not require mass to be said in the college chapel; but he answered, "not only was it unlawful, but it had been repealed by the act of Parliament requiring the use of the Book of Common Prayer." However, sentence was given that the election of Hough was void, and that he be deprived of his office of president. *Hough.* — "I do hereby protest against all your proceedings, all you have done, or shall hereafter do, in prejudice of me and my right, and I appeal to my sovereign lord the king in his courts of justice." "Upon which (says a contemporary account) the strangers and young scholars in the hall gave a *hum*, which so much incensed their lordships that the lord chief justice was not to be pacified, but, charging it upon the president, bound him in a bond of one thousand pounds, and security to the like value, to make his appearance at the King's Bench bar on the 12th of November; and, taking occasion to pun upon the president's name, said to him, "Sir, you must not think to *huff* us." He then ordered the door of the president's house to be broken open by a blacksmith; and a fellow observing, "I am informed that the proper officer to gain possession of a freehold is the sheriff with a *posse comitatus*," Wright said, "I pray who is the best lawyer, you or I? Your Oxford law is no better than your Oxford divinity. If you have a mind to a *posse comitatus*, you may have one soon enough."

Having ejected Hough, he issued a mandate for expelling all the contumacious fellows, and insured the expulsion of James from his throne, when the commissioners returned in triumph to London.

Wright was likewise a member of the Ecclesiastical Court of High Commission, of which Jeffreys was president, and he strenuously joined in all the judgments of that illegal and arbitrary tribunal, which, with a *non obstante*, had been revived in the very teeth of an existing act of Parliament. He treated with ridicule the scruples of Sancroft, the Archbishop of Canterbury, and others who refused to sit upon it, and he urged the infliction of severe punishment on all who denied its jurisdiction.

Although he was not a member of the Cabinet, he usually heard from the chancellor the measures which had been resolved upon there, and he was ever a willing tool in carrying them into effect.

When the clergy were insulted, and the whole country was thrown into a flame, by the fatal order in Council for reading the "Declaration of Indulgence" in all churches and chapels on two successive Sundays, he contrived an opportunity of declaring from the bench his opinion that it was legal and obligatory. Hearing that the London clergy were almost unanimously resolved to disobey it, he sent a peremptory command to the priest who officiated in the chapel of Serjeants' Inn to read the declaration with a loud voice; and on the famous Sunday, the 20th of May, 1688, he attended in person, to give weight to the solemnity. However, he was greatly disappointed and enraged to find the service concluded without any thing being uttered beyond what the rubric prescribes. He then indecently, in the hearing of the congregation, abused the priest as disloyal, seditious, and irreligious, for contemning the authority of the head of the church. The clerk ingeniously came forth to the rescue of his superior, and took all the blame upon himself by saying that "he had forgot to bring a copy," and the chief justice, knowing that he had no remedy, was forced to content himsef with this excuse.*

The seven bishops being committed to the Tower, and prosecuted for a conspiracy to defame the king and to overturn his authority, because they had presented a petition to him praying that they might not be forced to violate their consciences and to break the law, Wright, the lowest wretch that had ever appeared on the bench in England, was to preside

* The two clergymen who were most applauded on this occasion were the bold one, who, refusing to obey the royal mandate, took for his text "Be it known unto thee, O king, that we will not serve thy gods, nor worship the golden image which thou hast set up;" and the humorous one, who, having said, "My brethren, I am obliged to read this declaration, but you are not obliged to listen to it," waited till they were all gone, clerk and all, before the reading of the declaration began.

at the most important state trial recorded in our annals. The reliance placed upon his abject subserviency no doubt operated strongly in betraying the government into this insane project of treating as common malefactors the venerable fathers of the Protestant church, now regarded by the whole nation with affectionate reverence. The consideration was entirely overlooked by the courtiers, that, from the notorious baseness of his character, his excessive zeal might be revolting to the jury, and might produce an acquittal. It is supposed that a discreet friend of the government had given him a caution to bridle his impetuosity against the accused, as the surest way of succeeding against them; for, during the whole proceeding, he was less arrogant than could have been expected, and it is much more probable that his forbearance arose from obedience to those whom he wished to please, than from any reverence for the sacred character of the defendants or any lurking respect for the interests of justice.

They were twice placed at the bar before him — first when they were brought up by the lieutenant of the Tower to be arraigned, and afterwards when a jury was empannelled for their trial. On the former occasion the questions were whether they were lawfully in custody, and were then bound to plead. The chief justice checked the opposing counsel with an air of impartiality, saying, "Look you, gentlemen, do not fall upon one another, but keep to the matter in hand." And, before deciding for the crown, he said, "I confess it is a case of great weight, and the persons concerned are of great honor and value. I would be as willing as any body to testify my respects and regards to my lords the bishops, if I could see any thing in their objections worth considering. For here is the question, whether the fact charged in the warrant of commitment be such a misdemeanor as is a breach of the peace. I cannot but think it is such a misdemeanor as would have required sureties of the peace, and if sureties were not given, a commitment might follow." He was guilty of gross injustice in refusing leave to put in a plea in abatement; but he thus mildly gave judgment: "We have inquired whether we may reject a plea, and, truly, I am satisfied that we may if the plea is frivolous; and this plea containing no more than has been overruled already, my lords the bishops must now plead guilty or not guilty."

When the trial actually came on, he betrayed a partiality for which, in our times, a judge would be impeached; but, compared with himself, so decorous was he, that he was supposed to be overawed by the august audience in whose presence he sat. It was observed that he often cast a side glance towards the thick rows of earls and barons by whom he was watched, and who, in the next Parliament, might be his judges. One bystander remarked that "he looked as if all the peers present had halters in their pockets."

The counsel for the crown having, in the first instance, failed to prove a publication of the supposed libel in the county of Middlesex, and only called upon the court to suppose or presume it, the chief justice said: "I cannot suppose it; I cannot presume any thing. I will ask my brothers their opinion, but I must deal truly with you; I think there is not evidence against my lords the bishops. It would be a strange thing if we should go and presume that these lords did it when there is no sort of evidence to prove that they did it. We must proceed according to forms and methods of law. People may think what they will of me, but I always delare my mind according to my conscience." He was actually directing the jury to acquit, and the verdict of not guilty would have been instantly pronounced, when Finch, one of the counsel for the bishops, most indiscreetly said they had evidence on their side to produce. The young gentleman was pulled down by his leaders, who desired the chief justice to proceed. And now his lordship showed the cloven foot, for he exclaimed, "No, no, I will hear Mr. Finch. Go on; my lords the bishops shall not say of me that I would not hear their counsel. I have been already told of being counsel against them, and they shall never say I would not hear counsel for them. Such a learned man as Mr. Finch must have something material to offer. He shall not be refused to be heard by me, I assure you. Why don't you go on, Mr. Finch?"

At this critical moment it was announced that the Earl of Sunderland, the president of the council, — who was present in the royal closet when the bishops presented their petition to the king at Whitehall, — was at hand, and would prove a publication in Middlesex. The chief justice then said, with affected calmness, but with real exultation, "Well, you see what comes of the interruption. I cannot help it; it is your own fault." There being a pause while they waited for the arrival of the Earl of Sunderland, the chief justice, addressing Sir Bartholomew Shower, one of the counsel for the crown, whom he had stopped at an early stage of the trial, and against whom he had some private spite, observed with great insolence, "Sir Bartholomew, now we have time to hear your speech, if you will. Let us have it."

At last the witness arrived, and, proving clearly a publication in Middlesex, the case was again launched, and, after hearing counsel on the merits, it was to be left to the determination of the jury.

The chief justice, thinking to carry it all his own way, was terribly baffled, not only by the sympathy of the audience with the bishops, which evidently made an impression on the jury, but by the unexpected honesty of one of his brother judges, Mr. Justice John Powell, who had been a quiet man, unconnected with politics, and, being a profound lawyer, had been appointed to keep the Court of King's Bench from falling into universal contempt. Sir Robert Sawyer beginning to comment upon a part of the declaration which the bishops objected to, "that from henceforth the execution of all laws against nonconformity to the religion established, or the exercise of any other religion, should be suspended," *Wright, C. J.*, exclaimed, "I must not suffer this; they intend to dispute the king's power of suspending laws." *Powell, J.* — "My lord, they must necessarily fall upon the point; for, if the king hath no such power, (as clearly he hath not, in my judgment,) the natural consequence will be that this petition is no diminution of the king's regal power, and so not seditious or libellous." *Wright, C. J.* — "Brother, I know you are full of that doctrine; but, however, my lords the bishops shall have no occasion to say that I deny to hear their counsel. Brother, you shall have your will for once; I will hear them; let them talk till they are weary." *Powell, J.* — "I desire no greater liberty to be granted them than what, in justice, the court ought to grant; that is, to hear them in defence of their clients."

As the speeches for the defendants proceeded, and were producing a great effect upon all who heard them, the solicitor general made a very irregular remark, accompanied by a fictitious yawn — "We shall be here till midnight." The chief justice, instead of reprimanding him, chimed in with the impertinence, saying, "They have no mind to have an end of the cause, for they have kept it up three hours longer than they need to have done." *Serjeant Pemberton.* — "My lord, this case does require a great deal of patience." *Wright, C. J.* — "It does so, brother, and the court has had a great deal of patience; but we must not sit here only to hear speeches." In trying to put down another counsel, who was making way with the jury, he observed, "If you say anything more, pray let me advise you one thing — don't say the same thing over and over again; for, after so much time spent, it is irksome to all company, as well as to me."

When it came to the reply of Williams, the renegade solicitor general, who in his day had been "a Whig and something more," he laid down doctrines which called forth the reprobation of Judge Powell, and even shocked the chief justice himself, for he denied that any petition could lawfully be presented to the king except by the lords and commons in Parliament assembled. *Powell, J.* — "This is strange doctrine. Shall not the subject have liberty to petition the king but in Parliament? If that be law, the subject is in a miserable case." *Wright, C. J.* — "Brother, let him go on; we will hear him out, though I approve not of his position." The unabashed Williams continued, "The lords may address the king in Parliament, and the commons may do it; but therefore that the bishops may do it out of Parliament, does not follow. I'll tell you what they should have done: if they were commanded to do anything against their consciences, they should have acquiesced till the meeting of the Parliament." * (Here, says the reporter, the people in court hissed.) *Attorney General.* — "This is very fine indeed: I hope the court and the jury will take notice of this carriage." *Wright, C. J.* — "Mr. Solicitor, I am of opinion that the bishops might petition the king; but this is not the right way. If they may petition, yet they ought to have done it after another manner; for if they may, in this reflective way, petition the king, I am sure it will make the government very precarious." *Powell, J.* — "Mr. Solicitor, it would have been too late to stay for a Parliament, for the act they conceived to be illegal was to be done forthwith; and if they had petitioned and not shown the reason why they could not obey, it would have have been looked upon as a piece of sullenness, and for that they would have been as much blamed on the other side."

The chief justice, to put on a semblance of impartiality, attempted to stop Sir Bartholomew Shower, who wished to follow in support of the prosecution, and, being a very absurd man, was likely to do more harm than good. *Wright, C. J.* — "I hope we shall have done by and by." *Sir B. S.* — "If your lordship don't think fit, I can sit down." *Wright, C. J.* — "No! no! Go on, Sir Bartholomew — you'll say I have spoiled a good speech." *Sir B. S.* — "I have no good speech to make, my lord; I have but a very few words to say." *Wright, C. J.* — "Well, go on, sir; go on."

In summing up to the jury, the chief justice said: —

"This is a case of very great concern to the king and the government on the one side, and to my lords the bishops on the other. It is an information against his grace my lord of

* More than one American advocate for treating the fugitive slave act as a law, and submitting to it as such, till repealed, has preached precisely this doctrine. — *Ed.*

Canterbury and the other six noble lords, for composing and publishing a seditious libel. At first we were all of opinion that there was no sufficient evidence of publication in the county of Middlesex, and I was going to have directed you to find my lords the bishops not guilty; but it happened that, being interrupted in my direction by an honest, worthy, learned gentleman, the king's counsel took the advantage, and, informing the court that they had further evidence, we waited till the lord president came, who told us how the petition was presented by the right reverend defendants to the king at Whitehall. Then came their learned counsel and told us that my lords the bishops are guardians of the church, and great peers of the realm, and were bound in conscience to act as they did. Various precedents have been vouched to show that the kings of England have not the power assumed by his present majesty in issuing the declaration and ordering it to be read; but concessions which kings sometimes make, for the good of the people, must not be made law; for this is reserved in the king's breast to do what he pleases in it at any time. The truth of it is, the dispensing power is out of the case, and I will not take upon me to give any opinion upon it now; for it is not before me. The only question for you is a question of fact, whether you are satisfied that this petition was presented to the king at Whitehall. If you disbelieve the lord president, you will at once acquit the defendants. If you give credit to his testimony, the next consideration is, whether the petition be a seditious libel, and this is a question of law on which I must direct you. Now, gentlemen, anything that shall disturb the government, or make mischief and a stir among the people, is certainly within the case '*de libellis famosis;*' and I must, in short, give you my opinion — I do take it to be a libel. But this being a point of law, if my brothers have anything to say to it, I suppose they will deliver their opinions."

Mr. Justice Holloway, though a devoted friend of the government, had in his breast some feeling of shame, and observed, —

"If you are satisfied there was an ill intention of sedition or the like, you should find my lords the bishops guilty; but if they only delivered a petition to save themselves harmless, and to free themselves from blame, by showing the reason of their disobedience to the king's command, which they apprehend to be a grievance to them, I cannot think it a libel." *Wright, C. J.* — "Look you, by the way, brother, I did not ask you to sum up the evidence, (for that is not usual,) but only to deliver your opinion whether it be a libel or no." *Powell, J.* — "Truly, I cannot see, for my part, anything of sedition or any other crime fixed upon these reverend fathers. For, gentlemen, to make it a libel, it must be false, it must be malicious, and it must tend to sedition. As to the falsehood, I see nothing that is offered by the king's counsel, nor anything as to the malice; it was presented with all the humility and decency becoming subjects when they approach their prince. In the petition, they say, because they conceive the thing that was commanded them to be against the law of the land, therefore they do desire his majesty that he would be pleased to forbear to insist upon it. If there be no such dispensing power, there can be no libel in the petition which represented the declaration founded on such a pretended power to be illegal. Now, gentlemen, this is a dispensation with a witness; it amounts to an abrogation and utter repeal of all the laws; for I can see no difference, nor know of any in law, between the king's power to dispense with laws ecclesiastical, and his power to dispense with any other laws whatsoever. If this be once allowed of, there will need no Parliament: all the legislature will be in the king — which is a thing worth considering — and I leave the issue to God and your own consciences."

Allybone, however, on whom James mainly relied, foolishly forgetting the scandal which would necessarily arise from the Protestant prelates being condemned by a Popish judge for trying to save their church from Popery, came up to the mark, and, in the sentiments he uttered, must have equalled all the expectations entertained of him by his master: —

"In the first place," said he, "no man can take upon him to write against the actual exercise of the government, unless he have leave from the government. If he does, he makes a libel, be what he writes true or false; if we once come to impeach the government by way of argument, it is argument that makes government or no government. So I lay down, that the government ought not to be impeached by argument, nor the exercise of the government shaken by argument. Am I to be allowed to discredit the King's ministers because I can manage a proposition, in itself doubtful, with a better pen than another man? This I say is a libel. My next position is, that no private man can take upon him to write concerning the government at all; for what has any private man to do with the government? It is the business of the government to manage matters relating to the government; it is the business of subjects to mind only their private affairs. If the government does come to shake my particular interest, the law is open for me, and I may redress myself; but when I intrude myself into matters which do not concern my particular interest, I am a libeller. And, truly, the attack is the worse if under a specious pretence; for, by that rule, every man that can put on a good vizard may be as mischievous as he will, so that whether it be in the form of a supplication, or an address, or a petition, let us call it by its true denomination, it is a libel." He then examined the precedents which had been cited, displaying the grossest ignorance of the history as well as constitution of the country; and, after he had been sadly exposed by Mr. Justice Powell, he thus concluded: "I will not further debate the prerogatives of the crown or the privileges of the subject; but I am clearly of opinion that these venerable bishops did meddle with that which did not belong to them; they took upon themselves to contradict the actual exercise of the government, which I think no particular persons may do."

The chief justice, without expressing any dissent, merely said, "Gentlemen of the jury, have you a mind to drink before you go?" So wine was sent for, and they had a glass apiece; after which they were marched off in custody of a bailiff, who was sworn not to let them have meat or drink, fire or candle, until they were agreed upon their verdict.

All that night they were shut up, Mr. Arnold, the king's brewer, standing out for a conviction till six next morning, when, being dreadfully exhausted, he was thus addressed by a brother juryman: "Look at me; I am the largest and the strongest of the twelve, and, before I find such a petition as this a libel, here I will stay till I am no bigger than a tobacco-pipe."

The court sat again at ten, when the verdict of not guilty was pronounced, and a shout of joy was raised which was soon reverberated from the remotest parts of the kingdom.

One gentleman, a barrister of Gray's Inn, was immediately taken into custody in court, by order of the lord chief justice, who, with an extraordinary command of temper and countenance, said to him in a calm voice, — "I am as glad as you can be that my lords the bishops are acquitted, but your manner of rejoicing here in court is indecent; you might rejoice in your chamber or elsewhere, and not here. Have you any thing more to say to my lords the bishops, Mr. Attorney?" *A. G.* — "No, my lord." *Wright, C. J.* — "Then they may withdraw," — and they walked off, surrounded by countless thousands, who eagerly knelt down to receive their blessing.*

Justice Holloway was forthwith cashiered, as well as Justice Powell; and there were serious intentions that Chief Justice Wright should share their fate, as the king ascribed the unhappy result of the trial to his pusillanimity — contrasting him with Jeffreys, who never had been known to miss his quarry. This esteemed functionary held the still more important office of lord high chancellor, and, compared with any other competitor, Wright, notwithstanding his occasional slight lapses into conscientiousness, appeared superior in servility to all who could be substituted for him. † Allybone

* 12 State Trials, 183–523.

† It was supposed that he was jealous of Williams, the solicitor general, who had been promised by James the highest offices of the law if he could convict the bishops. This may account for a sarcasm he levelled at his rival during the trial. Williams, having accounted for a particular vote of the House of Commons in the reign of James II., when he himself was a member and suspected of bribery, said "there was a lump of money in the case." Wright, in referring to this, observed, "Mr. Solicitor tells you the reason, 'there was a lump of money in the case;' but I wonder, indeed, to hear it come from him." Williams, understanding the insinuation, exclaimed, "My lord, I assure you I never gave my vote for money in my life."

was declared to be "the man to go through thick and thin;" but, unfortunately, he had made himself quite ridiculous in all men's eyes by the palpable blunders he had recklessly fallen into during the late trial; and he felt so keenly the disgrace he had brought on himself and his religion, that he took to his bed and died a few weeks afterwards.

Thus, when William of Orange landed at Torbay, Wright still filled the office of chief justice of the King's Bench. He continued to sit daily in court till the flight of King James, when an interregnum ensued, during which all judicial business was suspended, although the public tranquillity was preserved, and the settlement of the nation was conducted by a provisional government. After Jeffreys had tried to make his escape, disguised as a sailor, and was nearly torn to pieces by the mob, Wright concealed himself in the house of a friend, and being less formidable and less obnoxious (for he was called the "*jackall* to the *lion*,") he remained some time unmolested; but upon information, probably ill-founded, that he was conspiring with Papists who wished to bring back the king, a warrant was granted against him by the Privy Council, on the vague charge of "endeavoring to subvert the government." Under this he was apprehended, and carried to the Tower of London; but after he had been examined there by a committee of the House of Commons, it was thought that this custody was too honorable for him, and he was ordered to be transferred to Newgate. Here, from the perturbation of mind which he suffered, he was seized with a fever, and he died miserably a few days after, being deafened by the cheers which were uttered when the Prince and Princess of Orange were declared King and Queen of England.

His pecuniary embarrassments had continued even after he became a judge, and, still living extravagantly, his means were insufficient to supply him with common comforts in his last hours, or with a decent burial. His end holds out an awful lesson against early licentiousness and political profligacy. He was almost constantly fighting against privation and misery, and during the short time that he seemed in the enjoyment of splendor he was despised by all good men, and he must have been odious to himself. When he died, his body was thrown into a pit with common malefactors; his sufferings, when related, excited no compassion; and his name was execrated as long as it was recollected.

It is lucky for the memory of Wright that he had contemporaries such as Jeffreys and Scroggs, who considerably exceeded him in their atrocities. Had he run the same career in an age not more than ordinarily wicked, his name might have passed into a by-word, denoting all that is odious and detestable in a judge; whereas his misdeeds have long been little known, except to lawyers and antiquaries.

It is a painful duty for me to draw them from their dread abode; but let me hope that, by exposing them in their deformity, I may be of some service to the public. Ever since the reaction which followed the passing of the reform bill, there has been a strong tendency to mitigate the errors and to lament the fate of James II. This has shown itself most alarmingly among the rising generation; and there seems reason to dread that we may soon be under legislators and ministers who, believing in the divine right of kings, will not only applaud, but act upon, the principles of arbitrary government. Some good may arise from showing in detail the practical results of such principles in the due administration of justice — the chief object, it has been said, for which man renounces his natural rights, and submits to the restraints of magisterial rule.*

* A similar and alarming reaction towards despotism has exhibited itself in America since the passage of the fugitive slave act of 1850, in the combination of so many distinguished jurists and divines to denounce the doctrine of a "higher law," and to advocate the "divine right" of Congress to make enactments according to its own pleasure and judgment, which enactments are to take precedence as rules of conduct of the individual conscience, which it is attempted to silence by stigmatizing it as a prejudice. Not only does there seem reason to dread that we may soon be under legislators and an executive who, believing in the divine right of those in authority, will not only applaud but act upon the principles of arbitrary government, we lately have been and still are, so far as the federal executive and the federal Senate are concerned, under precisely such ministers and legislators; and having lately had some such experience of the practical results of such principles in the administration of justice, what more natural than to compare our sufferings with those of our British forefathers, and to seek to learn from their experience the natural cure for such evils? — *Ed.*

# APPENDIX.

## No. I.

*The case of Passmore Williamson, as stated by himself in his petition for a habeas corpus, to the Supreme Court of Pennsylvania.*

*To the Honorable the Judges of the Supreme Court of Pennsylvania:*

The petition of Passmore Williamson respectfully sheweth: That your petitioner is a citizen of Pennsylvania, and a resident of Philadelphia; that he is a member of "The Pennsylvania Society for promoting the abolition of Slavery, and for the relief of free negroes unlawfully held in bondage, and for improving the condition of the African race," incorporated by act of Assembly passed the 8th day of December, A. D. 1789, of which Dr. Benjamin Franklin was the first president, and that he is secretary of the acting committee of said society.

That on Wednesday, the 18th day of July last past, your petitioner was informed that certain negroes, held as slaves, were then at Bloodgood's hotel, in the city of Philadelphia, having been brought by their master into the state of Pennsylvania, with the intention of passing through to other parts. Believing that the persons thus held as slaves were entitled to their freedom by reason of their having been so brought by their master voluntarily into the state of Pennsylvania, the petitioner, in the fulfilment of the official duty imposed upon him by the practice and regulations of the said society, went to Bloodgood's hotel for the purpose of apprizing the alleged slaves that they were free, and finding that they with their master had left said hotel, and gone on board the steamboat of the New York line, then lying near Walnut Street wharf, your petitioner went on board the same, found the party, consisting of a woman named Jane, about thirty-five years of age, and her two sons, Daniel, aged about twelve, and Isaiah, aged about seven, and, in presence of the master, informed the said Jane that she was free by the laws of Pennsylvania; upon which she expressed her desire to have her freedom, and finally, with her children, left the boat of her own free will and accord, and without any coercion or compulsion of any kind; and having seen her in possession of her liberty, with her children, your petitioner returned to his place of business, and has never since seen the said Jane, Daniel and Isaiah, or either of them; nor does he know where they are, nor has he had any connection of any kind with the subject.

Your petitioner used no violence whatever, except simply holding back Colonel Wheeler, their former master, when he attempted by force to prevent the said Jane from leaving the boat. Some half dozen negroes, employed, as your petitioner is informed, as porters and otherwise, at the wharf and in the immediate neighborhood, of their own accord and without any invitation of the petitioner, but probably observing or understanding the state of affairs, followed the petitioner when he went on board the boat. An allegation has been made that they were guilty of violence and disorder in the transaction. Your petitioner observed no acts of violence committed by them, nor any other disorder than the natural expression of some feeling at the attempt of Colonel Wheeler to detain the woman by force; that there was not any violence or disorder amounting to a breach of the peace is also fairly to be inferred from the fact that two police officers were present, who were subsequently examined as witnesses, and stated that they did not see anything requiring or justifying their interference to preserve the peace. And your petitioner desires to state explicitly that he had no preconcert or connection of any kind with them or with their conduct, and considers that he is in no way responsible therefor. Your petitioner gave to Colonel Wheeler, at the time, his name and address, with the assurance that he would be responsible if he had injured any right which he had; fully believing at the time, as he does still believe, that he had committed no injury whatever to any right of Colonel Wheeler.

On the night of the same day your petitioner was obliged to leave the city to attend an election of the Atlantic and Ohio Telegraph Company, at Harrisburg, and returned to Philadelphia on Friday, the 20th of July, between one and two o'clock, A. M. Upon his return, an *alias* writ of *habeas corpus* was handed to him, issued from the district court of the United States for the eastern district of Pennsylvania, upon the petition of the said John H. Wheeler, commanding him that the bodies of the said Jane, Daniel and Isaiah he should have before the Hon. John K. Kane, judge of the said district court, forthwith. To the said writ your petitioner the same day, viz., the 20th day of July last past, made return, that the said Jane, Daniel and Isaiah, or by whatever name they may be called, nor either of them, were not then, nor at the time of issuing said writ, or the original writ, or at any other time, in the custody, power, or possession of, nor confined nor restrained of their liberty, by your petitioner; therefore he could not have the bodies of the said Jane, Daniel and Isaiah before the said judge, as by the said writ he was commanded.

Whereupon and afterwards, to wit: on the 27th day of July aforesaid, it was ordered and adjudged by the court that your petitioner be committed to the custody of the marshal, without bail or mainprize, as for a contempt in refusing to make return to a writ of *habeas corpus* theretofore issued against him at the instance of Mr. John H. Wheeler; all which appears by the record and proceedings in the said case, which your petitioner begs leave to produce, and a copy of an exemplification of which is annexed to this petition. Thereupon, on the same day, a warrant was issued, commanding that the marshal of the United States, in and for the eastern district of Pennsylvania, forthwith take into custody the body of your petitioner, for a contempt of the honorable the judge of the said district court, in refusing to answer to the said writ of *habeas corpus*, theretofore awarded aganist him, the said petitioner, at the relation of Mr. John H. Wheeler, a copy of which is hereto annexed, and also a warrant, by and from the marshal of the United States, to the keeper of the Moyamensing prison, a copy of which is also hereto annexed; under which warrants your petitioner was committed to the said prison, and is now there detained, without bail or mainprize.

Notwithstanding the record is silent on the subject, your petitioner thinks it proper to state that, on the return of the writ of *habeas corpus*, the judge allowed the relator to traverse the said return by parol, under which permission the relator gave his own testimony, in which he stated that he held the said Jane, Daniel and Isaiah as slaves, under the law of Virginia, and had voluntarily brought them with him by railroad from the city of Baltimore to the city of Philadelphia, where he had been accidentally detained at Bloodgood's hotel about three hours; and certain other witnesses were examined. From the testimony thus given, though not at all warranted by it or by the facts, the said judge decided that your petitioner had been concerned in a forcible abduction of the said Jane, Daniel and Isaiah, against their will and consent, upon the deck of the said steamboat, but admitted that your petitioner took no personally active part in such supposed abduction after he had left the deck.

The hearing took place on the morning of Friday, the 20th of July, at ten o'clock, your petitioner having had the first knowledge of the existence of any writ of *habeas corpus* between one and two o'clock on the same morning. Under these circumstances, before the said testimony was gone into and afterwards, the counsel of your petitioner asked for time, until the next morning, for consultation and preparation for the argument of the questions which might arise in the case, which applications were refused by the court, and the hearing went on, and closed on the same morning between twelve and one o'clock.

On Tuesday, the 31st of July, 1855, your petitioner presented to the Hon. Chief Justice of this court a petition for a *habeas corpus*, which was refused.

Inasmuch as your petitioner is thus deprived of his liberty for an indefinite time, and possibly for his life, as he believes, illegally; inasmuch as he is a native citizen of Pennsylvania, and claims that he has a right to the protection of the commonwealth, and to have recourse to her courts for enlargement and redress; he begs leave respectfully to state some of the grounds on which he conceives that he is entitled to the relief which he now prays.

Whatever may be the view of the court as to the probability of his discharge on a hearing, your petitioner respectfully represents that he is clearly entitled to have a writ of *habeas corpus* granted, and to be thereupon brought before the court. Upon this subject the Pennsylvania *habeas corpus* act is imperative. Indeed, as the question of the sufficiency of the cause of his detention directly concerns his personal liberty, any law which should fail to secure to him the right of being personally present at its argument and decision, would be frightfully inconsistent with the principles of the common law, the provisions of our Bill of Rights, and the very basis of our government.

It is believed that no case, prior to that of your petitioner, is reported in Pennsylvania, of a refusal of this writ to a party restrained of his liberty, except the case of *Ex parte Lawrence*, 5 Binn. 304, in which it was decided that it was not obligatory on the court to issue a second writ of *habeas corpus* where the case had been already heard on the same evidence upon a first writ of *habeas corpus* granted by another court of the petitioner's own selection: in other words, that the statutory right to the writ was exhausted by the impetration and hearing of the first writ, and that the granting of a second writ was at the discretion of the court. This case, therefore, appears to confirm strongly the position of your petitioner, that he is absolutely entitled at law to the writ for which he now prays.

On the hearing there will be endeavored to be established on behalf of your petitioner, on abundant grounds of reason and authority, the following propositions, viz.: —

1. That it is the right and duty of the courts, and especially of the supreme court of this commonwealth, to relieve any citizen of the same from illegal imprisonment.

2. That imprisonment under an order of a court or judge not having

jurisdiction over the subject matter, and whose order is therefore void, is an illegal imprisonment.

3. That the party subjected to such imprisonment has a right to be relieved from it on *habeas corpus*, whether he did or did not make the objection of the want of jurisdiction before the court or judge inflicting such imprisonment; and that if he did not make such objection, it is immaterial whether he were prevented from making it by ignorance of the law, or by the want of extraordinary presence of mind, or by whatever other cause.

4. That the courts and judges of the United States are courts and judges of limited jurisdiction, created by a government of enumerated powers, and in proceedings before them the records must show the case to be within their jurisdiction, otherwise they can have none.

5. That if the record of any proceeding before them show affirmatively that the case was clearly without their jurisdiction, there can no presumption of fact be raised against such record for the purpose of validating their jurisdiction.

6. That no writ of *habeas corpus* can be issued to produce the body of a person not in custody under legal process, unless it be issued in behalf and with the consent of said person.

7. That at common law, the return to a writ of *habeas corpus*, if it be an unevasive, full and complete, is conclusive, and cannot be traversed.

8. That a person held as a slave under the law of one state, and voluntarily carried by his owner for any purpose into another state, is not a fugitive from labor or service within the true intent and meaning of the constitution of the United States, but is subject to the laws of the state into which he has been thus carried; and that by the law of Pennsylvania a slave so brought into this state, whether for the purpose of passing through the same or otherwise, is free.

9. That the district court of the United States has no jurisdiction whatever over the question of freedom or slavery of such person, or of an alleged abduction of him, nor any jurisdiction to award a writ of *habeas corpus* commanding an alleged abductor, or any citizen by whom he may be assumed to be detained, to produce him.

10. That in case of a fugitive from service or labor from another state, the district court of the United States has jurisdiction to issue a warrant for the apprehension of such fugitive, and in case he be rescued and abducted from his claimant, to proceed by indictment and trial by jury against such abductor, and on conviction to punish him by limited fine and imprisonment; but even in the case of a fugitive slave, said court nor

the judge thereof has no jurisdiction to issue a writ of *habeas corpus*, commanding the alleged abductor to produce such fugitive, or to enforce a return of such writ, or allow a traverse of the return thereof if made, or upon such traverse in effect convict the respondent, without indictment or trial by jury of such abduction, and thereupon punish him therefor by unlimited imprisonment in the name of a commitment, as for a contempt in refusing to return such writ of *habeas corpus*.

11. That generally it is true that one court will not go behind a commitment by another court for contempt; but that this is only where the committing court has jurisdiction of the subject matter; and your petitioner submits that when the circumstances of the supposed contempt are set forth upon the record of commitment, and it further appears thereupon that the whole proceedings were *coram non judice*, and that for that and other reasons the commitment was arbitrary, illegal and void, it is the right and duty of a court of competent jurisdiction, by writ of *habeas corpus*, to relieve a citizen from imprisonment under such void commitment.

12. That neither the district court of the United States nor the judge thereof had any shadow or color of jurisdiction to award the writ of *habeas corpus* directed to your petitioner, commanding him to produce the bodies of Jane, Daniel, and Isaiah, and that such writ was void; that your petitioner was in no wise bound to make return thereto; that the return which he did make thereto was unevasive, full, and complete, and was conclusive, and not traversable; that the commitment of your petitioner as for a contempt in refusing to return said writ is arbitrary, illegal, and utterly null and void; that the whole proceedings, including the commitment for contempt, were absolutely *coram non judice*.

13. That in such oppression of one of her citizens, a subordinate judge of the United States has usurped upon the authority, violated the peace and derogated from the sovereign dignity of the commonwealth of Pennsylvania; that all are hurt in the person of your petitioner, and that he is justified in looking with confidence to the authorities of his native state to vindicate her rights by restoring his liberty.

To be relieved, therefore, from the imprisonment aforesaid, your petitioner now applies, praying that a writ of *habeas corpus* may be issued, according to the act of Assembly in such case made and provided, directed to Charles Hortz, the said keeper of said prison, commanding him to bring before your honorable court the body of your petitioner, to do and abide such order as your honorable court may direct.

And your petitioner will ever pray, &c.

PASSMORE WILLIAMSON.

*Moyamensing Prison, August* 9, 1855.

## No. II.

*The Opinion and Decision of Judge Kane, referred to in the foregoing petition.*

*The U. S. A. ex. rel. Wheeler* agt. *Passmore Williamson* — Sur. *Habeas Corpus*, 27th July, 1855. — Colonel John H. Wheeler, of North Carolina, the United States Minister to Nicaragua, was on board a steamboat at one of the Delaware wharves, on his way from Washington to embark at New York for his post of duty. Three slaves belonging to him were sitting at his side on the upper deck.

Just as the last signal bell was ringing, Passmore Williamson came up to the party — declared to the slaves that they were free — and forcibly pressing Mr. Wheeler aside, urged them to go ashore. He was followed by some dozen or twenty negroes, who, by muscular strength, carried the slaves to the adjoining pier; two of the slaves at least, if not all three, struggling to release themselves, and protesting their wish to remain with their master; two of the negro mob in the meantime grasping Colonel Wheeler by the collar, and threatening to cut his throat if he made any resistance.

The slaves were borne along to a hackney coach that was in waiting, and were conveyed to some place of concealment; Mr. Williamson following and urging forward the mob; and giving his name and address to Colonel Wheeler, with the declaration that he held himself responsible towards him for whatever might be his legal rights; but taking no personally active part in the abduction after he had left the deck.

I allowed a writ of *habeas corpus* at the instance of Colonel Wheeler, and subsequently an *alias;* and to this last Mr. Williamson made return, that the persons named in the writ, "nor either of them, are not now nor was at the time of issuing of the writ, or the original writ, or at any other time, in the custody, power, or possession of the respondent, nor by him confined or restrained: wherefore he cannot have the bodies," etc.

At the hearing I allowed the relator to traverse this return; and several witnesses, who were asked by him, testified to the facts as I have recited them. The District Attorney, upon this state of facts, moved for Williamson's commitment: 1. For contempt in making a false return; 2. To take his trial for perjury.

Mr. Williamson then took the stand to purge himself of contempt. He admitted the facts substantially as in proof before; made it plain that he had been an adviser of the project, and had given it his confederate sanction throughout. He renewed his denial that he had control at any time over the movements of the slaves, or knew their present whereabouts. Such is the case, as it was before me on the hearing.

I cannot look upon this return otherwise than as illusory — in legal phrase — as evasive, if not false. It sets out that the alleged prisoners are not now, and have not been since the issue of the *habeas corpus*, in the custody, power or possession of the respondent; and in so far, it uses legally appropriate language for such a return. But it goes further, and by added words, gives an interpretation to that language, essentially variant from its legal import.

It denies that the prisoners were within his power, custody or possession, at any time whatever. Now, the evidence of respectable, uncontradicted witnesses, and the admission of the respondent himself, establish the fact beyond controversy, that the prisoners were at one time within his power and control. He was the person by whose counsel the so called rescue was devised. He gave the directions, and hastened to the pier to stimulate and supervise their execution. He was the spokesman and first actor after arriving there. Of all the parties to the act of violence, he was the only white man, the only citizen, the only individual having recognized political rights, the only person whose social training could certainly interpret either his own duties or the rights of others, under the constitution of the land.

It would be futile, and worse, to argue that he who has organized and guided, and headed a mob, to effect the abduction and imprisonment of others — he in whose presence and by whose active influence the abduction and imprisonment have been brought about — might excuse himself from responsibility by the assertion that it was not his hand that made the unlawful assault, or that he never acted as the jailer. He who unites with others to commit a crime, shares with them all the legal liabilities that attend on its commission. He chooses his company and adopts their acts.

This is the retributive law of all concerted crimes; and its argument applies with peculiar force to those cases, in which redress and prevention of wrong are sought through the writ of *habeas corpus*. This, the great remedial process by which liberty is vindicated and restored, tolerates no language, in the response which it calls for, that can mask a subterfuge. The dearest interests of life, personal safety, domestic peace, social repose, all that man can value, or that is worth living for, are involved in this principle. The institutions of society would lose more than half their value, and courts of justice become impotent for protection, if the writ of *habeas corpus* could not compel the truth — full, direct, and unequivocal — in answer to its mandate.

It will not do to say to the man, whose wife or whose daughter has been abducted, "I did not abduct her; she is not in my possession; I do not detain her; inasmuch as the assault was made by the hand of my subordinates, and I have forborne to ask where they propose consummating the wrong."

It is clear, then, as it seems to me, that in legal acceptance the parties whom this writ called on Mr. Williamson to produce, were at one time within his power and control; and his answer, so far as it relates to his power over them, makes no distinction between that time and the present. I cannot give a different interpretation to his language from that which he has practically given himself, and cannot regard him as denying his power over the prisoners now, when he does not aver that he has lost the power which he formerly had.

He has thus refused, or at least he has failed, to answer to the command of the law. He has chosen to decide for himself upon the lawfulness as well as the moral propriety of his act, and to withhold the ascertainment and vindication of the rights of others from that same forum of arbitrament on which all his own rights repose. In a word, he has put himself in contempt of the process of this court and challenges its action.

That action can have no alternative form. It is one too clearly defined by ancient and honored precedent, too indispensable to the administration of social justice and the protection of human right, and too potentially invoked by the special exigency of the case now before the court, to excuse even a doubt of my duty or an apology for its immediate performance.

The cause was submitted to me by the learned counsel for the respondent, without argument, and I have therefore found myself at some loss to understand the grounds on which, if there be any such, they would claim the discharge of their client. One only has occurred to me as, perhaps, within his view; and on this I think it right to express my opinion. I will frankly reconsider it, however, if any future aspect of the case shall invite the review.

It is this: that the persons named in this writ as detained by the respondent, were not legally slaves, inasmuch as they were within the territory of Pennsylvania when they were abducted.

Waiving the inquiry whether, for the purpose of this question, they were within the territorial jurisdiction of Pennsylvania while passing from one state to another upon the navigable waters of the United States — a point on which my first impressions are adverse to the argument — I have to say:

1. That I know of no statute, either of the United States, or of Pennsyl-

vania, or of New Jersey, the only other state that has a qualified jurisdiction over this part of the Delaware, that authorises the forcible abduction of any person or any thing whatsoever, without claim of property, unless in aid of legal process.

2. That I know of no statute of Pennsylvania, which affects to divest the rights of property of a citizen of North Carolina, acquired and asserted under the laws of that state, because he has found it needful or convenient to pass through the territory of Pennsylvania.

3. That I am not aware that any such statute, if such a one were shown, could be recognized as valid in a court of the United States.

4. That it seems to me altogether unimportant whether they were slaves or not. It would be the mockery of philanthropy to assert, that, because men had become free, they might therefore be forcibly abducted.

I have said nothing of the motives by which the respondent has been governed; I have nothing to do with them; they may give him support and comfort before an infinitely higher tribunal; I do not impugn them here. Nor do I allude, on the other hand, to those special claims upon our hospitable courtesy which the diplomatic character of Mr. Wheeler might seem to assert for him. I am doubtful whether the acts of Congress give to him and his retinue, and his property, that protection as a representative of the sovereignty of the United States, which they concede to all sovereignties besides. Whether, under the general law of nations, he could not ask a broader privilege than some judicial precedents might seem to admit, is not necessarily involved in the cause before me. It is enough that I find, as the case stands now, the plain and simple grounds of adjudication, that Mr. Williamson has not returned truthfully and fully to the writ of *habeas corpus*. He must, therefore, stand committed for a contempt of the legal process of the court.

As to the second motion of the District Attorney — that which looks to a committal for perjury — I withhold an expression of opinion in regard to it. It is unnecessary, because Mr. Williamson being under arrest, he may be charged at any time by the Grand Jury; and I apprehend that there may be doubts whether the affidavit should not be regarded as extra-judicial.

Let Mr. Williamson, the respondent, be committed to the custody of the marshal without bail or mainprize, as for a contempt of the court in refusing to answer to the writ of *habeas corpus*, heretofore awarded against him at the relation of Mr. Wheeler.

N. B. A motion of the prisoner's counsel for leave to amend the return was refused, and to a question for what time the imprisonment was to be, the judge replied — "While he remains in contempt."

## No. III.

*The opinion of the Supreme Court of Pennsylvania, delivered by Judge Black, declining to grant the petition of Passmore Williamson.*

This is an application by Passmore Williamson for *habeas corpus.* He complains that he is held in custody under a commitment of the district court of the United States, for a contempt of that court in refusing to obey its process. The process which he is confined for disobeying was a *habeas corpus* commanding him to produce the bodies of certain colored persons claimed as slaves under the law of Virginia.

Is he entitled to the writ he has asked for? In considering what answer we shall give to this question, we are, of course, expected to be influenced, as in other cases, by the law and the constitution alone. The gentlemen who appeared as counsel for the petitioner, and who argued the motion in a way which did them great honor, pressed upon us no considerations except those which were founded upon their *legal* views of the subject.

It is argued with much earnestness, and no doubt with perfect sincerity, that we are bound to allow the writ, without stopping to consider whether the petitioner has or has not laid before us any probable cause for supposing that he is illegally detained — that every man confined in prison, except for treason or felony, is entitled to it *ex debito justitiæ* — and that we cannot refuse it without a frightful violation of the petitioner's rights, no matter how plainly it may appear on his own showing that he is held in custody for a just cause. If this be true, the case of *Ex parte Lawrence*, 5 Binn. 304, is not law. There the writ was refused because the applicant had been previously heard before another court. But if every man who applies for a *habeas corpus* must have it as a matter of right, and without regard to anything but the mere fact that he demands it, then a court or a judge has no more power to refuse a second than a first application.

Is it really true that the special application, which must be made for every writ of *habeas corpus*, and the examination of the commitment, which we are bound to make before it can issue, are mere hollow and unsubstantial forms? Can it be possible that the law and the courts are so completely under the control of their natural enemies, that every class of offenders against the Union and the state, except traitors and felons, may be brought before us as often as they please, though we know beforehand, by their own admissions, that we cannot help but remand them immediately? If these questions must be answered in the affirmative, then we are compelled, against our will and contrary to our convictions of duty, to wage a constant warfare against the federal tribunals by firing off writs of *habeas corpus* upon them all the time. The punitive justice of the state would suffer still more seriously. The half of the Western Penitentiary would be before us at Philadelphia, and a similar proportion from Cherry Hill and Moyamensing would attend our sittings at Pittsburgh. To remand them would do very little good; for a new set of writs would bring them all back again. A sentence to solitary confinement would be a sentence that the convict should travel for a limited term up and down the state, in company with the officers who might have him in charge. By the same means the inmates of the lunatic asylums might be temporarily enlarged, much to their own detriment; and every soldier or seaman in the service of the country could compel his commander to bring him before the court six times a week.

But the *habeas corpus* act has never received such a construction. It is a writ of right, and may not be refused to one who shows a *prima facie* case entitling him to be discharged or bailed. But he has no right to demand it who admits that he is in legal custody for an offence not bailable; and he does make what is equivalent to such an admission when his own application and the commitment referred to in it show that he is lawfully detained. A complaint must be made and the cause of detainer submitted to a judge before the writ can go. The very object and purpose of this is to prevent it from being trifled with by those who manifestly have no right to be set at liberty. It is like a writ of error in a criminal case, which the court or judge is bound to allow if there be reason to suppose that an error has been committed, and equally bound to refuse if it be clear that the judgment must be affirmed.

We are not aware that any application to this court for a writ of *habeas corpus* has ever been successful where the judges, at the time of the allowance, were satisfied that the prisoner must be remanded. The petitioner's counsel say there is but one reported case in which it was refused, (5 Binn. 304;) and this is urged in the argument as a reason for supposing that in all other cases the writ was issued without examination. But no such inference can fairly be drawn from the scarcity of judicial decisions upon a point like this. We do not expect to find in reports so recent as ours those long-established rules of law which the student learns from his elementary books, and which are constantly acted upon without being disputed.

The *habeas corpus* is a common law writ, and has been used in England from time immemorial, just as it is now. The statute of 31 Char. II. c. 2, made no alteration in the practice of the courts in granting these writs. (3 Barn. and Ald. 420 to Chitty's Reps. 207.) It merely provided that the judges in vacation should have the power which the courts had previously exercised in term time, (1 Chitty's Gen. Prac. 686,) and inflicted penalties upon those who should defeat its operation. The common law upon this subject was brought to America by the colonists; and most, if not all of the states, have since enacted laws resembling the English statute of Charles II. in every principal feature. The constitution of the United States declares that " the privilege of a writ of *habeas corpus* shall not be suspended unless when, in cases of rebellion or invasion, the public safety may require it." Congress has conferred upon the federal judges the power to issue such writs according to the principles and rules regulating it in other courts. Seeing that the same general principles of common law on this subject prevail in England and America, and seeing also the similarity of their statutory regulations in both countries, the decisions of the English judges, as well as of the American courts, both state and federal, are entitled to our fullest respect, as settling and defining our powers and duties.

Blackstone (3 Com. 132) says the writ of *habeas corpus* should be allowed only when the court or judge is satisfied that the party hath probable cause to be delivered. He gives cogent reasons why it should not be allowed in any other case, and cites with unqualified approbation the precedents set by Sir Edward Coke and Chief Justice Vaughan in cases where they had refused it. Chitty lays down the rule (1 Cr. Law, 101; General Prac. 686-7.) It seems to have been acted upon by all the judges. The writ was refused in *Rex* v. *Scheiner*, (1 Burr. 765,) and in the case of the three Spanish sailors, (3 Black. Rep. 1324.) In Hobhouse's case, (2 Barn. and Ald. 420,) it was fully settled by a unanimous court, as the true construction of the statute, that the writ is never to be allowed, if upon view of the commitment it be manifest that the prisoner must be remanded. In New York, when the statute in force there was precisely like ours, (so far I mean as this question is concerned,) it was decided by the supreme court (5 Johns. 282) that the allowance of the writ was a matter within the discretion of the court, depending on the grounds laid in the application. It was refused in Huster's case, (1, 2 C. 136) and in *Ex parte Ferguson*, (9 Johns. Rep. 139.) In addition to this we have the opinion of Chief Justice Marshall, in Watkins's case, (3 Peters, 202) that the writ ought not to be awarded if the court is satisfied that the prisoner must be remanded.

It was accordingly refused by the supreme court of the United States in that case, as it had been before in Kearney's case.

On the whole, we are thoroughly satisfied that our duty requires us to view and examine the cause of detainer now, and to make an end of the business at once, if it appear that we have no power to discharge him on the return of the writ.

This prisoner, as already said, is confined on a sentence of the district court of the United States for a contempt. A *habeas corpus* is not a writ of error. It cannot bring a case before us in such a manner that we can exercise any kind of appellate jurisdiction in it. On a *habeas corpus*, the judgment, even of a subordinate state court, cannot be disregarded, reversed or set aside, however clearly we may perceive it to be erroneous, and however plain it may be that we ought to reverse it if it were before us on appeal or writ of error. We can only look at the record to see whether a judgment exists, and have no power to say whether it is right or wrong. It is conclusively presumed to be right until it is regularly brought up for revision. We decided this three years ago at Sunbury, in a case which we all thought one of much hardship. But the rule is so familiar, so universally acknowledged, and so reasonable in itself, that it requires only to be stated. It applies with still greater force, or at least for stronger reasons, to the decisions of the federal courts. Over them we have no control at all, under any circumstances, or by any process that could be devised. Those tribunals belong to a different judicial system from ours. They administer a different code of laws, and are responsible to a different sovereignty. The district court of the United States is as independent of us as we are of it — as independent as the supreme court of the United States is of either. What the law and the constitution have forbidden us to do directly on writ of error, we, of course, cannot do indirectly by *habeas corpus*.

But the petitioner's counsel have put his case on the ground that the whole proceeding against him in the district court was *coram non judice*, null and void. It is certainly true that a void judgment may be regarded as no judgment at all; and every judgment is void which clearly appears on its own face to have been pronounced by a court having no jurisdiction or authority in the subject matter. For instance, if a federal court should convict and sentence a citizen for libel, or if a state court, having no jurisdiction except in civil pleas, should try an indictment for a crime and convict the party — in these cases the judgments would be wholly void. If the petitioner can bring himself within this principle, then there is no judgment against him; he is wrongfully imprisoned, and we must order him to be brought out and discharged.

What is he detained for? The answer is easy and simple. The commitment shows that he was tried, found guilty, and sentenced for *contempt of court*, and nothing else. He is now confined in execution of that sentence, and for no other cause. This was a distinct and substantive offence against the authority and government of the United States. Does any body doubt the jurisdiction of the district court to punish contempt? Certainly not. All courts have this power, and must necessarily have it; otherwise they could not protect themselves from insult, or enforce obedience to their process. Without it they would be utterly powerless. The authority to deal with an offender of this class belongs exclusively to the court in which the offence is committed, and no other court, not even the highest, can interfere with its exercise, either by writ of error, mandamus, or *habeas corpus*. If the power be abused, there is no remedy but impeachment.

The law was so held by this court in M'Laughlin's case, (5 W. & S. 275,) and by the supreme court of the United States in Kearney's case, (7 Wharton, 38.) It was solemnly settled as part of the common law, in Brass Crossley's case, (3 Wilson, 183,) by a court in which sat two of the foremost jurists that England ever produced. We have not the smallest doubt that it is the law; and we must administer it as we find it. The only attempt ever made to disregard it was by a New York judge, (4 Johns. Rep. 345,) who was not supported by his brethren. This attempt was followed by all the evil and confusion which Blackstone and Kent and Story declared to be its necessary consequences. Whoever will trace that singular controversy to its termination will see that the chancellor and the majority of the supreme court, though once outvoted in the Senate, were never answered.

The Senate itself yielded to the force of the truths which the supreme court had laid down so clearly, and the judgment of the court of errors in Yates's case (8 Johns. 593) was overruled by the same court the year afterward in *Yates* v. *Lansing*, (9 Johns. Rep. 403,) which grew out of the very same transaction, and depended on the same principles. Still further reflection at a later period induced the Senate to join the popular branch of the legislature in passing a statute which effectually prevents one judge from interfering by *habeas corpus* with the judgment of another on a question of contempt.

These principles being settled, it follows irresistibly that the district court of the United States had power and jurisdiction to decide what acts constitute a contempt against it; to determine whether the petitioner had been guilty of contempt; and to inflict upon him the punishment which in his opinion he ought to suffer. If we fully believed the petitioner to be innocent — if we were sure that the court which convicted him misunderstood the facts, or misapplied the law — still we could not reëxamine the evidence or rejudge the justice of the case, without grossly disregarding what we know to be the law of the land. The judge of the district court decided the question on his own constitutional responsibility. Even if he could be shown to have acted tyrannically or corruptly, he could be called to answer for it only in the Senate of the United States.

But the counsel for the petitioner go behind the proceeding in which he was convicted, and argue that the sentence for contempt is void, because the court had no jurisdiction of a certain other matter which it was investigating, or attempting to investigate, when the contempt was committed. We find a judgment against him in one case, and he complains about another, in which there is no judgment. He is suffering for an offence against the United States; and he says he is innocent of any wrong to a particular individual. He is conclusively adjudged guilty of contempt; and he tells us that the court had no jurisdiction to restore Mr. Wheeler's slaves.

It must be remembered that contempt of court is a specific criminal offence. It is punished sometimes by indictment, and sometimes in a summary proceeding, as it was in this case. In either mode of trial the adjudication against the offender is a conviction, and the commitment in consequence is execution. (7 Wheat. 38.) This is well settled, and I believe has never been doubted. Certainly the learned counsel for the petitioner have not denied it. The contempt may be connected with some particular cause, or it may consist in misbehavior which has a tendency to obstruct the administration of justice generally. When it is committed in a pending cause, the proceeding to punish it is a proceeding by itself. It is not entitled in the cause pending, but on the criminal side. (Wall. 134.)

The record of a conviction for contempt is as distinct from the matter under investigation, when it was committed, as an indictment for perjury is, from the cause in which the false oath was taken. Can a person convicted of perjury ask us to deliver him from the penitentiary, on showing that the oath on which the perjury is assigned, was taken in a cause of which the court had no jurisdiction? Would any judge in the commonwealth listen to such a reason for treating the sentence as void? If, instead of swearing falsely, he refuses to be sworn at all, and he is convicted, not of perjury, but of contempt, the same rule applies, and with a force precisely equal. If it be really true that no contempt can be committed against a court while it is enquiring into matter beyond its jurisdiction, and if the fact was so in this case, then the petitioner had a good defence, and he ought to have made it on his trial. To make it after conviction is too late. To make it here is to produce it before the wrong tribunal.

Every judgment MUST be conclusive until reversed. Such is the character, nature, and essence of all judgments. If it be not conclusive, it is not a judgment. A court must either have power to settle a given question finally and forever, so as to preclude all further inquiry upon it, or else it has no power to make any decision at all. To say that a court may determine a matter, and that another court may regard the matter afterward as open and undetermined, is an absurdity in terms.

It is most especially necessary that convictions for contempt in our courts should be final, conclusive, and free from reëxamination by other courts on *habeas corpus*. If the law were not so, our judicial system would break to pieces in a month. Courts totally unconnected with each other would be coming in constant collision. The inferior courts would revise all the decisions of the judges placed over and above them. A party unwilling to be tried in this court, need only defy our authority, and if we commit him, take out his *habeas corpus* before an associate judge of his own choosing, and if that judge is of opinion that we ought not to try him, there is an end of the case.

The doctrine is so plainly against the reason of the thing, that it would be wonderful, indeed, if any authority for it could be found in the books, except the overruled decision of Mr. Justice Spencer of New York, already referred to, and some efforts of the same kind to control the other courts made by Sir Edward Coke, in the King's Bench, which are now universally admitted to have been illegal, as well as rude and intemperate. On the other hand, we have all the English judges, and all our own, disclaiming their power to interfere with or control one another in this way. I will content myself by simply referring to some of the books in which it is established, that the conviction of contempt is a separate proceeding, and is conclusive of every fact which might have been urged on the trial for contempt, and among others want of jurisdiction to try the cause in which the contempt was committed. (4 Johns. Rep. 325, *et sequ.* The opinion of Chief Justice Kent, on pages 370 to 375. 6 Johns. 503. 9 Johns. 423. 1 Hill. 170. 5 Iredell, 190. Ib. 153. 9 Sandf. 724. 1 Carter, 160. 1 Blackf. 166. 25 Miss. 836. 2 Wheeler's Criminal Cases, p. 1. 14 Ad. and Ellis,

556.) These cases will speak for themselves; but I may remark as to the last one, that the very same objection was made there and here. The party was convicted of contempt in not obeying a decree. He claimed his discharge on *habeas corpus* because the chancellor had no jurisdiction to make the decree, being interested in the cause himself. But the Court of Queen's Bench held that if that was a defence it should have been made on the trial for contempt, and the conviction was conclusive. We cannot choose but hold the same rule here. Any other would be a violation of the law which is established and sustained by all authority and all reason.

But certainly the want of jurisdiction alleged in this case would not even have been a defence on the trial. The proposition that a court is powerless to punish for disorderly conduct, or disobedience of its process in a case which it ought ultimately to dismiss, for want of jurisdiction, is not only unsupported by judicial authority, but we think it is new even as an argument at the bar. We, ourselves, have heard many cases through and through before we became convinced that it was our duty to remit the parties to another tribunal. But we never thought that our process could be defied in such cases more than in others.

There are some proceedings in which the want of jurisdiction would be seen at the first blush; but there are others in which the court must inquire into all the facts before it can possibly know whether it has jurisdiction or not. Any one who obstructs or baffles a judicial investigation for that purpose, is unquestionably guilty of a crime, for which he may, and ought to be tried, convicted, and punished. Suppose a local action to be brought in the wrong county; this is a defence to the action, but a defence which must be made out like any other. While it is pending, neither a party, nor an officer, nor any other person, can safely insult the court, or resist its order. The court may not have power to decide upon the merits of the case; but it has undoubted power to try whether the wrong was done within its jurisdiction or not. Suppose Mr. Williamson to be called before the circuit court of the United States as a witness in a trial for murder, alleged to be committed on the high seas. Can he refuse to be sworn, and at his trial for contempt, justify himself on the ground that the murder was committed within the limits of a State, and thereby triable only in a State court? If he can, he can justify perjury for the same reason. But such a defence for either crime, has never been heard of since the beginning of the world. Much less can it be shown, after conviction, as a ground for declaring the sentence void.

The wish which the petitioner is convicted of disobeying was legal on its face. It enjoined upon him a simple duty, which he ought to have understood and performed without hesitation. That he did not do so is a fact conclusively established by the adjudication which the court made upon it. I say the wish was legal, because the act of Congress gives to all the courts of the United States the power "to issue writs of *habeas corpus*, when necessary for the exercise of their jurisdiction, and agreeable to the principles and usages of law." Chief Justice Marshall decided in Burr's trial, that the principles and usages referred to in this act were those of the common law. A part of the jurisdiction of the district court consists in restoring fugitive slaves; and the *habeas corpus* may be used in aid of it when necessary. It was awarded here upon the application of a person who complained that his slaves were detained from him. Unless they were fugitive slaves they could not be slaves at all, according to the petitioner's own doctrine, and if the judge took that view of the subject, he was bound to award the writ. If the persons mentioned on it had turned out on the hearing to be fugitives from labor, the duty of the district judge to restore them, or his power to bring them before him on a *habeas corpus*, would have been disputed by none except the very few who think that the constitution and law on that subject ought not to be obeyed. The duty of the court to enquire into the facts on which its jurisdiction depends is as plain as its duty not to exceed it when it is ascertained. But Mr. Williamson stopped the investigation *in limine;* and the consequence is, that every thing in the case remains unsettled, whether the persons named in the writ were slaves or free.

Whether Mr. Wheeler was the owner of them — whether they were unlawfully taken from him — whether the court had jurisdiction to restore them — all these points are left open for want of a proper return. It is not our business to say how they ought to be decided; but we doubt not that the learned and upright magistrate who presides in the district court would have decided them as rightly as any judge in all the country. Mr. Williamson had no right to arrest the inquiry because he supposed that an error would be committed on the question of jurisdiction, or any other question. If the assertions which his counsel now make on the law and the facts be correct, he prevented an adjudication in favor of his proteges, and thus did them a wrong, which is probably a greater offence in his own eyes than any thing he could do against Mr. Wheeler's rights. There is no reason to believe that any trouble whatever would have come out of the case, if he had made a true, full, and special return of all the facts; for then the rights of all parties, black and white, could have been settled, or the matter dismissed for want of jurisdiction, if the law so required.

It is argued that the court had no jurisdiction, because it was not averred that the slaves were fugitives, but merely that they owed service by the laws of Virginia. Conceding, for the argument's sake, that this was the only ground on which the court could have interfered — conceding that it is not substantially alleged in the petition of Mr. Wheeler — the proceedings were, nevertheless, not void for that reason.

The federal tribunals, though courts of limited jurisdiction, are not *inferior* courts. Their judgments, until reversed by the proper appellate court, are valid and conclusive upon the parties, though the jurisdiction be not alleged in the pleadings nor on any part of the record. (10 Wheaton, 192.) Even if this were not settled and clear law, it would still be certain that the fact on which jurisdiction depends need not be stated *in the process*. The want of such a statement in the body of the *habeas corpus*, or in the petition on which it was awarded, did not give Mr. Williamson a right to treat it with contempt. If it did, then the courts of the United States must get out the ground of their jurisdiction in every subpœna for a witness; and a defective or untrue averment will authorize the witness to be as contumacious as he sees fit.

But all that was said in the argument about the petition, the writ, and the facts which were proved or could be proved, refers to the *evidence* in which the conviction took place. This has passed *in rem judicatam*. We cannot go one step behind the conviction itself. We could not reverse it if there had been no evidence at all. We have no more authority in law to come between the prisoner and the court to free him from a sentence like this, than we would have to countermand an order issued by the commander-in-chief to the United States army.

We have no authority, jurisdiction, or power to decide any thing here except the simple fact that the district court had power to punish for contempt, a person who disobeys its process — that the petitioner is convicted of such contempt — and that the conviction is conclusive upon us. The jurisdiction of the court on the case which had been before it, and every thing else which preceded the conviction, are out of our reach, and they are not examinable by us — and, of course, not now intended to be decided.

There may be cases in which we ought to check usurpation of power by the Federal courts. If one of them would presume, upon any pretence whatever, to take out of our hands a prisoner convicted of contempt in this court, we would resist it by all proper and legal means. What we would not permit them to do against us we will not do against them.

We must maintain the rights of the State and its courts, for to them alone can the people look for a competent administration of their domestic concerns; but we will do nothing to impair the constitutional vigor of the general government, which is "the sheet anchor of our peace at home and our safety abroad."

Some complaint was made in the argument about the sentence being for an indefinite time. If this were erroneous it would not avail here, since we have as little power to revise the judgment for that reason as for any other. But it is not illegal nor contrary to the usual rule in such cases. It means commitment until the party shall make proper submission. (3 Lord Raymond, 1108. 4 Johns. Rep. 375.)

The law will not bargain with anybody to let its courts be defied for a specific term of imprisonment. There are many persons who would gladly purchase the honors of martyrdom in a popular cause at almost any given price, while others are deterred by a mere show of punishment. Each is detained until he finds himself willing to conform. This is merciful to the submissive and not too severe upon the refractory. The petitioner, therefore, carries the key of his prison in his own pocket. He can come out when he will, by making terms with the court that sent him there. But if he choose to struggle for a triumph — if nothing will content him but a clean victory or a clean defeat — he cannot expect us to aid him. Our duties are of a widely different kind. They consist in discouraging as much as in us lies all such contests with the legal authorities of the country. *The writ of habeas corpus is refused.*

---

## No. IV.

*The dissenting opinion of Judge Knox in favor of granting the petition.*

Knox, J. I do not concur in the opinion of the majority of this court refusing the writ of *habeas corpus*, and shall state the reasons why, in my judgment, the writ should be granted.

This application was made to the court whilst holding a special session at Bedford, on the 13th day of August; and upon an intimation from the counsel that in case the court had any difficulty upon the question of awarding the writ, they would like to be heard, Thursday, the 16th of August, was fixed for the hearing. On that day an argument was made by Messrs. Meredith and Gilpin, in favor of the allowance of the writ.

I may as well remark here, that upon the presentation of the petition I was in favor of awarding the *habeas corpus*, greatly preferring that the right of the petitioner to his discharge should be determined upon the return of the writ. If this course had been adopted, we should have had the views of counsel in opposition to the discharge, and, moreover, if necessary, we could, after the return, have examined into the facts of the case.

I am in favor of granting this writ, first, because I believe the petitioner has the right to demand it at our hands. From the time of Magna Charta the writ of *habeas corpus* has been considered a writ of right, which every person is entitled to *ex debito justiciæ.* "But the benefit of it," says Chancellor Kent, "was in a great degree eluded in England prior to the statute of Charles II., as the judges only awarded it in term time, and they assumed a discretionary power of awarding or refusing it." 2 Kent Commentaries, 26. And Bacon says, "Notwithstanding the writ of *habeas corpus* be a writ of right, and what the subject is entitled to, yet the provision of the law herein being in a great measure eluded by the judge as being only enabled to award it in term time, as also by an imagined notion of the judges that they had a discretionary power of granting or refusing it," the act of 31 Charles II. was made for remedy thereof.

I am aware that both in England and this country, since the passage of the statute of Charles II., it has been held that where it clearly appeared that the prisoner must be remanded, it was improper to grant the writ; but I know of no such construction upon our act of 18th February, 1785. The people of the United States have ever regarded the privileges of the *habeas corpus* as a most invaluable right, to secure which, an interdiction against its suspension, "unless when in cases of rebellion or invasion the public safety may require it," is inserted in the organic law of the Union; and in addition to our act of 1785, which is broader and more comprehensive than the English statute, a provision in terms like that in the constitution of the United States is to be found in the constitution of this State.

It is difficult to conceive how words could be more imperative in their character than those to be found in our statute of 1785. The judges named are authorized and required, either in vacation or term time, upon the due application of any person committed or detained for any criminal or supposed criminal matter, except for treason or felony, or confined or restrained of his or her liberty, under any color or pretence whatsoever, to award and grant a *habeas corpus*, directed to the person or persons in whose custody the prisoner is detained, returnable immediately. And the refusal or neglect to grant the writ required by the act to be granted, renders the judge so neglecting or refusing liable to the penalty of three hundred pounds.

I suppose no one will doubt the power of the legislature to require this writ to be issued by the judges of the commonwealth. And it is tolerably plain that where, in express words, a certain thing is directed to be done, to which is added a penalty for not doing it, no discretion is to be used in obeying the mandate.

The English statute confined the penalty to a neglect or refusal to grant the writ in vacation time, and from this a discretionary power to refuse it in term time was inferred, but our act of Assembly does not limit the penalty to a refusal in vacation, but is sufficiently comprehensive to embrace neglect or refusal in vacation or in term time.

I have looked in vain through the numerous cases reported in this State to find that the writ was ever denied to one whose application was in due form, and whose case was within the purview of the act of Assembly.

In *Respublica* v. *Arnold*, 3 Yates, 263, the writ was refused because the petitioner was not restrained of his liberty, and therefore not within the terms of the statute; and in *Ex parte Lawrence*, 5 Binney, 304, it was held that the act of Assembly did not oblige the court to grant a *habeas corpus* where the case had already been heard upon the same evidence by another court. Without going into an examination of the numerous cases where the writ has been allowed, I believe it can be safely affirmed that the denial of the writ in a case like the present is without a precedent, and contrary to the uniform practice of the bench, and against the universal understanding of the profession and the people; but what is worse still, it appears to me to be in direct violation of the law itself.

It may be said that the law never requires a useless thing to be done. Grant it. But how can it be determined to be useless until the case is heard? Whether there is ground for the writ is to be determined according to law, and the law requires that the determination should follow, not precede the return.

An application was made to the chief justice of this court for a writ of *habeas corpus* previous to the application now being considered. The writ was refused, and it was stated in the opinion that the counsel for the petitioner waived the right to the writ, or did not desire it to be issued, if the chief justice should be of the opinion that there was not sufficient cause set forth in the petition for the prisoner's discharge. But this can in nowise prejudice the petitioner's right to the writ which he now demands. Even had the writ been awarded, and the case heard, and the discharge refused, it would not be within the decision in *Ex parte Lawrence*, for there the hearing was before a court in term time, upon a full examination of the case upon evidence adduced, and not at chambers; but the more obvious distinction here is that the writ has never been awarded. And the agreement of counsel that it should not be in a certain event, even if binding upon the client there, would not affect him here.

Now, while I aver that the writ of *habeas corpus, ad subjiciendum*, is a writ of right, I do not wish to be understood that it should issue as a matter of course. Undoubtedly the petition must be in due form, and it must show upon its face that the petitioner is entitled to relief. It may be refused if, upon the application itself, it appears that, if admitted to be true, the applicant is not entitled to relief; but where, as in the case before us, the petition alleges an illegal restraint of the petitioner's liberty, under an order from a judge beyond his jurisdiction, we are bound in the first place to take the allegation as true; and so taking it, a probable cause is made out, and there is no longer a discretionary power to refuse the writ. Whether the allegation of the want of jurisdiction is true or not, is determinable only upon the return of the writ.

If one has averred in his petition what, if true, would afford him relief, it is his constitutional right to be present when the truth of his allegations is inquired into; and it is also his undoubted right, under our *habeas corpus* act, to establish his allegations by evidence to be introduced and heard upon the return of the writ. To deny him the writ is virtually to condemn him unheard; and as I can see nothing in this case which requires at our hands an extraordinary resistance against the prayer of the petitioner to show that his imprisonment is illegal, that he is deprived of his liberty without due course of law. I am in favor of treating him as like cases have uniformly been treated in this commonwealth, by awarding the writ of *habeas corpus*, and reserving the inquiry as to his right to be discharged until the return of the writ; but as a majority of my brethren have come to a different conclusion, we must inquire next into the right of the applicant to be discharged as the case is now presented.

I suppose it to be undoubted law that in a case where a court acting beyond its jurisdiction has committed a person to prison, the prisoner, under our *habeas corpus* act, is entitled to his discharge, and that it makes no difference whether the court thus transcending its jurisdiction assumes to act as a court of the Union or of the commonwealth. If a principle, apparently so just and clear, needs for its support adjudicated cases, reference can be had to *Wise* v. *Withers*, 3 Cranch, 331; 1 Peters, Condensed Rep. 552; *Rose* v. *Hinely*, 4 Cranch, 241, 268; *Den* v. *Harden*, 1 Paine, Rep. 55, 58 and 59; 3 Cranch, 448; *Bollman* v. *Swartout*, 4 Cranch, 75; Kearney's case, 7 Wheaton, 38; *Kemp* v. *Kennedy*, 1 Peters, C. C. Rep. 36; *Wickes* v. *Calk*, 5 Har. and J. 42; *Griffith* v. *Frazier*, 8 Cranch, 9; *Com.* v. *Smith*, Sup. Court Penn., 1 Wharton Digest, 321; *Com. ex relatione Lockington* v. *The Jailer*, &c., Sup. Court manuscript, 1814, Wharton's Digest, vol. i. 321; *Albec* v. *Ward*, 8 Mass. 86.

Some of these cases decide that the act of a court without jurisdiction is void; some, that the proper remedy for an imprisonment by a court having no jurisdiction is the writ of *habeas corpus;* and others, that it may issue from a state court to discharge a prisoner committed under process from a federal court, if it clearly appears that the federal court had no jurisdiction of the case; altogether, they establish the point that the petitioner is entitled to relief, if he is restrained of his liberty by a court acting beyond its jurisdiction.

Neither do I conceive it to be correct to say that the applicant cannot now question the jurisdiction of the judge of the district court because he did not challenge it on the hearing. There are many rights and privileges which a party to a judicial controversy may lose if not claimed in due time, but not so the question of jurisdiction; this cannot be given by express consent, much less will acquiescence for a time waive an objection to it. (See U. S. Digest, vol. i. p. 639, Pl. 62, and cases there cited.) It would be a harsh rule to apply to one who is in prison "without bail or mainprize," that his omission to speak on the first opportunity forever closed his mouth from denying the power of the court to deprive him of his liberty. I deny that the law is a trap for the feet of the unwary. Where personal liberty is concerned, it is a shield for the protection of the citizen, and it will answer his call even if made after the prison door has been closed on him.

If, then, the want of jurisdiction is fatal, and the inquiry as to its existence is still open, the only question that remains to be considered is this: Had the judge of the district court for the eastern district of the United States power to issue the writ of *habeas corpus*, directed to Passmore Williamson, upon the petition of John H. Wheeler? The power of that court to commit for a contempt is not denied, and I understand it to be conceded as a general rule by the petitioner's counsel, that one court will not reëxamine a commitment for contempt by another court of competent jurisdiction; but if the court has no authority to issue the writ, the res-

35 *

pondent was not bound to answer it, and his neglect or refusal to do so would not authorize his punishment for contempt.

The first position which I shall take in considering the question of jurisdiction, is that the courts of the United States have no power to award the writ of *habeas corpus* except such as is given to them by the acts of Congress.

"Courts which originate in the common law possess a jurisdiction which must be regulated by the common law; but the courts which are created by written law, and whose jurisdiction is defined by written law, cannot transcend their jurisdiction. The power to award the writ by any of the courts of the United States must be given by written law." *Ex parte, Swartout*, 4 Cranch, 75. *Ex parte Barre*, 2 Howard, 65. The power of the United States to issue writs of *habeas corpus* is derived either from the fourteenth section of the act of 24th September, 1789, or from the seventh section of the act of March 2, 1833.

The section from the act of 1789 provides that "all the courts of the United States may issue writs of *scire facias*, *habeas corpus*, and all other writs not especially provided for by statute, which may be necessary for the exercise of their respective jurisdictions, and agreeable to the principles and usages of law. And either of the justices of the supreme court, as well as the judges of the district courts, may grant writs of *habeas*, for the purpose of inquiry into the cause of commitment; but writs of *habeas corpus* shall in no case extend to prisoners in jail, unless they are in custody under or by color of the authority of the United States, or are committed for trial before some court of the same, or are necessary to be brought into court to testify." The seventh section of the act of 2d March, 1833, authorizes "either of the justices of the supreme court, or judge of any district court of the United States, in addition, to the authority already conferred by law, to grant writs of *habeas corpus* in all cases of a prisoner or prisoners in jail or confinement, where he or they shall be committed or confined on or by authority of law, for any act done, or omitted to be done, in pursuance of a law of the United States, or any order, process, or decree of any judge or court thereof, any thing in any act of Congress to the contrary notwithstanding."

Now, unless the writ of *habeas corpus* issued by the judge of the district court was necessary for the exercise of the jurisdiction of the said court, or was to inquire into a commitment under, or by color of the authority of the United States, or to relieve some one imprisoned for an act done, or omitted to be done, in pursuance of a law of the United States, the district court had no power to issue it, and a commitment for contempt in refusing to answer it is an illegal imprisonment, which, under our *habeas corpus* act, we are imperatively required to set aside.

It cannot be pretended that the writ was either asked for or granted to inquire into any commitment made under or by color of the authority of the United States, or to relieve from imprisonment for an act done or omitted to be done in pursuance of a law of the United States, and therefore we may confine our inquiry solely to the question whether it was necessary for the exercise of any jurisdiction given to the district court of the United States for the eastern district of Pennsylvania.

This brings us to the question of the jurisdiction of the courts of the United States, and more particularly that of the district court. And here, without desiring, or intending to discuss at large the nature and powers of the federal government, it is proper to repeat what has been so often said, and what has never been denied, that it is a government of enumerated powers, delegated to it by the several States, or the people thereof, without capacity to enlarge or extend the powers so delegated and enumerated, and that its courts of justice are courts of limited jurisdiction, deriving their authority from the constitution of the United States, and the acts of Congress under the constitution. Let us see what judicial power was given by the people to the Federal government, for that alone can be rightly exercised by its courts.

"The judicial power" (says the second section of the third article) "shall extend to all cases in law and equity arising under this constitution, the laws of the United States, and treaties made, or which shall be made under their authority, to all cases affecting embassadors, other public ministers and consuls, to all cases of admiralty and maritime jurisdiction, to controversies to which the United States shall be a party, to controversies between two or more States, between a State and citizen of another State, between citizens of different States, between citizens of the same State, claiming lands under grants of different States, and between a State, or the citizen thereof, and foreign States, citizens or subjects."

The amendments subsequently made to this article have no bearing upon the question under consideration, nor is it necessary to examine the various acts of Congress conferring jurisdiction upon the courts of the United States, for no act of Congress can be found extending the jurisdiction beyond what is given by the constitution, so far as relates to the question we are now considering. And if such an act should be passed it would be in direct conflict with the tenth amended article of the constitution, which declares that "the powers not delegated to the United States by the constitution, nor prohibited by it to the States, are reserved to the States respectively, or to the people."

If this case can be brought within the judicial power of the courts of the United States, it must be either—

1st. Because it arises under the Constitution or the laws of the United States.

Or, 2d. Because it is a controversy between citizens of different States, for it is very plain that there is no other clause in the Constitution which, by the most latitudinarian construction, could be made to include it.

Did it arise under the Constitution or the laws of the United States? In order to give a satisfactory answer to this question, it is necessary to see what the case was.

If we confine ourselves strictly to the record from the district court, we learn from it that, on the 18th day of July last, John H. Wheeler presented his petition to the Hon. J. K. Kane, judge of the district court for the eastern district of Pennsylvania, setting forth that he was the owner of three persons held to service or labor by the laws of the State of Virginia; such persons being respectively named Jane, aged about thirty-five years, Daniel, aged about twelve years, and Isaiah, aged about seven years, persons of color; and that they were detained from his possession by Passmore Williamson, but not for any criminal or supposed criminal matter. In accordance with the prayer of the petition, a writ of *habeas corpus* was awarded, commanding Passmore Williamson to bring the bodies of the said Jane, Daniel, and Isaiah, before the judge of the district court, forthwith. To this writ, Passmore Williamson made a return, verified by his affirmation, that the said Jane, Daniel, and Isaiah, nor either of them, were at the time of the issuing of the writ, nor at the time of the return, nor at any other time, in the custody, power, or possession of, nor confined, nor restrained their liberty by him; and that, therefore, he could not produce the bodies as he was commanded.

This return was made on the 20th day of July, A. D. 1855. "Whereupon, afterwards, to wit: On the 27th day of July, A. D. 1855, (says the record,) the counsel for the several parties having been heard, and the said return having been duly considered, it is ordered and adjudged by the court that the said Passmore Williamson be committed to the custody of the marshal, without bail or mainprize, as for a contempt in refusing to make return to the writ of *habeas corpus*, heretofore issued against him, at the instance of Mr. John H. Wheeler."

Such is the record. Now, while I am willing to admit that the want of jurisdiction should be made clear, I deny that in a case under our *habeas corpus* act the party averring want of jurisdiction cannot go behind the record to establish its non-existence. Jurisdiction, or the absence thereof, is a mixed question of law and fact. It is the province of fact to ascertain what the case is, and of law to determine whether the jurisdiction attaches to the case so ascertained. "And" says the second section of our act of 1785, "that the said judge or justice may, according to the intent and meaning of this act, be enabled, by investigating the truth of the circumstances of the case, to determine whether, according to law, the said prisoner ought to be bailed, remanded, or discharged, the return may, before or after it is filed, by leave of the said judge or justice, be amended, and also suggestions made against it, so that thereby material facts may be ascertained."

This provision applies to cases of commitment or detainer for any criminal or supposed criminal matter, but the fourteenth section, which applies to cases of restraint of liberty "under any color or pretence whatever," provides that "the court, judge, or justice, before whom the party so confined or restrained shall be brought, shall, after the return made, proceed in the same manner as is hereinbefore prescribed, to examine into the facts relating to the case, and into the cause of such confinement or restraint, and thereupon either bail, remand, or discharge the party so brought, as to justice shall appertain."

The right and duty of the supreme court of a State to protect a citizen thereof from imprisonment by a judge of a United States court having no jurisdiction over the cause of complaint, is so manifest and so essentially necessary under our dual system of government, that I cannot believe that this right will ever be abandoned or the duty avoided; but, if we concede, what appears to be the law of the later cases in the Federal courts, that the jurisdiction need not appear affirmatively, and add to it that the want of jurisdiction shall not be proved by evidence outside of the record, we do virtually deny to the people of the State the right to question the validity of an order by a Federal judge consigning them to the walls of a prison "without bail or mainprize."

What a mockery to say to one restrained of his liberty, "True, if the judge or court under whose order you are in prison acted without jurisdiction, you are entitled to be discharged, but the burden is upon you to show that there was no jurisdiction, and in showing this we will not permit you to go beyond the record made up by the party against whom you complain!"

As the petitioner would be legally entitled, upon the return of the writ, to establish the truth of the facts set forth in his petition, so far as they bear upon the question of jurisdiction, we are bound before the return to assume that the facts are true as stated, and so taking them, the case is this:

John H. Wheeler voluntarily brought into the State of Pennsylvania three persons of color, held by him in the State of Virginia as slaves, with the intention of passing through this State. While on board of a steamboat near Walnut Street wharf, in the city of Philadelphia, the petitioner, Passmore Williamson, informed the mother that she was free by the laws of Pennsylvania, who, in the language of the petition, "expressed her desire to have her freedom; and finally, with her children, left the boat of her own free will and accord, and without coercion or compulsion of any kind; and having seen her in possession of her liberty with her children, your petitioner (says the petition) returned to his place of business, and has never since seen the said Jane, Daniel, and Isaiah, or either of them, nor does he know where they are, nor has he had any connection of any kind with the subject."

One owning slaves in a slave State voluntarily brings them into a free State, with the intention of passing through the free State. While there, upon being told that they are free, the slaves leave their master. Can a judge of the district court of the United States compel their restoration through the medium of a writ of *habeas corpus* directed to the person by whom they were informed of their freedom? Or, in other words, is it a case arising under the constitution and laws of the United States?

What article or section of the constitution has any bearing upon the right of a master to pass through a free State with his slave or slaves? Or, when has Congress ever attempted to legislate upon this question? I most unhesitatingly aver that neither in the constitution of the United States nor in the acts of Congress can there be found a sentence which has any effect upon this question whatever. It is a question to be decided by the law of the State where the person is for the time being, and that law must be determined by the judges of the State, who have sworn to support the constitution of the State as well as that of the United States — an oath which is never taken by a Federal judge.

Upon this question of jurisdiction it is wholly immaterial whether by the law of Pennsylvania a slaveholder has or has not the right of passing through our State with his slaves. If he has the right, it is not in virtue of the constitution or laws of the United States, but by the law of the State, and if no such right exists, it is because the State law has forbidden it, or has failed to recognize it. It is for the State alone to legislate upon this subject, and there is no power on earth to call her to an account for her acts of omission and commission in this behalf.

If this case, by any reasonable construction, be brought within the terms of the third clause of the second section of article four of the constitution of the United States, jurisdiction might be claimed for the federal courts, as then it would be a case arising under the constitution of the United States, although I believe the writ of *habeas corpus* is no part of the machinery designed by Congress for the rendition of fugitives from labor.

"No person (says the clause above mentioned) held to service or labor in one State under the laws thereof escaping into another shall, in consequence of any law or regulation therein, be discharged from such service or labor, but shall be delivered up on claim of the party to whom such service or labor may be due." By reference to the debates in the convention, it will be seen that this clause was inserted at the request of delegates from southern states, and on the declaration that in the absence of a constitutional provision the right of reclamation would not exist unless given by state authority. If it had been intended to cover the right of transit, words would have been used evidencing such intention. Happily there is no contrariety in the construction which has been placed upon this clause in the constitution. No judge has ever so manifestly disregarded its plain and unequivocal language as to hold that it applies to a slave voluntarily brought into a free State by his master. On the contrary, there is abundant authority that such a case is not within either the letter or the spirit of the constitutional provision for the rendition of fugitives from labor. Said Mr. Justice Washington, *Ex parte Simmons*, 6 W. C. C. Reports, 396: — "The slave in this case having been voluntarily brought by his master into this State, I have no cognizance of the case, so far as respects this application, and the master must abide by the laws of this State, so far as they may affect his right. If the man claimed as a slave be not entitled to his freedom under the laws of this State, the master must pursue such remedy for his recovery as the laws of the State have provided for him."

In *Jones* v. *Vanzandt*, 5 Howard, 229, Mr. Justice Woodbury uses language equally expressive: "But the power of national law," said that eminent jurist, "to pursue and regain most kinds of property in the limits of a foreign government is rather an act of comity than strict right, and hence as property in persons might not thus be recognized in some of the states in the Union, and its reclamation not be allowed through either courtesy or right, this clause was undoubtedly introduced into the constitution as one of its compromises for the safety of that portion of the Union which did not permit such property, and which otherwise might often be deprived of it entirely by its merely crossing the line of an adjoining state; this was thought to be too harsh a doctrine in respect to any title to property of a friendly neighbor, not brought nor placed in another state under state laws by the owner himself, but escaping there against his consent, and often forthwith pursued in order to be reclaimed."

Other authorities might be quoted to the same effect, but it is unnecessary, for if it be not clear that one voluntarily brought into a state is not a fugitive, no judicial language can ever make him so. Will we then, for the sake of sustaining this jurisdiction, presume that these slaves of Mr. Wheeler escaped from Virginia into Pennsylvania, when no such allegation was made in his petition, when it is expressly stated in the petition of Mr. Williamson, verified by his affirmation, that they were brought here voluntarily by their master, and when this fact is virtually conceded by the judge of the district court in his opinion? Great as is my respect for the judicial authorities of the federal government, I cannot consent to stultify myself in order to sustain their unauthorized judgments, and more particularly where, as in the case before us, it would be at the expense of the liberty of a citizen of this commonwealth.

The only remaining ground upon which this jurisdiction can be claimed, is that it was in a controversy between citizens of different states, and I shall dismiss this branch of the case simply by affirming — 1, that the proceeding by *habeas corpus* is in no legal sense a controversy between private parties; and 2, if it were, to the circuit court alone is given this jurisdiction. For the correctness of the first position, I refer to the opinion of Mr. Justice Baldwin in *Holmes* v. *Jennifer*, published in the appendix to 14 Peters, and to that of Judge Betts, of the circuit court of New York, in *Berry* v. *Mercein et al.* reported in 5 Howard, 103. And for the second, to the 11th section of the judiciary act, passed on the 24th of September, 1789.

My view of this case had been committed to writing before I had seen or heard the opinion of the majority of the court. Having heard it hastily read but once, I may mistake its purport, but if I do not, it places the refusal of the *habeas corpus* mainly upon the ground that the conviction for contempt was a separate proceeding, and that, as the district court had jurisdiction to punish for contempts, we have no power to review its decision. Or, as it appears from the record that the prisoner is in custody upon a conviction for contempt, we are powerless to grant him relief.

Notwithstanding the numerous cases that are cited to sustain this position, it appears to me to be as novel as it is dangerous. Every court of justice in this country has, in some degree, the power to commit for contempt. Can it be possible that a citizen once committed for contempt is beyond the hope of relief, even although the record shows that the alleged contempt was not within the power of the court to punish summarily? Suppose that the judge of the district court should send to prison an editor of a newspaper for a contempt of his court in commenting upon his decision in this very case; would the prisoner be beyond the reach of our writ of *habeas corpus?* If he would, our boasted security of personal liberty is in truth an idle boast, and our constitutional guaranties and writs of right are as ropes of sand. But in the name of the law, I aver that no such power exists with any court or judge, state or federal, and if it is attempted to be exercised, there are modes of relief, full and ample, for the exigency of the occasion.

I have not had either time or opportunity to examine all of the cases cited, but, as far as I have examined them, they decide this and nothing more — that where a court of competent jurisdiction convicts one of a contempt, another court, without appellate power, will not reëxamine the case to determine whether a contempt was really committed or not. The history of punishments for contempts of courts, and the legislative action thereon, both in our State and Union, in an unmistakable manner teaches, first, the liability of this power to be abused; and second, the promptness with which its unguarded use has been followed by legislative restrictions. It is no longer an undefined, unlimited power of a star chamber character, to be used for the oppression of the citizen at the mere caprice of the judge or court, but it has its boundaries so distinctly defined that there is no mistaking the extent to which our tribunals of law may go in punishment for this offence.

In the words of the act of Congress of 2d March, 1831, "The power of the several courts of the United States to issue attachments and inflict summary punishments for contempts of court, shall not be construed to extend to any cases except the misbehavior of any person or persons in the presence of said courts, or so near thereto as to obstruct the administration of justice, the misbehavior of any of the officers of the said courts in their official transactions, and the disobedience or resistance by any officer of the said courts, party, jurors, witness, or any other person or persons, to any *lawful* writ, process, order, rule, decree or command of said courts."

Now, Passmore Williamson was convicted of a contempt for disobeying a writ of *habeas corpus*, commanding him to produce before the district court certain persons claimed by Mr. Wheeler as slaves. Was it a lawful writ? Clearly not, if the court had no jurisdiction to issue it; and that it had not I think is very plain. If it was unlawful, the person to whom it was directed was not bound to obey it; and, in the very words of the statute, the power to punish for contempt "shall not be construed to extend to it."

But, says the opinion of the majority, he was convicted of a contempt of court, and we will not look into the record to see how the contempt was committed. I answer this by asserting that you cannot see the conviction without seeing the cause: 1, the petition; 2, the writ and the alias writ of *habeas corpus*; 3, the return; and 4, the judgment.

"It is ordered and adjudged by the court that the said Passmore Williamson be committed to the custody of the marshal without bail or mainprize, as for a contempt in refusing to make return to the writ of *habeas corpus* heretofore issued against him at the instance of Mr. John H. Wheeler." As I understand the opinion of a majority of my brethren, as soon as we get to the word contempt the book must be closed, and it becomes instantly sealed as to the residue of the record. To sustain this commitment we must, it seems, first presume, in the very teeth of the admitted fact, that these were runaway slaves; and second, we must be careful to read only portions of the record, lest we should find that the prisoner was committed for refusing to obey an unlawful writ.

I cannot forbear the expression of the opinion that the rule laid down in this case by the majority is fraught with great danger to the most cherished rights of the citizens of the State. While in contests involving the right of property merely, I presume we may still treat these judgments of the United States courts, in cases not within their jurisdiction, as nullities; yet, if a single judge thinks proper to determine that one of our citizens has been guilty of contempt, even if such determination had its foundation in a case upon which the judge had no power to pronounce judgment, and was most manifestly in direct violation of a solemn act of the very legislative authority that created the court over which the judge presides, it seems that such determination is to have all the force and effect of a judgment pronounced by a court of competent jurisdiction, acting within the admitted sphere of its constitutional powers.

Nay, more. We confess ourselves powerless to protect our citizens from the aggressions of a court, as foreign from our state government in matters not committed to its jurisdiction as the Court of Queen's Bench in England, and this upon the authority of decisions pronounced in cases not at all analogous to the one now under consideration. I believe this to be the first recorded case where the supreme court of a state has refused the prayer of a citizen for the writ of *habeas corpus* to inquire into the legality of an imprisonment by a judge of a federal court for contempt, in refusing obedience to a writ void for want of jurisdiction.

I will conclude by recapitulating the grounds upon which I think this writ should be awarded.

1. At common law, and by our statute of 1785, the writ of *habeas corpus ad sufficiendum* is a writ of right, demandable whenever a petition in due form asserts what, if true, would entitle the party to relief.

2. That an allegation in a petition that the petitioner is restrained of his liberty by an order of a judge or court without jurisdiction, shows such probable cause as to leave it no longer discretionary with the court or judge to whom application is made whether the writ shall or shall not issue.

3. That where a person is imprisoned by an order of a judge of the district court of the United States for refusing to answer a writ of *habeas corpus*, he is entitled to be discharged from such imprisonment if the judge of the district court had no authority to issue the writ.

4. That the power to issue writs of *habeas corpus* by the judges of the federal courts is a mere auxiliary power, and that no such writ can be issued by such judges where the cause of complaint to be remedied by it is beyond their jurisdiction.

5. That the courts of the federal government are courts of limited jurisdiction, derived from the constitution of the United States and the acts of Congress under the constitution, and that when the jurisdiction is not given by the constitution or by Congress in pursuance of the constitution, it does not exist.

6. That when it does not appear by the record that the court had jurisdiction in a proceeding under our *habeas corpus* act to relieve from an illegal imprisonment, want of jurisdiction may be established by parole.

7. That where the inquiry as to the jurisdiction of a court arises upon a rule for a *habeas corpus*, all the facts set forth in the petition tending to show want of jurisdiction are to be considered as true, unless they contradict the record.

8. That where the owner of a slave voluntarily brings his slave from a slave to a free State, without any intention of remaining therein, the right of the slave to his freedom depends upon the law of the State into which he is thus brought.

9. That if a slave so brought into a free State escapes from the custody of his master while in said State, the right of the master to reclaim him is not a question arising under the constitution of the United States or the laws thereof; a judge of the United States cannot issue a writ of *habeas corpus* directed to one who it is alleged withholds the possession of the slave from the master, commanding him to produce the body of the slave before said judge.

10. That the district court of the United States for the eastern district of Pennsylvania has no jurisdiction because a controversy is between citizens of different States, and that a proceeding by *habeas corpus* is, in no legal sense, a controversy between private parties.

11. That the power of the several courts of the United States to inflict summary punishment for contempt of court in disobeying a writ of the court, is expressly confined to cases of disobedience to "lawful" writs.

12. That where it appears from the record that the conviction was for disobeying a writ of *habeas corpus*, which writ the court have no jurisdiction to issue, the conviction is *coram non judice*, and void.

For these reasons I do most respectfully, but most earnestly, dissent from the judgment of the majority of my brethren refusing the writ applied for.

---

## No. V.

*How Passmore Williamson was finally discharged.*

Previously to the application on Williamson's behalf to the supreme court of Pennsylvania, Jane Johnson, the woman who, and her two sons, were claimed as slaves by Wheeler, had appeared before Judge Culver of New York, and had made an affidavit that the plan of claiming her freedom and that of her children had originated entirely with herself; that it was through her means that Williamson was made acquainted with her desire in that behalf; and that all he had done, after coming on board the boat, was to assure her and her claimant that she and her children were free, to advise her to leave the boat, and to interfere to prevent Wheeler from detaining her. The same facts she had afterwards testified to in open court in Philadelphia, on the trial for assault and riot of the colored men who had assisted her to escape.

After the failure of the application to the supreme court of Pennsylvania, certain persons, indignant at this refusal of justice and at the continuation of Williamson's false imprisonment, but acting wholly independently of him, induced Jane Johnson to present a petition to Judge Kane, setting forth all the above facts, and praying that as the writ of *habeas corpus* obtained by Wheeler under pretence of delivering her from imprisonment and detention had been obtained without her privity or consent, and on false pretences, the writ and all the proceedings under it might be quashed. After argument upon the question of allowing this petition to be filed, Judge Kane delivered a long and very elaborate opinion, embracing three principal topics. He began with a very elaborate eulogy upon the writ of *habeas corpus*, coming with a very singular grace from a judge who had prostituted that writ to so vile a use, viz.: an attempted kidnapping and the false imprisonment for a pretended contempt of the man who had encouraged and assisted Jane Johnson to vindicate her rights under the laws of Pennsylvania. Next followed Judge Kane's version of his proceedings in committing Williamson, and an attempt to vindicate himself therein; and to which succeeded a very labored effort at enforcing his favorite doctrine, on which his whole proceeding had been based, that slaveholders have a right to transport their slaves through Pennsylvania.

He refused to receive the petition of Jane Johnson, or to pay any attention to its suggestions, on the following grounds:

"The very name of the person who authenticates the paper is a stranger to any proceeding that is or has been before me. She asks no judicial action for herself, and does not profess to have any right to solicit action on behalf of another. On the contrary, her counsel have told me expressly that Mr. Williamson has not sanctioned her application. She has therefore no *status* whatever in this court."

After the delivery of this opinion a little episode followed, evidently got up with a view to relieve Judge Kane from a part of the odium under which he was laboring, of which episode the following account was given in the newspaper reports of the proceeding: —

"On the conclusion of the delivery of this opinion, John Cadwallader, (a member of the bar, but not engaged in this case,) in order to remove a false impression from the public mind, said, from his recollection of the circumstances attending the commitment of Passmore Williamson, a proposition was made to amend the return to the writ, when Judge Kane replied: — 'I will not receive an amendment now, but will be prepared to receive it when the record has been completed.'

"No such motion was subsequently made, and the public impression that permission to amend was refused, was not warranted by facts.

"Judge Kane replied that his (Mr. Cadwallader's) impression was correct. He had been prepared to receive a supplementary return from Mr. Williamson's counsel, but none had been offered.

"Mr. Cadwallader suggested that an addition be made to the opinion of the court, embracing the remarks of a member of the bar not engaged in the case, and the reply of the judge. He was induced to make the suggestion by the best feeling towards a worthy but mistaken man, hoping it might lead to the adoption of such a course as would end in his liberation.

"Mr. Cadwallader is to embody the remarks he made, when the judge will follow with his answer, so as to complete the record." *

Some days after, (Oct. 26,) Messrs. Gilpin and Meredith, of counsel for Williamson, appeared in Judge Kane's court, and asked leave to read a petition from Williamson. This petition contained a statement of the facts in relation to his connection with the liberation of Jane Johnson and her children, similar to that contained in his petition to the supreme court of Pennsylvania, Appendix No. I. The following account of the proceedings on this motion is taken from the *Philadelphia Gazette*: —

Judge Kane said, 'The court cannot hear an application from a party in contempt, except to absolve him. I understand there is an application, by petition, in the name of Passmore Williamson, which is not to relieve himself from the contempt, but —'

Mr. Meredith then remarked something in an inaudible tone, and Judge Kane said: 'Let us not be misunderstood — I am not prepared to receive an application from Passmore Williamson, who is incarcerated for contempt of this court, unless such petition be to relieve himself from contempt by purgation. I am of opinion, unless otherwise instructed, that that is an independent preliminary to any other application from him.

'If, therefore, the counsel arise to present an application from Mr. Williamson, it must be for purgation. The counsel do not inform the court whether they are here to purge Mr. Williamson from the contempt. As at

* Jane Johnson's suggestions, on the ground that she was a stranger to the proceeding, were allowed no weight towards the liberation of Williamson, and were refused admittance on the files of the court. At the same time, the suggestions of Mr. Cadwallader, another stranger, were eagerly clutched at and put upon the record, with a view to better the position of Judge Kane.

present advised, I have no power to hear their application, whatever it may be, in his behalf.'

Mr. Meredith said there were two kinds of contempts; one of personal insult to the bench, with which Passmore Williamson is not concerned; but the contempt consisting in not making a proper return to the process of the court.

Mr. Meredith then proceeded to argue that such a contempt could be purged by making an answer to the court and paying the costs, which he was now prepared to do.

Judge Kane said, that up to this moment there has been, on the part of the individual to whom the function of the court has been delegated and exercised in this matter, not a single particle of conscious excitement. He did not believe it was in the power of the entire press of the United States, after he had honestly administered his duty to the best of his ability, to give him a pang, or produce one excited feeling; therefore, now as heretofore, he looked upon the question as one that has no feeling on the bench.

If he understood the remarks of Mr. Meredith, he meant to say to the court that Passmore Williamson was desirous of testifying now his willingness to obey the exigencies of the writ of *habeas corpus*. If so, he had a simple, straightforward, honorable course to pursue. He has no need of making a narrative of facts or arguments of protest; let him come forward into court, declaring that he is willing to obey the writ issued by this court; and when he has done that, in the estimation of the judge, he is purged of his contempt.

Nothing on his part of personal offence was evinced to the court; his demeanor was entirely respectful; but he failed to obey the writ which the law issued to him; and when he has obeyed that writ, it will be the duty of this court to free him. What is understood by 'purgation' is not simply a mere form of words. It matters not about that, provided he received, from the party who is in contempt for having disobeyed the process of the court, the assurance that he is now prepared to obey such process, and, until he is prepared to announce his disposition to obey, he could not hear him upon any other subject which asserts that the court has erred either in point of fact or law, or has exercised a jurisdiction which does not belong to it. He said he would hear the counsel upon the question whether the court can legally hear any other petition than the one of purgation.

The respondent's counsel then proceeded to argue the right of the court to hear a petition, other than of purgation, from Passmore Williamson.

Mr. Meredith said he had found nothing in the authorities, either English or American, where persons were held guilty of a contempt in responding to a writ of *habeas corpus* unless the return was evasive. He referred to a case in 3 Mason, where, in a return to a writ before Judge Story, there was clearly an evasion shown on the face of the return.

Under these circumstances, Judge Story declared that the course of practice was to propound interrogatories and compel the respondent to disclose more fully. Mr. M. submitted whether it was not proper to subject the petitioner in this case to a further questioning. He could not find in English or American books any other course.

Mr. M. supposed that the respondent was committed until he should answer interrogatories. Why had they not been propounded in the form that the court might think proper to put them? No case could be shown in which a defendant was to be committed for contempt, until he presented a prayer to have interrogatories propounded to him. How is he to answer what has not been filed?

According to the books, the defendant may come into court at any time, and take advantage of an omission to file interrogatories within four days. If another view should be taken by the court, he would then ask that an order be made to show the defendant what he was to do to rid himself of the contempt.

Judge Kane said that the defendant could make a declaration, that he was now ready to answer interrogatories.

Mr. Meredith asked that the court make an order submitting certain interrogatories, such as it would deem sufficient, to the prisoner, the proper answers to which would be enough to purge him of the contempt.

The court then said, 'In some of the cases mentioned we know that the party adjudged to be in contempt submitted himself to interrogatories, either by writing or *per se.* I see no difficulty in the way of the court's giving this decision in the form of an order.

'The suggestion of the counsel now has frequently been intimated by the court. The prisoner might at any time, under a proper application, have been before the court. If there was a misunderstanding of the position of the case by the counsel for Mr. Williamson, it is a matter of sincere regret to me.'

Mr. Meredith said he could not find any case of petition that interrogatories should be filed, in any of the English books.

*Judge Kane.* — The gentleman, Mr. Williamson, is now recusant, and I often think that forms *sometimes* have meaning; and I cannot interfere otherwise than to say as I have said above.

*Mr. Meredith.* — I can enlarge the remark and say that forms *always* have meaning. He argued that the purging interrogatories must be filed. If not filed, the party was entitled to his discharge. He argued from the 'Chancery Practice' of Smith, that the defendant ought only to be imprisoned until he shall have properly answered the interrogatories put to him.

Mr. Van Dyke, the district attorney, then said that the question now was whether a person, in contempt, had any standing in court whatever. So far as Mr. Williamson is concerned, he has no standing. The argument of the gentlemen on the other side must be taken as arguing against the adjudication of this court. How far can a man in contempt come into court and purge that contempt? How did the counsel get over the fact, that his client was in contempt? He must first submit himself to the court by asking to be permitted to purge himself of contempt.

Mr. Meredith closed the argument, and the proceeding was closed by an entry on the part of Judge Kane of the following order on the record.

*The United States* v. *Williamson.* And now, October the 29th, 1855, the court having heard argument upon the motion for leave to read and file among the records, in this case, a certain paper writing purporting to be the petition of Passmore Williamson, and having considered thereof, do refuse the leave moved for, inasmuch as it appears that the said Passmore Williamson is now remaining in contempt of this court, and that by the said paper writing he doth in no wise make purgation of his said contempt, nor doth he thereby pray that he may be permitted to make such purgation; wherefore the said Passmore Williamson hath not at this time a standing in this court.

To the end, however, that the said Passmore Williamson may, when thereunto minded, the more readily relieve himself of his said contempt, it is ordered that whenever by petition, in writing, to be filed with the clerk, Passmore Williamson shall set forth, under his oath or solemn affirmation that 'he desires to purge himself of the contempt because of which he is now attached, and to that end is willing to make true answers to such interrogations as may be addressed to him by the court, touching the matters heretofore *legally* enquired of by the writ of *habeas corpus* to him directed, at the relation of John H. Wheeler,' then the marshal do bring the said Passmore Williamson before the court, if in session, or if the court be not in session, then before the judge at his chambers, to abide the further order of the court in his behalf. And it is further ordered that the clerk do furnish copies of this order to the said Passmore Williamson, and to the attorney of the United States, and to the marshal.

Under this order Williamson presented the following petition:

*United States of America* v. *Williamson, District Court of the United States, Eastern district of Pennsylvania.*

*To the Honorable the Judge of the District Court of the United States for the Eastern district of Pennsylvania:*

The petition of Passmore Williamson respectfully showeth: That he desires to purge himself of the contempt because of which he is now attached, and to that end is willing to make true answers to such interrogatories as may be addressed to him by the court, touching the matter heretofore inquired of him by the writ of *habeas corpus* to him directed at the relation of John H. Wheeler. Wherefore he prays that he may be permitted to purge himself of said contempt by making true answers to such interrogatories as may be addressed to him by the honorable court touching the premises. P. WILLIAMSON.

Affirmed and subscribed before me, Nov. 2, 1855.

CHARLES F. HEAZLITT, U. S. Com.

Judge Kane hesitated to receive this petition because it did not conform to his order by containing the word *legally*, before the phrase "inquired of," (thus confirming the legality of the proceedings under the original writ of *habeas corpus* directed to Williamson.) But finding that Williamson was resolved to make no such concession, Judge Kane finally concluded to receive the petition, and made the following reply to it:

'PASSMORE WILLIAMSON: The court has received your petition, and, upon consideration thereof, have thought right to grant the prayer thereof. You will therefore make here in open court your solemn affirmation, that in the return heretofore made by you to the writ of *habeas corpus*, which issued from this court at the relation of John H. Wheeler, and in the proceedings consequent thereupon, you have not intended a contempt of this court or of its process. Moreover, that you are now willing to make true answers to such interrogatories as may be addressed to you by the court, touching the premises inquired of in the said writ of *habeas corpus*.'

The required affirmation was then made in the form dictated by the judge.

Mr. Van Dyke, the district attorney, then submitted an interrogatory in writing, which was not read aloud at that time.

Mr. Gilpin said Mr. Williamson was perfectly willing to answer the interrogatory submitted by the district attorney, but as he did not know what other interrogatories might follow this, he thought it best that it and its answer should be filed.

Mr. Van Dyke said he was willing either to file the interrogatory or to submit it for an immediate reply.

Mr. Gilpin and Judge Kane both remarked that they had understood the district attorney to intimate, that if the question propounded was answered in the affirmative, he would be satisfied. The court further said, that it was for the petitioner to make his election whether or not the interrogatories and the replies should be filed.

After consultation with his counsel, the petitioner preferred that the questions and answers should be filed.

The court directed that the interrogatories should be filed.

Mr. Gilpin then read the interrogatory that had been propounded, and the reply of Mr. Williamson.

The interrogatory was as follows:

'Did you at the time of the service of the writ of *habeas corpus*, at the relation of John H. Wheeler, or at any time during the period intervening between the service of said writ and the making of your return thereto, seek to obey the mandate of said writ, by bringing before this honorable court the persons of the slaves therein mentioned? If to this interrogatory you answer in the affirmative, state fully and particularly the mode in which you sought so to obey said writ, and all that you did tending to that end.'

The reply made was as follows:

'I did not seek to obey the writ by producing the persons therein mentioned before the court, because I had not, at the time of the service of the writ, the power over, the custody or control of them, and, therefore, it was impossible for me to do so. I first heard of the writ of *habeas corpus* on Friday, July 20, between one and two o'clock A. M., on my return from Harrisburg. After breakfast, about nine o'clock, I went from my house to Mr. Hopper's office, when and where the return was prepared. At ten o'clock I came into court, as commanded by the writ. I sought to obey the writ by answering it truly; the parties not being in my possession or control, it was impossible for me to obey the writ by producing them. Since the service of the writ I have not had the custody, possession or power over them; nor have I known where they were, except from common rumor, or the newspaper reports in regard to their public appearance in the city or elsewhere.'

Some discussion arose between the district attorney and the counsel of Mr. Williamson. Mr. Van Dyke contended that the reply of the defendant was evasive and contradictory. The judge said the difficulty, he thought, could be easily overcome by amending the answer, and at the suggestion of the court it was amended in the following manner:

'I did not seek to obey the writ by producing the persons in the writ mentioned before this court. I did not seek, because I verily believed that it was entirely impossible for me to produce the said persons, agreeably to the command of the court.'

This answer was then accepted by the court and ordered filed.

Mr. Van Dyke then submitted another interrogatory, the substance of which was, whether or not Mr. Williamson had been guilty of mental reservations in his reply to the first interrogatory?

The court overruled this interrogatory as superfluous and improper.

Mr. Van Dyke withdrew this interrogatory and offered another, which was also overruled by the court, on the ground that it led to such replies as had already been objected to by the district attorney.

Mr. Van Dyke also withdrew this question.

Judge Kane then remarked that the district attorney had been invited to aid the court in this case, but that he would bear in mind that his relation to Mr. Wheeler was now suspended. This was only an inquiry as to what injury had been done the process of the court.

Mr. Van Dyke said he was aware of the position he occupied.

Judge Kane then said: 'The contempt is now regarded as purged and the party is released from custody. He is now reinstated in the position he occupied before the contempt was committed. Mr. Williamson is now before me on the return to the writ.'

Mr. Van Dyke then arose and addressed the court.

After Mr. Van Dyke had concluded, Mr. Meredith inquired: 'Is Mr. Williamson discharged?'

Judge Kane replied, 'He is. I understand from the remarks of the district attorney, that a *nolle prosequi* has been entered in the case in this court.'

The court then adjourned. Mr. Williamson was congratulated by his friends on his restoration to liberty. *

* The account of the final proceedings is from the Philadelphia *Evening Bulletin*.

www.ingramcontent.com/pod-product-compliance
Lightning Source LLC
LaVergne TN
LVHW021142110826
845150LV00005B/1101

* 9 7 8 1 4 2 5 5 4 7 4 8 6 *